History on Trial

HISTORY ON TRIAL

Culture Wars and the
Teaching of the Past

GARY B. NASH
CHARLOTTE CRABTREE
ROSS E. DUNN

ALFRED A. KNOPF NEW YORK 1997

THIS IS A BORZOI BOOK
PUBLISHED BY ALFRED A. KNOPF, INC.

Grateful acknowledgment is made to Cherry Lane Music Publishing Company, Inc.,
for permission to reprint an excerpt from "What Did You Learn in School Today," words and
music by Tom Paxton. Copyright © 1962, copyright renewed 1990 by Cherry Lane
Music Publishing Company, Inc. (ASCAP)/DreamWorks Songs (ASCAP). Worldwide rights
for DreamWorks Songs administered by Cherry Lane Music Publishing Company, Inc.
All rights reserved. Used by permission.

Library of Congress Cataloging-in-Publication Data
Nash, Gary B.
History on trial : culture wars and the teaching of the past /
by Gary B. Nash, Charlotte Crabtree, and Ross E. Dunn. — 1st ed.
p.   cm.
Includes index.
ISBN 0-679-44687-7 (hc : alk. paper)
1. History—Study and teaching (Elementary)—Standards—United States.
2. History—Study and teaching (Secondary)—Standards—United States.
3. Culture conflict—United States.
I. Crabtree, Charlotte A.   II. Dunn, Ross E.   III. Title.
LB1582.U6N37   1997
907.1'073—dc21   97-2819
CIP

Manufactured in the United States of America
First Edition

ILLUSTRATION CREDITS

PAGE 14: Chicago Historical Society; PAGE 44: *The American Legion Magazine;*
PAGE 126: ROB ROGERS, reprinted by permission of United Features Syndicate, Inc.;
PAGE 190: JEFF DANZIGER, reprinted by permission of *The Christian Science Monitor;*
PAGE 250: Karen Diegmueller and Debra Viadero, "Playing Games with History," *Education Week*

*This book is dedicated to
the nation's history teachers.*

Contents

Preface

For most of the twentieth century, public education in America has been a battleground where competing forces have struggled to shape the school curriculum. Nowhere have these conflicts been more bitterly fought than in the arena of history. The reasons for this are not hard to find. The American people care deeply about the history their children learn. Study of the past, after all, embodies many of the most fundamental messages we, as a nation, wish to send to young citizens. The past we choose to remember defines in large measure our national character, transmits the values and self-images we hold dear, and preserves the events, glorious and shameful, extraordinary and mundane, that constitute our legacy from the past and inspire our hopes for the future.

In researching this book, the authors have discovered much evidence across the country of excellence in history education. Dedicated teachers are inspiring students to scrutinize primary documents, conduct their own historical investigations, debate critical turning points in American and world history, analyze thorny historical issues, and listen to authentic voices from the past. These classrooms are alive with the love of history, and out of them come students equipped with understandings and skills to become responsible citizens and voters.

At century's end, however, the school history curriculum is not in a healthy state. Recent studies affirm that many American students are not learning much history and are enjoying the subject even less. Dismayed by evidence that youngsters were not performing as well academically as their counterparts in many other countries, the nation turned in 1992 to building new national standards of excellence in five school subjects, including history. For a time this initiative enjoyed a rare blend of bipartisan political support and public goodwill. That same year the authors of this book became involved in a project to develop, through a national consensus-building process, voluntary national standards for history. Two federal agencies funded the project. The collaborative team included virtually all the stakeholders in history education. Taking part were some thirty organizations representing the nation's parents, history teachers, school administrators, curriculum specialists, librarians, independent schools, professional historians, and educational groups. This participatory structure was unparalleled in any other nation that has revamped its history curriculum. It was also unique for bringing together academic historians, precollegiate history teachers, and a wide array of educators to work together as colleagues and partners.

In the fall of 1994, even before the National History Standards appeared in print, they were the object of a searing attack, soon to be followed by a barrage of op-ed page indictments, radio talk show confrontations, and TV debates that continued for eighteen months. The high—or low—point of this debate came in January 1995, when the United States Senate, intervening in educational matters heretofore left to the states, voted a sense-of-the-Senate resolution that, in effect, condemned the voluntary standards.

To understand why an ambitious, widely embraced, and promising undertaking to improve history in the schools became a sensational national controversy requires the telling of three related stories. First, this book explores the extraordinary blossoming of historical research, writing, and teaching that has taken place in this country in the twentieth century as the history profession has become more diverse, more methodologically sophisticated, and more committed to an inclusive American history and a genuinely globe-encircling world history. Second, the book shows that the recent war over the National History Standards has had many precedents in earlier decades of the twentieth century. Not everyone liked the idea that historians were shedding so much new light on the past, and some charged that new textbooks and programs disturbed hallowed national memories, undermined students' patriotism, pulled down cherished heroes, and even threatened national security. Third, we examine the "long walk" that academic historians took away from the schools in the decades following World War I. An unfortunate result of this estrangement between scholars and public education professionals was that both history teachers and the public at large remained largely unaware of the great broadening of the past that occurred over these years.

Only by braiding together these three strands from the late nineteenth century to the 1980s can we fathom the history standards controversy of the mid-1990s. Readers will see that our story parallels Lawrence Levine's recent account of struggles in colleges and universities over the last century "to open themselves to new areas of learning, to new ways of structuring education, and to new constituencies of students among the middle and working classes, women, immigrants, and minorities."[1] Situating the attacks on the history standards in the larger culture wars of the last decade allows a greater appreciation of what is at stake and how history education in the schools can be held hostage to political agendas.

If the attack on the history standards replays other similar episodes in our past, the end of this recent war may be far more promising. As the century draws to a close, we are witnessing a national surge of interest in history. A major reason for this is that more democratically conceived recountings of the past are being written—ones in which all citizens of the world's most diverse democracy can see their struggles, aspirations, contributions, and sacrifices. Nobody involved in writing the national standards will expect this book to produce tranquillity over the interpretation of history. But we hope that it will make a contribution to a sturdier democracy by showing the American people, particularly parents and grandparents of youngsters in the schools, that they can take satisfaction in the way historical scholarship has changed; the fruitful new ways schoolteachers, academic historians, and museum curators are collaborating; and the way national, state, and local organizations and agencies are sharing responsibilities for educational reform, thereby setting a standard for a nation that means to live up to its founding credo.

Acknowledgments

In the summer of 1994, none of the three of us dreamed we would write this book. As the National Standards for History moved toward publication, we looked forward to returning to our academic research and to the various projects of the National Center for History in the Schools. Then suddenly history war broke out, obliging us to put off our plans and devote more than two years to explaining, debating, and refining the standards. We also spent much time helping to rally history and social studies educators to confront a political campaign to discredit both the standards and indeed several decades of historical scholarship and pedagogy. Not long after the morning news broadcasters, the national press, the talk-show hosts, and, finally, the United States Senate jumped into the controversy, we began talking about how we would tell this remarkable story. We sketched out an outline of a book in March 1995, the same month that political critics of the standards were testifying before committees of Congress. In the ensuing months, our manuscript evolved along with the controversy. When the book went to press in April 1997, President Clinton was reviving the movement for national standards, and the drama was still unfolding.

Only one of us has academic expertise in the history of social studies education, and two of us normally labor in research fields far removed from the topic of this book. All of us, however, were eyewitnesses to, and indeed actors in, the most tumultuous debate over history, national identity, and American values ever to occur in this country. We make no claim to being nonpartisan academic observers of the history war. Modern historiography has taught us that historians can never fully detach their scholarly work from their own education, attitudes, ideological dispositions, and culture. For us to claim otherwise would be disingenuous. However, with the help of one another and the urgings of colleagues and editors, we have tried to climb the hill overlooking the battlefield and to present our version of the story fairly and without rancor. We have also attempted to situate the contention over the history standards within a much broader context of American struggles over national identity and the meaning of the past, and to compare our history wars with those in other countries. Looking backward and sideways is usually illuminating.

Several valued colleagues, some of whom were involved in writing or critiquing the National History Standards and some who were not, read early drafts of the book and offered cogent criticisms and suggestions: Joyce Appleby, University of California, Los Angeles; Arnita Jones, executive director of the Organization of American Historians; Michael Kammen, Cornell University; Stanley Katz, president of the American Council of Learned Societies; and Edmund Lindop, retired teacher in the Los Angeles Unified School District. Christopher Cross, president of the Council for Basic Education, and Charles Quigley, director of the Center for Civic Education, offered important comments on Chapter 9. For their suggestions on Chapter 6 we thank Edward Beasley, as well as British educators Sue Bennett, Martin Booth, Ian Colwill, Robert Phillips, and Ian Steele. For their helpful ideas and prodigious memories we are grateful to Linda Symcox, past associate director of the National Center for History in the Schools, and David Vigilante, retired San Diego history teacher. Rebecca Lowen of the Sandra Dijkstra Literary Agency also made valuable suggestions.

Several talented graduate students at UCLA and San Diego State University provided research assistance and computer skill: Margaret Dennis, Michael Fickes, Rebecca Frey, Jennifer Honigman, Jennifer Koslof, Thomas Materla, and Edie Sparks. We must also specially thank the History Center's indomitable Marta Hill.

Finally, we pay hearty tribute to the hundreds of teachers, professors, curriculum specialists, school administrators, and numerous other professional educators who conceived, drafted, argued over, and polished both the first and second editions of the National History Standards. And we owe a profound debt to those colleagues and citizens who contributed thoughtfully to the great history debate of 1994–96.

History on Trial

Abbreviations

AFT:	American Federation of Teachers
AHA:	American Historical Association
ASCD:	Association for Supervision and Curriculum Development
CBE:	Council for Basic Education
CCSSO:	Council of Chief State School Officers
CS4:	Council of State Social Studies Specialists
DAR:	Daughters of the American Revolution
DES:	Department of Education and Science (Britain)
ED:	U.S. Department of Education
GAR:	Grand Army of the Republic
GOPAC:	GOP Political Action Committee
NAEP:	National Assessment of Educational Progress
NCEST:	National Council on Education Standards and Testing
NCHS:	National Center for History in the Schools
NCSS:	National Council for the Social Studies
NEA:	National Endowment for the Arts
NEGP:	National Education Goals Panel
NEH:	National Endowment for the Humanities
NESIC:	National Education Standards and Improvement Council
NGA:	National Governors' Association
OAH:	Organization of American Historians
OHT:	Organization of History Teachers
OTL:	Opportunity to Learn Standards
UCLA:	University of California, Los Angeles

CHAPTER 1

In the Matter of History

It is true that history cannot satisfy our appetite when we are hungry, nor keep us warm when the cold wind blows. But it is true that if younger generations do not understand the hardships and triumphs of their elders, then we will be a people without a past. As such, we will be like water without a source, a tree without roots.

—Wall inscription, New York
Chinatown History Project

In the predawn hours of October 20, 1994, Gary B. Nash, Charlotte Crabtree, and other Californians helping to develop the National History Standards were rattled out of their slumber. East Coast friends, having scanned their morning copies of the *Wall Street Journal*, were phoning, the three-hour time difference forgotten in their stunned reaction to Lynne Cheney's editorial page article attacking the standards. The banner headline pronounced "The End of History."[1] The public had not yet read the standards because their release was scheduled for later that month. In one of the nation's most widely read newspapers, Cheney had delivered a preemptive strike against the new guidelines.

"Imagine an outline for the teaching of American history," began the former chairman of the National Endowment for the Humanities, "in which George Washington makes only a fleeting appearance and is never described as our first president. Or in which the founding of the Sierra Club and the National Organization for Women are considered noteworthy events, but the first gathering of the U.S. Congress is not." If those comments were not enough to raise readers' ire, she had more to offer. "The general drift of the document," she warned, "becomes apparent when one realizes that not a single one of the 31 national standards mentions the Constitution." True, she reported, the Constitution was described as "the culmination of the most creative era of constitutionalism in American history." But this description appeared only in what she alleged was "the dependent clause of a sentence that has as its main point . . . the paradox that the Constitution side-tracked the movement to abolish slavery that had taken rise in the revolutionary era." As for the extensive treatment of the Constitution throughout the standards, Cheney allowed only an offhand admission that "true, it [the Constitution] does come up in the 250 pages of supporting materials."

Cheney also charged that the U.S. History Standards presented a "grim and gloomy" portrayal of American history. Why so much attention, she asked, to topics such as the Ku Klux Klan and McCarthyism? Why did this curricular framework save its "unqualified admiration" for "people, places, and events that are politically correct?" By way of evidence, she cited one out of the nearly twelve hundred illustrative classroom activities, included to support the standards on what young Americans should learn. This particular example invited students to conduct a trial of John D. Rockefeller on his business practices. Students taking the roles of prosecutor, defense attorney, judge, and jury would investigate his piratical dealings—of the kind a PBS documentary on him had explored several years before.

Citing other teaching examples rather than the standards themselves, Cheney found six references to Harriet Tubman, an escaped slave who used the Underground Railroad to rescue scores of other slaves. In contrast, such white males as Ulysses S. Grant and Robert E. Lee were mentioned only one and zero times, respectively. The standards give no hint, she complained, "of the spell-binding oratory of such congressional giants as Henry Clay and Daniel Webster." And Alexander Graham Bell, Thomas Edison, Albert Einstein, Jonas Salk, and the Wright brothers, she claimed, "make no appearance at all."

"What went wrong?" Cheney asked. She found her answer in the disclosures of one member of the National Council for History Standards, the group that oversaw the three-year project to develop the guidelines. In the words of this informant, who asked not to be named, those "pursuing their revisionist agenda no longer bothered to conceal their great hatred of traditional history" once Bill Clinton's election in 1992 had "unleashed the forces of political correctness." Thereafter, the informant told Cheney, "nobody dared to cut the inclusive part" of the standards that "various political groups such as African American organizations and Native American groups" had forced on the council.

Farfetched as this explanation was of the consensus-building process through which the standards had been written, it was no more astonishing than Cheney's assessment of the World History Standards. She had not reviewed these guidelines, so she relied on the assessment of another unnamed informant. In this case, she reported authoritatively, the American Historical Association—the century-old historians' equivalent to the American Medical Association—grew "particularly aggressive" after Clinton's victory and "threatened to boycott the proceedings if Western civilization was given any emphasis" and "from that point on, hijacked standards-setting."

Cheney concluded her *Journal* attack with a call to arms. National certification of these standards, she warned, must at all cost be blocked or "much that is significant in our past will begin to disappear from our schools." She urged that the standards be stopped in their tracks because they were the rubbish produced by an "academic establishment that revels in . . . politicized history."

Four days after Cheney's blast, commentator Rush Limbaugh told his radio audience that the standards were part of the America-bashing multicultural agenda that he had cautioned viewers and listeners about. For many months, he had excoriated historians who had "bullied their way into power positions in academia" in order to indoctrinate students with the message that "our country is inherently evil."[2] He told his listeners that the standards, which had been "worked on in secret," should simply be flushed "down the sewer of multiculturalism."[3] "When you bring [students] into a classroom," he informed TV viewers on October 28, "and you teach them that America is a rotten place, . . . and they don't have a chance here . . . you have a bunch of embittered people growing up, robbing and stealing and turning to crime because they've been told all their young lives that there's no future for them. . . . This country does not deserve the reputation it's getting in multicultural classrooms, and the zenith of this bastardization of American history has been reached with new standards that have been written as part of Goals 2000 to standardize history."

Limbaugh then gave his audience a dramatic demonstration of what Cheney claimed would be the fate of America's traditional heroes if the standards were made official. "If you're a parent of a child anywhere from grade five through twelve, I want to show you what's in store for your kid in history," Limbaugh raged. Presenting the history standards as a textbook from which kids would study rather than a framework that teachers might voluntarily use as a resource, he began tearing pages out of a history book. "Here's Paul Revere. He's gone," exclaimed Limbaugh as a crumpled page hit the TV studio floor. "Here's George Washington as president. Look at all these pages in this book. He's gone. . . . Here's Thomas Edison. He's gone. J. P. Morgan—he's gone. The Wright brothers . . . let's rip them out. They're gone. This is what we're doing to American history with this stupid new book, folks." Limbaugh's conclusion? The standards are "a bunch of p.c. crap."

Limbaugh catechized the audience on just what historical correctness is and isn't. "History is real simple. You know what history is? It's what happened," he told his audience. "The problem you get into is when guys like this try to skew history by [saying], 'Well, let's interpret what happened because maybe we can't find the truth in the facts, or at least we don't like the truth as it's presented. So let's change the interpretation a little bit so that it will be the way we wished it were.' Well, that's not what history is. History is what happened, and history ought to be nothing more than the quest to find out what happened."

Limbaugh wrestled with questions about how wars occurred, how people were moved by religion or ideas, why one society developed differently from another. "Now, if you want to get into why what happened, that's probably valid too, but why what happened shouldn't have much of anything to do with what happened." He hoped millions of American parents would bear this history lesson in mind and agree that the National History Standards were radioactive enough to damage their children's minds.

In attacking the standards, Cheney and Limbaugh sent new shock troops into a culture war that had raged for a decade. Since the mid-1980s, Americans have been beset by controversies, criticisms, and contretemps over history. Was Columbus not an intrepid explorer but the world's greatest genocidist? Was Cleopatra black, the pride of Africa, rather than a heroine of Western civilization? Should the New York legislature stipulate that every schoolchild study the Irish potato famine of the 1840s? What other famines in history should legislatures mandate? Should one of Virginia's most hallowed Civil War battlefields be obliged to share space with a mega-theme park where American families could learn versions of history produced in Disney's imagineering laboratory? Did the curators of "The West as America" exhibit at the National Museum of American Art in Washington become part of the "embarrassed to be American" crowd when they suggested that the stunning paintings by Bierstadt, Remington, Catlin, and others might be looked at in many ways—as reflections of imperialism and racism as much as Arcadian depictions of the frontier?

Why was Colonial Williamsburg staging an eighteenth-century slave auction, heartrending but allegedly degrading, even if the producer was a talented young black woman who wanted people to understand the brutality of slavery? Were the Smithsonian Institution's curators and consulting historians really "hijacking history," practicing "political correctness," and demonstrating "anti-Americanism," when they planned an exhibit on *Enola Gay*, the B-52 that dropped the first atom bomb on Japan a half-century ago? Why did San Francisco's Art Commission agree to move an

800-ton monument showing a Spanish friar, with finger pointing to heaven, standing over a supine Indian while a *vaquero* raised his hand in triumph? All of these—a historical figure, a monument, a site, an event—became lightning rods for sulphurous debates over historical, heritage, and group sensibility.

It is not surprising that the political Right would open a history front in the culture wars. History, like politics, is about national identity. Hence the work of historians frequently comes under attack amid calls for refurbishing or restoring the national identity. "Today's moralists have successfully filled the Great Enemy Vacuum left by the end of the Cold War," writes James A. Morone. This time the enemy was to be found within, with the nation divided between "a righteous 'us' and a malevolent 'them.' "[4] For Pat Buchanan, speaking before the Republican National Convention in 1992, this was "a war for the soul of America."[5] For Irving Kristol, intellectual leader of neoconservatism, "there is no 'after the Cold War' for me. So far from having ended, my Cold War has increased in intensity, as sector after sector has been ruthlessly corrupted by the liberal ethos." Since historians are easily associated with "the liberal ethos," their province was naturally terrain to be attacked and, if possible, captured in the culture wars. "Now that the other 'Cold War' is over," warned Kristol, "the real Cold War has begun. We are far less prepared for this Cold War, far more vulnerable to our enemy, than was the case with our victorious war against a global Communist threat."[6]

Historians have been, by turns, amazed, amused, and aghast at the recent blitzkrieg on the profession's research of the past few decades. They have been drawn into a series of public disputes, often reluctantly but also because their own scholarship has precipitated shrill, bombastic arguments, especially when it has challenged cherished historical narratives. Historians have become personalities on the public stage, applying makeup for the TV cameras, miking up for radio talk shows, and writing op-ed essays for local newspapers.

History is hot. If Cecil B. De Mille was correct in arguing that there is no such thing as bad publicity, then historians ought to welcome the excitement. History is unceasingly controversial because it provides so much of the substance for the way a society defines itself and considers what it wants to be. The culture wars, though unnerving and nasty, offer the public a grand opportunity to talk with historians and history teachers about how history is written, how research has changed in recent decades, and how arguments about the past illustrate a democracy at work. If historians find themselves unorganized and relatively powerless to combat oversimplification and misrepresentation of their work, they can take satisfaction that their influence has spread from college and high school classrooms into public spaces as varied as museums, local historical societies, TV documentaries, historic sites, theme parks, and CD-ROM "textbooks."

History does matter, and it is important for Americans at the end of the twentieth century to understand how the recent history wars have unfolded, how these struggles are connected to earlier arguments over interpreting the past, and what this tells us about the state of our society. This book argues that contention over the past is as old as written history itself, that the democratizing of the history profession has led to more inclusive and balanced presentations of American and world history, and that continuously reexamining the past, rather than piously repeating traditional narratives, is the greatest service historians can render in a democracy.

What Is History? Why History?

The four most famous historians of the Greek and Roman world were Herodotus, Thucydides, Livy, and Tacitus. Together they established historical writing as both a literary genre and an intellectual discipline. Their re-creations of the past were transcribed, read aloud, and remembered. Centuries later, after the invention of printing, the work of the early classical historians took the form of books, which can be found today in libraries, schools, and homes.

But these historians, though the first to write history, were by no means the first historians. For thousands of years before the Greeks, a society's memory was transmitted orally from generation to generation. Bards, storytellers, priests, and griots handed down to their children the collective past worth remembering. Almost every people has folk sayings that express the great importance of memory as precious and socially sustaining. "A people without history is like wind upon the buffalo grass," goes an old Teton Sioux saying. The Yoruba in West Africa tell their children, "However far the stream flows, it never forgets its source." Thomas Jefferson prescribed history for all who wished to take part in democratic government because it would "enable every man to judge for himself what will secure or endanger his freedom." By reflecting on the past—other times, other people, other nations—citizens would be able "to judge of the future" and make up their own minds on the "actions and designs of men."

The human mind seems to require a usable past because historical memory is a key to self-identity, a way of comprehending one's place in the stream of time, and a means of making some sense of humankind's long story. It is nearly impossible to step outside of time, to cut oneself off from the past as if its hand were not upon us. The study of history, moreover, reveals the long, hard path of human striving for dignity. Historical knowledge and perspective, while helping people to think intelligently about contemporary issues, have the deeper potential to provide personal moorings, both secular and religious. Literature, philosophy, art, music, and science have the same potential. But history is the most integrative of all disciplines. For the historian, nothing is beyond notice in the quest to understand the nature and meaning of change, the complexities of human behavior, and the multitude of connections between the past and our world today.

That history matters is indisputable. Americans are devouring huge numbers of history books. They flock to movies such as *Glory* and *Gettysburg*. By the millions they tune in to such television series as *Roots* and *The Civil War*. They visit historical sites in record-breaking numbers, often watching citizen "reenactors" make scenes from the past come alive. They reach deep into their pockets to help preserve, restore, and present the past.

History as Interpretation

In this education-minded nation, where every autumn more than 13 million Americans go to college, students who take history courses know what Rush Limbaugh doesn't: that written history is based on carefully gathered evidence but that historians must weave facts into plausible explanations of the human experience. History without explanation, without analysis, without pattern is barren chronicle. Most students also quickly learn that a great many facts of history come to us in somewhat less than pure form.

In today's history wars, phrases such as "revisionist history" and "historical revisionism" are bandied about as damning indictments of historians, who are seen as misled or malevolent creatures who "kidnap" or "steal" what traditionalists think is a single, agreed-upon history that exists "out there." Even centuries ago, intelligent people would have laughed at the notion that the past is nothing but a set of agreed-upon facts.

Before considering some examples, let us ask a simple question: How are facts determined, and how can all facts be gathered and authenticated before the writing of a history book begins? The number of "facts" is limitless, restricted only by the number of documents that have survived floods, fires, and the trash barrel. But if we could somehow find *all* the facts on a subject, the history of medieval England, for example, or the American westward movement, how would we establish their authenticity and neutrality?

Every individual document—whether in the form of official correspondence, diaries, autobiographies, private letters, legislative proceedings, diplomatic communiqués, newspapers, business accounts, or old Sears Roebuck catalogs—can tell us, as historian Edward Hallett Carr says, no more than "what the author of the document thought—what he thought had happened, what he thought ought to happen or would happen, or perhaps only what he wanted others to think he thought, or even only what he himself thought he thought."[7] Moreover, as the philosopher of history H. Stuart Hughes puts it, "Historians—in contrast to investigators in almost any other field of knowledge—very seldom confront their data directly. The literary or artistic scholar has the poem or painting before him; the astronomer scans the heavens through a telescope; the geologist tramps the soil he studies. . . . The historian alone is wedded to empirical reality and condemned to view his subject matter at second remove. He alone must accept the word of others before he even begins to devise his account."[8]

Even material artifacts from the past—tombstones, campaign buttons, farm tools, dolls, powder horns, claw-footed bathtubs, potsherds, and much more—are inert, and become evidence only when historians ask questions about them. Three of today's historians put it this way: "These traces, alas, never speak for themselves. . . . Usually they remain where people left them in discarded trunks in attics, in inscrutable notations in ledgers, in the footings of abandoned buildings; sometimes they are collected in repositories and archives. Some of this physical residue lies forgotten, but close enough to the surface of life to be unexpectedly happened upon. Then like hastily buried treasure or poorly planted land mines they deliver great surprises."[9]

Any work of history is necessarily selective because historians must choose the most relevant evidence in order to make sense of some part of the past. It is a "preposterous fallacy," as Carr puts it, that historical "facts" exist "objectively and independently of the interpretation of the historian."[10] "What I want is facts," says Mr. Gradgrind in Dickens's *Hard Times*, "Facts alone are wanted in life." But anyone who studies history for social and cultural nourishment will get a poorly balanced diet if nothing but Rush Limbaugh's factoids are served. The history-as-facts argument is not simply an uneducated view. It is also an ideological position of traditionalists and the political Right that particular facts, traditions, and heroic personalities, all untainted by "interpretation," represent the "true" and "objective" history that citizens ought to know.

We are living in an era when unusually strident claims are made about how reinterpreters of history dishonor American traditions and demean Western values. The sky is falling, they say, because new faces crowding onto the stage of history ruin the symmetry and security of older versions of the past. The argument masquerades under claims of objectivity and neutrality. In fact, one of the most important of all American traditions is education and citizenship that requires open inquiry and healthy skepticism about any account of the past, and open-mindedness to the possibility of new historical perspectives. This kind of tolerance and receptivity is itself a cardinal tenet of Enlightenment thought.

If interpretation—based carefully on information sifted from many sources—is the heart of historical inquiry, it is little different from the work of a lawyer who gathers evidence and builds a case to present to a jury. As detectives collect clues, following one bit of data to the next, so do historians. As lawyers write briefs, so do historians. As journalists amass facts in order to report and analyze today's happenings, so historians gather evidence to write stories that interpret yesterday's events.

To understand the *act* of writing history we must also recognize, as Thucydides did twenty-five hundred years ago, that the past is necessarily embedded in the present human condition. Frederick Jackson Turner, whose "Frontier Thesis" in American history made him famous, understood that to comprehend the United States on the eve of World War I "demands that we should rework our history from the new points of view afforded by the present."[11] Carl Becker, a much revered historian of the same generation, spoke of the humility that all scholars ought to have in their search for the most convincing re-creation of the past: "In the history of history a myth is a once valid but now discarded version of the human story, as our now valid versions will in due course be relegated to the category of discarded myths."[12] England's Lord Christopher Hill echoes this: "History has to be rewritten in every generation because, although the past does not change, the present does; each generation asks new questions of the past, and finds new areas of sympathy as it re-lives different aspects of the experiences of its predecessors."[13]

If today's conservative politicians who yearn for an American golden age find it to their advantage to regard historical revision as an un-American activity, they will have to convince the public that there is, or has ever been, one indisputably true history. Again, the words of Carl Becker are useful: "It should be a relief to us to renounce omniscience, to recognize that every generation, our own included, will, must inevitably, understand the past and anticipate the future in the light of its own restricted experience."[14]

Lawrence Levine, a recent president of the Organization of American Historians, has reiterated the necessity of continuously reevaluating the past. We cannot escape viewing history "through the prism of a changing present," he writes, and need not regard this prism as "a prison" that condemns historians to a "flawed vision." On the contrary, the present is "not merely a hindrance; it ... provides new ways of seeing things, new tools, new perceptions of human motivation or economic forces that help us to gain a surer sense of past generations."[15]

Arguing that history is an interpretive practice does not compromise a commitment to accuracy, procedures for documentation and verification, and fair, balanced reconstruction of events. No historian wants to be labeled a propagandist, a peddler of polemics, or an intellectual charlatan. Anyone who has such inclinations is unlikely to get tenure in an American college or university. In fact, the writing of history today is conducted in a stringently professional way, and the standards of scholarly journals and academic publishers are very high. One of these standards, Joan Scott writes, is the idea that "the meanings attributed to events of the past always vary, that the knowledge we produce is contextual, relative, open to revision and debate, and never absolute."[16]

In making sense of the history battles swirling around us today, we might think for a moment about science and science education. The recently released National Science Standards, which were produced in a way parallel to the National History Standards, have occasioned a mild debate about how much science young Americans should learn, in what grades, and by what processes. But the science standards have not evoked attacks on science educators, charging them with "bastardizing" their discipline because they draw on new research. No one so far is protesting that scientific revisionism is subversive or that teachers and scholars are "science thieves" or "science bandits" because they built standards on new knowledge—the existence of uranium, radon, and the isotope carbon 14, for example—that was unavailable several generations ago. Nor would American parents want their college-bound children to major in science if they were not going to learn $E = mc^2$, a formula unknown two generations ago.

Yet the pursuit of historical and scientific knowledge is remarkably similar. Scientists, like historians, search for new facts—or empirical evidence. To be sure, the two groups take on problems that are very different: "Humanists study action which is responsive to intentions, whereas naturalists investigate the bounded world of behavior."[17] Yet all scholars, whatever their discipline, use evidence to build new interpretations, or theories— for scientists, about the behavior of the physical world; for historians, the human world in the past. Both make conceptual "breakthroughs" in their fields by asking questions that derive from their present concerns and the present condition of the world—questions that predecessors did not or could not ask because of the way society, culture, and the limits of knowledge restricted their investigations.

This is not to argue that fraud, propaganda, and deliberate misrepresentation, either in history or science, are unknown. However, historians and scientists take pride in ferreting out cooked evidence, false analogies, plagiarism, and other forms of rogue scholarship. The Institute for Historical Review has published pamphlets and articles for more than a decade denying that the Holocaust occurred. To expose such cruel canards, along with hoaxes such as the Piltdown man, Hitler's diaries, and the Protocols of the Elders of Zion (which fed anti-Semitism for years), is part of the historian's responsibility. Academic scientists are equally committed to uncloaking bizarre projects such as the Nazi experimental pseudoscience that denied quantum mechanics and relativity, labeling it "Jewish physics."

The parallel between science education and history education goes further. Scientists, like historians, believe that "literacy" in their field "is not simply a mastery of facts," as two prominent scholars have put it, "but a way of thinking—an analytical process through which we reach conclusions."[18] Both historians and scientists rely on "pattern recognition"—"perceptible relationships among important facts," as William H. McNeill has said. "That and that alone constitutes an intelligible pattern, giving meaning to the world, whether it be the world of physics and chemistry or the world of interacting human groups through time, which historians take as their special domain."[19]

Finally, both science and history educators share the view that if American students are to measure up to their counterparts in other nations, they must "learn to identify their assumptions, think logically and consider alternative explanations. They should be able to apply the knowledge they acquire, not merely memorize facts long enough to repeat them on the next exam."[20] If science educators want to train students to consider "alternative explanations," should history educators find this inappropriate? The notion of alternative explanations and multiple perspectives is, as we will see, anathema to the traditionalist history-as-facts, history-as-it-has-always-been school. But if students do not learn that a corner on truth is hard to come by, they will measure up poorly against their counterparts in other countries.

Moreover, if interpretation and alternative explanations are not allowable, then almost all written history since Livy and Tacitus will have to be purged from the libraries. If contending perspectives on the past are inadmissible, how might a parent resolve the confusion of a child who learns about Sir Francis Drake first in a classroom in England and later in a school in Spain? In British schoolbooks, Drake is a gallant, steely Elizabethan sea dog who enriched Protestant England by capturing Spanish galleons carrying gold and silver from Peruvian and Mexican mines to Spain. He helped repulse the Spanish Armada in 1588. The queen decorated him lavishly for his exploits. His statue graces British and American historic sites. Commuters in California's Marin County drive Sir Francis Drake Boulevard on their way to work, and their children attend Sir Francis Drake High School. In textbooks in Spain, however, Drake is "El Pirato," a bloodthirsty captain who unleashed murderous English sea louts to pillage and destroy Spanish towns in Central and South America. No statues or schools in Spain commemorate El Pirato any more than Aztecs would have glorified the conquering Cortés.

A 1927 comment on the question of who owns history
Chicago Daily Tribune, October 19, 1927

History and Patriotism

In all modern nations, educators and political leaders have regarded history as a vehicle for promoting *amor patriae*, for instilling in young people knowledge and attitudes that promote national cohesion and civic pride. Even the controversial 1991 report of the New York Commission on a new social studies framework, criticized for promoting corrosive multiculturalism, adheres to the idea that "the teaching of the nation's history, our national traditions and values, and a common loyalty are purposes commonly accepted as appropriate to the social studies."[21] In other words, the charms of Clio, the muse of history, are closely connected to her ability to elicit *civisme*, to contribute to the forming of educated and concerned citizens. This is a transnational phenomenon. A century ago, France's principal textbook writer expressed what all nations believe today: "A natural instinct binds us to our ancestors with a sort of sacredness. . . . It gives us a feeling of continuity."[22]

History wars frequently turn on the issue of patriotism. However, arguments over history can easily be misrepresented and oversimplified as pitting unpatriotic historians against patriotic citizens. For some Americans, history that dwells on unsavory or even horrific episodes in our past is unpatriotic and likely to alienate young students from their own country. "Grim and gloomy" history is seen as undermining the national goal to educate loyal, proud Americans rather than pessimists and cynics.

On the other side of the issue are those who believe that exposing students to grim chapters of our past is *essential* to the creation of informed, responsible citizens. Historians are not trying to trash America when they examine and analyze the brutality of slavery, the genocidal displacement of indigenous people, the exploitation of child labor, the frailty of national leaders, or contradictions between lofty political principles and shabby practices. Most historians are reformers by nature, and they critique the past in order to improve American society and to protect dearly won gains.

The argument is in fact between two visions of patriotic history. On one side are those who believe that young people will love and defend the United States if they see it as superior to other nations and regard its occasional falls from grace as short pauses or detours in the continuous flowering of freedom, capitalism, and opportunity. Thus, the Right sees no need to examine blemishes that in any case have been historically removed. On the other side are most historians, who believe that *amor patriae* is nurtured by looking squarely at the past, warts and all. Only this clear-sightedness will obviate the cynicism that sugar-coated history produces when youngsters get older and recognize "the lies my teacher told me."[23]

We argue here that nothing can serve patriotism worse than suppressing dark chapters of our past, smoothing over clearly documentable examples of shameful behavior in public places high and low, and airbrushing disgraceful violations of our national credo such as the actions of the Ku Klux Klan or the internment of Japanese Americans during World War II. If events like these are seen as mere footnotes to history, America's youth are unlikely to swallow the story, especially when they see around them systemic problems that eat at the national fabric. Sooner or later they will discover that a self-congratulatory version of American history sheds little light on how we got to the place we now occupy. Surely not all of America's problems began in the 1960s.

Let us take a single example of what the traditionalist Right would regard as a "grim and gloomy" presentation of American history and consider how it might affect the patriotism of high school students. Textbooks of an earlier time described the Spanish-American War of 1898 as a smashing victory over Spain's corrupt colonial government and as the freeing of Cubans and Filipinos from oppressive masters. Surely this was an example of American democracy on the march, a war in which Americans could take great pride.

Today's textbooks describe the American victories but also analyze the role of William Randolph Hearst's yellow journalism in whipping up hatred against Spain for its purported sabotaging of the battleship *Maine*. Some new books also recount the war that American forces waged against Filipinos fighting for independence. In these texts, students learn that Filipino revolutionaries initially welcomed American troops to their country as liberators and that the United States promised to support Philippine independence if nationalists fought with the Americans against Spain. Students also learn that to justify annexation of the islands, expansionists promoted President William McKinley's argument that he would end "anarchy," and would "educate," "uplift," and "civilize" the Filipinos. Newer history books explain that behind these lofty intentions other considerations lurked: The Philippines could provide a rich variety of natural resources, as well as a foothold in Asia—a naval stop on the way to China. When Americans raised their flag and took control of the country, nationalists waged guerrilla war at full force until 1902 and sporadically until 1906. One new history book for eleventh-graders quotes Mark Twain's comment on the supreme irony of the situation:

There must be two Americas: one that sets the captive free, and one that takes a once-captive's new freedom away from him, and picks a quarrel with him with nothing to found it on; then kills him to get his land.[24]

What effect will reading such passages have on Americans approaching voting age? Will learning about the eight-year war against Filipino revolutionaries, who called nationalist leader Emilio Aguinaldo the George Washington of their country, make young Americans hate their nation or want to emigrate to some other land? Today, most educators believe that it would be dishonorable to ignore this long war, in which forty-two hundred Americans died, along with fifteen thousand Filipino rebels and some two hundred thousand civilians. These teachers and scholars think that American students old enough to fight in this nation's wars are mature enough to reflect upon the Philippines episode and thus develop more thoughtful and nuanced perspectives on American foreign policy. Everyone fighting in Desert Storm understood the war to be a justifiable action to thwart a despicable Iraqi dictator; but nearly everyone also knew that the war was partly about oil reserves in Kuwait. No one was under the illusion the war aimed to restore democracy to Kuwait, which was then and still is an authoritarian oligarchy.

In the current culture wars, where the ultraconservatives' object is to sway the emotions of as many people as possible with charges of "political correctness," "America-bashing revisionism," and "balkanizing multiculturalism," a telling double standard rears its head. Ideologues contemptuous of American historians who reexamine and reinterpret the American past are jubilant that Russia, Germany, and Japan have revised their history textbooks so that students will learn about such things as the Russian appeasement of Hitler, Stalin's slaughter of twenty-one thousand Polish army officers, the Ukrainian genocide against Kiev's Jews, the Japanese enslavement of Korean women for wartime sexual services, and the Holocaust. Almost all Americans would agree that children in other nations must look squarely at the dark side of their history. Is the same wisdom not applicable in the world's leading democracy?

The First American History Wars

In light of today's charges that historians are tampering with the past and thrusting twisted truths on the nation's children, we should recall that historical revisionism in this nation began in the afterglow of the American Revolution. Political leaders fenced over the meaning of the Revolution even before the battle scars had healed. John Adams, who occupied the political center stage at the time, was sure that the record was being distorted. "The history of our Revolution," he complained, "will be one continued lie from one end to the other. The essence of the whole will be that Dr.

Franklin's electric rod smote the earth and out sprang George Washington. That Franklin electrified him with his rod, and henceforward these two conducted all the policy negotiations, legislatures, and war."[25] Such an interpretation appalled Adams all the more because he had such a dim view of Franklin, with whom he served as a diplomat in France during the war. "I never knew but one man who pretended to be wholly free from [vanity]," grumbled Adams, "and him I know to be in his heart the vainest man, and the falsest character I have ever met with in life."[26]

Debates over the character, meaning, and legacies of the independence movement continued throughout the careers of the Founding Fathers. They argued furiously about the Revolution and one another's role in it. Adams lamented "the superstitious veneration that is sometimes paid to General Washington," thinking that "I feel myself his Superior."[27] He also thought that Franklin, whom he loved to call "the great Deceiver" and the "old Conjuror," was vastly overrated. The nation's second president was reduced to sputtering when someone asked him his opinion of Thomas Paine, whose *Common Sense* galvanized the vacillating public and the Continental Congress in early 1776 to declare independence from mighty England. Paine was "a mongrel between pig and puppy, begotten by a wild boar on a bitch wolf. . . . Never before in any age of the world" was such a "poltroon" allowed "to run through such a career of mischief."[28]

Jefferson also took his lumps—and administered a few. He regarded Adams as impossible. "He hates Franklin, he hates Jay, he hates the French, he hates the English," wrote Jefferson in 1783.[29] Adams returned the favor. After losing to Jefferson in the presidential campaign in 1800, he called his rival so "warped by prejudice and so blinded by ignorance as to be unfit for the office he holds." New England's Congregational ministers especially hated the third president. One predicted that Americans "will rue the day and detest the folly, delusion, and intrigue, which raised him [Jefferson] to the head of the United States." Other clergymen bombarded their congregations with descriptions of Jefferson as an adulterous atheist and a toadying lover of the hopelessly corrupt French, whose revolution was as lovable as a plague.[30]

We will return in a later chapter to see how new research on the American Revolution has broadened our view of the nation's birth. But never was that event an agreed-upon story to which everyone subscribed. Revising the Revolution began approximately one day after the Paris Peace Treaty was signed on September 3, 1783. The revisions will continue as long as Americans—and people around the world—see that the revolutionary ideology echoes across the centuries, speaks to their own aspirations, and matters to their own times.

By the mid-1790s, in fact, Americans could not celebrate the Fourth of July together. So divided were they over the legacy of the Revolution that men who had fought side by side in the "glorious cause" found it necessary to organize separate parades, partake of separate feasts, hear different orations, and raise glasses to astoundingly conflicting toasts. Until the Federalist Party collapsed four decades after the Revolution, there would be no community celebrations of July 4—only separate commemorations of the nation's birthday by deeply divided Americans.

The 1840s give us another glimpse of the contention about the past. At a time when abolitionists were determined to root out slavery from the American republic, many Southerners railed against "the wandering incendiary Yankee schoolmaster" with "his incendiary school books" marching under "the piratical ensign of abolitionism."[31] Southerners had long since adopted the argument that slavery was good for Africans and their descendants. Under attack from abolitionists, they could ill afford to have their children read books that pointed out the discrepancy between the nation's founding credo of inalienable rights and the perpetuation of dehumanizing slavery. From the white Southerners' point of view, the history books created in the North consisted of unacceptably revised, polemical history.

After the Civil War, Notherners and Southerners continued to argue over the proper way to tell the story to young learners. In fact, the war nearly guaranteed that a unitary version of American history would be impossible to achieve, at least so long as martial glory and self-justification preoccupied those who fought in blue and gray. Publishers bravely tried to produce textbooks that split the difference between Northern and Southern points of view, "leaving the reader to his own conclusion as to the right or wrong of it," as the Grand Army of the Republic (GAR), the patriotic organization of federal army veterans, bitterly complained.[32]

But given the intensity of the conflict and the extent of the bloodletting, neither section of the country was ready to accept fresh interpretations, even in the 1880s. Staking out positions to preserve war memories and the rectitude of their respective ideological positions, Northern and Southern veterans turned textbook treatments of the Civil War into codas on Bull Run and Antietam. The GAR charged in 1888 that pro-Southern textbooks justified secession, defiled Lincoln as a warmonger, and pictured Confederate leaders as selfless patriots. The time had come, the GAR wrote, "to cease toying with treason for policy, and to cease illustrating the rebels as heroes. . . . It is not reviving sectional issues or animosities to advocate that this matter be dealt with strictly in accordance with the true facts of history."[33]

The veterans of the Confederacy had a different set of "true facts" in mind. Scrutinizing the currently used books, they could hardly find a "true and reliable history" that would vindicate white Southerners who fought in the war. In 1911, the United Confederate Veterans resolved that "every text-book on history and literature in Southern schools should be tested" against Mildred L. Rutherford's *A Measuring Rod for Text-Books*. This small primer called for rejection of any text that, among other things, "says the South fought to hold her slaves" or "speaks of the slaveholder of the South as cruel or unjust to his slaves." Librarians were enjoined to inscribe on the title page of any book not measuring up to *A Measuring Rod* the words "Unjust to the South."[34]

The history battles over presentation of the Civil War became so heated that the Wisconsin section of the GAR proposed a commission of educators to write a history amenable to both North and South.[35] No such book ever appeared. Beset by veterans' groups in both North and South, publishers abandoned volumes presenting different perspectives and instead issued separate Northern and Southern versions of U.S. history. For decades, young people from North and South would discover that they had been taught widely, indeed wildly, different versions of the Civil War, in each case believing that their textbooks had provided the "true facts."

Though students absorbed either one or another version of the Civil War but never learned of several perspectives on it, they learned something in common—a superpatriotic history once the books got beyond the Civil War. But what did love of nation consist of? One of the main ideas of the American patriotic rendition of the past was that nature's law arranged the races of the world hierarchically, with Europeans on top and people ordered beneath them almost by the degree of pigment in their skins. If the student learned his or her history lessons properly, any American boy or girl would have been able to glance at a new schoolmate and know whether that child was capable of intellectual or social success. As the main surveyor of nineteenth-century textbooks puts it: "The child would question the wisdom of indiscriminate immigration to the United States; he would not expect the Negro to take an equal place in American civilization; he would expect race to be a determining factor in the development of the individual. Nor would he think the American melting pot capable of amalgamating racial traits into a homogeneous whole."[36]

Schoolchildren at the end of the nineteenth century would also read books that were thoroughly mistrustful of too much democracy and deeply averse to portraying the role of ordinary people in the making of history. Frederick Law Olmsted, the designer of Central Park in New York City and Golden Gate Park in San Francisco, wrote earlier in his career that "men of literary taste . . . are always apt to overlook the working-classes, and to confine the records they make of their own times . . . to the habits and fortunes of their own associates or to those of people of superior rank to themselves." Olmsted, who left us one of the most remarkable surveys of plantation life in the slave South, deplored that "the dumb masses have often been so lost in this shadow of egotism, that . . . it has been impossible to discern the very real influence their character and condition has had on the fortune and fate of nations."[37] But textbook writers were deaf to Olmsted's imprecations; the cultural arbiters of the late nineteenth century were little interested in the history of ordinary people, many of whom were engaging in bitter industrial war against the wealthy captains of industry.

Nor were the Founding Fathers immune from acidic treatment, especially if they seemed too democratically inclined. John Bach McMaster's popular eight-volume *History of the People of the United States* reviled Thomas Jefferson, saying he was "saturated with democracy in its rankest form" and "remained to the last day of his life a servile worshipper of the people."[38] Children's textbooks emphasized the theme of love of nation and liberty. But liberty was rarely defined. "The child reader," writes Ruth Miller Elson, "could be certain that it [liberty] is glorious, it is American, it is to be revered, and it deserves his primary loyalty. But for the child to find out from these books what this liberty is would be astonishing."[39]

Remember that if "the world created in . . . schoolbooks [was] essentially a world of fantasy—a fantasy made up by adults as a guide for their children, but inhabited by no one outside the pages of schoolbooks," that world was one where all but a small percentage of young Americans completed their schooling by eighth grade and then moved on to places of work.[40] In 1880, nearly ten million teenagers were enrolled in the grammar schools but only one hundred ten thousand in high schools.[41] The aim of history instruction, then, was to teach the morality of work and loyal citizenship. That study must inculcate "a firm and unanimous stand on matters of basic belief . . . love of country, love of God, duty to parents, the necessity to develop habits of thrift, honesty, and hard work in order to accumulate property, the certainty of progress, the perfection of the United States."[42] Youngsters in Germany, Japan, Russia, and Brazil learned a similarly rosy and stirring national history.

History and Controversy

This book will look at a number of episodes when historical revisionism came under attack. All these stories show that important works of history and new schools of scholarly inquiry have repeatedly triggered controversy.

Nearly two thousand years ago, Plutarch denounced Herodotus, saying he had slandered the greatest Greek cities, not least Thebes, which was in Plutarch's native region of Boeotia. Though others in his day told Tacitus that "your histories will be immortal," only a century later he was called "the glibbest of liars." As the centuries have rolled by, Tacitus's reputation has varied. He excited the scorn of Napoleon, who called him an "unjust slanderer of humanity," but he earned praise from Thomas Jefferson and John Adams, who equated the "morality of Tacitus" with the "morality of patriotism."

For many generations Americans have been involved in face-offs over what history should be taught in school. Perhaps it cannot be otherwise because history is a touchstone of contemporary concerns and a mirror that we hold before us to see who we are, where we came from, and where we are going. So long as history is a fluid, dynamic field, it will uneasily mingle commemoration and critique. Americans have never agreed on a single, unified version of our past, nor should they if our country is to remain democratic. Nor can anyone find a people anywhere in the world who agree on the course of their national history. Like Americans, they vigorously debate heroes and villains, high points and low points, tragic mistakes and towering successes.

Today's gunslingers in the history wars are dead sure, as Newt Gingrich has instructed us, that Americans until 1965 had a common understanding of the past, "from deTocqueville to Norman Rockwell's paintings." Senator Bob Dole, running hard for the Republican presidential nomination, told the American Legionnaires on Labor Day 1995 that a generation of historians were members of "intellectual elites who seem embarrassed by America."[43]

To make such claims requires a convenient forgetting of the long story of historical controversy in this nation. Arthur Schlesinger Sr., a leader of the history profession before World War II, was slammed by ultraconservatives in the middle of the 1920s for his *New Viewpoints in American History*, a book of essays that included such chapter titles as "The Influence of Immigration on American History" and "The Role of Women in American History." In 1927, the mayor of Chicago, reviling Schlesinger as a history thief and perpetrator of "un-American and unpatriotic statements," dispatched one of his staffers to burn a copy of the historian's "treason-tainted" book on the steps of the downtown public library.[44]

Should Americans be alarmed that history produces controversy? Is the moral fabric of our nation imperiled if historians challenge yesterday's version of the American Revolution, the Civil War, or the Salem witch trials? If Marcel Duchamp's painting "Nude Descending a Staircase" was controversial at the Armory show in New York City in 1913, should that picture have been suppressed? How does controversy over Albert Einstein's quantum theory in physics differ from controversy over reinterpretations of Columbus's character?

Today's apocalyptic predictions about "the end of history" and charges of the plundering of the honorable past by relativist-deconstructionist-revisionist historians, supposedly "tenured radicals" foisted on colleges and universities in the 1960s, actually come down to a simple question: Whose history? The sources of this argument, as we will see, are various. But the present debate, the occasion for writing this book, was born in reaction to the redistribution of the property in history that arose when the history profession began to resemble American society in all its diversity.

Two millennia ago Plato observed, "Those who tell the stories also hold the power." This sentiment is reflected succinctly in the words chiseled in marble inside the rotunda of the Library of Congress: "History is the biography of great men." That is the lesson that millions of schoolchildren learn when they visit the rotunda on spring vacation trips to Washington. In fact, until recently, their own school textbooks taught the same dictum: History was the story of great white men—for that matter, great white Protestant men.

Today the storyteller's power is held more diversely, both inside and outside the academy. This has led to an examination of vast dimensions of the human experience heretofore unnoticed. Why should a democratic people dedicated to equality not applaud the attention now given to the roles in history of women, African Americans, working people, religious denominations, and other groups relatively powerless in the formal political sense? Christopher Hill reminds us that "The experience of something approaching democracy makes us realize that most of our history is written about, and from the point of view of, a tiny fragment of the population."[45] Is this the voice of "political correctness" or a recognition of the link between a democratic society and a more historically complete and accurate rendering of the past?

In the United States and other countries, historians have since the 1960s opened up new fields of study, especially women's history, the history of minority groups, and the history of labor. Scholars have also "explored unchartered groups and institutions; made the expressive culture of the folk and of popular entertainment part of American culture; wondered openly about the direction of cultural diffusion and hypothesized that cultural influence could proceed from the socioeconomic bottom to the top as well as vice versa."[46] For most educators, this is cause for satisfaction. "It is no longer necessary," Christopher Hill wrote more than two decades ago, "to apologize profusely for taking the common people of the past on their own terms and trying to understand them."[47]

"The primary criticism of contemporary historiography," writes Lawrence Levine, "has little to do with what kind of history we practice and almost everything to do with the subjects of that history. This is really what is objected to by those who so fear the directions in which many contemporary historians are moving."[48] In subsequent chapters, we will examine this alteration in the writing and teaching of history and show how it has "grown out of the insistent democratization of American society."[49] We will argue that those who attack historians as cultural elitists are actually frightened by the shattering of elite control over history writing, by the subsequent widening of historians' lenses, by the "opening of the American mind" rather than its closing, and by the far more inclusive, often bittersweet history that young Americans are learning in school.[50]

CHAPTER 2

Hallowed History, New History

What did you learn in school today,
Dear little boy of mine?
I learned our government must be strong.
It's always right and never wrong....
That's what I learned in school.

—Song by Tom Paxton

By the eve of the Civil War, history for American students was a house built on a rock. Its foundation firm, it was a safe abiding place for patriotic certainties, national truths, and a knowable world. It was a storehouse of sacrosanct facts attesting to America's inherent greatness and unique virtue.[1] Of course, most adults knew better because they were still arguing passionately about the causes, character, and outcomes of the American Revolution. Theirs was a more complex view of history, but they agreed, in the main, that children would have time enough to learn that when they were older.

A half century later, the rock had developed cracks and fissures. History became a professional enterprise modeled on science, and its practitioners believed that once the present becomes the past, it can never be fully recovered. Rather, it must be reconstructed. More than that, the new historians recognized themselves as building contractors with different ideas about how those materials should be chosen and assembled into narratives and explanations. Religious beliefs, economic circumstances, ethnic affiliations, schooling, and numerous other variables deeply affected how different scholars approached and carried out their tasks. As the Age of Einstein opened, history builders also recognized that historical findings could never be completely detached from the individuals who discovered, organized, and interpreted the information. If this proposition was correct—if each new generation of historians reshaped the past in a new way—how could the nation be sure that any truth about itself was unquestionable?

By the early twentieth century, a condition of chronic tension was developing in this country between history as something to be analytically constructed using resources at hand with as much detachment and integrity as possible and history as a framework for reaffirming the rectitude and world mission of America and Western civilization. As a recent study puts it, "the open-ended search for information about the past collided with the vigilant censors of patriotic pride."[2]

Nationalist defenders of a glorious and immutable past knew, of course, that the most important incubator of patriotism was the schoolhouse. But to their dismay they discovered, in their view way too late, that the new history masters—with their critical questions, conflicting interpretations, and insistence on relativism and perspective—were taking control of the curriculum. Academic specialists, teachers, school superintendents, and educational sociologists had many factional quarrels, but all of them seemed to agree that civic allegiance and virtue should arise out of reflection, debate, and vigorous engagement with history. To the patriots who believed schools were places not to appraise and analyze America but to inspire imperturbable faith in its nobility, such views were shameful. Intellectual vandals, they said, should stay out of history's sacred temple.

Treason Texts

The first cannonades fired in this century's history wars were aimed at an unlikely target. David Saville Muzzey cut a poor figure as a propagator of seditious schoolbooks. A Massachusetts Brahmin from a line of preachers and teachers extending back to the Puritans, Muzzey held a doctorate from Columbia University and taught history there. In 1911, he published a secondary school text titled simply *An American History.* Written in lively prose and displaying a firm grip on the scholarship of his day, the book was a great success. It appeared in numerous editions and sold millions of copies.

Muzzey was a Progressive, believing that the rise of smokestack industry and the accompanying immigration of massive numbers from southern and eastern Europe had left the nation in need of refurbishment and reform. "It was inconceivable," he wrote, "that the great body of American citizens . . . will long allow one tenth of their number to stagnate in abject poverty."[3] He was also critical of the Mexican War of 1846–48 because it expanded slave territory and fueled bitter conflict among Americans. He thought slavery had been a cancer and wrote privately of how he was "sick of the pussy-footing of authors who know what a damnable cause the South fought for."[4]

Yet Muzzey was anything but a radical. He had a thoroughly patrician distaste for the labor organizing and conflict that occurred during the post-Reconstruction decades. Nor was he enlightened on the topic of race. Accepting conventional theories of the innate inferiority of blacks and others of stock supposedly less hardy than Anglo-American, he wrote in *An American History* that Indians displayed "a stolid stupidity that no white man could match."[5] On Reconstruction he instructed students that the Fourteenth and Fifteenth amendments were mistakes because enfranchising the freedmen "set the ignorant, superstitious, gullible slave in power over his former master."[6] Students also learned that state governments in the South were run by scalawags and inferior blacks who conducted "an indescribable orgy of extravagance, fraud, and disgusting incompetence—a travesty on government."[7]

Muzzey was a mainstream historian of his time, who wished merely to bring the flavor of recent scholarship into the classroom. Across the country children lugged his textbook back and forth to school. Even so, he might have had a hint of approaching trouble. In 1913, Charles Beard, a brilliant historian also at Columbia, came under public attack after publishing *An Economic Interpretation of the Constitution of the United States*. Working from sheaves of documents in the Treasury Department, Beard reconstructed the financial investments of the members of the Constitutional Convention of 1787. The research demonstrated that something more than abstract political theory filled the heads of the fifty-five delegates. Beard's group biography—an innovative methodology in itself—concluded that the new nation's propertied classes, loathing the popular democracy permeating some state legislatures, had sought a Constitution that would provide a strong federal bulwark against the likes of the rebellious Daniel Shays and the debt-ridden farmers who followed him.[8]

An Economic Interpretation would be read, discussed, and debated for decades; it still is today. But in 1913, Beard was attacked in terms that made Benedict Arnold seem like a model American. A headline in the newspaper in Marion, Ohio, proclaimed:

SCAVENGERS, HYENA-LIKE, DESECRATE THE GRAVES
OF THE DEAD PATRIOTS WE REVERE.

The ensuing story called Beard's book "libelous, vicious and damnable" for impugning the pure motives of the framers of the Constitution, and it urged all true Americans to "rise to condemn him and the purveyors of his filthy lies and rotten aspersions."⁹ Seattle banned Beard's book from the public schools and ordered city library officials to move it to "closed and restricted reserve," where lurid and scatological materials were sequestered.¹⁰

The early revised editions of Muzzey's *An American History* paid little attention to Beard's provocative thesis, but in 1921, after the book had enjoyed a decade of success in the schools, Muzzey suddenly found himself accused of writing a "treason text" and contaminating young minds with anti-Americanism. Other Progressive historians also became targets of superpatriotic hostility.

The attacks on the way these historians were interpreting the American experience must be set against the climate of the times. Out of the Great War, which ended in 1918, the United States emerged as a muscular, rapidly growing, intensely polyglot nation. The 1920s in some ways paralleled the 1990s as a period when the country's economic, demographic, and cultural personality was being transformed. Growing pains were to be expected. For example, the victory of the Bolsheviks in the Russian Revolution produced in this country a surge of antiforeign feeling that led in 1919 to the Red Scare. More than thirty-six hundred labor strikes, some of them violent, hit cities coast to coast. Sacco and Vanzetti, immigrant anarchists, and Joe Hill, songwriter for the radical Wobblies, captured headlines throughout long court trials that ultimately sent them to their deaths. When Sacco and Vanzetti were executed in 1927, riots broke out in numerous cities abroad.

Amid these agitations, Charles Grant Miller, a syndicated writer for the Hearst newspapers, launched a campaign to convince school boards across the nation that Muzzey and other historians who subscribed to the new professionalism were producing textbooks "unfit for public-school use because subversive of the American spirit," "grossly defamatory," and "un-American." These texts were filled, he said, with "alien allegiances" and "distortions, perversions and outright falsifications of vital historical truths," and they assaulted impressionable minds with "sneering deprecations" of the nation's founders and other eminent Americans.¹¹

Such charges of subversion suggest that critics had exposed Muzzey and other scholars as wild-eyed radicals disseminating Bolshevik versions of American history. In fact the presumed virus infecting the schoolbooks was not left-wing radicalism but Anglophilia, purportedly pro-British distortions of the American Revolution and the War of 1812. Miller's book, *The Poisoned Loving-Cup*, laid out the charges against Muzzey and his colleagues, and it is instructive in light of today's attacks on historical revisionism. Miller's title was a reference to Anglo-American "coalition propaganda." Instead of imbibing draughts of patriotism from the loving-cup of history, schoolchildren were swallowing a bitter brew of anti-Americanism, "contemptuous hostility toward heroes of the Revolution and other founders and defenders of our Republic." The wretched "revisionists," he wrote, "minimize or omit many of the vital principles, heroes, and incidents of the Revolution, hitherto held sacred in American history." As detestable a man as Benedict Arnold was, "his weapon was sword against sword in a man-to-man warfare. But the treason of today insidiously directs against the minds of our children the poison gas of alien propaganda to deaden patriotic spirit and stupefy the national soul into unthinking submission to unknown imperialistic designs."[12]

Miller enlisted the support of alarmed patriotic organizations: the Veterans of Foreign Wars, the American Legion, the Sons of the American Revolution, the United Daughters of 1812, the Patriotic Order of the Sons of America, and others. His harangues readily convinced them that Muzzey, Carl Becker, Andrew McLaughlin, Albert Bushnell Hart, Charles and Mary Beard, and other textbook writers subjected students to "perversion, distortion and pollution." Even more darkly, Miller asserted that "such school men ... owe their promotion and their attitude of mind to the organized influences which seek to undermine the American spirit." The youth of America would now march to "God Save the King" rather than to "Yankee Doodle Dandy."[13]

For Miller and his allies, Hart committed simple and deliberate treason when he told students, as he did in his textbook, that before the Stamp Act crisis of 1765 "the colonists liked to think of themselves as part of the British empire ... [and] were proud of being Britons."[14] This of course was patently true, for although the colonists, living locally circumscribed lives, nurtured affection for Virginia, Pennsylvania, and New Hampshire, they also cultivated cosmopolitan transatlantic ties, sending sons to England for legal and medical training, aping English fashions, and wearing with great pride the emblem "freeborn Englishman."

The Poisoned Loving-Cup singled out Muzzey for special treatment, assailing him for suggesting that the Founding Fathers and presidents were made of anything but marble. "Professor Muzzey does not know American history," wrote Miller, "and does not want to know it. All he knows is British history of America. What he knows is what he sees through King George's eyes."[15] Among the most odious of Muzzey's presumed lies was the assertion that many Americans refused to subscribe to "the glorious cause" in 1776. In response to Muzzey's contention that "the Tories or Loyalists were champions on one side of a debatable question, namely, whether the abuses of the King's ministers justified armed resistance," Miller railed: "On what grounds can it be contended that such doubts and questionings of the cause of the patriots are not just as treasonable today as they were then?"[16]

In his campaign, Miller used tactics that right-wing critics of the National History Standards would find useful seventy years later: Employ hyperbolic, overheated language; distort the content of the books; flood the press with scary stories denouncing the corruption of children's minds; and enlist support from national patriotic associations. Miller himself founded The Patriotic League for the Preservation of American History, raising money to issue a booklet titled *Treason to American Tradition: The Spirit of Benedict Arnold Reincarnated in United States History Revised in Textbooks.* The wide distribution of this tract was enough to bring a number of school superintendents under fire. In Portland, Oregon, Newark, New Jersey, and other cities, superintendents lost their jobs when Miller's patriots discovered the pro-British propaganda in their schools.

In an action presaging the Senate's censure of the National History Standards in 1995 for allegedly failing to show "a decent respect for . . . United States history, ideas, and institutions, to the increase of freedom and prosperity around the world," the Oregon legislature passed a law prohibiting the use of any textbook that "speaks slightingly of the founders of the republic, or of the men who preserved the union, or which belittles or undervalues their work."[17] The law did not say who would judge where such belittling and undervaluing had crept into the texts. Nor did it specify whether descriptions of such episodes as Puritans hanging Quakers on Boston Common in the 1650s or the Paxton Boys massacring praying Christian Conestoga Indians in 1763 were slights on the American character that should be eradicated from schoolbooks.

The American Historical Association (AHA) tried to rescue Muzzey and his colleagues by issuing a statement: "The clearly implied charges that many of our leading scholars are engaged in treasonable propaganda and that tens of thousands of American school teachers and officials are so stupid or disloyal as to place treasonable textbooks in the hands of children is inherently and obviously absurd."[18] Viewing the attacks on the new scholarship incorporated into school texts, James Truslow Adams, a popularizer of American history, asked the public to consider whether American democracy was up to its principles. "If democracy rejects the truth, will it slowly retire again, as in the Middle Ages, to the quiet cell of its cloistered votary?" If the American public "should come to prefer flattering local legend to critical analysis, if it should demand passionate propaganda in place of reasoned statement . . . then the outlook for the writing of history which should be both popular and truthful would indeed be dark."[19]

Miller's Patriotic League continued to fight its culture war on a broad front, convinced that it had uncovered "interlocking directorates between [a] text-book publishing firm and seven alien agencies." The offending corporation was Ginn & Company, Muzzey's publisher and the largest producer of schoolbooks in the United States at the time. The seven conspiring agencies were the World Court League, the League of Nations Union, the League of Nations Non-Partisan Association, the World Peace Foundation, the World Alliance for Promoting International Friendship Through the Churches, the New York Peace Society, and the New York Union for International Justice. Ginn's offices in New York, charged Miller, were "the largest breeding-nest and roosting-place in America of Anglo-American and pacifist organizations." Miller tagged George A. Plimpton, Ginn's senior officer, with the title "King George" Plimpton, and he exposed Nicholas Murray Butler, president of Columbia University (and a onetime Republican vice presidential candidate), as the head of the World Peace Foundation, an organization striving to "disarm America by destroying patriotic spirit and inculcating national pusillanimity in the name of peace."[20]

Though isolationist sentiment was strong enough to keep the United States from joining the League of Nations, relatively few teachers and school boards bought the idea that crazed professors at prominent universities were part of an Anglo-American plot to subvert the nation. Gradually, the furor over the "treason texts" subsided as America turned its attention to the decade's rollicking business boom. And though banned in some communities, Muzzey's books continued to be widely distributed. In 1927, William Hale Thompson, the new mayor of Chicago, launched a belated attack on allegedly pro-British textbooks. But Chicagoans, more interested in Prohibition and Al Capone, paid little attention. One political cartoon neatly poked Mayor Thompson in the eye. A Chicago police officer pulls over a suspicious-looking truck and demands to know what the driver is carrying. "Only booze," the trucker replies. "Drive on, brother," says the officer, "I thought it was history books."[21]

Even the American Legion, which commissioned a textbook on U.S. history in 1925, dismissed the contention that Muzzey and other scholars had sold out to the British or deliberately sullied the heroes of '76.[22] However, the organization did advise that until American students reached college they should not be exposed to the "blunders, foibles and frailties of prominent heroes and patriots" or even learn about unsavory aspects of the American past such as slavery or the displacement of Native Americans. Schoolbooks, counseled the American Legion, should never be vehicles for putting students in touch with "recent historical research." Rather, *amor patriae*, an undiluted patriotism, should be inculcated through triumphal and heroic storytelling.[23]

Public dispute over the proper relationship between history and national identity emerged as a serious twentieth-century problem. Professional historians found the prospects disturbing. Arthur M. Schlesinger Sr. reflected morosely "on the difficulties of a historian, if he must guide his pen to meet the requirements of one hundred percent American school committee politicians."[24] If the country had entered World War I to keep the world safe for democracy, what kind of society was to be honored at home in the books children read? Beard deplored the attempts of superpatriots to "standardize the minds of children" and commended "tendencies in research and learning that work in the opposite direction, towards enlightened intelligence as distinguished from formulas of salvation."[25] Another university professor who tried his hand at writing a textbook observed, "If the history of the United States were written exactly as it happened the author would probably be landed in jail."[26]

The New History

Part of the reason that history became more controversial after World War I was that many more Americans were learning it. At the end of the nineteenth century, the public school came of age as young people who in earlier decades would have spent their days in field, mine, and mill entered the nation's classrooms. Between 1880 and 1900, the standard of living of the average American went up and the number of high schoolers almost quintupled, rising from one hundred ten thousand to five hundred nineteen thousand.[27] By 1920, the high school population soared to 2.2 million. The Jeffersonian dream of a republic built on free public schools—the *sine qua non* of democracy—was beginning to come true.

Many of the new pupils standing at the blackboards were children of the great wave of immigration from southern and eastern Europe, and Asia, that spanned the nineteenth and early twentieth centuries. As schools proliferated and classrooms filled with children of many origins, legislators, school boards, and arbiters of culture looked for ways to Americanize this diverse throng. Public conviction was growing that the study of history, especially the American past, was one way to help assimilate the influx of newcomers whose roots were neither Anglo-Saxon nor Protestant and, in many cases, not even European. Educators and public officials were moved to firm up and unify the national consciousness of Americans, who had only lately been released from the brutal bloodletting and deep regional hatreds of the Civil War. Also, a curriculum combining American and European history would instill in all citizens, whether they were born in Indiana or Italy, Rhode Island or Russia, the sensibility of sharing a common heritage of Western civilization.

It was natural that the newly emerging corps of professional historians should be involved in this framework building. It was equally logical—in fact it was regarded as a responsibility—that they should not only transform colleges from schools for wealthy boys into modern, research-oriented universities but also turn their hands to writing textbooks for young learners. Today we remember little of this group of historians who plumped for making history an essential element of public education. Among them were Woodrow Wilson, who headed Princeton University before launching his political career; Andrew C. McLaughlin, the foremost constitutional historian of the early twentieth century and the son of a Michigan teacher and school superintendent; Charles Kendall Adams, a former schoolteacher who rose to become president of Cornell and the University of Wisconsin; Frederick Jackson Turner, whose essay on the role of the frontier in shaping American society made him a household name; and Albert Bushnell Hart, friend and Harvard classmate of Teddy Roosevelt.

These men, as well as Beard, Muzzey, and several others, proudly gave themselves the name of "New Historians" and declared their mission to be to write "New History." Rather than hobbyists and armchair intellectuals who dabbled in history on the side while practicing law or medicine, many of the new breed of scholars earned doctorates at German universities where they were taught "scientific" methods for exploring historical causation and meaning. These scholars established the first doctoral programs in history at American universities, founded the first national history organizations, launched scholarly journals, and brought new energy, ideas, and foresight to the state and local historical societies that had been spreading since the early decades of the nineteenth century.

The atmosphere of serious, professionalized inquiry brought about a striking change of attitude toward history in the schools, not only the *subjects* children should study but also *how* they should acquire knowledge and intellectual maturity. The New Historians, allying with Progressive school educators, told the nation that the traditional curriculum and its teaching methods were dysfunctional in a fast-changing, multiethnic society. The dry, limited subject matter, the mindless verbatim recitations, the monotonous memorization—all inflicted on children out of the quaint assumption that such practices exercised the "mind-as-muscle"—were ill-suited to educate Americans about the responsibilities of democratic citizenship. In the quest for an egalitarian, functional education, school subjects were not to be abandoned. Rather, they were to be expanded to include more of the "modern" studies—history, science, English, and modern languages—that began to penetrate the classical curriculum during the middle decades of the nineteenth century. History, according to the Progressive reformers, must emphasize not indoctrination or memory work but analysis and interpretation of the past based on rigorous weighing and judging of evidence from a variety of original sources. Historical studies grounded in "critical thinking" held the promise of an astute citizenry capable of independent reflection and reasoned judgment—precisely the skills a dynamic nation needed to confront problems for which past practices held few answers.

The New Historians found their first major opportunity to influence the schools through a task force organized in 1892 to make recommendations on curriculum. A revitalized National Education Association instituted the committee, and Charles Eliot, president of Harvard, headed it. The Conference on History, Civil Government, and Political Economy—more commonly referred to as the History Ten—constituted one of the council's nine subcommittees. This group included several luminaries among the New Historians: Charles Kendall Adams, president of the University of Wisconsin and chair; Albert Bushnell Hart of Harvard; James Harvey Robinson of Columbia; and Woodrow Wilson of Princeton.

The committee's 1893 report found history and its allied disciplines, insofar as they were taught through properly thought-provoking methods, to be worthy because these subjects served "to broaden and cultivate the mind, . . . counteract a narrow and provincial spirit, . . . prepare the pupil in an eminent degree for enlightenment and intellectual enjoyment in after years, . . . and assist him to exercise a salutary influence upon the affairs of his country."[28]

Thus, the committee advised that the chief purposes of history teaching should not be to impart facts but to train students to gather evidence, generalize upon data, estimate character, apply the lessons of history to current events, and lucidly state conclusions.[29] Instead of rote recitations and "historical catechism," classrooms should be alive with mock legislatures and debates, inquiry into original sources, broad reading in historical literature beyond the assigned textbook, and comparative analyses of institutions and events. Viewed a hundred years later, these recommendations have a fresh, contemporary ring, the sort of sound instructional practice that most dedicated history teachers still favor.

In 1896, the AHA formed a second commission, the Committee of Seven, to take up the question of college entrance requirements in history. The traditional nineteenth-century curriculum included little study of any history other than the ancient and Biblical past. The president of Harvard observed that as of the mid-1880s most colleges "make no requirement in history for admission, and have no teacher of history whatsoever."[30]

By the end of the century, however, history was gaining legitimacy as part of university education, and curricular linkages back to the high schools had become an important issue. In its 1899 report the History Seven, whose combined membership had a rich fund of experience in both secondary and college teaching, ratified virtually everything the History Ten had said about the value of critical inquiry over memory work. The committee's key action was to recommend that all young Americans devote themselves to a four-year block of high school history: Greek, Roman, and early medieval history, with attention to the Oriental background in grade 9; the Middle Ages and modern Europe in 10; English history in 11; and American history and government in 12. The committee also advised that teachers be trained in both "the essentials of historical study and historical thinking" and in the subject "as a growing, developing, and enlarging field of human knowledge."[31]

After the turn of the century, Charles McMurry codified the two commissions' ideas in *Special Method in History*, which became the leading guide for teacher education. Biographies of famous heroes would still have a place in the curriculum, serving as "examples and ideals to arouse enthusiasms, and having an unestimated power in giving the initial impulses toward the formation of character in children."[32] The common interests of society and the introduction of students to public issues must, however, occupy the larger share of history education. The New History also suggested a sounder approach to patriotic values than the traditional focus on nationalist emotion and nostalgia. McMurry advised:

It is often said that one aim of history is to teach patriotism. It might better be said that history should aim to clarify and purify the sentiment of patriotism. The crude feeling of patriotism is very strong and demonstrative in this country.... True patriotism, by common consent, does not consist in magnifying our own country at the expense of England, the North at the expense of the South, or America, right or wrong, at the expense of the world. To cultivate fair-mindedness and honesty, to see clearly both sides of an historical controversy, is, in this respect, the true standard of historical study. Americans have enough to be proud of without belittling those who chance to be their opponents, and without extravagant boasting as to their own deserts. Among other things we can well afford to understand our own mistakes and weaknesses, and to accept with fair-mindedness and honesty some of the superior excellences and institutions of other countries.[33]

Hence, elementary and secondary schools must develop in students "a well-balanced judgment in the weighing of arguments, and in estimating probabilities. This is a most useful form of reasoning, constantly needed in our everyday problems."[34]

Together the History Ten and the History Seven gave American schools the closest thing to a national curriculum in history and civics that educators would ever attempt. History secured a firm place in the academic day, and by 1916 the four-year course sequence was nearly universal in secondary institutions.[35] The critical and "scientific" methods of the New Historians, however, did not percolate down through the schools as quickly as members of the AHA might have liked. Before World War I many teachers were still only minimally educated, and, particularly in rural America, schoolmarms and masters continued for a long time to rap out lessons in the old-fashioned ways. Even so, reflective, analytical approaches to the study of history found wide support among Progressive educators committed to the formation of an alert, informed citizenry.

The New Historians had reason to be optimistic about both the revisionist history they were writing and the pedagogy that was gradually taking hold in the schools. Nevertheless, the cultural boundaries of these scholars and their work were still narrow compared to our own time. In 1895, the first issue of the *American Historical Review*, the journal of the AHA, signaled just how smugly satisfied the young profession could be about its own cultural pedigree. "We are Europeans of ancient stock," announced the editorial board, "[who] brought with us from England, Scotland, Ireland, Holland, Germany, and France," a "well-ordered, serious life."[36] The profession was to be understood as a cultivated patrician one, "a homogeneous class with a common mission" to curb the democratic but hurly-burly excesses of immigrants and laborers and to serve the nation, disorderly, dynamic, and muscular as it was, as a unifying and stabilizing force.[37]

This cramped social and cultural vision notwithstanding, the first generation of professional historians produced a remarkable body of scholarship. By 1915, a group of them under the leadership of Hart were hard at work on the twenty-eight volume *American Nation* series. By today's standards, these books are loosely woven and lightly documented, but they represented an early, ambitious effort to interweave new research in social and political history. Over several decades the volumes influenced the textbooks students read in both schools and colleges.

The Historians Take a Walk

Even before the end of World War I the alliance between historians and the schools was beginning to weaken. Ironically, the same progressive impulses that had produced the New History also brought forth critics of history's prominent position in the curriculum. One of the dimensions of Progressivism was the movement for "scientific management" of the nation's industry and, by extension, its educational infrastructure. The leaders of this crusade for accountability, cost-effectiveness, practicality, and "social efficiency" in the schools were not teachers or scholars but superintendents, principals, and curriculum specialists, the officials who directly confronted the myriad organizational problems of rapidly expanding school systems. Utility-minded administrators wanted young Americans to finish high school prepared to work diligently, consume intelligently, and vote responsibly. Therefore, they favored social education that emphasized current affairs, civic life, and the wisdom of the social sciences, which were not far behind history in becoming organized as professional disciplines. These apostles of social efficiency found such humanistic studies as ancient and medieval history insufficiently useful to young Americans training to fill social and occupational niches in the workaday world.

In 1916, when Woodrow Wilson was president and the United States was about to enter World War I, the National Education Association issued a report developed by a schools task force, the Commission on the Reorganization of Secondary Education. One of the commission's arms was the Committee on Social Studies, a body that, in contrast to the Committees of Ten and Seven, included a large number of administrators and teachers but not many university historians. This committee advised junior and senior high schools to rework their curriculums to emphasize modern and contemporary issues: geography and history in grades 7 and 8, civics in 9, a "problems of democracy" course in 12, and all history studies focusing on the last few centuries.

The group also called for a broader, more eclectic social education that would draw as much on political science, sociology, and economics as on history and geography. "Social studies" came into use as an umbrella term for those pursuits "whose subject matter relates directly to the organization and development of human society, and to man as a member of social groups."[38] The 1916 commission's recommendations, pushed enthusiastically by school officialdom, had a huge effect on curriculum in the ensuing years. The golden age of the four-year history curriculum, which in fact had lasted less than two decades, came to an abrupt end as community civics and problems of democracy courses became dominant features of the new social studies curriculum, a national pattern in place for the next seventy years.

A number of progressive historians, such as Charles Beard and James Harvey Robinson, agreed with the 1916 report that modern history, far more than Greek or Roman, illuminated the present in socially serviceable ways and that economic and social themes were as important as political history in training young minds for democratic citizenship. Most of the profession, however, watched in dismay as yearlong courses in ancient, medieval, and English history disappeared from the schools. Like John Dewey and other progressives of a more humanistic turn, they rued the extreme utilitarianism and intellectual presentism of the new breed of school bureaucrat. The great majority of college scholars and teachers, however, responded not by fighting on for high school history but by retreating gradually into their campus quads. Just when David Muzzey, whose lively textbooks pleased most progressive administrators, found himself at war with superpatriots and Anglophobes, his fellow historians were taking less and less interest in how their subject was taught in the schools.

The profession withdrew slowly. In 1921, the AHA helped finance the National Council for the Social Studies (NCSS), whose early membership consisted mostly of education professors, progressive historians, and teachers who favored the integration of history and the social sciences to better mold public-spirited citizens. At the end of the decade the AHA made one more effort at school involvement by forming yet another Commission on Social Studies. This group's fifteen volumes of materials and two major reports (1932 and 1934) advocated close links between history and the social sciences in the schools and reasserted history's preeminence as the integrating and synthesizing "crown" of the social studies curriculum.[39]

The reports also set a vision for the social studies firmly grounded in a reformist and social activist stance reflective of the early years of the Great Depression and the New Deal. Developed during a period of unprecedented federal planning, the commission's *Conclusions and Recommendations* advocated education as a form of social action that raised concerns about indoctrination. This final report affirmed the importance of the scientific method in order that students might learn "to seek and weigh evidence . . . and act with an informed rather than a prejudiced mind."[40] But it also argued for the development of the activist citizen as the central moral responsibility of the social studies.

This activist reform agenda disturbed and alienated many historians, and the AHA declined to endorse the study. When the seventeen hefty but inchoate volumes fell flat within the profession, historians hastened their retreat from the schools. One eminent scholar, Carlton Hayes, threw in the towel with this statement:

It is now *de rigueur* to regard history not merely as a step-sister of the social sciences but as an ugly and fallen sister, one whose very name should be avoided in polite circles and when referred to at all should be mentioned apologetically and with blushes. No longer, in any part of the country, or in any kind of schools, is there a history program.[41]

Hayes overstated the situation because history continued to hold a respectable place in high school curricula around the country. The public still expected children to know something about the national past, and in the great majority of states a battery of laws and directives protected the eleventh-grade U.S. survey. Also, a new generation of educators, while advocating social studies as a distinct and dynamic discipline, were themselves divided over the central purposes of their field and the place of history in it. Some were history haters, convinced that the discipline was devoted entirely to acquiring facts and did not prepare students to cope with the social, economic, and political problems engulfing the nation in the Depression. For them, sociology, economics, and political science were more relevant for an activist social studies curriculum focused on problems of the present day. Other educators were happy to maintain history at the curricular core. Amid this professional contention and public inertia, thousands of history-loving teachers went on with their subject as they always had.

They did so, however, with less and less help from the academicians. Although the AHA maintained contacts with the NCSS, the two organizations drifted apart, and the collegial network of relationships among professors and teachers slowly dissipated. Increasingly intent on well-rewarded research in more and more specialized university environments, the professoriate closed its eyes to precollegiate education. By the mid-1930s the halcyon days were finished, not to be restored for another half century.

A New Assault on History—1930s Style

However historians, teachers, social scientists, and school officials might argue over the best ways to socialize and Americanize the nation's growing population, virtually the entire educational field agreed in the 1920s and 1930s that social studies education should promote analytic and critical thought. Radical developments in science deeply affected the way Americans with advanced schooling, if not yet the general public, looked upon society, past and present. Before the Great War, modern science had provided "a vision of a comprehensible world: a model of certitude, of unambiguous truth; knowledge that was definite, and independent of the values or intentions of the investigator."[42] But in the 1920s, Einstein's theory of relativity and other astonishing hypotheses shook the foundations of empirical science and its Newtonian certainties.

Historians and social scientists could hardly ignore this revolution. Charles Cole, a scholar of Europe, observed that the theory of relativity compelled him and his colleagues to question the iron grip that factual objectivity had on historical writing. No longer, wrote Cole, would theories "cringe and cower like handmaidens before the queenly 'facts.' "[43] Scientific detachment could hardly sustain historical research if the old science was itself crumbling.

Consequently, scholars mounted what has been called "the pragmatic revolt in American history," a new set of guiding principles: Historical judgments are always tentative, subject to further investigation and evaluation; historical knowledge is contingent; multiple perspectives on the past must be explored because people under study are seldom of one mind; historical objectivity should be pursued, but it can never be completely achieved; and because, as Einstein declared, a scientist is himself part of the scientific "laws" he expounds, then the historian's writings can never be detached from the persona of the writer.

Despite the almost universal acceptance of these dicta among historians and social scientists, another stream in American society insisted that historical certitudes be reaffirmed, especially the stories and traditional truths that accord with the nation's self-image as great, good, and free. Muzzey discovered in the early twenties the price to be paid for placing himself between the rock of twentieth-century scholarship, with its new notions of contingency and relativism, and the hard place of immutable nationalist narrative. Muzzey's troubles abated at the end of the decade, but within a few years self-appointed guardians of the national memory found another malefactor: Harold Rugg.

Rugg was as unlikely an enemy of the people as Muzzey was. A ninth-generation New Englander who worked as a weaver in a Massachusetts textile mill in order to understand industrial labor and the quality of life at the bottom of the social hierarchy, Rugg acquired two degrees in civil engineering.[44] By 1910, however, he knew that his true calling was in education. After completing a Ph.D. in psychology and sociology, he taught briefly at the University of Chicago. When the country entered the Great War, he joined the psychological division of the U.S. Army. Later, he accepted an appointment as associate professor of education at Teachers College, Columbia, and as educational psychologist at the university's experimental Lincoln School.[45] Here he launched his career as an educational theorist, teacher, and textbook writer.

Rugg drew ideas and strategies from Progressivism that nourished the creative abilities of young learners. Rummaging through many disciplines, he took inspiration from Van Wyck Brooks, Thorstein Veblen, John Dewey, Frederick Jackson Turner, Charles Beard, John Maynard Keynes, R. H. Tawney, John R. Commons, Charles E. Merriam, and others among the leading historians, social scientists, educators, and cultural critics of the new century, most of whom were deeply influenced by the revolution in scientific inquiry. Rugg contrasted these intellectual draughts with his own limited childhood education at the hands of school-ruling traditionalists who worshiped at the altar of social conformity. "The narrow physical inheritance [of New England]," wrote Rugg,

> had produced its counterpart in the circumscribed mental horizon of the people. Life was thin and arid like the soil; norm domineered over the spirit. All social forces—home, community and education—made for acquiescence, molding my contemporaries and myself to the standards of adult life. Independence of thought was minimized; loyalty was canonized.[46]

Firmly committed to the progressive movement in education, Rugg figured prominently in Teachers College's John Dewey Society and in the pages of its journal, *The Social Frontier,* "the leading voice of educational reform."[47] In 1921 he also helped found the NCSS, which became the largest organization of K–12 history and social studies teachers. The particular mission of Rugg's intellectual circle at Columbia was to replace the pedagogy of memorization, harsh discipline, and passive learning with flexible, functional, child-centered social education. As a progressive, he also believed that studies in history must be relevant to contemporary society and its problems and must eschew austere factualism. Though lesser known than many of the progressive movers and shakers at Teachers College, this mild-mannered, highly moral man resolved to apply his theoretical convictions to the writing of textbooks.

In the social studies marketplace, Rugg was soon giving Muzzey's books a run for their money.[48] Producing texts for both elementary and secondary schools almost faster than children could read them—a series titled *Man and His Changing Society* had twenty volumes—Rugg introduced more of the emerging social and economic research than other books did, and his *History of American Civilization, Economic and Social* (1930) became something of a best seller.

In all his books he stressed the need for students to develop analytical judgment, reflective thought, and creative self-expression. He insisted that "pupils must learn to think critically about modern problems" and advised teachers to instill in their pupils "tolerant understanding," to ask over and over again, "Why do you think so?" "Are you open-minded about the matter?" "What is your authority?" "Have you considered all sides of the case?"[49] Rugg also made contributions to world history and culture. His *Changing Civilizations in the Modern World* focused on the histories and contemporary geography of ten countries—Great Britain, France, Germany, Russia, Japan, India, China, Argentina, Brazil, and Chile—and gave fairly balanced and respectful treatment to all of them.[50]

Rugg was particularly inspired by Charles and Mary Beard's efforts to present to American children a history "in which all members of the community would see themselves as somehow among the builders of a unique civilization."[51] He shared this sentiment with the American Federation of Labor (AFL), which for years had been protesting the near exclusion of working people, labor perspectives, controversial subjects, and the experiences of Italian, Chinese, Japanese, Jewish, and other minority groups from history texts. Both Rugg and the AFL also argued that "subjects should be presented not in the form of finished judgments and dogmatic rules . . . but rather as observations of the world about us" and that "in the case of highly controversial subjects, important dissenting views should be fairly and adequately presented."[52]

Rugg's textbooks included restrained criticism of some aspects of American life. He believed that rapid industrialization and laissez-faire economics had produced a consumer culture and higher standard of living for many but also had created corrosive competition, a materialistic mentality, and an impoverishment of the arts. As his biographer puts it, he was deeply devoted to "building a better America"; his social criticism was merely "a lover's quarrel" with his country.[53]

From the perspective of the late 1990s, Rugg's explorations of American and world history appear carefully constructed and ideologically mild, yet far ahead of fellow textbook authors in many of the open-ended questions that he posed. For example, in a section titled "The Red Man's Continent" in *A History of American Civilization* he asked: "In what spirit did the Indians and the Europeans receive each other? Did the white men buy the Indians' land that they settled upon? . . . Again ask yourself whether it was possible for two widely differing civilizations to live side by side in the same region. Consider also the ethical problem: Was it right for the more numerous Europeans to drive back the scattered tribes of Indians?"[54]

By the late 1930s, Rugg's widely admired books, constituting altogether some twenty-five thousand pages of printed material, had sold several million copies in more than five thousand schools.[55] Then, suddenly, the attacks began. Patrioteers who in the 1920s berated Muzzey and others as being pro-British shifted their ground in the following decade to assail Rugg as spreading communist lies. According to Diane Ravitch, this assault was "the first successful ambush by the Red-baiting vigilantes" of the 1930s.[56]

The *National Republic*, a conservative opinion weekly, trained its guns on Rugg in 1936, saying he was infatuated with "collectivism" and was "Sovietizing our children." The same publication attacked Carl Becker's *Modern History* as a "subversive textbook" that purportedly propagated Marxist teachings. It also published a feverish account of the 1936 meeting of the American Federation of Teachers (AFT) in Philadelphia. A "red mist," the article said, rose over the city as "1,000 radicals held high carnival" to mock "those American institutions and ideals that patriots love so well." Sweltering in August heat, these male conventioneers exhibited their leftist credentials by shedding their coats and even their neckties. Among the communists, the article announced, were Charles Beard, John Dewey, and George F. Counts, a colleague of Rugg's at Teachers College and one of the most influential educators in the country.[57]

That attack on Rugg sputtered out, but three years later, new groups brought up heavier artillery. This time the American Federation of Advertising took offense at Rugg's comment that one purpose of advertising was "to persuade the purchaser to buy whether he wants to or not."[58] The publicist for the National Association of Manufacturers, writing in *Liberty*, assailed Rugg, Counts, Carl Becker, and other reformist educators for supposedly promoting "Marxist teachings." (Ironically, Rugg and Counts were leading a censure movement against a communist faction in the faculty union at Teachers College.) B. C. Forbes, soon to found *Forbes* magazine, spearheaded the continuing condemnation of Rugg. Enlisting the American Legion in the cause, he urged its magazine to publish Rugg-beating tracts. In one piece, "Treason in the Textbooks," a cartoon depicted a leering teacher pouring slime on four books titled "Constitution," "Religion," "U.S. Heroes," and "U.S. History" while puzzled boys and girls looked askance.[59]

The assaults on Rugg, far better organized and more strenuous than the attacks on the New Historians of the 1920s, expanded into an ultranationalist crusade to eradicate allegedly anti-American textbooks from the public schools.[60] The stakes, everyone knew, were high. Since 1895, high school education had taken a gigantic leap forward. No longer was it restricted to the top 5 percent of teenage Americans; now it drew the great majority. When William McKinley became president in 1897, two hundred ten thousand Americans attended about twenty-six hundred high schools. As FDR moved toward his second term in 1935, 6 million American youths attended some twenty-nine thousand high schools.[61] The people attacking Rugg saw

One view of Harold Rugg's influence on history teaching
The American Legion Magazine, September 1940

calamity in the subjection of millions of youngsters to critical questioning of the nation's narrative of righteous progress.

In Bradner, Ohio, patrioteers publicly burned Rugg's textbooks, giving local students a counterlesson in First Amendment rights. Wayne Township, New Jersey, and Binghamton, Bronxville, and Mount Kisco, New York, removed his books from the schools. By early 1940, the National Association of Manufacturers had 6,830 "sentinels" posted in 1,338 communities. This infantry's "educational assignment" was to cleanse the schools of "creeping collectivism." "For a generation now," proclaimed association president H. W. Prentis Jr., "our free institutions and the heroes of the American republic have been derided and debunked by a host of puny iconoclasts, who destroy since they cannot build."[62]

A relatively small number coordinated the campaign to banish Rugg's books. Naming eight principal "merchants of conflict," Rugg later observed that they fomented fear in hundreds of communities "by using national publicity channels, especially the facilities of certain national organizations to distribute articles, letters, circular notices, what not."[63] Forecasting in a remarkable way the consequences of Lynne Cheney's 1994 attack on the National History Standards, Rugg noted that "a single article distributed by a national patriotic organization can alter, indeed has drastically altered, the mood of the people in hundreds of communities scattered widely over the country and has resulted in the censorship of schools."[64]

Rugg found himself defending his textbook discussion of the extent to which all Americans shared in the rising standard of living that industrial capitalism had stimulated. In fact, he wrote virtually nothing about the chronic industrial warfare that punctuated the late nineteenth and early twentieth centuries. Rather he confined himself to remarks explaining that the rapid increase in worker wages between 1850 and 1900 tailed off and that by the late 1920s national income was very unevenly distributed. Such revelations, however, were enough to touch off a wave of nationalist indignation on the grounds that young Americans exposed to Rugg's books would think poorly of their country and be incited to class conflict.

Among the persistent themes were charges that Rugg's books "undermine patriotism," "stress 'errors and evils' in our civilization," "belittle and malign America," "debunk our great heroes of the past," and present generally "subversive" and "un-American" points of view.[65] One searches his books in vain for evidence of America-bashing other than a single passage, repeated ad nauseam by Rugg's critics, regarding the Constitutional Convention. The offending words read: "The merchants, landowners, manufacturers, shippers and bankers were given what they wanted [at the Constitutional Convention]." The critics deftly ignored the passage that followed: "namely a government which would stabilize the money and trade, keep order within the country and defend the nation against foreign enemies."[66] In his autobiography, Rugg put his finger on a point that applied equally well to the denunciation of the National History Standards: "Obviously, a writer's meaning can be completely altered or destroyed by lifting statements out of context.... Certainly it is clear that without the indispensable contexts such statements lose their meaning and validity."[67]

Rugg's critics had deep suspicions of critical thinking and tended to equate open inquiry with cynicism and deficient loyalty. Mrs. Elwood Turner, the corresponding secretary of the Daughters of the Colonial Wars, expressed the authoritarian, paternalistic streak in the anti-Rugg campaign. This man, she declared, was trying "to give a child an unbiased viewpoint instead of teaching him real Americanism. All the old histories taught my country right or wrong. That's the point of view we want our children to adopt. We can't afford to teach them to be unbiased and let them make up their own minds."[68]

Rugg's defenders agreed with Charles Beard that "if the social studies are not to deceive pupils, if they are to prepare pupils for the actual world of rough and tumble, give and take, debate and discussion, then they must reckon with controversial issues."[69] In 1942 the American Committee for Democracy and Intellectual Freedom, an organization of leading historians, published a booklet appraising Rugg's writings. The five men who contributed to *The Textbooks of Harold Rugg, An Analysis* were all distinguished scholars and leaders at eminent universities. Cautioning that "attacking textbooks is easy; evaluating them fairly is hard," the authors fully upheld the integrity of Rugg's work. One writer deplored the "acrimonious controversy that generates more heat than light," and he lamented the "numerous onslaughts upon textbooks by groups that have condemned brief passages isolated from their contexts."[70] The reviews contended that Rugg's contributions to the spirit of free inquiry in America were very great.

The booklet helped Rugg continue his career in education, and the controversy died away as the country entered the war. Americans set about making history rather than debating it. However, the children of the war years read David Muzzey's texts more often than Rugg's, and advanced students were typically assigned new books by Henry Steele Commager and Samuel Eliot Morison, both of whom had dodged the public barrages. The criticism of Rugg hurt his sales badly, and after the war the publisher quietly dropped the texts from its list. More troubling, the dispute did serious damage to the Progressives' belief in the power of history—interpreted, reinterpreted, and argued over—to serve the nation's best interests. After the war most textbooks reverted to pallid and fact-soaked prose that was less objectionable to guardians of hallowed national myths but also less engaging to millions of schoolchildren.

General History in the Schools

While putting the writing and teaching of U.S. history on a fresh footing, the New Historians, together with school educators, also wrestled with questions about children's knowledge of the world beyond the country's borders. If America at the turn of the century was a "storm of strangers," what should young people know about the histories of other peoples?

Before World War I, history educators took it for granted that any study of the world's past meant courses on Europe and Europeans abroad. Virtually no controversy arose over issues of cultural inclusiveness and diversity in the study of non-American history because the medieval and modern histories of Asia, Africa, and Latin America did not register on the intellectual consciousness of teachers, historians, or the public.

The earliest secondary school courses in non-American history, called "General History," emerged in the nineteenth century from studies in Bible history and the classics. After about 1870, a time when public high schools began to grow, historians constructed textbooks for General History courses. All of them presented European history, defined to include Greek and Roman civilization, as if it were the history of the world, the only history that for the post-ancient centuries had serious significance for humankind. Moreover, race provided fundamental explanations for the way human society evolved. According to an 1874 textbook titled *Outlines of the World's History,*

> We see that history proper concerns itself with but one highly developed type of mankind; for though the great bulk of the population of the globe has . . . belonged, and does still belong, to other types of mankind, yet the Caucasians form the only true *historical* race. Hence we may say that civilization is the product of the brain of this race.[71]

The text further divided Caucasians into Aryan, Semitic, and Hamitic branches, ranking the first above the other two as the premier maker of history: "It is of interest to know that the race to which we belong, the Aryan, has always played the leading part in the great drama of the world's progress."[72]

The early General History schoolbooks did some justice to Egypt, Mesopotamia, Persia, India, and China as early contributors to civilization but then declared that at the end of ancient times all of these places fell into dead tradition and stasis. Thereafter, history gravitated westward to the Aegean Sea, then to Rome, then to Western and Central Europe. There the grand story of Christian and democratic civilization unfolded. The 1917 edition of a popular text for high schools and colleges contends that

> China was the cradle of a very old civilization, older perhaps than that of any other lands save Egypt and Babylonia; yet Chinese affairs have not until recently exercised any direct influence upon the general current of history. All through the later ancient and medieval times the country lay, vague and mysterious, in the haze of the world's horizon.[73]

As for Africans, their history was a total blank, "for since time immemorial they have been 'hewers of wood and drawers of water' for their more favored brethren."[74]

These textbooks reflected dominant Anglo-Saxon values and attitudes that set cultural standards in the United States and Europe in the decades before World War I. The nations of Western Europe collectively assumed global military control or economic domination, a fact that, despite Japan's participation in imperial enterprise, seemed to confirm the idea that the West was the exclusive agent of historical change. The Second Industrial Revolution was in full swing, and the industrializing, urbanizing countries of Europe and North America were changing so fast that by comparison the rest of the world seemed not to be changing at all. Pseudoscientific race theories explained basic cultural and historical differences among human groups, and racialist assumptions were a routine part of lessons in both school and church. Scholars of the new German-inspired "scientific" history practiced their craft mainly in the archives of Western nation-states. The study of "tribal" peoples and ancient Asian empires was considered to be the business of philologists, archaeologists, and the new specialists in anthropology, but not historians. To American educators of the turn of the century, Eurocentrism was not an intellectual position but a serene certainty.

The idea of world history as coincidental with the Western experience remained firmly entrenched in American schools through World War I, but the commonly taught course in General History fell on hard times. The two key reforming commissions of the 1890s deplored the General History "short course" as massive, unmanageable, and fact-heavy, a subject likely to turn young Americans off to history for the rest of their lives. The Committee of Seven's four-year sequence of high school history courses—classical, medieval/modern, English, and American—took General History's place in most schools. This shift represented a renunciation of the whole idea of the broad course in world history, even though the narrow definition of the world worth knowing did not significantly change. Thus, the one-year survey virtually disappeared from the schools—but only for a time.

After the 1916 Committee on Social Studies issued its recommendations, the one-year world history course, "son of General History," reappeared in more and more schools. Progressive educators, pushing a curriculum that would meet the tests of pragmatic payoff and civic value, not only wanted to free students from long journeys into the remote and, in their view, irrelevant past but also to create a "short course," most often slotted in at tenth grade, that could squeeze non-American history, world geography, and bits of government and sociology into a shipshape and socially efficient package. To them the old History Seven four-year model had too little flexibility and took up too much curricular time. As one educator said, "A three-year course-in-one to be taught on the sophomore level in high school seemed almost too good to be true."75

History professors, who had collaborated with teachers in devising the four-year cluster, dismissed one-year world history as an administrative ploy lacking thematic coherence and pedagogical justification. A school survey conducted for the NCSS in 1923–24 lamented: "Very often the new course is introduced simply to cover as much ground as possible in the one year of history other than American which is offered," and explained that the "conflicting demands of other social studies are the real explanation, rather than any recognition of a World Community or of the need for a new world history."[76]

As more and more university people conceded the field to the social studies professionals, and as the "sheepskin curtain," as Gilbert Allardyce calls it, descended between them, tenth-grade world history gradually became the national standard.[77] This did not mean, however, that overall student enrollments in non-American history declined. A Bureau of Education survey in 1933–34 showed that although far fewer students took courses in ancient, medieval, or English history, enrollments in world history increased steadily enough to make up for the loss.[78] Moreover, considering the rocketing population of high school students, by 1940 reaching 6.6 million in public schools and a half million in private schools, a growing proportion of the nation's youth was being exposed to at least two years of history.[79]

In the interwar period, educators and academic scholars continued to define world history as the story of Western progress, one that largely excluded the experiences of Africans, Asians, and Latin Americans. This attitude is not surprising because, after all, most American intellectuals of that era tended to equate the forces of modernity—science, technology, democracy, liberalism, and enlightened social scientific reasoning—with European civilization. Since the nineteenth century, educated Americans had linked this country's culture and institutions to the traditions and achievements of Europe. After 1918, they were even more zealous to present the United States to the world as a responsible member of the club of democratic nations that had won the war. More than that, the idea of the American nation as the culmination of centuries of struggles toward a more perfect liberty became part of the vocabulary of our national culture. For schoolchildren this meant, as Philip Curtin has written:

Instead of trying to explain the modern world in terms of its past or even tracing the rise of human civilizations, the older "world history" began with the United States and then searched for the roots of American civilization. It was, in effect, "history taught backward"—back to the colonial period on this continent, then back to Europe, and still further back to the

Western Middle Ages, Rome, Greece, and the ancient civilizations of the
Near East.[80]

Another historian describes this traditional "historical world-image of
the West" as having two key components. One was the idea of a "mainstream of history" consisting of "our own closest historical antecedents."
This included the Middle East and Egypt to the time of the Greeks but not
later; Greek history to the time of Rome, but not since; and the nations of
Europe and North America in modern times, but nothing else. The second
idea was that the world is divided historically into two parts. On one side is
the "West," which includes classical Greece but not the Byzantine empire,
the Mediterranean of Rome but not the Mediterranean of Islam. On the
other side is the "East" or "Orient," a place where all the civilizations of Asia
and North Africa may be conceptually heaped together as one, a notion that
"enables us to set up our West as conceptually equivalent to all the other
civilized regions taken together." According to the Western world-image,
moreover, regions such as Africa, Southeast Asia, or pre-Columbian America were to be dismissed as "sparsely inhabited" or at best semicivilized;
thus, their history "does not force itself on our attention."[81]

Not all writing about world history was as rigidly Eurocentric as this
during the interwar period. One reason is that both social studies professionals and New Historians believed that education for responsible citizenship should involve in-depth study of contemporary international issues,
including events beyond North America and Europe. The AHA's 1929–34
commission called in its final report for student understanding of the place
of the United States in a "world civilization" and for a social studies curriculum giving greater attention to international peace efforts and to contemporary developments in Asia, Africa, and Latin America.

Yet despite infusions of contemporary internationalism into the social
studies curriculum, the notion that Western civilization was the creative
center of progressive change throughout world history proved remarkably
tenacious. Carl Becker's *Modern History*, which carried great authority
among teachers and which explored new realms of social and economic as
well as political change, nevertheless defined the modern world in European terms: "While all history is our history in the sense that all history is
the work of human beings like ourselves, modern history is our history in a
special sense. Modern history is the history of our civilization, and of those
recent centuries during which our civilization has taken on the form with
which we are familiar."[82]

Virtually every textbook presented Africa in a way that helped condition
children's view of race. In one widely used book, Africa had no history of

its own. Rather, "Most of the inhabitants were dark of skin. Many of them were even darker of mind, for the light of civilization had not yet reached them.... The vast interior was unknown and untamed. It seemed securely guarded by deserts and distances, by jungles, fevers, and savage tribes."[83] Though the texts of the 1930s were an improvement over the nineteenth-century books, they continued to drag along the baggage of cultural arrogance. The much-used *World History* told children: "From the times of Pericles and Caesar to the present the chief roles in the great drama of history have been taken by the white men of Europe.... The European white man has taught, and if need be, has compelled, his yellow and brown and black brothers to adopt the ways of Europeans."[84]

Paralleling the growth of the Western-Civ-as-world-history course in high schools, universities increasingly adopted a conceptually similar program as a general education requirement for freshmen. College Western Civ had its genesis in the War Issues Course, which campuses across the nation offered during World War I in connection with the government's Student Army Training Corps. The course was designed to educate young American men on the causes of the war but also to build wartime morale. Students were to learn that the struggle in Europe pitted democracy against autocracy, morality against immorality, and civilization against barbarism. France, Britain, and the United States were fighting together to make the world decent and free; Germany and its allies represented the antithesis of all that democratic nations stood for. At Columbia College, the War Issues Course devolved in 1919 into Contemporary Civilization, whose explicit purpose was to impart democratic values and virtues and to reinforce the goal of instruction in U.S. history to unify socially all Americans, whatever their country of origin, and to instill in the growing educated class shared standards of thought and civic action. In other words, the Western Civ course started out not simply as an intellectual exploration of America's European cultural and political heritage. Rather, "it came into being with a significant amount of political and ideological content both during and after World War I."[85]

Ironically then, just when many AHA scholars were decrying the resurrection of the General History survey in the schools, the scholars at Columbia were creating a new survey of their own. The model for Contemporary Civilizations was more coherent than the typical high school course because it rigorously followed a central theme: the march of rationalism, science, and liberty in the West. Though the course explicitly focused on Europe, Columbia's James Harvey Robinson did not make a distinction between that topic and world history. One scholar observes that in the textbooks Robinson wrote to accompany his course, the past is subordinated to the present, recent history becomes "relevant" history, the human past becomes the prologue to European history, and Europe is interpreted as the seat of modernity, the source of "contemporary ways of doing and thinking.... Westerners, of course, had long universalized European history into the general history of mankind. More effectively than others of his generation, Robinson made this old general history into a "modern" history of Western civilization.[86]

From its beginnings at Columbia, the introductory Western Civ course prospered across the country in the interwar period as one of the pillars of college general education. Moreover, if the trend toward research specialization caused historians to view schools from across a widening chasm, Western Civ programs, which obliged academics to think about historical breadth and creative teaching methods, may have helped keep some of the bridges intact.[87] On the other hand, as Western Civ courses proliferated, they also tended to get more voluminous. Professors added their own favorite topics, more ancient and medieval history crept in, social and economic content expanded, and publishers strove as always to produce textbooks that would please everyone.

By World War II, therefore, college Western Civ was looking more and more like the overstuffed and scrambled tenth-grade world history class. Robinson's well-ordered theme of Western civilization's "genetic development" was not so much rejected as lost in a blizzard of historical detail.[88] Even so, Western Civ continued to tax the minds of thousands of college freshmen well into the post–World War II era and to be accepted tacitly as synonymous with world history.

For the time being, controversy over the teaching of non-American history in both colleges and schools was largely confined to professional arguments over which and how much history should be taught. The public had no quarrel with the basic logic of Western-Civ-as-world-history, which was to set the nation's experience within the wider context of Western political and cultural achievement. If Americans had little consciousness of Africa, Asia, or Latin America in medieval and modern times, this was partly because the great explosion of historical knowledge about these regions still lay in the future. Hence, not until after World War II and in the context of drastically changed conditions in both the world and the academy was the paradigm of world history as the West's "moral success story" called into question.[89]

CHAPTER 3

Postwar Paradoxes

The only way in which a human being can make some approach to know-
ing the whole of a subject is by hearing what can be said about it by per-
sons of every variety of opinion, and studying all modes in which it can
be looked at by every character of mind. No wise man ever acquired his
wisdom in any mode but this; nor is it in the nature of the human intel-
lect to become wise in another manner.

—John Stuart Mill, *On Liberty*

In the twenty years after World War II, the study of history in the United States underwent a series of transformations, traumas, and twists that, collectively, would fuel the history wars of the 1980s and 1990s. Many of the developments are paradoxical, and some are as familiar as an old sock worn out at the toe. On the one hand, established historians of the Cold War era began to refurbish national history in ways that minimized its conflicts and stressed what they imagined was the consensual nature of American society. On the other hand, the new generation of scholars entering the profession in those same years broke fresh ground in subject areas that had been neglected and that often involved conflict rather than consensus.

Among those subjects, African American history, labor history, and women's history figured importantly. The arctic winds of conservatism, however, blown up to hurricane force by McCarthyism, partially smothered this second emergence of New Historians, delayed the percolation of their work down to the textbooks used in schools, and fed the chill that had de-veloped between academic historians and social studies educators in the schools. Remarkably, the presentation of world history changed very little in these years, despite the new challenges of the Cold War, the rise of the United States to superpower status, and the emergence onto the world stage of many new nations. These developments called for a truly global history rather than a polished-up version of Western Civilization, but no such change occurred. This chapter, dealing with the period from 1945 to the mid–1960s, considers how these various developments were linked to post-war events and how they set the stage for later controversies.

The Great Mutation

Speaking at the annual meeting of the American Historical Association (AHA) in 1962, President Carl Bridenbaugh lamented the changes he saw occurring in the academic world. Himself from Protestant Middle America, Bridenbaugh deplored "the great mutation" in Clio's profession that was occurring as the post–World War II GI Bill ushered into the undergraduate and graduate programs people who could not have gone to college in the Depression. "Many of the young practitioners of our craft, and those who are still apprentices," Bridenbaugh lamented, "are products of lower middle-class or foreign origins, and their emotions not infrequently get in the way of historical reconstructions." They suffered from an "environmental deficiency" because they were urban-bred, rooted in the Old World traditions of their parents' homelands, and therefore lacking in the "understanding ... vouchsafed to historians who were raised in the countryside or in the small town. ... They find themselves in a very real sense outsiders on our past and feel themselves shut out. This is certainly not their fault, but it is true."[1]

Almost everyone who heard or read Bridenbaugh's references to urban, foreign-born outsiders, mutants tarnishing a noble profession, understood that he was speaking about Jews. This was far from the last lamentation about the wholesale change in the recruitment of historians in a period of extraordinary growth in higher education. Bridenbaugh's discomfort was shared widely because before World War II the history profession had been drawn overwhelmingly from the ranks of middle- to upper-class white Protestant men.

From this perspective, it was entirely fitting that only those of the highest intellect, the deepest American roots, and the most polished manners had the mettle to stand above the ruck and look dispassionately at the annals of human behavior. Such a view conformed to the old elite notion that ordinary people were ruled by emotion. Only the wealthy and urbane, remaining austerely impersonal, could transcend this state to achieve absolute neutrality and objectively set the record straight.

After World War II, however, the equivalent of a tectonic plate shift occurred in the writing of history. This second wave of New History, far more extensive than of the early twentieth century, changed what young Americans—and young people elsewhere in the world—learned in school.

This transformation did not occur all at once. For many generations a small number of women, African Americans, and white radicals had worked—without much recognition—to create alternative histories. As early as the 1780s, women had occasionally ventured onto male territory to write about the past. A few gained substantial numbers of readers. Mercy Otis Warren, sister of the Revolutionary firebrand James Otis, wrote one of the first histories of the American Revolution. The abolitionist-inspired histories by Lydia Childs, a Massachusetts Quaker, telling heroic stories of those who escaped slavery or fought against it, sold briskly in the 1840s and 1850s. Helen Hunt Jackson's *Century of Dishonor*, published in 1887, caused a sensation because she excoriated the long history of white genocide against Native Americans. Writing in a period when General Philip Sheridan's quip that "the only good Indian is a dead Indian" was considered a clever joke, Jackson denied that hers was an unpatriotic attempt to undermine the nation. But such remarkable women in no way altered the profession's decidedly male character.

Pioneering black historians also made important contributions. In 1855, William Nell's *Colored Patriots of the American Revolution* gave the public its first history by a black American. Not for another century, however, would the profession include more than a handful of black scholars. To be sure, that handful included such voices as W.E.B. Du Bois, one of the most noteworthy historians of the twentieth century. Though such sturdy dissidents challenged the profession for many decades, they wrote no textbooks, had little cachet within the profession, and for the most part did not hold academic appointments.

But after World War II, young historians of inconspicuous backgrounds began to discover history as a career. Even before Bridenbaugh's AHA address, history's gates were opening. At Yale, the old elite tried to hold the line when class barriers, along with religious restrictions, began to fall as bright young men with GI Bill benefits clamored for a place in the academy. The chairman of the history department wrote the university's president in 1957 that, though the doctoral program in English "still draws to a degree from the cultivated, professional, and well-to-do classes, by contrast, the subject of history seems to appeal on the whole to a lower social stratum." Looking over the applications to the Ph.D. program, he complained that "far too few of our history candidates are sons of professional men; far too many list their parents' occupation as janitor, watchman, salesman, grocer, pocketbook cutter, bookkeeper, railroad clerk, pharmacist, clothing cutter, cable tester, mechanic, general clerk, butter-and-egg jobber, and the like."[2]

The changing composition of graduate school programs hardly merited newspaper headlines or op-ed exposés. But the shifts, like the movement of glaciers, were slowly transforming the landscape. It is not surprising that new questions about the past would be posed by people representing segments of the American mosaic that had not been part of the storytelling. Step by step, new historians began to construct previously untold chapters of history and, along the way, as we will see, helped to overcome the deep historical biases that for many generations had afflicted a narrowly constituted profession.

As portrayed in Chapter 2, historians in the first half of the twentieth century unearthed fresh historical information and offered insights that introduced students to the complexity of history and, occasionally, to tragic chapters of the past. Even these endeavors, modest by today's standards, drew fire from those who wanted an affirmative version of American history. Such departures from celebratory history brought into question whether historians had abandoned "objectivity" by introducing subtleties and paradoxes. When prominent scholars insisted that all history is interpretive, patrioteers restated the need to stick to the facts, the plain facts, and nothing but the facts.

Such traditionalists welcomed developments after World War II. The advent of the Cold War and the nation's ideological mobilization against communism nearly erased the critical tone that had so offended critics of the New History. "From 1948 onward," writes Peter Novick, "among historians, as among other academics and intellectuals, there was an accelerating abandonment of dissidence, a rapid accommodation to the new postwar political culture."[3] The "retreat into quietude" was hastened by McCarthyism, which swept across American campuses in the 1950s. In the concerted effort to remove "reducators," hundreds of teachers, at every level of American education, lost their jobs. Thousands more adopted a cautious posture or a fear-driven self-censorship.[4] At the five University of California campuses, all but three historians bowed to the loyalty oaths that became a requirement for teaching at the nation's largest and finest public university system.

Making History Nice

From the Cold War era arose what is now called "counterprogressive" or "consensus" history. To be counterprogressive was to disparage earlier historians who had seen the struggle between the haves and have-nots and the role of conflict as central themes in American history. One of the leading consensus historians, Louis Hartz, argued that Americans were bound together by the glue of a liberal ideology—construed, in the European sense of "liberalism," as a deep commitment to laissez-faire capitalism and a restricted government supremely suited for people who had no medieval past and were "born free."

Going further, Daniel Boorstin argued that Americans had no ideology at all, having shed philosophical tendencies as a curse. "We do not need American philosophers," Boorstin explained, "because we already have an American philosophy, implicit in the American Way of Life." This was simple enough. "Why should *we* make a five-year plan for ourselves when God seems to have had a thousand-year plan ready-made for us?"[5] Most historians exhibited less flamboyant boosterism than Boorstin, and almost nobody could—or cared to—match him for expunging huge areas of American history as he wove his three-volume history, *The Americans.* Among those areas hidden from view were, as we will see, slavery and race.

While students read consensus history, highly popular historical sites had much greater influence on the public at large. Among them, and by far the most visited, was Colonial Williamsburg. In the 1930s, John D. Rockefeller Jr., underwrote a $79 million demolition of 720 buildings constructed after 1800 while restoring 82 surviving eighteenth-century structures and constructing 341. What emerged was a romantic version of a colonial town, the capital of Britain's most valuable North American colony. The mosquito-infested, ramshackle, virtually paintless village with foraging hogs and stray dogs became a spotlessly clean, garden-manicured, wartless town with perfectly maintained buildings dressed out in colors so appealing that suburban America soon clamored for housepaint of Williamsburg hues. Rockefeller's imaginary Williamsburg featured the brilliant Virginia cohort of Revolutionary leaders: Washington, Jefferson, George Wythe, Patrick Henry, George Mason, and others.

Americans loved it. And no untutored visitor could have guessed that two centuries ago the Founding Fathers in Williamsburg had mingled among their slaves, who represented half the town's population and undergirded Virginia's economy. Corporate capital had resurrected a heroic, unblemished planter elite in the cradle of the nation's birth. Who would not have wanted to live in such a place and time. As Michael Wallace writes, the town was "orderly, tidy, with no dirt, no smell, no visible signs of exploitation," a world where "respectable craftsmen run production, paternalistically and harmoniously; ladies run well-ordered households with well-ordered families in homes filled with tasteful precious objects." Colonial Williamsburg was, in short, "the DAR approach writ large." It was what every American in the Cold War era wanted to believe their nation had been and ought to be.[6]

In the 1970s, when Williamsburg's directors were convinced that Americans needed to face the past more honestly, visitors were shown a much more realistic Virginia capital—complete with unkempt sideyards, slave artisans, peeling paint, and an insane asylum. Spurred by Research Director Cary Carson's effort to graft the scholarship of the postwar generation onto Rockefeller's dream, the leaders of Colonial Williamsburg found that the American public loved Williamsburg not less but even more.

Historians Examine America's Achilles' Heel

If the Cold War encouraged a posture of consensus and conciliation among most historians, it did not dishearten the diverse scholars who by the 1960s were churning through Ph.D. programs in astounding numbers. In the 1930s, American universities annually produced about 150 history doctorates. By the mid-1960s, this number had soared fourfold. By 1970, about one thousand people received doctorates per year.[7] Beyond sheer numbers, this generation of historians was notable for its mixed social backgrounds. That alone guaranteed new vectors of scholarly research.

Fortified by unprecedented research support, and installed at new state university branches built to accommodate GI Bill veterans, American historians entered a new epoch of innovative research. In 1960, H. Stuart Hughes observed, "It is quite possible that the study of history today is entering a period of rapid change and advance such as characterized the science of physics in the first three decades of the twentieth century." Five years later, John Higham's survey of the changing history profession reached a similar conclusion. "Anyone who looks back at the frequently stiff and pedestrian articles in the leading journals during the Twenties and Thirties may feel reassured about the general level of contemporary work: it is more deft, often more perceptive, and usually more substantial."[8]

Despite the consensus history that settled over the profession in the 1950s, some of the newcomers researched several new topics that would sharply change the study of American history. The most important of these subjects was race. Before World War II, as noted in Chapter 2, American and world history were deeply tainted by scientific racism—the belief in the innate superiority of Anglo-Saxon people and the indelible inferiority of those descended from other groups.

A comparison of the treatment of slavery and African Americans in the earliest textbooks read by children in the new nation with those read after World War II is revealing. In the early nineteenth century, most textbooks, at least for the Northern market, condemned slavery as a moral evil and indicted the slave trade in particular as an abominable practice. Historians described slavery as a miserable institution. It drove many Africans to suicide, corrupted white slave owners (as Jefferson had eloquently expressed in his *Notes on Virginia*), and provoked often violent resistance among enslaved Africans.[9] During the high-water years of abolitionism in the 1830s and 1840s, textbook authors, save those writing for a Southern market, became even more strident in condemning slavery. Southern textbooks, by contrast, assured young readers that "the slave was happier under slavery than he would be as a free man in a free society."[10]

After the Civil War, Northern schoolbooks commended the emancipation of slaves, but historians usually approached the future of the nation's millions of black Americans with gloomy speculation. "The child influenced by these books," writes our best authority on nineteenth-century textbooks, "would be unlikely to see the Negro as a participant in and a contributor to American culture." Picturing black Americans as incapable of self-direction—the view of most Northerners as well as Southerners after the Civil War—textbook writers counseled that the future for blacks depended entirely on the charity of those whites who cared to uplift them gradually from the debilitating birthmarks of African descent.[11]

When pseudoscientific racism captured academic life in the late nineteenth century, the depiction of African Americans became even more distorted. A vast majority of whites accepted Louis Agassiz's pronouncements about the absurdity of racial equality. Such equality, he declared was a "natural impossibility" because blacks were "in natural propensities and mental abilities ... indolent, playful, sensual, imitative, subservient, good-natured, versatile, unsteady in their purpose, devoted, and affectionate."[12] This passage, quoted in James Ford Rhodes's widely admired eight-volume history of the United States, set the tone for almost all history textbooks for decades to come.

Even progressive writers such as Muzzey and Beard embraced pseudoscientific racism. Their textbooks often adopted the strategy of ignoring African Americans altogether, mentioning slavery only as a political issue debated by white Americans. A generation of schoolchildren learned their history from books barren of any information on slave life, slave resistance, slave culture, or the growth of free black communities in the North after the Revolution. As Frances FitzGerald put it, "In the vast majority of books, there were only 'the slaves'—slaves who had appeared magically in this country at some unspecified time and had disappeared with the end of the Civil War."[13]

Condemned for Anglophilia, Muzzey's textbooks provide evidence for FitzGerald's claim. Perusing his many editions from 1911 to 1945, one can find no mention of Richard Allen, Frederick Douglass, Harriet Tubman, George Washington Carver, W.E.B. Du Bois, or the leaders of slave rebellions such as Nat Turner, Gabriel, and Denmark Vesey. Beard's many textbooks were no better. Obliterated from the record were the horrors of the slave trade, the brutality of slavery, the resistance of enchained Africans, and the struggles of free blacks to gain full citizenship under the banner "All men are created equal."

From these books, students would never know that black Americans had fought in the American Revolution (probably in larger proportions than whites, though mostly with the British in order to gain their freedom); in the War of 1812; in the Civil War; and in the Mexican- and Spanish-American Wars. In the 1950s, textbooks made incremental changes to include two or three African Americans who were deemed significant in the course of a 350-year history—usually only Frederick Douglass, Booker T. Washington, and George Washington Carver.

While virtually all white historians suffered historical amnesia regarding the role of black Americans in the unfolding of American history, some took scientific racism to its logical extremes by explaining to schoolchildren that slavery was a blessing because it rescued Africans from eternal darkness in their savage homelands. The textbook commissioned in 1924 by the American Legion to replace the maligned Muzzey texts told readers that the slave ships were horrible and that slavery was "unrighteous." But it added, "In America itself the slaves' condition was usually much better than in their former African lives of fear and ignorance and misery. . . . The marked and advancing culture of the negro race has all been gained in America. . . . The blight of slavery fell less upon their race than on their masters."[14]

Regarding Reconstruction, schoolchildren using the book learned that nobody knew what to do with the 4 million "ignorant human beings" who had been suddenly emancipated. "During the war most of the negroes had remained loyally in their old homes, serving their masters despite the absence of almost all white men with the armies. There were no slave uprisings during these four years of suffering. This was proof of the kindly nature of the slaves as well as of the former kindness of their masters. Yet such slaves obviously knew little of the methods of directing and governing their own lives."[15]

Even luminous academic historians subscribed to such characterizations of slave-owner kindness and African incapacity. Henry Steele Commager and Samuel Eliot Morison's best-selling *The Growth of the American Republic*, first published in 1930, had only one name for 4 million enslaved Africans. "Sambo, whose wrongs moved the abolitionists to wrath and tears . . .

suffered less than any other class in the South from its 'peculiar institution.' . . . The majority of slaves were . . . apparently happy. . . . There was much to be said for slavery as a transitional status between barbarism and civilization. The negro learned his master's language, and accepted in some degree his moral and religious standards. In return he contributed much besides his labor—music and humor for instance—to American civilization."[16]

This viewpoint became the standard description of Africa—a cultureless land from which barbarous people left in chains almost eagerly since they could look forward to the benefits of civilized society on the other side of the Atlantic. Du Bois, the Harvard-trained historian, bitterly indicted this view: "I stand at the end of this writing, literally aghast at what American historians have done to this field. . . . [It is] one of the most stupendous efforts the world ever saw to discredit human beings, an effort involving universities, history, science, social life, and religion."[17]

As late as the 1950s, California's fifth-graders learned how the chattel slavery system operated in the plantation South in these sentences: "Perhaps the most fun the little masters and mistresses have comes when they are free to play with the little colored boys and girls. Back of the big house stand rows of small cabins. In these cabins live the families of Negro slaves. The older colored people work on the great farm, or help about the plantation home. The small black boys and girls play about the small houses. They are pleased to have the white children come to play with them."

That slaves would be contented in this pleasant world was not surprising. Textbooks told children:

> In time many people came to think that it was wrong to own slaves. Some of them said that all the Negro slaves should be freed. Some of the people who owned slaves became angry at this. They said that the black people were better off as slaves in America than they would have been as wild savages in Africa. Perhaps this was true, as many of the slaves had snug cabins to live in, plenty to eat, and work that was not too hard for them to do. Most of the slaves seemed happy and contented.[18]

Even through the 1960s, many students imbibed views of black Americans from textbooks that had hardly changed since the 1920s. For example, Alabama fourth-graders, whether white or black, learned that under "terrible carpetbag rule" during Reconstruction, freed slaves were so ignorant that they bought colored sticks from mercenary Northern carpetbaggers in the belief that "they could own the land where they put those sticks." They also learned that "loyal white men," trying "to protect their families," formed the Ku Klux Klan "to bring back law and order." Never violent, the Klansmen protected Alabamans from "bad lawless things," persuaded the "lawless men who had taken control of the state" to go back North, and persuaded "the Negroes who had been fooled by the false promises of the carpetbaggers to get themselves jobs and settle down to make an honest living."[19]

Reviewing these textbooks confirms the judgment of Leon Litwack that "no group of scholars was more deeply implicated in the miseducation of American youth and did more to shape the thinking of generations of Americans about race and blacks than historians."[20] But the racist consensus was so pervasive that only with the civil rights movement of the 1960s was the mold shattered and consciousness raised about how unthinkingly white teachers and students absorbed patently racist descriptions of Africans and African Americans.

Efforts to break this mold had begun in the 1930s when a small number of historians revolted against the deeply racist treatments of African Americans in textbooks. But not until the 1950s did scholars undertake a thorough revamping of slavery, the African past, the Reconstruction era, and nearly every other chapter of American history in which race figured prominently. Even while the Cold War silenced many dissident historians and influenced scholarship that stressed consensus while minimizing conflict in the American past, some historians forged ahead with a scholarly agenda that irrevocably changed the way Americans thought about their history. Their scholarship on race—including the history of Native Americans and Asian Americans, but especially African Americans and white-black relationships—swam vigorously against the tide of consensus history.

Scholars such as Kenneth Stampp, John Hope Franklin, Benjamin Quarles, Herbert Aptheker, Philip Foner, Howard Beale, C. Vann Woodward, and others turned on its head the commonly accepted textbook version of slavery and the character of enslaved Africans. Rather than benign slavery was brutal. Rather than passively accepting chattel bondage, enslaved Africans resisted it along a spectrum of defiance that ran from tool breaking to running away to outright rebellion. Rather than innately inferior, Africans enduring the "middle passage" brought to the Americas agricultural know-how, valuable understandings about pharmacopeia and smallpox inoculation, enduring religious beliefs, and rich aesthetic traditions.

Behind the dismantling of the racist consensus lay several converging factors. One was the way in which black Americans, along with some white liberals and radicals, turned World War II into an antiracist crusade—a campaign that drew sustenance from the Cold War imperative to convince Third World nations that the United States was not the racist stronghold that the Soviet Union delighted in exposing.

Second, a number of anthropologists and sociologists led assaults on scientific racism. The anthropologist Melville Herskovits's *Myth of the African Past* ushered in a new era for African and African American history. Herskovits's evidence that enslaved Africans brought viable cultural attributes to the Americas and grafted them upon the slavemasters' societies amounted to a stunning reformulation of the black experience. A team of social scientists, led by the Swedish sociologist Gunnar Myrdal, produced *An American Dilemma*, which demolished the reigning paradigm about Negro inferiority. "No historian of the institution [of slavery]," wrote Kenneth Stampp, "can be taken seriously any longer unless he begins with the knowledge that there is no valid evidence that the Negro race is innately inferior to the white, and that there is growing evidence that both races have approximately the same potentialities."[21]

Third, black historians, though small in number, got a hearing through appointments outside the black colleges where they had pursued their careers. Benjamin Quarles's pioneering book *The Negro and the American Revolution*, published in 1961, restored to historical consciousness the role that enslaved Africans and a small number of free blacks played in the character and course of the Revolution. The work of John Hope Franklin, already developing as a towering figure in Southern history at Howard University, secured him an appointment at Brooklyn College and then at the University of Chicago.

Fourth, as part of the Cold War contest for the allegiance of emerging Third World nations, the Ford Foundation and other funders established African Studies centers at a number of universities. These institutes committed themselves to the first serious investigation of African history. Even in this budding stage, historians working with anthropologists prepared the groundwork for a frontal assault on the bankrupt notion of Africa as the "dark continent."

Last, the early stages of the civil rights movement in the 1950s inspired those who looked for scholarly avenues they might pursue in directions other than consensus history. As Novick phrases it, "By the late 1950s, as the civil rights movement gathered steam, an increasing number of young historians found in that struggle an outlet for social energies and idealism bottled up in the previous period of political quiescence."[22] As we will see in the next chapter, the multifaceted scholarship of the post-1950 period took some sharp turns, created vibrant debates within the profession, and triggered conservative counterattacks, but, withal, it enormously enlarged the store of historical knowledge in U.S. and world history.

Who Built America?

Nearly twenty years ago, Frances FitzGerald, surveying U.S. history textbooks published over the last century, traced the peculiar presentations of
the American economic system and noted how social stratification, the distribution of income and wealth, and the degree of opportunity had begun
to emerge as topics of historical consideration. Harold Rugg's attempts at
"social realism" in the 1930s to explain the lives of Mr. Very Poor Man, Mr.
Average Worker, Mr. Average White Collar Man, Mr. Prosperous Business-
man, and Mr. Cultured Man infuriated patriotic groups and such defenders
of business as the National Association of Manufacturers. Responding to
their outrage, textbook publishers cleansed their books after World War II
of any discussion of income distribution or inequality. From the 1940s
through the 1970s, FitzGerald reports, "The books were as purely booster-
ish as a Radio Free Europe broadcast," leaving the baby boomers "wholly
ignorant of the virtues as well as the vices of their own economic system."[23]
    While economic history was ignored in textbooks, laboring Americans
went equally unnoticed. For generations, schoolchildren studied their
nation's history without encountering historical figures who might have reminded them of their parents and grandparents. The textbooks were also
silent on the history of poverty. From elementary school books children
would have had the impression that they lived in "a wall-to-wall middle-
class suburbia."[24] From high school books they would have learned that "by
1815, America was a country of middle-class people and of middle-class
goals."[25]
    In this version of the United States as a classless society the word "pov-
erty" was inconvenient. Hence, it appears infrequently in the textbooks, almost always in connection with the Great Depression, or in a discussion of
Lyndon Johnson's Great Society (where textbook writers had to discuss the
"war on poverty" by admitting the existence of the poor). "Its cause is unknown," writes FitzGerald, "its cure is hotly debated, and yet somewhere—
somewhere in the regions yet unprobed by science—there is a vaccine
against it."[26] Like discussions of discrimination, poverty can be held to nobody's account.
    In the "great mutation" overtaking the history profession after World
War II, young scholars embarked for the first time on studies of social stratification, wealth distribution, and—more generally—laboring people. Perhaps it was natural that the first sizable number of sons and daughters of the
working classes to earn doctorates in history would cast their gaze on blue-
collar America; it was also natural that national attention to inequality, aris-

ing from the civil rights and women's movements, would lead historians to explore the roots of poverty and inequality as more than an occasional cancer on the American body politic.

On the face of it, nothing could be more democratic than history that addressed *all* the people and whose authors believed they were writing their books for *all* the people. Indeed, the mission of labor history has been to trace "the changing nature of work that built, sustained, and transformed American society over the course of almost four centuries and the changing conditions, experiences, outlooks, and conduct of the people who performed that essential labor."[27] In the course of a quarter century, hundreds of books have emerged that analyze the lives of ordinary Americans, compare the myth and reality of the immigrant experience, explore gender and racial discrimination in labor's ranks, reveal stories of labor conflict, enrich the understanding of labor's role in American politics, and give voice— usually through oral history—to those rendered voiceless, faceless, and mindless in the standard history textbooks.

The Big Chill

One of the ironies of the "great mutation" in the history profession is that although the diversified and democratized academics produced a cornucopia of studies that looked at neglected chapters of history, they exercised only limited influence upon the history that was taught in the schools. However, the much-celebrated Civil War historian Allan Nevins triggered national interest with his much-publicized attack on social studies in 1942. American history, he claimed, was seriously neglected in the schools and colleges, with "probably a majority of American children never [receiving] a full year's successful work in our national history."[28] A month later the *New York Times* reported that 82 percent of the nation's colleges and universities required no American history for graduation, and 72 percent required none for admission.[29] Reviewing this survey, the *Mississippi Valley Historical Review* called for schools and colleges to redress these problems by offering more and better courses in history.[30]

One year later, with the war going badly for the Allies, the *New York Times* published the results of a test administered to seven thousand freshmen in thirty-six colleges, which revealed "a striking ignorance of even the most elementary aspects of United States history."[31] Alarmed, newspaper editors and members of Congress conducted a campaign against those held responsible for this state of affairs: namely, social studies "extremists," the National Council for the Social Studies (NCSS), and "its twin brother,

Teachers College, Columbia," all of which were accused of having "contempt for the facts of American history."[32]

History and social studies devotees fought back, certain that opponents of the social studies were interested in ultrapatriotic history rather than in bringing the rich harvest of the New History into the schools. University of Wisconsin's William B. Hesseltine refuted the test's "narrow, factualist approach" to history and ridiculed the "Committee to Defeat America by Memorizing the Presidents."[33] Merle Curti, along with many others in the AHA, voiced concern that "a legitimate demand for a wider and better understanding of American history [would] play into the hands of isolationists and reactionary chauvinists."[34] His concerns were echoed by UCLA's John D. Hicks:

> The opposition to the Social Studies program out here [California] comes from people who are utterly uninterested in either content or method. All they want is indoctrination: (1) against the U.S. ever again abandoning Washington's doctrine of isolation, (2) that Great Britain is the chief enemy of the human race, and (3) that the American system of free enterprise, *as they interpret it,* is sacrosanct.[35]

Seeking to distance themselves from the controversy unleashed by Nevins and the *Times* survey and to regain the initiative, the AHA, the Mississippi Valley Historical Association, and the NCSS established a Committee on American History in the Schools and Colleges. The committee developed its own test of U.S. history and administered it not only to high school students but also to ROTC undergraduates, social studies teachers, *Who's Who* listees, and other adults not involved in the teaching of history. Reporting its findings, the committee admitted that "Americans do not know their own history as well as they might," and concluded that a serious deficiency existed, given the importance of history in the education of citizens.[36]

The flurry over historical illiteracy, arising as it did in the midst of a war hardly rippled the surface of American public opinion in 1943–44; winning the war preoccupied the nation. After the war, however, academic historians abandoned what remained of their interest in history for schoolchildren. Signifying its withdrawal from the field, the AHA surrendered its editorial and financial responsibility for the teachers magazines published by the NCSS. The AHA's representative to the editorial board of NCSS's *Social Education* in the late 1940s observed that whereas in the 1930s it had been "accepted as sound doctrine that the . . . direction and leadership of instruction in history on all levels was an important obligation of our Association . . .

this vital function . . . has in the past few years been virtually surrendered."[37] In his presidential address to the Mississippi Valley Historical Association in 1953, James L. Sellers announced that the association's services to history in the schools had all but ended.[38] The two leading historical associations confirmed that the historians' long walk away from the schools, begun two decades before, was complete. It was to be a costly journey.

Inoculating the Baby Boomers

Although historians and social studies educators continued on their separate paths throughout the 1950s, the same forces that shaped the development of "consensus history" in the universities also influenced social studies education in the schools. The exigencies of World War II, the advent of the Cold War, and the years of McCarthyism only accentuated the retreat already under way from the activist social studies programs of the 1930s. Deradicalized by the revelations of Stalin's brutal purges of educators in the Soviet Union, and by the high-handed tactics of communist factions in the labor movement vying for control of the teachers unions, activist educators had long grown disenchanted with Marxist-Leninist claims.[39] The journal *Social Frontier*, which George Counts founded in 1934 as a forum for those who saw the mission of the schools as reconstructing society, was by 1939 openly rejecting communism. By 1943, the magazine had ceased publication altogether.

The 1950s witnessed a relatively noncontentious emphasis upon "Education for Democratic Citizenship" as the dominant social studies program in the schools. It was variously interpreted as "internationalist" in its commitment to preparing students for the challenge of international organization and postwar planning;[40] as "intercultural" in its postwar commitment to addressing problems of anti-Semitism in American society and "to building more democratic human relations among multiple groups and cultures";[41] or as "participatory" in providing for students' active involvement in citizenship education projects in their schools and communities.[42]

Although history did not figure large in these programs, the "internationalist" focus in citizenship education encouraged expansion in the content of the tenth-grade world history course, struggling at the time to incorporate something of the contemporary non-Western world in what was still an essentially Western Civ curriculum. At the same time, U.S. history teachers were called upon to prepare students for the international responsibilities their nation had undertaken in the postwar years. It was a daunting challenge, given the state of history textbooks. Historians on both sides of the Atlantic found a disturbing level of ethnocentric bias in these books. Examining thirteen American history textbooks widely used in American junior and senior high schools and twenty-four English history textbooks used in English grammar and secondary modern schools, a committee of British and American historians found nationalistic bias to be "as persistent in today's schoolbooks as in those used a generation ago."[43]

Although textbook writers could seldom be charged "with the sins of their nineteenth-century predecessors who deliberately distorted the truth to magnify the virtues of their national heroes and discredit their nation's enemies," the committee nonetheless found in these texts many of the same distortions influencing students' historical understandings. These books, they judged, passed along to a new generation of students disproven folklore that glorified both national and white racist superiority. Omitting the failings of the nation, these texts also exaggerated stirring victories and heroic men while failing to credit the achievements of other countries, even those as closely linked in culture and heritage as Britain and the United States.

Social studies educators also called upon U.S. history courses to contribute to improved "intergroup understandings," a hallmark of citizenship education. Textbook publishers dutifully added chapters on immigration that included eastern and southern European newcomers in addition to the northern European Protestants whose stories had dominated in years past. But true to the spirit of "consensus history," these immigrant studies were generally bland, expunged of conflict, and celebratory of the opportunities new Americans enjoyed. They were also largely unrelated to the struggles of students in the newly born civil rights movement which, in the years following *Brown v. Board of Education* (the Supreme Court decision that in 1954 called for desegregation of the schools), confronted young people with the challenges of integrated schools in a racially divided nation.

Even these relatively innocuous approaches to postwar education, however, did not protect the social studies profession from attacks unleashed in the heyday of McCarthyism. Throughout the 1950s, critics repeated statements lifted from early 1930s issues of *Social Frontier* as proof of their claims that progressives and communists were conspiring to use the schools to subvert the "American way of life." As the title of one book proclaimed, *Progressive Education is REDucation.* Such books twisted interpretations of statements gleaned from early writings of thinkers such as George Counts, Charles Beard, and Harold Rugg.

In the 1950s, those intent on ferreting out communist subversion trained their sights on public school teachers. More than half the states required teachers to sign loyalty oaths. Thirty-three states passed legislation authorizing the dismissal of teachers found to be "disloyal." Fourteen required teachers to affirm, as a condition of employment, that they were not members of the Communist Party or any other organization advocating the forcible overthrow of the government.

In the early 1950s, the House Un-American Activities Committee and the Senate Internal Security Subcommittee launched investigations into alleged cases of subversion in schools. Though the public widely supported the dismissal of communists from teaching posts, and the Supreme Court upheld a New York state law requiring the certification of teachers' loyalty in 1952, the social studies profession, like those in academia, feared that the loyalty oaths and governmental investigations threatened basic guarantees of civil liberties and academic freedom.

The climate was ripe for conducting witchhunts in neighborhood schools. Pressure groups formed in hundreds of communities, spurred on by tracts such as "They Want Your Child!" by speakers skilled in delivering such hell-raisers as "How Red Is the Little Red Schoolhouse?" and by organizations such as the Minute Women, who opposed the United Nations, racial integration, federal aid, and "progressive education."

In many communities and states new battles of the books erupted. For example, in Meriden, Connecticut, in 1961, the evening newspaper ran a shocking story about how un-American textbooks were brainwashing the children of this model community. Armed with a report commissioned by the Daughters of the American Revolution (DAR), which examined 220 textbooks and determined 170 of them to be subversive, several Meriden citizens did their duty.⁴⁴ Two local Republicans discovered that most of the textbooks were on the DAR's Red-tainted list. They found plenty of damning evidence: pictures of American slums and lines of unemployed citizens during the Great Depression, attention to subjects such as the United Nations, prejudice, and mental health; and music books with "too many 'work tunes' and 'folk songs' (as distinguished from native and national airs)." Equally offensive to the DAR were mentions of further reading that steered students to the writings of "liberal, racial, socialist or labor agitators." Among them were Theodore H. White, Margaret Mead, Richard Wright, Pearl Buck, Langston Hughes, Norman Cousins, Henry Steele Commager, Allan Nevins, Burl Ives, and Bill Mauldin. Also unacceptable were "socialist slants" in textbook chapter subheadings such as "Industrialization Brings Problems as Well as Benefits," "Congress Attempts to Curb the Trusts," and "Panics and Depression Become More Severe."

The contretemps over textbooks in Meriden fizzled out within a year, after most of the teachers and clergy, the local newspaper's editors, and even the American Legion chapter declined to climb on the bandwagon.

But Meriden-like incidents were occurring in every corner of the country. The most successful textbook in American civics, Frank Abbott Magruder's *American Government*, was pilloried in many states and banned in Houston; Little Rock, Arkansas; Lafayette, Indiana; and throughout the state of Georgia in the early 1950s, even though it had been in use for nearly four decades. Critics charged that the latest version of *American Government* would pervert the minds of America's youth. It was bad enough to find references to the United Nations. But much worse, the leading critic insisted, Magruder's explanation of democracy went "straight from Rousseau, through Marx, to totalitarianism." By defining democracy as "that form of government in which the sovereign power is in the hands of the people collectively, Magruder was peddling Soviet collectivism." The critic neatly ignored the clause that completed this sentence: "and is expressed by them either directly or indirectly through elected representatives."[45]

In Texas, by 1961, the legislative hearings on books assigned in the public schools "proved as wild as a Texas rodeo."[46] After reading the legislature's resolution that "the American history courses in the public schools [should] emphasize in the textbooks our glowing and throbbing history of hearts and souls inspired by wonderful American principles and traditions," school libraries yielded up dozens of books deemed subversive and dangerous to the health of schoolchildren. In Amarillo, for example, the school board ordered four libraries to remove ten novels, four of which had won Pulitzer Prizes. Among the banned novels were Aldous Huxley's *Brave New World*, John Steinbeck's *Grapes of Wrath*, Thomas Wolfe's *Of Time and the River*, Herman Wouk's *Marjorie Morningstar*, Oliver LaFarge's *Laughing Boy*, and George Orwell's *1984*.[47] One defender of the textbooks deplored the tendency of publishers to expunge passages that raised the ire of almost anyone. The publishers, warned J. Frank Dobie, "are so compliant that most of them would print the texts in Hindu if the buyers preferred. Their aim is to offend nobody." Nonetheless, more and more school districts adopted the Washington, D.C., formula for avoiding controversy. "We try to make sure," explained the deputy superintendent, "that the books we select are not objectionable to anyone."[48]

Preparing Youth for America's Century

As McCarthyism played itself out in the late 1950s, the nation turned its attention once again to improving education. Setting the tone of this undertaking was the President's Commission on National Goals, appointed by Dwight Eisenhower to "develop a broad outline of coordinated national policies and programs" to meet the special challenges confronting the nation in the 1960s.[49] The commission, led by the president of Brown University, was composed of education, corporate, labor, judicial, military, and State Department leaders. Contributing to the work were some one hundred experts in various fields of domestic and international concern.

The commission's 1960 report, intended to launch a national discussion, identified eleven domestic and four international goals. The report unequivocally endorsed equality of treatment and opportunity for every American regardless of race, gender, or economic status. It also stressed that freedom of expression, free inquiry, and free exchange of views, however controversial, were the foundation of a democratic society. Mindful of McCarthyism, the report declared:

> The notion that ideas and individuals must be rejected merely because they are controversial denies the essence of our tradition. Schools and institutions of higher education, and the trustees, board members and legislators responsible for them, have a particular responsibility to ensure freedom of expression by students, faculty and administrators alike. We must bring up young men and women to believe in the individual and to act upon that belief. There are subtle and powerful pressures toward conformity in the economic, social, and political world. They must be resisted so that differences of taste and opinion will remain a constructive force in improving our society.

"Unity of purpose," the report emphasized, "must never be confused with unity of opinion."[50]

Among its eleven domestic goals, the report declared that "education at every level and in every discipline [must] be strengthened and its effectiveness enhanced." To that end, greater resources, national as well as state and local, had to be mobilized. Knowledge on every front had to be advanced—science and technology foremost but also history and social sciences, which are "vital to understanding, to the capacity to feel and communicate, to a sense of values." These disciplines were of even greater urgency "as the conditions of living have become more complex." They provided nothing less, the commission concluded, than the standards by which posterity would judge "the success of the United States as a civilized society."[51]

The Soviet Union's Sputnik launch in 1957 almost guaranteed national action on these education proposals. Congress promptly provided liberal federal funding, some of which initiated the New Math and New Science projects. Social scientists soon became involved in projects federally funded as the New Social Studies. Working independently and through their professional associations, social scientists stepped forward with new services and curricula for the schools, many specifically drafted to connect with the challenges set forth in the commission's report.

Historians, by contrast, remained almost as disengaged from the schools as they had been for thirty years. The AHA did form a Committee on Teaching of History in the Schools in 1952, as well as a Service Center for Teachers that produced book lists and pamphlets providing historical material on a host of topics useful to precollegiate educators. Beyond these initiatives, historians were loath to go. In effect, they wanted to be "on tap but not on top."[52] Thus, the New Social Studies was enriched by the latest scholarship in political science, economics, geography, anthropology, sociology, and social psychology, but it benefited little from the scholarship of the New History. The profession's continuing standoffishness was costly, leaving most teachers unfamiliar with the rich new work of social historians, and most students deprived of new perspectives on race, class, and gender issues that might have helped them more intelligently confront the social upheavals of the 1960s.

The Eisenhower commission made strong recommendations for programs in international education to meet four global challenges: the defense of the free world; foreign trade and aid to less developed nations emerging from the breakup of the European and Japanese empires; international disarmament; and the strengthening of the United Nations, including the support of UN programs offering technical assistance to new nations, controlling violence, and settling disputes. In the report's concluding words:

> Man has never been an island unto himself. The shores of his concern
> have expanded from his neighborhood to his nation, and from his nation
> to his world. Free men have always known the necessity for responsibility.
> A basic goal for each American is to achieve a sense of responsibility as
> broad as his world-wide concerns and as compelling as the dangers and
> opportunities he confronts.[53]

A European-style ministry of education in Washington in the 1960s might have directed a major shift toward truly global studies so that young Americans would learn about the history and cultures of those societies that Americans were now seeking to influence, and would understand the transnational forces of change that challenged their country. But in a democracy where decisions over curriculum have always rested at the state and local level no such ministry existed, nor would it have been welcomed.

Nonetheless, social scientists in colleges and universities responded to the Eisenhower commission report with ideas and materials to help schools teach global citizenship and contemporary issues courses, which were just what most social studies theorists wanted. The commission's report seemed also to call for broadening the definition of world history in the schools. But even though universities were beginning to hire and train significant numbers of specialists in the history of Africa, Asia, and Latin America, and to open new avenues to comparative history, most schools continued to teach the tenth-grade Western Civ-as-world-history course.

Part of the problem was the sheer inertia of the program, which one writer has described as "the oldest history course in public high schools and the most despised by teachers and students alike."[54] Another factor may have been a postwar melding of the traditional idea of "Western civilization" with the Cold War concept of the "West" as the "free world" of European and Atlantic democracies. The defense of the West against communist aggression and infiltration required that Americans understand and appreciate the ideas and values of the ancient republics, the Enlightenment, and the democratic revolutions. That in turn meant that young people must continue diligent study of Western civilization.

A few historians argued that of course students should gain a grasp of the modern development of representative democracy, constitutionalism, the Bills of Rights, abolitionism, and so on, but that the proper geosocial context for such study was not just the countries at the western end of Eurasia but the world as a whole. After all, the argument ran, those ideas and institutions were not *inherently* and *eternally* Western; rather they went out to the world, and, by the nineteenth or twentieth century, peoples around the world were grappling with them in a multitude of ways. In the early 1960s, Leften Stavrianos, a Balkan history specialist at Northwestern University, set up a World History Project to promote this line of reasoning and put genuine globe-encircling history into the schools. Many secondary teachers appreciated what he was doing, but the academy, including much of his own history department, eschewed involvement with precollegiate education.[55]

Thus, despite the internationalist spirit that seized the United States in the Eisenhower and Kennedy years and that activated social scientists to introduce themselves to the schools, most historians seemed not to mind that the non-American curriculum was not only bland and fact-clogged, but gave far too little attention to regions of the world whose history and destiny were so intricately bound up with our own. K. S. Latourette, who a half century earlier had made a case for teaching Asian history, was still a voice crying in the wilderness:

The world is becoming a unit, and in the future our half can ignore the other only at its peril. . . . There is open to historians a great opportunity to aid in furthering world-wide understanding between great and divergent peoples, and to prepare the way for intelligent action. If we persist in our provincialism, in our neglect of half of the human race, the nation may well accuse us of blindness to our task and faithlessness to our trust.[56]

CHAPTER 4

Years of Ferment

If men at twenty learn to see the events of history in a certain frame-work, and if they learn it without acquiring imagination and elasticity of mind, then we can say . . . that by the study of history a merely probable national disaster can be converted into a one hundred per cent certainty.

—Herbert Butterfield

No one who lived through the 1960s would say that the decade was anything less than a time of stirring national drama. Some Americans, regarding that turbulent period as one of the most significant eras of social reform and democratic revitalization, long for another one just like it. Others revile the 1960s as the awful period when a confidently united country became disunited, when left-wing revisionists seized our unified history and ripped it to pieces. However, the idea that the nation's history broke down requires believing that historical revisionism is new, that our past ought to be frozen in amber, and that disunity never vexed the United States until that fateful decade. Only severe historical amnesia would erase from memory the fiery political battles of the 1790s, when the Federalist Party tried to silence its opposition by locking up democratic-republican newspaper editors; the 1830s, when race riots roiled Eastern cities; the massive industrial wars at the turn of the twentieth century, when nitroglycerine was the weapon of choice from one side of the country to the other; and a hundred other episodes of friction, faction, fission, and fragmentation as Americans strove for that "more perfect union."

Ideologues of the Right speak of the 1960s as the beginning of a "cultural meltdown" of American society and the collapse of shared values and cultural consensus. They indict historians and other academics trained in that era as conspirators in deliberate attempts to poison Middle America's cultural wells and pollute malleable young minds. If one believes the rhetoric, demolition squads moved out from academia to plant dynamite in the mainstreams of American and Western history. Ruled by intellectual anarchism, so the theory runs, college historians, the people who write the textbooks children learn from, asserted multiple truths, relative truths, or even no truths at all. Charles Colson, one of the convicted Watergate conspirators, has recently warned that history departments from one end of the country to the other have "caved in to deconstructionism," a new "ism" where all truth is relative, objectivity is scorned, and history is a plaything of the Left. His indictment of the profession is unqualified: "Radical subjectivism," which he decries as "particularly destructive in interpreting American history," is practiced by all our history departments.[1]

History's New Horizons

The caricaturing of the 1960s as a *decennium horrible* that hatched a generation of Marxists and nihilists with advanced degrees has received much media attention. But the past quarter century has seen vital and stimulating developments in the ways we investigate and learn about the past. One of these has been the flood of creative research and writing that draws on new sources, methods, and formulations. Quite simply, historians, archaeologists, and other social scientists have together reconstructed more of human history in the past twenty-five years than at any time since the birth of history as a modern discipline.

As scholars have found more innovative ways to get at the record of the past, they have produced a "new history" that is more socially inclusive, that extends to more of the world's people, and that embraces wider and wider realms of human experience. This new work in social, cultural, intellectual, technological, environmental, nutritional, and epidemiological history has been accompanied on one hand by radical proposals challenging the very idea of historical truth and on the other by impassioned demands for a national history made up mostly of political "facts" and biographies of great men. Amid the ferment, the research of the past decades has slowly filtered into school classrooms.

The great expansion of our historical consciousness since the 1960s has begun to recover the experiences of social groups and categories heretofore neglected. Fifty years ago a college student might sit through a year of history lectures and rarely or never hear the words "women," "workers," "Jews," or any designation for African Americans. This is no longer true. The danger of the past several decades, however, has been the tendency among some to imagine that whites, African Americans, Latinos, Native Americans, and Asian Americans exist as self-contained groups, each with a separate and different ethos, outlook, and history. As the past generation's historical research has shown, America's social, cultural, and economic life has been far too complex and interactive for that to be possible. Unfortunately, government agencies, TV reporters, social scientists, and even multicultural educators have too often fallen into the habit of using drastically oversimplified and stereotyped definitions of ethnoracial groups and their historical experiences.[2]

"Multiculturalism" as applied to the historical enterprise is a term that threads through this book. Initially, this neologism was the property of liberal educators—those who strove to write more inclusive studies of society, culture, and history and labored to introduce that work into their classrooms. Scholars and teachers who enlisted in the multicultural campaign were a thoroughly mixed lot but included almost all feminists and people of color in the profession.

Broadly construed, "multiculturalism" refers to the many cultural affiliations that Americans hold and to the complex fusion of cultural identities and attitudes that each of us carries in our mind. Culture is acquired, but never through one's genes. Nor can it be displayed merely in the hue of one's skin. Rather, each person shapes and reshapes his or her cultural personality in connection with individual upbringing, religion, gender, social status, family allegiance, schooling, sexual preferences, and more. We manifest culture through speech, aesthetic sensibilities, cuisine, holiday celebrations, work habits, literary predilections, and so on.

Multicultural perspectives in history involve intersecting pathways of historical scholarship in which no one's social and cultural experience is off limits to investigation, not that of suburban women, nor slaves, nor dirt farmers, nor CEOs. Behind all of this scholarship resides a simple and—on the face of it—noncontroversial notion: One cannot study any nation's history as the whole without understanding the parts in all their variety. This obliges historians to pay heed to "the consciousness and actions of workers, women, ethnic, religious, racial, and national minorities, immigrants and their progeny, who participated in a myriad of separate geographical, occupational, fraternal, and religious communities that together constituted the larger society."[3]

In relation to non-American studies, multiculturalism has signified a commitment to teach children about the experiences of a variety of the world's peoples, not just North Americans and Europeans, and to look anywhere on the globe for answers to questions about how the world came to be the way it is. A multicultural perspective embodies the idea that historical and cultural studies are too important (and too interesting) to American students to permit them to be confined to just one part of the world or to politics, constitutions, and wars.

For about a decade, however, "multiculturalism" has been a battle cry, blamed for making race- or ethnic-based truth claims and thereby "balkanizing" America. But the great opening up of social history in the 1960s has occurred in *three* broad areas: in gender and class, as well as ethnoracial history. Like the flow of glaciers that gradually recarve the landscape, the new research has cumulatively altered our understanding of the past, affecting the way textbooks have been written and revised, museums have presented exhibits, and movies and TV have enlivened history for a new generation of viewers. Consider some examples.

The movie *Glory* on the black Massachusetts 54th Regiment and Ken Burns's *Civil War* documentary series on PBS were vastly enriched by thirty years of scholarship in African American history. The much-praised exhibit at the Valentine Museum in Richmond, Virginia, on black Americans' Civil War in the South could never have been installed except for this research. One of the authors of this book has compiled a bibliography of African American history for the period from 1765 to 1830 for the forthcoming *Harvard Guide to Afro-American History.* More than three hundred books and six hundred articles pertaining to this era have been published since 1965. *The Harvard Guide* will detail thousands of books, articles, and doctoral dissertations on a topic that commanded little attention before the 1960s. Does this scholarship represent an excess of multiculturalism and undermine American unity? On the contrary, it enriches our past by including those African Americans who played critical roles in building the national economy, who contributed to the polychromatic canvas of American culture, and who held political leaders to account for failures to enforce our charter of founding documents.

In 1988, when the Smithsonian Institution opened its "Field to Factory" exhibit on the great migration of Southern black tenant farmers to Northern cities in the early twentieth century, thousands of African Americans flocked to see it. Here was a portrayal of their own experiences and those of their parents and grandparents. The Smithsonian show unveiled in 1990 on the internment of Japanese Americans during World War II also drew crowds because the museum had pried open a chapter of our history that not many citizens knew anything about. The exhibition revealed not only how some one hundred and ten thousand Japanese Americans endured the internment and prevailed over its calamitous effects but also prompted citizens to consider how civil liberties have been compromised and curtailed in time of war.

In 1993, record numbers of people visited the Chicago Historical Society to see "We the People," an exhibit focusing on the lives of plain folk in the American Revolution. This program gave citizens an opportunity to see, feel, and read about the many ways that ordinary people, as well as textbook heroes, shaped and guided the Revolution. That same year the Historical Society of Pennsylvania opened an exhibition called "Finding Philadelphia: Visions and Revisions." Here curators and guest historians strove to present Philadelphia—from the time of William Penn's "green country town" to the 1940s—through the eyes of people high and low, white and black, male and female, young and old. This was the most successful exhibit the society ever mounted. Responding so warmly to these expositions, the public demonstrated its desire to have the curtains drawn back on the ways that people of every class and condition experienced the past. History from the perspective of field, factory, dock, mine, tunnel, kitchen, hospital bed, and alley engages citizens as much as the scene from legislative halls, governors' mansions, plantation homes, and counting houses.

In exhibitions in cities and towns all across the country, curators have drawn on a huge body of research in social history to bring to life previously unexamined dimensions of our past. It is as if historians have stumbled across Leo Tolstoy's dictum in *War and Peace*: "To study the laws of history we must completely change the subject of our observation, must leave aside kings, ministers, and generals, and study the common, infinitesimally small elements by which the masses are moved."[4] This challenge to Thomas Carlyle's axiom that "the history of the world is but the biography of great men" has been taken up only in recent years as young men and women of diverse backgrounds and ethnoracial affiliations have joined the historical profession's ranks.

That American history textbooks until recently left out the record of common folk seems extraordinary in a democratic society where we live by the motto "of, for, and by the people." Social historians have never denied that the great figures of our national pantheon are important. But the vital task is to teach history that shows dynamically how political leaders, religious luminaries, scientific geniuses, captains of industry, and military commanders not only influenced but *were influenced by* the ideas, deeds, protests, and inventions of ordinary citizens.

We cannot, for example, understand the Great Awakening of the 1740s, the first mass movement in American history, without delving into the roles of Jonathan Edwards, George Whitefield, and other clergymen. But neither can we understand this religious revival without noticing that women and youth, servants and slaves, farmers and artisans transformed and extended the Great Awakening, often offending the purported leaders in the process. The American Revolution would have looked very different, indeed might even have failed, without its steadfast Washington, its charismatic Franklin, its sagacious Jefferson, and many other storied heroes. But neither could it have succeeded without the massive participation of the multitude, who, once involved, altered its course, sometimes to the dismay of the standard bearers. The antislavery movement of the antebellum period had its Garrisons, Welds, and Grimkes, but without thousands of anonymous individuals, black and white, male and female, taking unpopular and often dangerous stands, it would have foundered. Hence, our nation's story is incomplete—and therefore distorted—if we do not show how social, political, and religious movements changed as wealthy and powerful elites persuaded and enlisted ordinary people and how at the same time ordinary people pushed forward their own agendas in ways that influenced and sometimes displaced leaders.

The new social history has uncovered much buried treasure in the American past, but it has also transformed the way historians look at all parts of the world. Innovative research methods and techniques, together with broader attitudes about whose history is worth investigating, have opened broad new panoramas on the history of Africa, Asia, and Latin America. The small, grainy, black-and-white screens of pre-1960s history featured European explorers, settlers, soldiers, and businessmen, together with a small supporting cast of local Westernized elites, imposing modernity and civilization on sullen savages and docile natives. Today the history of the world's major regions is told, as it were, in Omnimax and Dolby Sound. The European explorers are still in the picture, but so are Central Asian caravan merchants, North American mound builders, Turkish slave soldiers, Muslim women's rights activists, Angolan revolutionaries, and twelfth-century Chinese scientists. The study of African, Asian, and Latin American history has become thoroughly professionalized, and, despite the persistence of crude stereotypes in film and television, the peoples of these regions are gradually finding their place in the nation's college and K–12 textbooks.

For example, research of the past quarter century has transformed our understanding of the nearly four-hundred-year history of the Atlantic slave trade. Older representations of the trade in terms of crude dichotomies—savage vs. civilized, white vs. black, peaceful Africans vs. rapacious Europeans, "good" African slavery vs. "bad" American slavery—have given way to much more nuanced depictions. In the new accounts the forced movement of Africans to the Americas is to be seen as both a social disaster and a great human migration. African men and women of that era are to be viewed not only as victims of the trade but also as agents of history, interacting with Europeans and with one another in a multiplicity of ways amid the turbulent conditions of a complex and rapidly changing world economy.

Closely allied to the new social history are the projects of recent decades to fathom the deeper, slower currents of the human past. One example is an approach to historical research known as the "Annales school." Taking its name from a scholarly journal founded in France in 1929, Annaliste historians explored those patterns of change in nature and society that unfolded largely below the surface of human awareness. Climatic transformations, changing disease environments, the spread of new technology, long-range economic cycles, and demographic shifts have all been typical subjects of Annaliste investigation. The leading figures of this school—French historians Marc Bloch, Lucien Fevebre, and Fernand Braudel the most famous among them—believed that by combining historical methodologies with those of the social sciences and by integrating the study of long- and medium-term change with the record of short-term events, they could arrive at "total history," a grand synthesis of the human experience.

The Annalistes had their detractors, as proponents of new approaches invariably do. But they also profoundly influenced scholars and teachers in the United States by demonstrating that historical explanation must take into account, not only the conscious thoughts and deeds of individuals and groups, but also the "unconscious" phenomena—rainfall patterns, epidemic diseases, urban diets, child-rearing practices—that contribute to the way visible events are played out on the surface of human experience.

Another development of the past several years has been the "new cultural history." Drawing heavily on anthropology and literary theory, historians of culture "dig beneath the formal productions of law, literature, science, and art to the codes, clues, hints, signs, gestures, and artifacts through which people communicate their values and their truths."[5] Starting from the premise that all human thought and action operate within concrete cultural frameworks, these historians probe the cultural and mental universes of past societies to more fully understand how peoples of earlier times gave meaning to events and made sense of the world.

A classic example of cultural history is Robert Darnton's account of "The Great Cat Massacre."[6] One day in the late 1730s a group of Parisian workers in the printing trade went on a neighborhood rampage in which they captured, tortured, and ritually executed dozens of cats. They thought that what they were doing was side-splittingly funny. To late twentieth-century minds such a ghoulish display of cruelty seems horrifying. Why did the workers kill the cats, Darnton asked, and why did they think the murders were so hilarious? These questions led him deep into archives and libraries to find an explanation. He discovered some intriguing answers and, in the process, shed light on the values, beliefs, and fears of urban laborers in eighteenth-century Europe.

In assimilating the insights of the Annales school, cultural history, and other subdisciplines of the profession, scholars have had to recognize the great extent to which the deeds of both aristocrats and commoners are hemmed in by cultural walls and economic and social conditions. On the other hand, most practicing historians also believe that even though humans are carried along on currents of change they cannot fully comprehend, the individual, acting alone or with his fellows, is still a nimble, creative, courageous shaper of history. Social historians have exhibited the greatest respect for "the folk whom they now began to see not as inarticulate, impotent, irrelevant historical ciphers continually processed by forces over which they had no control but rather as actors in their own right who, to a larger extent than we previously imagined, were able to build a culture, create alternatives, affect the situation they found themselves in, and influence the people they found themselves among."[7] In college and school classrooms this dual question—what have been the limits on human endeavor, and how have men and women persistently surmounted them?—is what brings history alive.

A Case in Point: The American Revolution

Consider how new approaches to the past have enriched our understanding of this country's pivotal event, the American Revolution. For more than a quarter century social historians have written much sharper, subtler, more inclusive histories of the Revolution and the nation's founding than pre-1960s scholarship ever produced. But only in recent years has this research been included in school textbooks.

Traditionally, textbook discussions of the Revolution have passed over the experiences and the involvement of large groups in colonial society or have simply homogenized all colonial Americans into one undifferentiated mass. Therefore, the popular understanding of the Revolution has rested primarily on the great man theory of history. Washington, Jefferson, Franklin, John and Samuel Adams, and a few other leaders have occupied center stage. Students have had little idea of what the Revolution meant to the one-fifth of the colonial population that was black, to the thousands of Native Americans caught up in the struggle, to women of different races and social position, or to white males of different classes, occupations, and regional backgrounds. Textbooks have presented the Revolution almost exclusively as a war for independence, paying scant attention to the "war at home," that is, the intense struggle to redefine social and political relations that accompanied the military drama. By failing to examine the Revolution in its multiple dimensions, the textbooks have denied its complexity, robbed it of its radical character, and underplayed the contingency of its outcomes.

Traditional texts, for example, have consistently ignored the complicated process of drafting state constitutions. After renouncing the English charters, the law under which their provincial societies had functioned, Americans cast themselves into a state of nature, as it were, and had to begin anew. They had to decide what kinds of laws, political structures, and constitutionally protected liberties they wished to enshrine and by what means new governmental arrangements should be created. The immigrant Thomas Paine captured some of this challenge in his widely read and breathtakingly bold *Common Sense*: "We have it in our power to begin the world over again. A situation similar to the present has not happened since the days of Noah until now. The birthday of a new world is at hand."[8] Ten weeks after the Declaration of Independence was signed, Paine again prophesied a millennial sunrise: "The answer to the question, can America be happy under a government of her own, is short and simple, viz. As happy as she please; she hath a blank sheet to write upon."[9]

This was the opportunity but also the problem. The sheet may have been blank, but people were hardly of one mind about what to write on it. United in their desire to begin anew, they were nonetheless divided by region, class, religion, ethnicity, and a keen sense of having experienced the colonial era in different ways. They brought diverse agendas to the bargaining table and contrasting notions of how to redefine American society. In some states it took most of the war for the participants to frame their demands and negotiate agreements, and knotty unresolved questions carried over into the postwar period.

The Revolution is an epic of people at all levels of society—in the plantation South, the urban North, the rural hinterland—taking part in a historical transformation. Nearly every colonist had to make difficult choices, decide what freedom was worth, and calculate whether revolutionary promises were worth dying for. Some saw more of their revolutionary agenda accomplished than did others, while the Tories disavowed it. Some suffered keen disappointment but drew upon revolutionary principles as they understood them to continue their struggles after the war. Nearly all induced to join the disorderly but exhilarating campaign had not only to win a war but to invent a republic.

Why, for example, should American students not learn that Ebenezer MacIntosh, a poor Boston shoemaker and son of a Scots-Irish immigrant, led the Stamp Act riots? Why should this twenty-something street general, whom respectable Boston leaders shortly hustled out of the way because he appealed to the poor and disinherited, be omitted from the textbooks?

Why should it be forgotten that Philadelphia artisans and shopkeepers led revolutionary agitation against English policies, pushing social superiors such as John Dickinson and Benjamin Franklin along the road to war and independence?

The majority of the inhabitants of the thirteen colonies were either women, African Americans, or Native Americans. None of these categories represented a monolithic group sharing the same revolutionary ideas and experience. But all three were profoundly affected by the Revolution and helped shape its course. For African Americans, the Revolution offered a new opportunity to overthrow the institution of chattel slavery. Drawing on the rhetoric of inalienable rights, slaves petitioned for their freedom and in some cases tried to enlist in the revolutionary cause or fight in place of their masters. Black Americans joined with white allies to expose the contradiction between resistance to British oppression and the reality of slavery.

When it became clear that the Revolution would bring no general emancipation, slaves tried to liberate themselves whenever possible. Indeed the British stratagem of offering freedom to slaves who reached royalist lines changed the character of the war, especially in the South, where white Revolutionists found themselves fighting not only the British army and colonial loyalists but also escaped slaves, who provoked what amounted to the largest slave insurrection in American history. Among the consequences of the black presence in the Revolution were new pressures to abolish slavery in both the North and Southern border states; the exodus of ex-slaves who had fought for the British, first to Nova Scotia, then to Sierra Leone in West Africa; and the emergence of a cadre of black leaders who after the war established churches, schools, fraternal organizations, and mutual aid societies and thereby sustained free black communities from Charleston to Boston and kept abolitionism alive. This chapter of the American Revolution is still only edging its way into school textbooks.

For some two hundred thousand Native Americans living between the Atlantic Ocean and the Mississippi River, the Revolution was also a time "to try men's souls." Like the majority of African Americans, most Indians believed that they could best achieve their revolutionary goals by sticking to the British side. The logic of nearly two hundred years of contact with Europeans and their descendants governed the choice: It was colonial settlers who most threatened Indian autonomy, but royal power that in some measure protected native lands and sovereignty by prohibiting colonial expansion west of the Appalachians.

In the end, Indians who fought alongside the revolutionists—among them the Catawba, Oneida, and Stockbridge—lost out after the war no less than those who sided with the British. Their efforts for the cause of independence won them little protection from land-hungry settlers and speculators. However, this does not gainsay the important effects that Indians had on the course of the war or their continuing desires to secure the life, liberty, and the pursuit of happiness that the new republic proclaimed. When Ethan Allen, leader of the insurgent Green Mountain Boys, sailed to England in chains to answer for treasonous conduct, he shared space on the vessel with Joseph Brant, the Mohawk chief who was on his way to discuss with the king's ministers the spreading Revolution and the destiny of the Iroquois Confederation. Thus, a genuinely multicultural approach to the revolution includes Native Americans not because they represent a politically correct "interest group" but because they were deeply involved in the military campaigns, because they challenged American consistency in keeping faith with revolutionary principles, and because their wartime experience deeply affected their postwar strategies as the republic expanded westward over the Appalachian crest.

Critics of multiculturalism have denigrated efforts to infuse the experience of women into every era of American history. The work of scholars such as Linda Kerber and Mary Beth Norton on women in the American Revolution should convince history students otherwise. As market-goers and consumers, American women were crucial to the organizing of boycotts against tea, textiles, and other British goods in the years leading up to the war. From Georgia to Maine, women began spinning yarn and weaving cloth, turning every fireside, as John Adams recalled after the war, into "a theater of politics." Nor can the American military victory be fully understood without factoring in women as providers of food for armies on the march, as fund-raisers for the war effort, as nurses for the wounded, and as companions to soldiers both in the campgrounds and on the battlefields.

In "the war at home" men and women reexamined family and social relationships and redefined them more broadly. As male leaders talked of England's intentions to "enslave" its colonial subjects, women began to rethink their own social and legal situations. The enlightened rhetoric of the Revolution reminded women all too readily of their own domestic "subjecthood." Abigail Adams's call to her husband, John, not to "put such unlimited power into the hands of the husbands" in creating the nation's new laws and her warning that women would not "hold ourselves bound by any laws in which we have no voice or representation" is but one of many examples of women pressing forward to write upon Tom Paine's "blank sheet."[10] John Adams laughed at his wife's claims to political voice and equitable laws, reminding her that men would not give up "their masculine power." But in a stroke Abigail carried the political principles of the revolution onto new social and moral terrain. It would be many generations before women acquired suffrage and equitable legal treatment, but the process began in the Revolutionary era and is part of its story.

An inclusive version of the American Revolution—messier, sometimes paradoxical, often bittersweet—may be more difficult for teachers to present, more troublesome for students to understand. Perhaps a mythic, sanitized telling of the Revolution makes some students feel good about their country. Surely, however, the story of the nation's birth will seem more real, concrete, and just plain interesting when students explore the Revolution as an event both terrifying and inspiring, heroic and mundane, divisive and binding.

The Turbulent Sixties and the Pursuit of Relevancy

Though historical scholarship boomed in the 1960s, the tumult associated with the civil rights movement and then the national trauma of the Vietnam War produced severe strains within the public schools. These tensions, often breaking into violent disruptions, occurred at the very time when public education became nearly universal in the country.

The grand American experiment, begun in the nineteenth century to educate all the nation's children through public elementary schooling, expanded in the twentieth century to an even grander vision: to provide universal secondary education and, by the postwar years, to ensure equality in educational opportunities. Of these two goals, the first—expanding public access to secondary education—proved by far the easier to achieve. By 1960, 8.3 million American youths were in public high schools; by 1970, the number had leaped to 13 million—very near universal attendance. Ensuring equality of education proved much more elusive—in fact, so difficult to achieve and so divisive in the measures undertaken in its behalf—that it caused wave upon wave of criticism from all parts of the political spectrum.

It is easy to criticize the way educators faced the problems that tested the country's agility at accommodating wholesale change. Charles Silberman's *Crisis in the Classroom* (1970) charged that at the end of the 1960s "the public schools are in disarray, torn apart by conflicts over integration, desegregation, decentralization, and community control." But teachers of proud heart and good intentions were trying to cope with rapid changes of a kind unprecedented in their experiences. First, they had to confront national events that conspired to shake students' confidence in the nation's public institutions and led them to challenge what they were being taught in school. The most visible signs of a nation at war with itself occurred in the assassi-

nations of Martin Luther King Jr. and Robert F. Kennedy in 1968; the conflicts unleashed by the long-deferred federal resolve to reverse centuries
of discrimination against African American citizens; the escalation of the
Vietnam War and its extension into Cambodia; the rising militancy of public protests of the war; the scandal of Watergate reaching into the highest
levels of the White House; and the resignation of a sitting president in
disgrace.

Second, teachers had to grapple with the counterculture movement of
the 1960s, which inspired students to respond to the militant world they saw
swirling around them with a wave of militancy of their own. They joined
protest movements, organized student strikes, and occupied principals' and
deans' offices of high schools and colleges alike. They protested against the
war and against discriminatory practices on the campuses. Minority students railed against the failure of schools—and their textbooks—to recognize their heritage and their contributions to building the American nation.
In some schools, they demanded ethnic studies programs where they could
study their own cultural traditions apart from the dominant culture. Students were not prepared to leave these concerns quietly at the schoolhouse
door.

Third, teachers were directly and daily influenced by a silent demographic revolution occurring across the nation, a transformation that was
changing the face of American classrooms. Since the 1950s, the second great
migration of African Americans out of the Deep South doubled and even
tripled the proportion of black students in most Northern urban schools.
On top of this, the Immigration Act of 1965, reopening doors that had been
relatively closed since the restrictions of the early 1920s, brought into the
public schools millions of young newcomers, especially from Asia, Mexico,
and Central America. In many schools, teachers who had looked out over
mostly white faces now taught African American, Puerto Rican, Mexican,
Salvadorean, Taiwanese, Vietnamese, Cambodian, Korean, and Filipino
children.

Fourth, teachers and administrators were adjusting to the wave of federal
legislation of the Great Society years when Congress attempted to redress
the injustices of pervasive racial discrimination and inequality. The resulting education legislation enacted by the 88th and 89th Congresses brought
major changes to the schools and the programs they offered. For example,
the Equal Educational Opportunities Program of the Civil Rights Act of
1964 provided money to desegregate school districts, instructed the commissioner of education to monitor inequality in educational opportunities,
and empowered the government to withhold money from programs in violation of antidiscrimination laws. In 1965, the Elementary and Secondary

Education Act furnished special assistance for schools heavily populated by the children of low-income families. In 1974, the Women's Educational Equity Act, signed by President Nixon, aimed at ending sex discrimination in educational opportunities and sex stereotyping in the curriculum.

Social studies, like other curricular fields, struggled to cope with the new and often conflicting demands of students, parents, teachers, administrators, and federal regulations. Under pressure to socialize immigrant children to American culture, to teach them English, and to reconfigure education in general to achieve equal educational opportunities, teachers adopted "relevance" as their watchword. If these demands overpowered the schools' quest for educational excellence that began in the post-Sputnik years, teachers were not to blame. Schools did not operate in a vacuum, immune from the social changes and upheavals sweeping American society.

Some prominent social studies educators saw only a fragmented curriculum and a rush for relevance, if not a caving in to political agendas of particular "interest groups." "The student as academic inquirer," one history educator observed, "was replaced by the student as social activist in search of an individual or group identity"—a change, she concluded, that fragmented the social studies curriculum.[11]

Other educators were even more shaken by student activism. In 1977, James Shaver, a foremost champion of citizenship education as the organizing core of the social studies, attacked the "mindlessness" into which the field had fallen.[12] Its uncritical acceptance of trendy areas of study, and its failure to question fundamental assumptions had, he charged, left the field adrift. Four years later, Howard Mehlinger, president of the National Council for the Social Studies, declared that the subject suffered from terminal illness, if it was not already dead.[13] The field, he judged, was "goal-rich and content-poor." It had cut itself loose from its academic moorings, leaving itself susceptible to fads and political pressures. Like others, Mehlinger found the field mindlessly bending to every breeze that came along, admitting multitudes of elective "minicourses" and encouraging the spread of the "cafeteria high school."

In many schools, intellectually challenging programs in the social sciences, organized by academic disciplines, were indeed replaced with activist projects on ethnicity, urban problems, law, war, peace, poverty, crime, social inequality, racism, sexism, drug use, and the environment. Values clarification, which involved inculcating no particular values but sought instead to help students define their own choice of personal values, entered the curriculum for a time until research demonstrated its inadequacy. Some deplored all these developments. But to dismiss out of hand the changes that many students, parents, and teachers demanded is to ignore the sources of such demands and the legitimacy of complaints about the education of children who were not white and prosperous.

World History Blues

As many American teachers began to look out on classrooms filled with the children of newly arrived immigrants, they might well have seen the need for world history programs that would connect the experience of youngsters learning to be American with the lives of native-born children. Or, they might have noticed how the transnational reach of the United States demanded a globe-encircling world history. In fact, no major shift took place in the 1960s and 1970s in the ways non-American history was taught. Most states continued, as before the war, to let students graduate from high school without studying any non-American history or geography at all. As of the early 1960s, about half the country's high school students took world history, usually the tenth-grade course that in the 1930s had largely replaced the three-year sequence of ancient, medieval/modern, and English history.[14] More often than not, high school world history was an elective, not a requirement. The junior high social studies curriculum had no coherence nationally, but world cultures and geography courses that mixed in a bit of history were common, notably for sixth- and ninth-graders. In the 1970s, enrollments in non-American history and geography continued to decline. The standard tenth-grade course appears to have held its own, but as of 1977 only about 70 percent of the country's high schools even offered world history.[15]

Somewhat like a Christmas tree, tenth-grade world history retained the solid trunk and branches of Western civilization that it had possessed since the 1930s, but teachers continued to festoon it, indeed load it down, with the results of new research in social, economic, and cultural history. Though one scholar, writing around 1940 on the problem of the Western Civ college survey, declared that "we have probably put into these introductory courses by now all that they will ever hold,"[16] teachers and textbook publishers discovered more and more ornaments to hang on the tree. Although they still left out most of the medieval and modern history of Asia and nearly all history of Africa and pre-Columbian America, they introduced more material on recent affairs in non-Western countries. And even though teachers tended to look out on Africa, Asia, and Latin America "from the deck of a gunboat," as one teacher put it,[17] they paid increasing attention to the history of European overseas expansion. In short, as the United States became the world's mightiest nation, the traditional world history course lost its original *raison d'etre* to give students a uniform, progressive, immutable history of the civilization of Europe. Now world history became a Fibber McGee's closet of facts and generalizations—Plato to NATO, homo sapiens to the Hungarian Revolt.

In the 1960s and 1970s, social studies educators registered much discontent over the non-American curriculum. "In terms of enrollment," Gilbert Allardyce writes, high school world history "was one of the great success stories in the history of American education; in terms of everything else, it was a running failure"—unfocused, elephantine, and stale.[18] Leften Stavrianos, an incisive critic of the Western Civ approach, surveyed the situation in 1964:

> We have the privilege of living in what is without a doubt the most exciting and significant era in history. What man is achieving now is beyond compare, and what he will be achieving in the next few decades is almost beyond imagination. And yet, in this very day and age, the world history course is the one most criticized by teachers and students alike! Incredible as it seems, it is criticized most frequently because it is dull and irrelevant![19]

If tenth-grade world history made students' heads nod, "world cultures" courses at the elementary or junior high school level administered the sleeping pills. These classes tended to be a hodgepodge of geographical, cultural, and historical information about this nation and that. Martin Mayer parodied the typical course: Students learn that "Tokyo is the largest city in the world; the Dutch reclaim land from the sea and grow tulips; Egyptians farm the sediment deposited by the Nile; birds drop guano along the Chilean shore; ... America has everything, almost."[20]

Interesting information perhaps, but how did these courses contribute to students' systematic understanding of the world in which they lived and to their powers of critical and analytical thought? No one seemed sure. Of course, when a skilled and spirited teacher entered the classroom, whether sixth-grade or senior high, children rose to the occasion despite the dreary textbook and course outline. The problem here was not so much the deficiencies of teachers (though teacher training in non-American history was decidedly inadequate in most states) as it was the failure of Eurocentric, grab-bag history and superficial culture studies to make sufficient sense in the atomic age.

Sheer institutional inertia kept traditional courses largely in place, but new ideas were brewing in the 1960s and 1970s. The same explosion of knowledge and interpretive controversy that pushed out the postwar frontiers of American history opened minds to wider and wider worlds. The same social and political currents that helped transform research in U.S. history stimulated fresh angles of vision on the history of Europe, Asia, Africa, Latin America, and the Middle East. In the interwar period, the Western-Civ-as-world-history model superficially served America's self-conception as the flagship of Atlantic democracy and perhaps its deep ambivalence about too much involvement with the rest of the world. In the aftermath of World War II and the icing over of Soviet-American relations, however, the United States was no longer simply a North American power but a South Atlantic, Pacific, and Indian Ocean presence as well. Economic, political, and cultural intertwinings with Japan, India, Algeria, Iran, Guatemala, and Angola were now no less important than the long-standing bonds of trade, diplomacy, and sentiment that connected Americans to Britain, France, and Italy. This new world cried out for a new kind of world education for American citizens.

Toward this end, one of the most important developments was the movement in the 1950s to establish foreign area studies programs at major universities. The public stood resolutely behind the proposition that our government, business leaders, and military should know a great deal more about African nationalism, Soviet politics, Latin American economies, and Japanese culture. The new programs aimed to create cadres of young citizens with multidisciplinary knowledge of all the countries of the world. By itself, this required mastery of not just the French, German, and Spanish languages, but Arabic, Chinese, and Swahili. Graduate students went forth to do field research in Africa, Asia, and Latin America, bringing new social scientific and linguistic skills to bear on dissertations that would gradually broaden America's understanding of the world and contribute, as a matter of national interest, to global peace and prosperity. Beginning in 1958, federal dollars poured into area studies programs through the National Defense Education Act. The title of the legislation pointed conspicuously to Congress's recognition of the connection between national identity and our knowledge of the past and present world.

Just as new research in American history uncovered hitherto unknown chapters of the past, so area studies scholars posed questions about history and society in far corners of the earth that older attitudes and modes of thinking had precluded. Few Americans would have blinked at the standard pronouncements about Africa that appeared in prewar textbooks. "Until comparatively recently," one book informed students, "this vast area, except the northern and southern extremities, was peopled by savage tribes of blacks living amidst the most primitive conditions, and almost wholly cut off from the outside world."[21] Even in 1963, the distinguished British historian Hugh Trevor-Roper declared confidently that the continent's history was merely "the unrewarding gyrations of barbarous tribes in picturesque but irrelevant corners of the globe" and therefore not worth any scholar's attention.[22]

Yet by this time, North American historians and social scientists, skilled in the requisite languages, were traveling to African countries in increasing numbers and collaborating with European and African academics to reconstruct the continent's rich past, drawing on written records in Arabic and European languages that no one had analyzed before and making use of sophisticated research techniques in archaeology, linguistics, ethnobotany, and oral tradition. In the mid-1950s, Africanist historians in the United States numbered no more than a few dozen. By the end of the 1970s, there were about six hundred of them.[23] As research proceeded, and books, articles, and dissertations proliferated, the world's understanding of the African past was transformed. The old paradigm of savage, static, anthropological Africa—existing outside history altogether—soon collapsed, not so much because American education promoted tolerance or cultural relativism but because the weight of research demonstrated empirically that Trevor-Roper's image of the continent was simply silly.

Unfortunately, the ocean separating academic specialists from social studies teachers was so wide in the 1960s and 1970s that the new research, not only on Africa, Asia, and Latin America, but also on women, peasants, and ethnic peoples in European history, seeped into K–12 classrooms and textbooks at a very slow pace. In those two decades both universities and schools moved seriously to internationalize the curriculum, and they did so for many of the same reasons—the challenge of Sputnik, the Soviet threat, the Vietnam War, the rise of dozens of new nations, and a general appreciation of the realities of global interdependence, a sentiment the public largely shared. Even so, the sheepskin curtain remained more tightly drawn than ever. College professors buried in their important researches in Czechoslovakia, Senegal, or Peru were scarcely aware of the problems tenth-grade history teachers faced in trying to make sense of the world as a whole.

In the colleges and universities the established course in Western civilization sustained wounds in the great battle of the mid- and late sixties over the meaning and purpose of a common core of learning. In institutions all across the country, though by no means in all of them, general education programs that had earlier been required were loosened up or dismantled, faculty were encouraged to teach their specialties in the name of rigorous standards, and freshmen were permitted to pick what courses they liked and to "do their own thing." As Allardyce sees it, this challenge to general education meant a challenge to Western Civ as well. For connected to the absolutes of general education were the absolutes of the original Western Civ idea: the belief in the oneness of history, in the potential of the historical method to integrate human experience, and in Western history as the "high history" of mankind.[24]

Also, the burgeoning history departments of the 1960s included many young scholars just back from field research in Africa, Latin America, or Asia. They tended to look upon introductory Western Civ, which an older generation of professors taught implicitly but inaccurately as world history, with disinterest or contempt.

But the Young Turks who derided the narrow vision and cultural arrogance of Western-Civ-as-world-history were themselves largely apathetic about developing more effective introductory courses. After all, specialized research led to grants, sabbaticals, publication, promotion, and tenure. Teaching innovative courses to freshmen led to extensive lecture writing, stacks of essays, and a pat on the head from the academic dean. William McNeill, whose 1963 book *The Rise of the West* offered perhaps the first coherent framework for the whole of human history, sorely lamented the profession's rush to dynamite Western Civ without coming up with a viable alternative, "something worth teaching to undergraduates en masse: something all educated persons should know; something every active citizen ought to be familiar with in order to conduct his life well and perform his public duties effectively."[25]

The concern was not so much that students would not take an introductory survey but that if professors taught only their special fields of expertise, then most students would not take history at all. To McNeill it was "self-evident" that "the only frame suitable for introducing students to the world in which they live is world history."[26] McNeill made this proposal in 1976, but it would be several more years before the movement to introduce large numbers of college freshmen to a world history not shackled to the old Western "mainstream" paradigm would gain favor. In the meantime, media attention to controversy over core curricula at such prestigious institutions as Columbia, Harvard, and Stanford obscured the fact that many state universities and small colleges continued to teach Western Civ straight through the period of tumult. And freshmen continued to learn the Western tradition without being told that it was not world history.

These struggles in the universities over the value and relevance of mandated liberal arts programs were hardly heard in the schools. There the challenge in the 1960s and 1970s to the tenth-grade world history course came not from university scholars, who had other fish to fry, but from social studies educators supporting internationalization, indeed "globalization," of the curriculum. These globalists were not radical advocates of world government but mainly school of education faculty and other social studies professionals who saw an urgent need to prepare young citizens to live in a world that was continuously restructuring itself—economically, politically, environmentally—and that subjected all Americans, whether or not they liked it, to the push and tug of transnational forces.

Social studies globalists spoke the language of astronauts and cosmonauts: spaceship Earth, global village, world-mindedness, global consciousness, big blue marble. One treatise on global studies sponsored by the National Education Association warned: "More than ever before, Americans need to develop a species view, a humankind or global perspective, if they are to understand and function effectively in the global society in which they live."[27]

Educators holding such sentiments might have been expected to champion solid non-American history programs in the schools. In fact, many globalists, like the advocates of the New Social Studies, were mostly interested in having children study contemporary international issues and social scientific approaches to them. Some regarded the traditional one-year world history course as hopelessly Eurocentric (which in large measure it was) and the historical discipline as relentlessly dedicated to rote memorization of facts about English kings and Balkan diplomacy (which emphatically it was not). Historians noted the irony of social studies internationalizers wanting to throw out world history, convinced that "the global village was no place to dig up the past."[28] History teachers, in turn, accused globalists of rampant presentism and pushing sixth-graders not to become historically literate but to resolve the arms race.

Stavrianos tried to reconcile the contending parties by proposing that the schools activate a "shift from Western civilization to genuine world history by dealing with the various regions of the world in accord with an integrated, globally oriented approach."[29] He made an impact with a thoughtful new global history textbook that reconceptualized Europe up to A.D. 1500 as one of four major Eurasian "centers of civilization" whose past was driven not so much by internal mechanisms inherited from Mesopotamia and Greece as by "powerful interregional historical forces."[30]

Yet in spite of such pioneering work, neither Stavrianos, the globalists nor the New Social Studies proponents made much of a dent in the way that non-American history was taught in the schools. The major change was the drop in enrollments as new courses in anthropology, psychology, and other social sciences competed with optional world history. The academic scholars, who were accumulating vast stores of knowledge about the history of all the world's regions, showed little interest in developing new organizing principles for their own survey courses, much less in helping the high schools do it.

Throughout the 1960s and 1970s, the American public left the debate over globalization and Western versus non-Western history mostly to education insiders. In those years the public was on the whole friendly toward the ideals of international education. Political conservatives in a few states made fun of internationalization in the schools as "globaloney" or as the work of liberals determined to lead United Nations raids on American sovereignty. But as yet no politicians or newspaper columnists railed against world history as an assault on patriotism or "Western values." Multiculturalism had not yet become a subject of grave national dispute.

Uncertainty in the Schools

Overall, how did the status of history in schools fare amid these troubled years? In 1969, when the social science movement was in full flower, churning out innovative and captivating programs in a profusion that virtually overwhelmed the schools, Berkeley's Charles G. Sellers, one of the few historians who still voiced an interest in precollegiate education, asked, "Is history on the way out of the schools, and do historians care?" Peter Novick, recently assessing the state of affairs at the time, has judged the answer to these questions to be, respectively, "yes" and "no."[31] More than historians held this view. Irving Morrisett, professor of economics and executive director of the Social Science Education Consortium, told Crabtree in 1963 that "history will soon be as dead as Latin in the schools."

Six years later, a joint committee of the American Historical Association and the Organization of American Historians reported a "very dynamic situation" in the schools, with most of the movement away from history, at least as history had been traditionally defined and taught.[32] Where courses in the discipline were holding strong, state legislatures had often mandated study of U.S. history for high school graduation.

These legal requirements did not, however, guarantee the quality of the history taught, particularly where the requirements were resisted. "History would doubtless be much more neglected in the schools of Tennessee if the statutory requirements were repealed," suggested the report from that state. As it was, some Tennessee schools had reduced their U.S. history course to less than a semester and were using the remainder of the year for other social sciences. The Arkansas report said that the emphasis on history in that state "is due to the requirement by the State Department of Education . . .

and does not reflect genuine interest in history as a subject." North Carolina no longer required history above the ninth grade, and the subject had disappeared from the state curriculum for grades ten through twelve. Maryland reported that "history has been clearly deemphasized and is now generally incorporated into social studies units. . . . The general trend is toward the multidisciplinary approach."

Similar reports came from the Midwest and West. Iowa disclosed that "major changes in both content and method are under way and . . . the thrust of these changes has been toward teaching less history of the traditional sort, eroding any sense of a differentiated past and unique time perspectives, and turning students away from historical study or an appreciation of its importance." Illinois reported that "recent legislation mandating consumer education in public schools has led districts and departments to respond by substituting courses in economics, consumer economics, and career education for world history." Oklahoma communicated that "present-day students have no time to study the past." In New Mexico, high schools replaced history courses with "ethnocultural courses of which history is only one aspect of the class." Nearly all school districts in Utah reported moving "toward more emphasis on interdisciplinary content, economics, current events, American problems, and sociology." In Hawaii history had lost its former dominance in the curriculum to what was called an "Inquiry-Conceptual Program" integrating all the social sciences in courses focused upon "making decisions and taking action on social and civic problems."

In places where changes of these sorts were under way, public contention, not surprisingly, broke out. The Arizona report revealed how history had become a "focal point of political controversy." Conservative opponents of change demanded that United States history be taught "undefiled," with a primary goal of inculcating in students national pride. To that end, they influenced formation of a Basic Goals Commission, which called upon teachers of a new eleventh-grade course in U.S. history "to teach positive, rather than negative aspects of the American past, to eschew conflict as a theme, inculcate pride in the accomplishments of the nation, and show the influence of rational, creative, and spiritual forces in the shaping of the nation's growth." In hearings before the Arizona State Board of Education, critics charged the proposed course "expressed an anti-Indian bias, ignored the roles of blacks and Mexican Americans, was self-congratulatory, extolled rural virtues, and provided very little preparation for life in an urban industrial society."

The ferment of the 1960s and 1970s did indeed destabilize history and social studies curricula across the nation. But it also produced an unprecedented burst of creative research and writing in U.S. and world history. The new scholarship not only opened panoramic new vistas on the past but also helped to expose the fact that historical understanding among the nation's children was shockingly narrow, fragmentary, and distorted. By the 1980s, the loss of collective memory among the young was so apparent that education leaders and other citizens cried out for something to be done.

CHAPTER 5

History, Culture, and Politics

He who controls the past controls the future.
He who controls the present controls the past.

—George Orwell, *1984*

In the 1980s and 1990s, a powerful movement to strengthen history education seemed about to accomplish what no nation had done before:
offer students an inclusive history of the country based on copious new
scholarship, recognize that globe-encompassing history serves the nation's
international interests and responsibilities, and ensure that children develop the analytic skills and level-headed perspectives that the contemporary world demands. The United States was gathering a head of steam to
overcome history illiteracy.

Anyone might have imagined that the United States was entering a new
period of maturity in history education, a dawning of consciousness akin to
the nation's acceptance of responsibilities for global leadership following
World War II. Speaking on the issue of isolationism in 1941, Henry A. Wallace, Franklin D. Roosevelt's vice president, said, "We of the United States
can no more evade shouldering our responsibility than a boy of eighteen
can avoid becoming a man by wearing short pants. The word 'isolation'
means short pants for a grown-up United States."[1] By the early 1990s Americans seemed ready to wear long-pants history. Perhaps the time had come
when citizens would be "capable of looking at their own history soberly,"
and avoiding the "snares of trivializing, sanitizing, and sanctifying the past
into which other nations have fallen."[2]

As we shall see, the hope that American society was divesting itself of
jingoistic, myopic, short-pants attitudes toward teaching and learning history was not yet to be realized. In fact, the movement to strengthen history
in the schools and universities was fraught with irony. Education leaders of

traditionalist mind and right-to-center politics provided much of the initial inspiration to restore history to the school curriculum, but they also took a dim view of research that to them seemed to gallop off in all directions and to threaten an immutable national narrative to which all Americans might subscribe. Instead of capturing the high ground that might have provided pedagogical models for countries emerging from communist control or struggling with ethnoracial conflicts, the United States fell into fights over history as nasty as those of the 1920s and 1930s.

Multiculturalism, which until the late 1980s had been a largely benign ideal in American education, suddenly became a slogan in the culture wars. Our multicultural society was no longer seen as one in which ethnoracial diversity has simply enriched the citizenry collectively but a place of angry arguments and disputed claims over social recognition, justice, and equality for various groups, that is, a country in the grip of "identity politics." According to most media reporting in the late 1980s, liberals and leftists were presumably for multiculturalism, conservatives and "real patriots" against it, though what exactly multiculturalists wanted and antimulticulturalists opposed became an increasingly murky issue. Moreover, politicians, pundits, government representatives, and even educators increasingly acquired the habit of talking about American society as though it were divided into fixed ethnoracial groups, each possessing its distinct culture, world view, and history extending backward to a selected set of ancestors of particular origin and color. Such a notion tended to encourage people who wished to promote history as "social and political therapy," as Arthur Schlesinger Jr. calls it.[3]

Such an ideology has led militant monoculturalists of the Right to demand history that extols Ozzie and Harriet patriotism and exclusive celebration of the Western tradition. Militant multiculturalists, on the other hand, have romanticized the history of their particular group, or world regions other than Europe, out of all recognition, and stigmatized Western civilization as the world's oldest evil empire. And so battle lines formed once again over the old question of the purpose of history and history education in a democratic society. A recent work on this subject sums up the enduring problem:

Democracy and history always live in a kind of tension with each other. Nations use history to build a sense of national identity, pitting the demands for stories that build solidarity against open-ended scholarly inquiry that can trample on cherished illusions. Here the pressing question is which human needs should history serve, the yearning for a self-

affirming past, even if distorted, or the liberation, however painful, that
comes from grappling with a more complex, accurate account?[4]

The New Historical Scholarship: A Threat to the Nation?

In the 1980s new approaches to the American past, especially social history,
produced some discontent inside the colleges and universities, though no
more than usual whenever new subjects are introduced and methodologi-
cal shifts are in progress. Outside the academy, by contrast, near panic broke
out among those on the political Right.

A minority of university scholars worried that social historians, by focusing on particular groups, distinct communities, and small bits of the
larger national story, were fragmenting American history. Some argued that
history as collections of particularistic studies, "a melange of isolated, un-
connected truths," as one historian put it, jeopardizes the integrated vision
and coherent story line that make history courses digestible for college students. Worse, succeeding waves of new interpretive, often conflicting, research might make American history unusable in the schools, where the
focus should be on national character formation.[5] One scholar saw "sheer
disarray and confusion in the proliferation of analytical historiography."[6]
Another characterized his young colleagues as a field full of solitary go-
phers, each digging its own tunnel.[7]

These were sober reflections on the surging wave of social history.
Undeniably the outpouring of scholarship on particular groups—Italian
immigrants in Buffalo, Irish laborers in Boston, African Americans in Philadelphia, women on the Montana frontier, Japanese Americans in the San
Joaquin Valley, Mexican Americans in Santa Barbara—complicated the national experience and made it nearly impossible to imagine one seamless,
tidily packaged history. Indeed, the traditional story, focusing on national
politics, elite society, and traditional heroes, had been elegant, linear, and
unconfusing precisely *because* it left out so much. As one historian put it, this
"sacred story with strong nationalist overtones . . . derived much of its coherence from the groups it ignored or dismissed."[8]

Those who defended the "old" history, which in truth was far from
monolithic, were sure that the "new" history decenters and marginalizes the
themes that gave the past coherence. Consider the lament of Gertrude
Himmelfarb, a leading critic of social history: "It is difficult . . . to see how
the subjects of the new [social] history can be accommodated in any single
framework, let alone a national and political one. . . . How can all these
groups, each cherishing its uniqueness and its claim to sovereign attention,

be mainstreamed into a single, coherent, integrated history?"⁹ One can argue whether historians of women or African Americans, or any other group have ever demanded "sovereign attention," and whether a single framework based on eternal verities has lasted more than a generation or two.

But can social history be made a part of a single framework? Can a plurality of stories and jarring perspectives fit into a coherent understanding of the American past? Quite simply, the particularities of social history *can* be mainstreamed readily enough by changing the governing narrative from the rise of democracy, defined in terms of electoral politics, to the struggle to fulfill the American ideals of liberty, equal justice, and equality. This new narrative, arising out of a democratized historical practice, would speak to contests and conflicts over power and how such contests reflect the long struggles among various groups to elbow their way under the canopy of the nation's founding promises. This narrative is as simple as the opening words of the Constitution: "to create a more perfect union."

Can there be any grand narrative more powerful, coherent, democratic, and inspiring than the struggles of groups that have suffered discrimination, exploitation, and hostility but have overcome passivity and resignation to challenge their exploiters, fight for legal rights, resist and cross racial boundaries, and hence embrace and advance the American credo that "all men are created equal"? Is it not a coherent, integrated history that portrays "the dignity of common people who quietly struggle under difficult conditions and who, in large and small ways, refuse to submit passively to abuse, discrimination, and exploitation"?¹⁰ This is nothing less than the story of the uncompleted project of making Americanism "a matter of heart and mind rather than race or ancestry."¹¹

Compare how American history textbook titles have spoken to the old narrative's spinal cord. Signatures of this narrative can be quickly identified by titles such as *The Great Republic, Triumph of the American Nation* and *America: The Glorious Republic.* New textbooks that are infused with social history, but social history braided with political, economic, and intellectual subjects, bear signature titles such as *America Will Be, A More Perfect Union,* and *A People and a Nation.* Rather than triumphally saluting a completed national agenda and celebrating an undiluted record of achievement, a new synthesis of the old and new history presents a multicultural nation and a continuously replenished immigrant society engaged in a ceaseless and often bittersweet crusade to narrow the gap between principles enunciated in charter documents and the actual conditions of life.

This is the America of Emerson when he wrote, "What is man born for but to be a reformer; a remaker of what man has made; a renouncer of lies?" No contradiction exists between telling a national story on the one hand

and on the other hand incorporating the work of historians who have respect, as Lawrence Levine puts it, for

> the folk whom they now began to see not as inarticulate, impotent, irrelevant historical ciphers continually processed by forces over which they had no control but rather as actors in their own right who, to a larger extent than we previously imagined, were able to build a culture, create alternatives, affect the situation they found themselves in, and influence the people they found themselves among.[12]

One of the peculiarities of today's history wars is that those who believe that particularistic studies of women, African Americans, Asian Americans, religious minorities, and working people will balkanize America do not reflect on whether groups that have been ignored, demeaned, or marginalized can be expected to feel part of the *unum* when they are not counted among the *pluribus*. New studies of the previously unstudied cannot disunify this nation unless it is a united nation ripe for disunification. Surely unity is more likely to emerge when those who read history books do not see their own kind ignored or insulted.

Though academics who expressed their doubts about social and other forms of "new" history were for the most part political conservatives, they did not stand as far to the right as the group of culture critics that emerged in the early 1980s. Speaking from platforms mostly outside the schools and universities, these critics charged that much of the new scholarship was left-wing, nihilistic, divisive, and "politically correct." The notion of political correctness, which one study defines as a term of derision used by the Right "to refer to a kind of regimented sympathy shown to the nation's minorities and women,"[13] has been applied to several aspects of American life—hiring policies, college living arrangements, administrative terminology, literature curricula, and so on. Politically correct history is that which presumably gives too much attention to women, minorities, and the laboring masses in comparison with traditionally celebrated groups and leaders; bashes cherished American and Western values, though letting non-Western perpetrators of political oppression, widow burning, and clitoridectomy off the hook; declares that the past is never other than what group A or group B thinks it should be; and denies the reality of objective historical truth.

Like self-appointed censors of textbooks in the 1920s and 1930s, the enemies of presumed politically correct history argue that America's future is profoundly jeopardized by failure to affirm a stable, proud, unitary past. They repeatedly raise images of "a chaotic present and disastrous future," then set this scary state of affairs against "a nostalgic vision of an intact and uncontested intellectual world that we are losing or have already lost."[14]

The great public debate over *unum, pluribus*, and the crisis of American national identity rose several decibels in the middle years of Ronald Reagan's presidency. Conservatively funded think tanks such as the Hudson Institute and the American Enterprise Institute issued proclamations about the excesses of multiculturalism and relativistic thought. William Bennett and Lynne Cheney became, especially after being appointed by President Reagan to high office, two of the most articulate critics on the Right. Bennett served first as chairman of the National Endowment for the Humanities (NEH), then as secretary of education; Cheney succeeded Bennett at NEH from 1986 to 1992. At the NEH, the Advisory Council took on a strong conservative and traditionalist flavor and moved sharply to limit funding of research on topics having to do with women, labor, racial groups, or any project focusing on conflictual aspects of American history.

One former NEH staffer reports that "projects dealing with Latin America, the Caribbean, some women's studies, and anything appearing as vaguely left wing are seen as suspect. Controversy is a central issue: Will this cause a headline and get us in hot water with our conservative constituency?"[15] While heralding the NEH's commitment to the search for truth, Cheney "packed her Advisory Council with critics of multiculturalism and women's studies" and, "as the darling of the conservatives in Congress and the White House . . . deep-sixed any grant she didn't like."[16]

As William Bennett, ever keen-witted and provocative, toured the country telling audiences what was wrong with the universities and American education in general, the media put out its antennae for any sign of culture war. In 1987–88 stories were published about trouble among faculty and students at Stanford University over a decision to replace a freshman core course in Western Culture with a series of humanities offerings that were modestly less Western-oriented. The faculty decision to revise the course was clearly motivated far less by political ideology than by recognition of the broadening of horizons that had occurred in humanistic scholarship and creative writing in the previous three decades.

Bennett, then secretary of education, chose to interpret the change as a left-wing faculty *putsch* to "drop the West." Never one to skirt enemy territory, he traveled straight to Stanford, where he charged that the curriculum revision was "an unfortunate capitulation to a campaign of pressure politics and intimidation" and that the university was ruled by a "left-wing political agenda" based on a combination of feminism and Marxism. Donald Kennedy, president of Stanford, retorted that Bennett was "either ill-informed or irresponsible."[17] Even so, Stanford's initially intramural disagreement ballooned quickly into a national dispute "over what the next generation of Americans should learn about their intellectual heritage: Were standards being lowered? Was the American mind at Stanford opening—or closing?"[18]

By the end of 1990, the American media, which had traditionally paid little attention to the cultural and curricular life of universities, went, in Todd Gitlin's phrase, "into full panic." Egged on by conservative press stars such as Bennett, Dinesh D'Souza, George Will, and Allan Bloom ("the barbarians are not at the gate; they, without our knowing it, have taken over the citadel"[19]), the thought police of the Right roamed the country's campuses looking for antiwhite discrimination, tenured radicals, and left-wing, postmodernist storm troopers. By 1991, Gitlin writes, things were reaching a fever pitch:

> Ridicule, indignation, and uproar rippled outward through talk shows and news reports, and flowed through millions of eddies and inlets of private conversation into the great sea of opinion and mood where popular sentiment forms. . . . Among the periodicals in the NEXIS database, the term "politically correct" and its variants appeared 7 times in 1988, 15 times in 1989, 66 times in 1990, 1,553 times in 1991, 2,672 times in 1992, and 4,643 times in 1993.[20]

Conservative politicians were quick to see the possibilities of a national crusade against political correctness and multiculturalism. According to Midge Decter, a prominent conservative, Reagan's presidential victories "bore witness not so much to a wish for radical new policies as to an open declaration of war over the culture. And a culture war, as the liberals understood far better than did their conservative opponents, is a war to the death."[21] Pat Buchanan, former Nixon speech writer and later Republican presidential hopeful, told audiences: "Our Judeo-Christian values are going to be preserved, and our Western heritage is going to be handed down to future generations and not dumped into some landfill called multiculturalism."[22]

John Wilson's book *The Myth of Political Correctness* argues persuasively that the evidence for a Great Fear in the universities had astonishingly little substance to it. Rather, conservative writers and rhetoricians recycled then recycled again, a not-very-long list of anti–politically correct anecdotes having mainly to do with a few major research universities. Most stories were to one degree or another inaccurate—for example, D'Souza' largely fictional account of the Stanford episode.[23] Wilson writes: "A casual observer of the conservatives' attacks on diversity might conclude that the universities are swarming with leftists who ruthlessly inculcate student with deconstructionist philosophy, pop culture, feminist theory, and Marxist proclamations masquerading as multiculturalism."[24] His survey of what is actually taught and assigned on college campuses exposed these canards. He claimed not that the literary canon wasn't changing, as it always has, but that the "vast majority of classes still teach the same canonical texts, with most of the changes happening on the margins, and usually to the improvement of education."[25]

The primary targets of the Right were not historians, but English departments, ethnic studies programs, dormitories, student newspapers, and other corners of universities where political correctness might be discovered. Nevertheless, conservatives were wary of the influence of the new social and cultural history, as well as innovative methods and concepts in the discipline. These suspicions contributed to the Right's abhorrence of multiculturalism. It is a fascinating irony of the 1980s, therefore, that not a few of the same federal officials and traditionalist educators who rued the presumed decomposition of the humanities and social sciences in the universities also demanded that the schools teach a lot more history.

The Civil War Was When?
A New Debate over History in the Schools

The 1980s found the United States once again in the throes of self-flagellation over the plight of the schools. In 1983 the National Commission on Excellence in Education, a body appointed by President Reagan's secretary of education, released *A Nation at Risk*, a sober report warning that the multiple failures of public education were putting America in grave danger. Decrying the mediocrity of the schools, the report warned grimly that "if an unfriendly foreign power had attempted to impose on America the mediocre education performance that exists today, we might well have viewed it as an act of war. As it stands, we have allowed this to happen to ourselves.... We have, in effect, been committing an act of unthinking, unilateral educational disarmament."[26]

Hard on the heels of this woeful admonition came a host of studies, commission reports, books, and articles offering myriad diagnoses of the schools' troubles and proposing a national mobilization against this "enemy within." In the multipolar, economically dizzying world of the 1980s the oft-heard watchword of the new reform was "educational excellence." American political and business leaders were awakening, however tardily, to the new realities of global economic competition and to the critical connection between national education policy and the momentous shifts taking place in worldwide patterns of production and trade.

These transformations meant that rich countries were going to stay rich only if the working population became increasingly literate, numerate, and skillful. Was not education an industrially advanced country's most precious asset and probably its economic salvation? Moreover, the United States faced growing public expenditures, soaring deficits, taxpayer unrest, and uncertain economic forecasts. Consequently, citizens demanded not only that schools and universities educate young people better but that they do it cheaper, more efficiently, and in ways that would make educators fully accountable for results achieved.

Because history was a basic subject at least somewhere in the K–12 curriculum in all fifty states, the reform movement addressed that discipline along with science, math, and English. Not surprisingly, however, the same culture wars that were beginning to rack the universities—or at least the media representation of the universities—also affected the debate over school reform. If American children were to learn more history, then whose history and what history should it be? Whenever these questions had come up in the past, national agendas invariably clashed. In the late 1980s they clashed again, and this time more loudly than ever before.

The argument was messy. Traditionalists praised the "old history"[27] centered on political events and institutions, celebratory of well-known heroes, and reverential toward Western civilization. From a slightly different angle came the proponents of "cultural literacy," a movement to endow all Americans with a common fund of knowledge they assumed was essential to intelligible public discourse and mature nationhood. In 1987, E. D. Hirsch's book *Cultural Literacy: What Every American Needs to Know* rose on the best-seller lists. An English professor at the University of Virginia, Hirsch argued that "the great hidden problem in American education" was the system's failure to provide a "network of information that all competent readers possess."[28] If all citizens had a common store of basic knowledge that permitted them to "talk the same language," our society would be more equitable, just, and unified.

To illustrate what all Americans should know, his book presented a sixty-four-page, double-columned list of names, terms, and expressions constituting information that genuinely literate citizens should possess. Critics promptly pointed out that a deeply traditionalist, culturally cramped view of the world informed the choice of items on it. If this list were to be a guide for literate men and women of the late twentieth century, they would know quite a lot about American and European history and culture but remain in sublime ignorance of the rest of the world or the dynamics of international social and economic change.

Lynne Cheney, too, vigorously advocated that all Americans should carry a shared backpack of knowledge. "Among good teachers," she wrote, "the idea persists that teaching is about transmitting culture."[29] In contrast to some of her arch-conservative cohorts, however, she argued that recent scholarship about women, minorities, and non-Western societies should have a significant place because "such efforts broaden knowledge and enlarge understandings."[30] But she also urged that these inclusions must be put to a litmus test of "telling the truth," a phrase that many found to be a code for sheltering American children from too much "new history," critical analysis, or searching assessment of the shape and meaning of the American past.

Probably most history educators sympathized with the general goals of the cultural literacy movement. College and senior high school teachers much preferred that classroom references to Mesopotamia, Moses, the *Mayflower*, or the Marshall Plan ring bells in students' brains rather than echo through empty chambers. But teachers, from kindergarten to college, also understood that children would not be able to make sense of their world or communicate effectively in the global arena, which they would assuredly be expected to do, if the curriculum ignored the historical experiences of large numbers of Americans, the world beyond Europe, or the big issues of economic, social, and cultural change. Most K–12 and college teachers, in short, recognized that the body of shared history subscribed to in the 1950s was not sufficient for the new millennium.

Academics on the political Left charged that in the name of educational excellence traditionalists were trying to force their cultural and intellectual hegemony on the production and control of knowledge. Whatever the merits of this assertion, history teachers did not need a Marxian ideological framework to argue that an inclusivist, internationally oriented curriculum simply made practical sense in our small and crowded world. Surely knowledge of the Meiji Restoration, the Mexican Revolution, the Middle Passage, and Nelson Mandela were as vital to cultural literacy as the biography of Gustav Mahler.

Yet another point of view came from a large group of social studies professionals centered in university and state departments of education. As we have seen in earlier chapters, K–12 social studies programs had always included history, but the heart of the movement was citizenship education, including a strong emphasis on the skills and processes of critical thought—skills that social studies teachers judged to be essential for an active citizenry in a democratic nation. Educators in this camp now saw reason to worry. While traditionalist reformers took persistent jabs at newfangled social history, they reserved their left hooks for social studies, which they largely blamed for the country's rampant ignorance of history.

As social studies educators entered the debate in response to such rebukes, the threads of advocacy became more tangled. Champions of social education tended to perceive the most vocal history reformers as promoting a return to dry facts, patriotic indoctrination, and "history for its own sake," rather than teaching the subject "so that historical data are brought to bear directly on the larger questions facing our nation and the world, questions that impinge on students' lives."[31] They were particularly bitter that reformers blamed them for the decline of history teaching. It had not, they claimed, declined much, especially in high schools, since the 1960s or even the 1940s. And insofar as enrollments had dropped, the fault lay in chroniclelike, "narrative mode" teaching ("This happened, then that happened") when the curriculum should have been even more solidly organized around lively study of "societal issues and problems."[32]

Most history professionals agreed that critical analysis of current issues was a worthy part of K–12 education. Historians worried, however, that too many social studies educators thought history was mainly useful for laying out "background" for the study of up-to-the-minute national and international events. On this issue, many historians tended to line up with moderately conservative critics, sharing their view that the rich, four-year history curriculum of the early twentieth century had been a good idea, that history should be taught chronologically, and that children might better devote less time to "solving" political crises abroad or social problems at home and more to gaining the historical perspectives and understandings they would need to address public problems in adulthood, when those issues would for the most part have changed.

None, however, but the most rigid traditionalists—at least in the 1980s— wanted students to spend most of their time memorizing "objective facts" or to be indoctrinated with an ideologically driven history. Diane Ravitch, a prominent educator viewed by some social studies critics as neoconservative, well understood the interpretative nature of history:

> I don't know of any historian who thinks he or she is writing the Truth. I don't know of any historian who does not recognize the reality of conscious selection, and the reality that what one selects is influenced by the perspective of one's own life and culture and society. . . . This means that you don't write about the past to suit your own ideology.[33]

This would stir no argument from most history or social studies professionals. Both groups, on the other hand, tended to suspect traditionalists of accepting uncritically the axiom that children should learn information first, and think about it later—a nineteenth-century notion that research in learning had discredited. As this debate raged, good history teachers continued to work from a premise they had long accepted: students acquire both knowledge and higher-order thinking skills most effectively when these two pursuits go forward together, mutually reinforcing one another.

A key event in the reform controversy was publication in 1987 of *What Do Our 17-Year-Olds Know? A Report on the First National Assessment of History and Literature*.[34] Diane Ravitch and Chester Finn initiated the assessment to get hard evidence concerning students' basic knowledge of history and literature and thereby alert the nation to the schools' deficient performance in these subjects. William Bennett's NEH funded the project, and the National Assessment of Educational Progress (NAEP), which Congress had authorized in 1969 as a national testing program, was called on to administer it. Various commission reports had appeared in previous years, but, as Ravitch and Finn noted, virtually no data on student achievement in history were available to support reform. "There were powerful arguments to be made," they wrote, "about the importance of history and literature in transmitting and enriching our culture, in developing critical intelligence, in cultivating understanding, character, and judgment. But these arguments were seldom made and, when they were made, not often heard by policy-makers."[35]

The history assessment was made up of questions designed to "plumb whether students do or do not know the basic facts of American history." The authors had no problem with a test that emphasized factual recall, convinced that it is "fatuous to believe that students can think critically or conceptually when they are ignorant of the most basic facts of American history."[36] Among the eight thousand students who took the test the average score was 55 percent correct answers. Ravitch and Finn judged this performance to be "extremely weak," and expressed astonishment that only 32 percent of the test takers were able to place the Civil War in the correct half century.

Critics of *What Do Our 17-Year-Olds Know?* quickly pointed out that not a single test item required students to engage in historical analysis, interpretation, or inference. The study, reviewers said, also failed to show that remembering the right facts contained in this particular test had anything to do with critical intelligence, character, or judgment, the qualities that Ravitch and Finn claimed were cultivated by the study of history. Responding to their critics, the authors countered that the test showed plainly enough that something in American education was "gravely awry." The nation tended to agree, and publication of the report was favorably greeted by educators and the media.

In 1990 NAEP published the results of its first comprehensive test of American history, administered to sixteen thousand students.[37] The results here were more encouraging, as most test takers seemed to possess a beginner's knowledge base. On the other hand, only 5 percent of the high school seniors who took the test could interpret more challenging historical information and ideas. So the news was still far from satisfactory. Both the Ravitch-Finn and NAEP studies seemed to confirm the worst: The United States was earning a C− in history.

New Strategies to Raise America's History Grade

By 1987, definite moves were under way to strengthen the history curriculum. One sign of progress was the blooming romance, after a half century of estrangement, between academic historians and K–12 teachers. A few scholars such as William McNeill and Leften Stavrianos had been arguing since the 1960s or 1970s that if the academic elite did not do something to help stimulate schoolchildren's interest in history or join in discussions over what precollegiate social studies should teach, colleges would find their history majors disappearing. Indeed, that is precisely what happened throughout the 1970s. By the next decade, however, the profession was awakening to the possible connections among several phenomena: the lifeless, unengaging character of too many junior and senior high school history courses; the erosion of history's place in the curriculum; the decline in college history enrollments; the historical illiteracy of most Americans; and the research-absorbed loftiness of the professoriate, which didn't seem to care much about the erosion of the country's collective memory.

The professors indeed had something to offer teachers—the fruits of the new social, cultural, and international history. As historians ended their "long walk" from the schools and struck up fresh alliances, teachers responded to information about the new subjects, resources, methods, and questions that represented the profession's great achievement over the previous quarter century. As many studies showed, students rated history as their least-liked subject. But now teachers believed that social, cultural, and genuinely world-scale history, woven into rather than replacing political, legal, institutional, and biographical studies, might rekindle classroom interest. Infused with rich, potentially engrossing content, history education might, as Diane Ravitch wrote, achieve its goals "not just through books, but through simulations, debates, role-playing, dramatics, computer games, videodiscs, field trips, movies, and anything else that teachers can find or devise to get their students to understand that the past was a different world, inhabited by people who had hopes and dreams, fears and problems."[38]

Academic historians and K–12 teachers renewed their long-neglected vows in connection with a number of innovative projects. In 1980, the

American Historical Association (AHA), the Organization of American
Historians (OAH), and the National Council for the Social Studies (NCSS)
formed the History Teaching Alliance to promote professional development of K–12 instructors, professors, and public historians through collaborative seminars. Funded by the NEH and private foundations throughout
the 1980s, this project recalled the early 1920s when the AHA and NCSS
worked hand in glove.

Also in 1980, teachers and scholars founded National History Day, an independent program that invited middle and high school students to take
part in an annual series of local, state, and national history project contests.
This history student's equivalent of spelling bees encouraged young people
from across the nation to design displays, hold debates, create dramatiza-
tions, and present original research on a designated historical theme. In
1982, history professionals founded the World History Association on an
explicit platform of collaboration among teachers at all levels, and throughout the decade both the AHA and the OAH campaigned to recruit more
K–12 history teachers into their organizations. In 1985, the OAH launched
Magazine of History, a journal for teachers that presented up-to-date research, original documents, and lively lesson plans on historical topics.

The late 1980s also saw the formation of two important new commissions,
both involving collaboration between K–12 and postsecondary educators. In
1987, the Educational Excellence Network, founded by Ravitch and Finn,
established the Bradley Commission on History in Schools. Seventeen academic historians, classroom teachers, and curriculum leaders made up the
task force. The group's report, *Building a History Curriculum*, recommended
that because "the knowledge and habits of mind to be gained from the study
of history are indispensable to the education of citizens in a democracy, . . .
history should . . . be required of all students." It follows, the commission declared, that grades K–6 social studies should be history-oriented, that
grades 7–12 should include no fewer than four years of history, and that history education should encompass all regions of the world, as well as ethnic
minorities and men and women of all social classes. The task force also recommended that certification of social studies teachers in middle and high
schools include "a substantial program in history."[39]

The great majority of Americans appeared to agree with the commission's premise that "an historical grasp of our common political vision is
essential to liberty, equality, and justice in our multicultural society,"[40] and
greeted its recommendations without controversy. Most historians, too,
responded positively to the report. After all, it advocated a fairly radical
shift from the dominant social studies approach by calling upon schools
to center their entire K–12 program on history. Indeed, the commission

respectfully evoked the 1892 Committee of Ten and the four-year "common democratic curriculum" that high schools across the country had adopted in the early twentieth century. It explicitly endorsed, in addition to Western Civ, a year's study of world history, recommending that "every student should have an understanding of the world that encompasses the historical experiences of peoples of Africa, the Americas, Asia, and Europe."[41]

A second task force, the National Commission on Social Studies in the Schools, also had a stellar membership. The commission, cosponsored by the NCSS, the AHA, the OAH, and the Carnegie Foundation, included major leaders in the social studies, distinguished scholars from history and the other social sciences, state legislators, and educators from state and local school agencies.

The commission's report, *Charting a Course* (1989), recommended social studies reform that gave almost as much attention to history as did the Bradley Commission,[42] though history was just one of seven social sciences recommended for study. Moreover, the commission boldly recommended that U.S. and world history be merged, thus "teaching our nation's history as part of the general story of humanity."[43] World history crusaders favored this idea, but many in the NCSS found unacceptable the focus on chronologically organized history at the expense of current issues analysis and ethnic studies. Although its membership chose not to approve the report when released in 1989, the NCSS continued to disseminate *Charting a Course*, and its influence has been felt in Florida, among other states, where a number of its recommendations have been incorporated, including merging modern U.S. and world history, in the state social studies framework developed shortly after.

Even before these reports had been completed, California's State Board of Education mounted the most momentous institutional reform of these years. Adopted in 1987, its new History–Social Science Framework called for three years of U.S. history at grades 5, 8, and 11 and three years of world history at grades 6, 7, and 10.[44] History also permeated the K–4 social studies curriculum. Not since the early part of the century, if then, had any state awarded so much room for history in the school curriculum. Both Diane Ravitch and Charlotte Crabtree played key roles in the curriculum's development, and Bill Honig, California's superintendent of public instruction and a longtime history buff, pushed enthusiastically for this groundbreaking shift. The framework unambiguously endorsed a curriculum that would embody broadly inclusive American history, global-scale world history, controversial issues, and more forthright study of religions and ethical traditions than publishers had dared offer students for half a century. "The express purpose of the [California] undertaking," wrote the *New York Times*,

'is to force a sharp reversal of the decades-old trend of watering down textbooks to avoid controversy and appeal to the widest possible market."[45]

Traditionalist educators tended to see the new curriculum as a victory
for history over social studies. "California is the only state in the nation,"
Diane Ravitch rejoiced, "that actually has a history curriculum that meets
the demanding specifications set by the Bradley Commission."[46] Lynne
Cheney regarded the California reform as a model for the nation. In
general, the history community responded warmly to the new program.
California social studies teachers at first reacted apprehensively because
their history training had not prepared them for the demands of the new
program. But high school teachers welcomed the focus on modern world
and twentieth-century U.S. history in grades 10 and 11, an arrangement that
for the first time gave students sufficient time to plumb the momentous
events and critical issues of the contemporary world. Some education professors argued that more history, particularly "tell a story" history, was not
the answer.[47] Some social scientists were gloomy as well. Although the new
history courses were to be braided with geography, economics, literature,
and contemporary issues, separate courses in the social sciences, except for
government and economics, were given only elective status.

Amid much national reporting of the California reform, other states
roused themselves to examine it. In most parts of the country in the late
1980s tenth-grade world and eleventh-grade American history survived as
the only history courses in the curriculum, and the elementary grades were
weak on history altogether. But no state or school district could have failed
to hear the hue and cry over America's insensibility to its own and the
world's past. The California decision was a stunning victory for the back-
to-history movement, and several other states, large and small, soon organized reform projects of their own.

Related to this success was a decision to create a national center for
improving history education in the schools. In 1988, the NEH under
Cheney's chairmanship funded the National Center for History in the
Schools at UCLA under the direction of Charlotte Crabtree and Gary B.
Nash. A child of the great history debate, the new center was applauded by
both the history profession and leading traditionalists. Cheney would, on
her retirement from the NEH four years later, refer to it as one of her notable accomplishments.[48] The center embarked immediately on a number
of projects to gather data on history teaching in the schools, develop new
classroom materials and curriculum guides, sponsor workshops, and organize a nationwide network of history educators.

As the 1980s ended, and as history made its biggest advances in the curriculum since the end of the nineteenth century, disagreements between
the professional community and conservative educators over social history,

new methodologies, and global approaches seemed to be fading away.
The public, which had always thought that the young should know their
American history, had few complaints about this trend in education. During the same years, however, political antagonisms over national identity
and culture were spreading across the land like so many prairie brush fires.
Separating history education from identity politics would soon prove
impossible.

Book Battles

If K–12 social studies curricula were changing in favor of history, then textbooks would have to change too. As Frances FitzGerald demonstrates,
American history texts of the late 1970s were far from cleansed of elitist and
Eurocentric bias, but they had begun to incorporate sidebars, add-ons, and
illustrations on women, ethnoracial groups, workers, and other forgotten
Americans.[49] The federal Women's Educational Equity Act of 1974, which
required equity for girls in school curriculum policy, had some effects on
book content. The new social history scholarship also filtered into the
schools through the College Board's Advanced Placement program, which
offered high school students college credit in American and European history if they passed a national exam. Most Advanced Placement courses
used college-level textbooks that included the new themes. On the other
hand, U.S. history texts written for the high school market continued to
ignore economic life, labor strife, social and economic inequality, and
poverty.[50] Many textbooks still portrayed a relatively classless colonial society that bequeathed to the nineteenth and twentieth centuries a land of
boundless opportunity. One social historian concerned about the K–12 curriculum observed that even though the College Board urged schools to
catch up with research in social history and the humanities, "the new scholarship . . . had barely penetrated most public school curricula" by the early
1980s.[51]

The situation in world history was, by the 1980s, somewhat more promising. The market for the traditional Western Civilization textbook was
rapidly drying up, though such stalwarts as Palmer and Colton's *A History of
the Modern World*, which in fact omitted the majority of the world's peoples,
continued to be popular in independent schools and Advanced Placement
classes in European history.[52] Texts published for the high school world history course began to display at least a tentative awareness that Chinese,
Arabs, West Africans, and other non-Europeans had quite a lot to do with
how the world got to be the way it is. *A Global History of Man* by Lefter

Stavrianos had been on the market since 1962, and publishers gradually took lessons from its modest success.

Most of the new texts, however, tended to retain their Western Civ spines with various Asian, African, and Latin American limbs attached. And because most teachers, both new and veteran, had not gotten much training in non-Western let alone world history in college, they frequently resorted to lopping off chapters on Africa or other parts of the world when they felt their own knowledge was inadequate.

As the 1980s wore on, however, genuinely globe-encompassing world history courses slowly took hold in schools, community colleges, and universities. At the postsecondary level, introductory world history courses began replacing, or more often supplementing, long-standing Western Civ offerings. At the K–12 level, school districts began routinely insisting that texts offer "global coverage." This drift toward genuinely spherical world history at both the K–12 and postsecondary levels, while halting and ambiguous, was nonetheless unmistakable. Indeed, the arguments for history and social studies education that embraces the whole human experience, not just the European or North American part of it, grew so compelling in those complicated times that public lobbying to restrict school history to Western civilization was almost nonexistent. Plenty of fights over the issue broke out inside red-brick walls. But even there the contention moved steadily from the issue of whether world history should replace Plato-to-NATO Western Civ to the problem of how to present the human venture to students in a way that is intelligible and engaging.

In the early 1990s, publishers responded more vigorously to issues of inclusion and diversity. A major breakthrough came with Houghton Mifflin's publication of a new history program for kindergarten through eighth grade. Activated by the new California history framework and Superintendent Honig's insistence that not a single textbook in print could meet its criteria, a small development company named Ligature ventured to produce a series correlated to the California curriculum. (Gary B. Nash was the history author of the series.) Most publishers doubted that the books would ever sell nationally, but Houghton Mifflin bought the program. "Never before," a *New York Times* reporter observed, "have elementary-school texts made such an effort to include the broad sweep of history and the divergent cultures that flow into the American mainstream." The books also treated historical subjects more realistically and with greater candor than publishers had previously dared to do:

The fifth grade volume devotes roughly 50 pages to slavery in the South, with vivid, firsthand descriptions of its cruelty, and contains fairly frank

treatment of the brutality visited on American Indians by European settlers. Among the primary sources quoted are Olaudah Equiano (an
African slave), Abigail Adams, Marco Polo, Black Hawk, and Jane Ad-
dams, the founder of Hull House. It quotes the writings of an escaped
slave, the Rev. Josiah Henson, who described his mother, on her knees,
begging the man who had just bought her to buy her baby too; she was
kicked senseless.[53]

In the 1960s, Mel and Norma Gabler of Longview, Texas, had developed
a small-growth industry evaluating American history and other textbooks
from a right-wing, religiously fundamentalist point of view and appearing
before state and local school boards to oppose the adoption of materials
tainted in their view with Marxism, evolutionism, and secular humanism.
However, when the Houghton Mifflin books came up for state adoption in
Sacramento in the spring of 1990, right-wing and fundamentalist groups did
not complain, and traditionalists lauded the series as one more nail in the
coffin of the social studies. This time the attacks came from the cultural far-
left, Afrocentrists, and a number of ethnoracial and religious organizations,
first in hearings before the State Board of Education, then in Oakland the
following year in connection with a local adoption decision. In a series of
raucous public meetings, reported in the national press, critics from these
camps denounced the books as racist, Eurocentric, colonialist, and ex-
ploitative of people of color.

Considering that these texts introduced elementary and junior high
students to far more social, inclusivist, and world history than any school
books then in use or on the market, why did the controversy occur? One
reason, Todd Gitlin suggests, was simply festering public rancor, particularly among minority populations, over perennial education funding crises
and all policies and programs that seemed to favor white, middle-class Californians and their children.[54] Another factor was the perception, way off
the mark as it turned out, that both the Houghton Mifflin books and the
curriculum framework were the work of a network of conservative and
neonativist educators.[55] A third element was the aspect of 1990s identity
politics that demanded the purging of any evidence of bias in the historical
or cultural representation of particular groups.

Opponents of the books tended to make sweeping charges supported
with scattered references to words or illustrations here and there, an attack
strategy that the Right would later perfect in trashing the National History
Standards. Even so, some critics made valuable suggestions, and a number
of revisions were made—removal, for example, of a pictorial representation of the Prophet Muhammad, a feature that offended practicing Mus-
lims. In the end, following the broadest public review ever held in the

nation, the California Curriculum Commission and California State Board of Education approved the revised texts, and within a short time all but three of the state's 693 school districts adopted them.

Though some conservatives concluded that if the program was under assault from the Left, it therefore must be good, the Right did not absolve every new book that came along. In 1994, Holt, Rinehart, and Winston published a revision of *The American Nation*, a history text by Merle Curti and Paul Lewis Todd that had been in use for forty years. Paul Boyer, the historian at the University of Wisconsin who prepared the revised edition, wove into it many of the threads of the "new history" that illuminated the experiences of men and women of all classes and ethnicities.[56]

Though the book was consistent with the Houghton Mifflin series and did nothing more than incorporate up-to-date scholarship, columnist John Leo in *U.S. News & World Report* complained that such inclusive accounts of history presented a "balkanized view of America." "What's next?" he taunted, "maybe describe the impact of the Los Angeles earthquake on Polish-Americans or explain how the people of Minneapolis feel about Rodney King?"[57] Gilbert Sewall, the founder and president of the small American Textbook Council, charged that Boyer had produced the "triumph of textbook trendiness," "affirmative action history," "revisionist folly"—all a consequence of the publisher's caving in to multiculturalist "pressure groups."[58]

Boyer responded that an antiseptic, univocal history of the United States hardly befits a democratic nation that honors and encourages spirited contention over ideas. The publisher chided Sewall for speaking of the " 'nation's official record of its past' as if that record were static and immutable. We would be doing a disservice to our young people of today were we to teach them that such is the case, and we would be doing a disservice to the study of history. . . . History is a process, and interpretation of the past is subject to revision."[59]

The attack on *The American Nation*, though a small episode, showed that history's curricular successes over present-mindedness in the social studies did not represent even a temporary alliance between the professional community and those conservatives who thought a robust national identity required a positive and unchanging rendition of the past.

Afrocentrism and the History Curriculum

Teaching children romantic or mythologized history in order to induce emotional attachment to particular values and institutions was by no means an ideology limited to the Right. The benign credo of multiculturalism instructed schools to nurture respect for the dignity of all individuals, no matter their ethnoracial affiliation, and to encourage fair-mindedness toward people, at home or abroad, whose cultural traditions were different from their own. Few responsible Americans disagreed with those principles. However, multiculturalism also took on the important mission to correct the racist, culturally arrogant, and stereotypical assumptions that continued to pervade news reporting and schoolbooks into the 1970s and beyond. Those assumptions were so pervasive that rectification required a sustained and energetic effort.

Sometimes even the best-intentioned of multicultural theorists and teachers overcompensated. As white racism and Eurocentric vanity were exposed and cut down to size, ethnic minority and non-Western cultures tended to grow taller and more beautiful. The challenge was to teach history that was inclusive of major ethnoracial groups and civilizations without giving in to temptations to engage in reverse romanticizing or to play games of cultural tit-for-tat—notions, for example, that sixteenth-century Europeans were uniformly violent, crude, and rapacious but Africans lived in peace and communal harmony, or that European empires were big and rich but that African or Mesoamerican empires were bigger and richer.

Some groups, however, abandoned multiculturalism altogether in favor of a cultural separatism and aggrandizement that mirrored the self-glorifying Eurocentrism of earlier decades. By far the most conspicuous of these movements has been Afrocentrism, particularly its more extreme ideological wing.

Defining Afrocentrism is difficult because it includes an assorted, often inconsistent bundle of ideas and assertions, only some of which have to do with the presentation of history. The movement has focused on introducing African American children to, indeed immersing them in, the cultural heritage of ancestral Africa and the African diaspora in the United States and other lands. According to Molefi Asante, a professor at Temple University and the movement's leading theorist, Afrocentrism "means treating African people as subjects instead of objects, putting them in the middle of their own historical context as active human agents. It is not the implementation of a particular world view as if it is universal." Asante has also declared that "to replace Eurocentric with Afrocentric is simply committing another crime, replacing one orthodoxy with another.... In a multicultural society, the Afrocentric curriculum becomes an organic piece that is fused into the general curriculum."[60] Any educator who believes that all American schools should seriously teach African and African American history would find little to argue with here.

On the other hand, as Afrocentrism became an issue of public debate, Asante did not divorce himself from a number of ideas about history and culture that ranged from the questionable to the bizarre to the deeply offensive. Afrocentric writers have focused much attention on ancient Egypt, arguing "the centrality of the ancient Kemetic (Egyptian) civilization and the Nile Valley cultural complex as points of reference for an African perspective."[61] Though the traditional Western Civ approach to ancient history wrongly took Africans out of Egypt and Egypt out of Africa (relocating it to the Middle East and thus to "Western" ancestral territory), extreme Afrocentrists have stood culturally arrogant Eurocentrism on its head, claiming that the Nile Valley of the pharaohs was a categorically "black" civilization as opposed to a "white" one; that it was the original fount of civilization worldwide; that medieval and modern Europe derived most of its mathematics, science, philosophy, and art from there; that Greece "stole" its civilization from the Nile; and that Egypt, rather than Atlantic-facing West and Central Africa, should be the main reference point for studying the African diaspora. The *Social Studies African-American Baseline Essay*, a document developed in the mid-1980s that presents a comprehensive foundation for an Afrocentric curriculum, devotes more than three times as much space to the history and culture of ancient Egypt as to West and Central Africa for historical periods before the Atlantic slave trade.[62]

Leonard Jeffries and some other advocates for the movement have advanced an immoderate Afrocentrism that combines overt racial hatred with crackpot history. Jeffries preaches that the slave trade was a conspiracy of Jewish entrepreneurs; that Jews, working closely with the Mafia, have consciously built "a financial system of destruction of black people"; that world history should be understood as a race war between "Ice People" (Europeans) and "Sun People" (dark-skinned tropical people); and that melanin in the skin goes along with physical and intellectual superiority.[63] John Henrik Clarke, author of the history section of the *Social Studies African-American Baseline Essay*, rejects all religion and urges black parents to turn their backs on the black churches. "At what point," Clarke says, "do we stop this mental prostitution to a religion invented by foreigners? . . . All the major religions of the world are male chauvinist murder cults."[64] Wade Nobles, San Francisco's leading Afrocentrist, teaches that all education for black children has to be cleansed of white Western influence. "When we adopt other people's theories, we are like Frankenstein doing other people's wills. It's like someone drinking some good stuff, vomiting it, and then we have to catch the vomit and drink it ourselves."[65] Such views are of course contrary to multiculturalism's principled aims. Henry Lewis Gates Jr., a Harvard scholar, decries the strands of "ethnic fundamental-ism" in Afrocentrism, including its penchant for reducing "the astonishing diversity of African cultures to a few simple-minded shibboleths."[66]

Afrocentrism has become an educational phenomenon of some significance. As of 1991, when cultural politics was rapidly replacing anti-communism as this country's major ideological preoccupation, dozens of public and private schools advertised Afrocentric curricula.[67] Afrocentric education has been particularly appealing in some of the nation's largest cities, where many of the most economically disadvantaged American children live. More than a few black citizens, especially in blighted urban areas, found ideas and programs of cultural separatism to be useful avenues for expressing frustration and rage over the failed promises of racial equality. Historically, cultural nationalism, which tends to absolutize racial differences, has had its greatest appeal in times when minority groups stopped believing that the gap between America's universalist ideas and the realities of daily life could be closed. "The only issue for us," says Jeffrey Fletcher of the Black United Front for Education Reform in Oakland, California, "is how we can get out of this plight. It's like if you have someone around your throat choking you. It's nice to know about the baseball scores and other cultures, but the only thing you need to know is how to get those fingers off your neck."[68]

A scholarly Afrocentrism that advocates knowledge and understanding of peoples of Africa and the diaspora as "active human agents," as Asante puts it, has a pedigree going back at least a century. H. L. Kealing, the editor of the *African Methodist Episcopal Review*, wrote in 1899 that "the greatest bane of slavery to the American negro is that it robbed him of his own standard and replaced it with the Grecian."[69] In the 1930s, Carter G. Woodson, a leading black educator and historian, argued that the educated minority of African Americans, schooled in European-centered curricula, had left the black masses behind and lost touch with their own cultural ancestry.[70] Almost none of the most prominent Afrocentric intellectuals has a degree in history. But like most scholars of the African and ethnoracial past, they have been well aware that the "cultural literacy" that Americans informally acquire has since the nineteenth century consistently included a great deal of outrageous miseducation about African wildness, tribalism, and cultural retardation. Images of Tarzan's Africa, false though they are, have unfortunately become part of American culture. If Afrocentric thought has too often been nasty or even bizarre, it has also stimulated black children's interest in history and cultural studies. Moreover, it has jump-started scholarly debates on the effects of pseudoscientific racism on European and American perceptions of Africa, as well as the cultural relationships among ancient Greece, Egypt, and Semitic Asia.

At the center of these debates is an unlikely figure. Between 1987 and 1991 Martin Bernal, a white, Jewish, Chinese politics expert at Cornell University, published two volumes of *Black Athena*, a massive study arguing for profound Egyptian and Semitic influences on the formation of Greek civilization.[71] He did not explicitly argue that the goddess Athena, the Greeks, or the Egyptians were categorically black, but he did reaffirm the fundamental fact that, as Africanist scholars have known for a long time, Egypt was an *African* civilization. His work was in no sense an Afrocentric polemical tract, but nevertheless he became an Afrocentric hero.

Black Athena was a breathtaking book that produced much contentious discussion at academic meetings. Classical history scholars who normally spent their time reading undergraduate blue books or musing over Greek or Latin texts suddenly found themselves on the public stage. Mary Lefkowitz, a classicist at Wellesley College, published a judicious refutation of a number of Afrocentric claims about Egypt and Greece, as well as a learned critique of Bernal.[72] Several of the movement's key assertions, such as the notion that Queen Cleopatra was "black," made easy targets for Lefkowitz. Even so, both she and Bernal demonstrated that the interpretation of historical developments occurring two thousand to four thousand years ago could echo in the American identity politics of the 1990s. Both authors became overnight media stars, and their books sold briskly.

Most academics and history teachers, whatever their political tendencies, have either ignored Afrocentrism's peculiar cultural politics, or else criticized it for distorting American democratic and pluralistic ideals as much as the most rigid Eurocentrism. As David Hollinger has written,

> Bernal's achievement reminds us that much of the culture of the West traditionally carried by American schools was already cast in ethno-racial terms and was much in need of the demystifying scrutiny to which it has been subjected in recent years. . . . Correcting this need not mean cynically turning the tables and indulging this will on behalf of some other contemporary group. . . . Certainly we want to know as much as we can about the society and culture of ancient Egypt and Greece, and we do not want racist interpretations to go uncorrected. But honest efforts to find the truth should not be understood to place at risk the relative self-esteem of black and white children in contemporary America. Egypt, surely, belongs to us all, and so, too, does democracy.[73]

Such reasoned engagement with Afrocentric claims has been of little interest to the cultural referees of the Right. Leonard Jeffries, Gitlin suggests, "seemed to have been sent directly from Central Casting to kindle indignation" among ultraconservatives.[74] To right-wing media heroes, Afrocentrism has been a dream-come-true of political correctness, a phenomenon to be blown out of proportion and compared derisively to the absolute and noble truths that presumably belong exclusively to Western—not black, not African—civilization. With typical hyperbole, Dinesh D'Souza writes that "the 'revolutionary commitment' to which Molefi Asante refers is evident in the hardened gleam in many Afrocentric eyes. . . . Gradually but unmistakably, Afrocentrists are severing the bonds of empathy and understanding that are the basis for coexistence and cooperation in a multiracial society."[75]

Confronting Afrocentrism with incendiary, my-culture-is-better-than-yours rhetoric has only helped confine the public debate over history and culture to the gladiatorial arena of identity politics. If the conflict over Afrocentrism disappears, it won't be by crushing the movement with Western cultural arrogance.[76] More likely, the multiethnic realities of American society will dissolve this particular conflict. The migrations of Hispanic, Asian, Middle Eastern, and African newcomers to America has turned city schools into mosaics where cultural and social identities are continually negotiated and contested. As an assistant principal in Massachusetts put this point in 1991, a school of twenty-three hundred students representing seventy nationalities has no room "for any one 'centrism.' "[77]

Commemoration or Interpretation?

Culture war on the history front took place not only in universities, schools, and popular magazines but also on the lawns around commemorative statues and in the echoing halls of museums. The 500th anniversary of Christopher Columbus's first voyage to the Western Hemisphere provided a prelude of struggles to come. Compare the 1992 quincentennial with the national celebrations a hundred years before. Then, Americans marked the 400th anniversary with festivals, parades, fireworks, and speeches in honor of a man who nearly everyone agreed was a great and courageous explorer, a cultural hero who brought two worlds together and initiated the "rise of the West." In New York City, parades went on for three days, and Italian Americans swelled with pride. In Chicago, the World Exposition of 1893 featured a Columbian jubilee with crowds turning out in numbers that the city has never since matched. In the nineteenth century more cities and counties were named for Columbus than for George Washington.

By contrast, 1992 featured mock trials of Columbus as a genocidist. The National Council of Churches resolved that the quincentenary should be observed with penitence, not merrymaking. "For the descendants of the survivors of the subsequent invasion, genocide, slavery, 'ecocide' and exploitation of the wealth of the land," the resolution declared, "a celebration is not an appropriate observance of this anniversary."[78] A fiery argument over the 1992 Rose Bowl parade dissolved only when the organizing committee invited a Native American to serve as comarshal. When an officer in the Spanish navy and blood descendant of Columbus addressed an auditorium full of freshmen at San Diego State University, a history instructor rose up and roundly accused the bewildered gentleman of being personally implicated in the crimes of his famous ancestor. Most conservative commentators dismissed these protestations as politically correct, multiculturalist nonsense, and the press had a field day chronicling the intrepid mariner's public debunking.

The controversy over Columbus actually had little to do with accurate interpretations of history and a great deal to do with the condition of America's storehouse of sacred symbols. Defenders of the treasury saw Columbus—individualistic, visionary, action-prone—as the prototype of a unique American personality and an emblem of the fusion of American identity with "Western institutions and Judeo-Christian values" originating in Europe. To the protesters, tributes to the voyager were an insult to the Native Americans and Africans who suffered and died as a result of his intrusion and still had to fight for justice and equality a half millennium later. Columbus became, as one scholar put it, "a convenient personification and embodiment—at least for this year—of that contest for control over the past."[79] As the country changes, in other words, so does the Columbian image. As one cultural historian tells us, Columbus "has been interpreted and reinterpreted as we have constructed and reconstructed our own national character."[80]

The quincentennial brought forth not only public controversy but also a flood of books and exhibits that advanced our knowledge of the late fifteenth-century world where European ship captains, for good or ill, linked not only Europe with America but every region of the earth with all the others. The 500th anniversary was also the first in which the history and culture of those who greeted the Genoese sailor at the water's edge received serious attention. The Smithsonian Institution's exhibition "Seeds of Change: A Quincentennial Commemoration," which opened in 1991, inspired visitors with vivid artifacts and images depicting the epic convergence of Europeans, Africans, and Native Americans, as well as their plants, animals, and microorganisms. This exhibit reflected three decades of innovative and revisionist scholarship, and few contested its merit.

At the Smithsonian's National Museum of American Art, however, a show titled "The West as America" opened the same year to remonstrations from the Right. This exhibit presented celebrated paintings by Frederic Remington, Thomas Cole, Albert Bierstadt, George Caleb Bingham,

George Catlin, Thomas Moran, Karl Bodmer, and other American artists. But a loud fight quickly erupted over the writing on the wall—dozens of labels that invited viewers to interrogate the paintings for evidence of romanticizing and mythologizing subtexts. Drawing on the scholarship of a new school of historians of the American West, the curators pointed out elements of nationalism, racism, and imperialism that might be discerned in the painters' representations of the frontier.

Heavy criticism enveloped the Smithsonian curators. Such irreverent revisionism, said Daniel Boorstin, librarian of Congress, had created "a perverse, historically inaccurate, destructive" exhibit.[81] (Years before, Boorstin had published a history of the United States whose first volume on "the colonial experience" neatly elided all mention of slavery.) Even the use of words such as "race," "sexual stereotype," and "class" was enough to provoke charges of political correctness.[82] Senators Ted Stevens of Alaska and Slade Gorton of Washington threatened to cut the Smithsonian's appropriations. As a result of the feud, the museum's director rewrote five exhibition labels that were particularly offensive to certain critics. The show was to travel to museums in St. Louis and Denver, but both cities canceled it. Yet the exhibit was a great success in Washington, almost doubling attendance at the National Museum of American Art and inspiring visitors to fill up three comment books. The remarks ran the gamut from "I didn't need to be told that Catlin's pictures were propaganda—phooey! I'm happy with the myth" to "Most engaging and thought-provoking, A new way to enjoy and look at art. As the comments suggest, you've gotten people to think—that is a great accomplishment, especially for my seventh-grade students."[83]

Despite such a pragmatic and modulated approach to American history, curators who opened mythic versions of the past to new interpretation clearly were painting targets on their own backs. As the museum community recoiled from the thought of members of Congress censoring art exhibits and threatening funding cuts because historians and curators were doing what they had done since the time of Thucydides—reevaluating the past—an even more ferocious storm was brewing. While the American West show was running, Smithsonian curators were planning a commemoration of the dropping of the first atomic bomb on Hiroshima in 1945. Scheduled to open in 1995 in the Smithsonian's Air and Space Museum as a fiftieth anniversary observance, "The Last Act: The Atomic Bomb and the End of World War II" was destined to become the most bitterly contested museum exhibition in U.S. history.

The controversy began in earnest in 1994 when the Air Force Association and other veterans groups censured the exhibition script, complaining that the curators planned to ask visitors to consider the moral and political dimensions of Truman's decision to drop the bomb and to look at photographs of charred women and children in Hiroshima. This, the veterans said, would arouse the idea that the Japanese were victims rather than military aggressors in World War II. When Smithsonian officials agreed to revise the script by eliminating, for example, all references to the fact that Truman's government intensely debated the advantages and disadvantages of dropping the bomb at all, historians retorted that the script was being "historically cleansed." "Unfortunately," wrote one member of the exhibit's advisory committee,

> the eagerness of critics to demonize the Smithsonian obscured a central issue: the inevitable tension between the commemorative voice and the historical voice when history becomes the focus of a public exhibit or ceremony. . . . "The Last Act" was caught between memory and history. Those who believed that the National Air and Space Museum was a temple whose function was to celebrate American technology wanted an exhibit that would commemorate the atomic bomb as the redemptive ending of a horrible war. . . . Those who believed that the museum was a forum whose function was to present diverse interpretations of complex historical events wanted an exhibit that would discuss the 50-year-old controversy about the decision to drop the bomb, remind visitors of the devastation caused by it, and underscore the enduring nuclear danger.[84]

No doubt, in the first draft the curators and advisory board were inadequately sensitive to the emotional and moral concerns of Americans who fought in the war, but they were not obdurate about sticking to the original plan. In fact, they revised the script many times after negotiating with several veterans groups.

The election of November, 1994, however, sharply intensified the debate and reduced the maneuvering room for a satisfactory compromise. Ultraconservatives on Capitol Hill, emboldened by the Republican capture of both houses of Congress, turned up the heat on the curators, insisting that the Air Force veterans should have veto power over the way this particular story was told. The Republican-controlled Senate fueled the controversy by threatening hearings on the exhibit and voting unanimously for a resolution condemning the exhibit's script as "revisionist, unbalanced, and offensive."

After months of rhetoric, the struggle ended in a two-part climax. In January 1995, I. Michael Heyman, the Smithsonian's new director, agreed to cancel the exhibit and replace it with a display of the *Enola Gay* fuselage accompanied by a simple identifying plaque. In May, with eighty-one members of Congress calling for his head, exhibit director Martin Harwit resigned his post as director of the Air and Space Museum.

Congressional Revisionist History Museum
Pittsburgh Post Gazette, January 31, 1995

The decision to cancel carried a heavy price. In a democracy, curators asked, is a historical exhibit not suitable unless it passes a congressional litmus test? Cannot a democratic people both honor hallowed artifacts and reflect on their meaning in complex historical contexts? Is a literate, informed citizenry compromised by pondering evidence that President Truman listened carefully to General Eisenhower, Admiral Leahy, and others who advised against dropping the bomb? A *New York Times* editorial drove to the heart of the matter:

> It is understandable that veterans who fought in the war and might have been ordered to invade Japan view the bombing . . . as a life-saving reprieve. To question the decision, even in a balanced exhibit, may strike them as unpatriotic. But the real betrayal of American tradition would be to insist on a single version of history or to make it the property of the state or any group. History in America is based on freedom of inquiry and discussion, which is one reason why Americans have given their lives to defend it.[85]

The *Enola Gay* affair signaled that politicians were prepared to proclaim what is historically correct or incorrect—in other words, to create "official history." One observer of the museum wars concluded that "curators at the Smithsonian and the Library of Congress operate entirely in a realm of politics now, with projects driven more by the absence of their power to offend than by the strength of their ideas."[86] A former chief of history for the U.S. Air Force regards the cancellation of the exhibit as possibly "the worst tragedy to befall the public presentation of history in the United States in a generation."[87]

In such a climate, the credo that the president of the Association of American Museums enunciated in 1990 lies in a shambles: "Museums are places where the members of a pluralistic society may contemplate, reflect, and learn, and where we may examine not only the evidence of what affirms our values, but at times what challenges them."[88] If the cold northern winds of ultrapatriotism continue to blow, then museums will become mausoleums housing "sacred icons for reverential observation."[89] And as historian Joan Scott reminds us, "There can be no democracy worthy of the name that does not entertain criticism, that suppresses disagreement, that refuses to acknowledge difference as inevitably disruptive of consensus, and that vilifies the search for new knowledge."[90]

History wars, whether fought in museums, galleries, schools, or universities, invariably signal that a nation's self-definition is being contested. This has been true not only in the United States, but in other countries as well—in stable democracies like ours, in states that have undergone radical changes of regime, and in nations just being born. In the next chapter we look at history wars in other lands.

CHAPTER 6

History Wars Abroad

Perhaps the hardest battle I fought on the national curriculum was about history. Though not an historian myself, I had a very clear—and I had naively imagined uncontroversial—idea of what history was. History is an account of what happened in the past.... No amount of imaginative sympathy for historical characters or situations can be a substitute for the initially tedious but ultimately rewarding business of memorizing what actually happened.

—Margaret Thatcher,
The Downing Street Years

In the same years that Americans were contending for the nation's collective memory in textbook adoption meetings, art museums, congressional hearing rooms, and talk-show studios, history wars were also flaring up in other lands. Virtually every modern country founded on a nationalist ideology has had to strive to reconcile the texts, images, and symbols that represent what it stands for and where it came from with the fact that social, cultural, and economic life simply will not stand still. No society in a world that is continually restructuring itself can ever expect to decide once and for all the history its citizens ought to remember and its children learn.

A brief look at controversies over history teaching in a few other countries throws into relief the unique and not-so-unique elements in America's ceaseless dialogue with its past. Wherever history wars have broken out, national identity and collective memory are invariably the fundamental issues. As the world changes, so do the ways all nations imagine themselves, their achievements, and their place in the international scene. However, nations have probed and rethought history education for young citizens in decidedly different ways, notably in the role central governments and their educational agencies play in determining the knowledge and interpreti-

explanations that children will be taught. Here the American approach to rethinking history has been atypical.

New Governments, New Nations, New Histories

That a rash of history wars should occur in the United States and several other countries in the 1980s and 1990s is no coincidence. The baffling complexities of global communication and trade, the emergence of new centers of economic and military power, the winding down of the Cold War, and the dissolution of the Soviet Union all contributed to national soul searchings, notably in countries whose international situation and prospects were changing. One consequence of these global transformations has been a surge of educational reform movements in countries around the world.

No single event—no Sputnik—provoked the new spirit of innovation. In virtually all the industrialized democracies of the Northern Hemisphere, political leaders only gradually roused themselves to examine the connections between a well-educated citizenry and success in the global economy, a marketplace that no longer consisted of countries of the North Atlantic rim but now also included several Asian and two or three Latin American powerhouses. Assembly-line industries were moving to countries with lower wage structures, automation was spreading, and the explosion of information technology demanded that more and more workers know how to use computers and other complicated machines. In short, established democracies that lacked highly skilled and literate populations might do poorly indeed in the dog-eat-dog arena of international trade.

In other parts of the world, reform movements were by-products of the radical reconfiguring of geopolitics that began in 1988. After the collapse of the Soviet Union and the communist regimes of Eastern Europe, fifteen new sovereign states emerged, and revolutions swept away several national governments. Consequently, new education systems had to be created and existing ones restructured along radically different ideological lines. When authoritarian regimes that had enforced an "official history" on the schools fell in disgrace, new ministries of education had to work overtime to propose fresh versions of history untainted by discredited ideologies.

In the countries that once constituted the Soviet Union, state and society have changed so drastically that national perspectives on history have been thrown into utter confusion. When the Soviet empire collapsed, its official historical identity collapsed with it. Until the late 1980s, public disputation over the Soviet history curriculum was unthinkable. Government committees in Moscow created a syllabus for all children, checked it for Marxist-

Leninist purity, and submitted it to Communist Party headquarters for approval. The state determined the "facts" to be taught and gave all students equal opportunity to ingest and regurgitate them. After Mikhail Gorbachev introduced glasnost, teachers were permitted to remove Marxist blinders and look at the turbulent Soviet past from new angles. But as teachers took up the invitation to question the official narrative, so much turmoil arose over the issue of whose history and what history *ought* to be taught that in 1988 the government felt obliged to cancel national exams for high school seniors.[1]

Since the breakup of the Soviet Union, Russia and the other new states have had to confront the problem of reconciling history with new national identities. If Marxist-Leninist ideologues no longer own the past, then who does? What should now be remembered that was forgotten before? While Americans might argue over which national heroes and landmarks schoolbooks should privilege, leaders in such places as Kazakhstan, Uzbekistan, and Belarus set about *rediscovering* national heroes and events that had been all but eradicated from the collective memory. As one Russian teacher commented in 1991, "My students don't really have any heroes from our past because so many of their childhood heroes have turned out to be false heroes. They're much more likely to pick Arnold Schwarzenegger as a hero. But I think this is OK. I'd much prefer that they think freely rather than unquestioningly love Lenin."[2]

Today the problem of a usable past continues to be in as much flux in the lands of the former Soviet Union as are most all cultural and social institutions. Serious history wars may yet be fought in some of these nations, but for the time being energies must go into reinventing entire educational systems and principles. For example, in the same period that some countries have opted for greater governmental involvement in curriculum choices, Russia has enthusiastically repudiated centralized control of education as one of the evils of the communist political order. In almost all the old Soviet republics, as well as the former communist countries of Eastern Europe, Marxist-Leninist history has been disavowed. But whose truths are to replace it? That post-communist Russia was eager to debate the question became apparent in 1994, when 20 million children received new textbooks—books "determinedly devoid of ideology" and Soviet-speak. Education Minister Yevgeny Tkachenko declared that the books will nurture "an ability to analyze and to make independent decisions, ... the opposite of what we had before." One 16-year-old student welcomed the breath of fresh air: "Before, they taught everything from one point of view: everything Soviet was good and everything non-Soviet was bad." Now her teacher "gives us the right to formulate our own point of view."[3]

If the new books brought Russian history education more into line with standards of critical inquiry as practiced in the United States, the proponents of sweeping innovations came under fire from none other than unregenerate communists. Some charged that the new books were too pro-American, lauded capitalism, dwelled too much on odious chapters of the Soviet past, and gave short shrift to the Third World. Gennadi Zyuganov, communist candidate for president in 1995, attacked the new history for being insufficiently patriotic, for failing to teach young Russians to love the Motherland, and for dwelling on grim and gloomy crimes and repressions of the Stalin era.[4]

Most educators, however, welcomed historical revisionism because they understood it to be an essential part of the struggle for democracy. "The approach is different," said one teacher with an ironic smile. "There is no Soviet triumphalism, no more 'This is the best-in-the-world system which provides the best-in-the-world opportunities.'" Meanwhile, very young students scratch their heads when asked to identify Vladimir I. Lenin. One 10-year-old made a stab at the answer: "He used to play in a rock band called the Beatles."[5] Other youngsters, however, were sharpening new thinking skills. "Older students," reports one journalist, "discuss high and low points of Soviet rule using contemporary documents and family memories and arrive at their own conclusions. The artificial simplicity of the past has gone."

The past has certainly become more complicated in South Africa, where the destruction of the apartheid system and the election of Nelson Mandela to the country's presidency necessitated a reordering of the national consciousness comparable in some ways to the Russian experience. Under apartheid all children of whatever racial or linguistic category learned history almost exclusively as the narrative of Western civilization and white South Africa. According to the rigidly controlled state curriculum, the country had no history before the mid-seventeenth century, when the first Europeans arrived. Indeed, neither black Africans nor people of Asian origin participated in any period of history as active agents; rather they appeared in textbooks essentially as "problems" that the white minority confronted as it strove to create a more perfect Christian civilization. As for the rest of the African continent, it had no history whatsoever worth acknowledging. Teachers of all races were expected to drill into students these state-mandated "facts" and use government-prescribed textbooks. Though a few progressive schools began to take liberties with the curriculum in the 1980s, South Africa, like the Soviet Union, prohibited teaching children skills of historical inquiry and analysis.

Since the coming of majority rule in 1994, educators have argued vigorously over the form and content of a new history for South Africa that

would embrace the entire population, not just the formerly dominant seg-
ment of it. Plenty of information on the country's past, going back millennia, is readily available because scholars have written about black South
African history for decades. The government simply prevented this scholarship from penetrating schoolrooms. On some subjects teachers are now being asked to turn the past upside down. Until 1990, for example, textbooks
vilified Nelson Mandela, if they mentioned him at all, as a terrorist and
enemy of the nation. He is now the country's much-revered president, and
so the "facts" of his life must be radically revised.

Simply because a national history designed to legitimate white domination has been thrown out does not mean that an alternative vision is entirely
obvious. Should South African schools now institute an "Afrocentric" curriculum that would represent the pre-European past as a happy African
golden age and all that happened after Dutch settlers first arrived as the
record of resistance to colonial oppression? Or, should each racial and linguistic group—Zulu, Xhosa, Venda, Afrikaner, English, and so on—have its
own self-contained history in order to preserve and celebrate particularist
cultural traditions? Should history be put into the service of multicultural
nation building, emphasizing the unity and harmony of all, even though
such an approach might involve a degree of indoctrination? Should history
teachers focus on critical skills, training students to nurture the new democracy by questioning the political and social values of the new South
Africa as much as the old?[26] All of these points of views have their advocates
and consensus has by no means been achieved.

In 1994 school authorities began permitting teachers to edit classroom
materials to remove white supremacist myths. But only in 1997 did the first
post-apartheid textbooks began to appear. In the old books history began in
1652, when Jan van Riebeeck, the first European immigrant, settled at the
Cape of Good Hope. One of the new texts tells children that South African
history began many centuries earlier, though the book does not romanticize
the deeper African past. According to one textbook author, "Now Van
Riebeeck is three-fourths into the book in a debate called 'The Struggle
Over Land.' ... Neither side is portrayed as heroes. It's not about goodies
and baddies. It's about understanding people's motives for what they did."
The new texts also encourage students to engage in creative discussion and
critical thought, which for South Africa is a revolutionary step.

In a country where half the adults cannot read or write, where every aspect of education is being reinvented, and where some conservative white
groups insist on retaining "their own" version of the past, opening the
nation's memory to free public scrutiny will not be easy. "The problem is
massive," one curriculum writer lamented. "It will take a generation to

solve."[8] Ironically, finding definitive solutions to the objectives and content of history education is not in all respects compatible with emerging democratic culture. As South Africa and Russia are finding, endemic history war is in some measure a sign that democracy is flourishing.

Indeed, interpretations of the past may arouse considerable national passion in countries where the political and social terrain, compared with the former Soviet countries, is relatively stable. The urge to revise the national past can spring up without the nation being revolutionized. In Mexico, for example, a furious public dispute broke out in 1992 over the content of new government-sponsored textbooks for elementary school children. Critics charged that the texts altered accepted understandings of the Mexican revolutionary period, whitewashing the politically repressive but economically prosperous regime of President Porfirio Díaz (1877–80, 1884–1911). In contrast, the books played down the role of social reformers such as Emiliano Zapata in order to legitimize the pro-business economic policies of Carlos Salinas de Gortari, who was president from 1988 to 1994. Critics also accused Salinas of allowing textbooks to put a rosy glow on Díaz's concessions to foreign investors in the late nineteenth century in order to boost the image of Mexico as a player in the world capitalist economy and to help persuade the United States to sign the North American Free Trade Agreement.[9] The texts had to be rewritten.

In Europe, perplexing economic and political change in the 1980s provoked new rivalries among intellectuals and politicians over the proper rendering of the national past. In France, for example, the 1989 bicentennial celebration of the French Revolution ignited a public quarrel over the causes and consequences of those momentous events. Contention arose mainly over the political Right's assertion that France should bury memories of the revolution because it was a bloody, radical-democratic affair whose excesses offer no legitimate model for the late twentieth century.[10] In French education circles, competing narratives of the revolution and its significance severely tested the balance between honored national memory and free inquiry. The clamor was so loud that the education ministry felt obliged to erase all questions about the Revolution from high school examinations that year.[11] On the other hand, the French nation was not weakened, and perhaps made stronger, by such a democratic airing of its revolutionary past.

In both the German Federal Republic and Japan fierce public debates erupted in the 1980s over national identity and the collective remembrance of World War II. Both countries were economic miracles of the postwar decades, shedding their identities as defeated fascist powers for brand-new ones as dynamic, democratic consumer societies and big players in global trade. In both countries a large body of opinion, especially among political conservatives, favored reshaping the national personality in ways that would dispel guilt, rumination, and embarrassment over fascist deeds and release young citizens to look back beyond the dark episodes of the 1930s and 1940s to prouder eras of the national past. An opposing body of opinion argued that both national consciousness and international respect were best served by insisting that schools squarely confront the evils of the war years and teach plain truths about Nanking, Pearl Harbor, and Auschwitz.

Before the 1980s, school history in the German Federal Republic hardly ever incited controversy because teachers for the most part shunned nationalistic content and even avoided the Nazi period altogether. However, in the mid-1980s, at a time when the federal government had taken a turn to the right under Chancellor Helmut Kohl, German academic scholars engaged in a tumultuous contest over the question of war guilt and the proper interpretation of Nazism. The "war of the German historians"[12] played itself out as a major media event in about a year and a half, but it jolted schoolteachers into more engaged, controversial teaching about Hitler and the National Socialist era. Nationalist-minded teachers in particular became progressively more willing to emphasize the political continuities of Germany's long past and to suggest less condemnatory, guilt-infused interpretations of the Nazi period.

Wherever the trend of history teaching in the Federal Republic was heading in the mid-1980s, confusion reigned again following unification because the schools of East Germany had their own Marxist-Leninist account of the past, one that for World War II emphasized communist heroism, the evils of Nazi capitalism, and the righteousness of all Stalin's wartime policies. Marxist history has now been expelled from the schools of a united Germany, but the reshaping of the national past is still under way.[13]

In Japan, whose education system is highly centralized, public controversy centered on the content of textbooks. In 1965, Ienaga Saburo, the author of a school text titled *A New History of Japan*, filed suit challenging the right of the ministry of education to demand that writers revise their textbooks as a precondition for official certification. The government, Saburo argued, wished to allay war guilt by imposing censorship and approving only textbooks that played down Japan's responsibility for military atrocities and the war in the Pacific. Education officials indeed insisted on what they regarded as a balanced account of the war. "If atrocities by Japanese troops are described, similar actions by Soviet forces should also be included or the text will be biased. And what about the Americans?"[14]

Saburo fought a running legal battle with the ministry for many years.

Successive court decisions were inconclusive, but they provided grist for a continuous national debate over the meaning of the war and a textbook controversy that took on international dimensions. In 1982, the ministry released a new list of certified textbooks. Several newspapers subsequently ran stories accusing the government of forcing authors to replace a particular word meaning "aggression" with a more neutral term to describe Japan's invasion of northern China in the 1930s. Although the story later proved inaccurate, the press in both China and South Korea quickly picked it up, adding additional criticisms of the approved books. Consequently, both countries lodged formal protests, accusing the Japanese government of concealing the facts about imperial outrages.

Japan made a number of conciliatory statements to defuse the issue, but right-wing nationalists responded by sponsoring publication of a history textbook espousing pro-imperial interpretations of the war. Though the ministry refused to certify the book unless numerous changes were made, South Korea complained again that Japanese children were being fed militarist history. In time, extensive revisions were made and the nationalists' text was published.

As Japan has moved to assert active economic and political leadership in Asia, the public has more freely recognized that, as one Tokyo University professor put it, the country "will never have normal relations with its Asian neighbors as long as it continues to try to hide its past."[15] One study shows, for example, that Japanese teachers have tended, in contrast to their American counterparts, to avoid detailed study of the events of the war, focusing instead on postwar reconstruction and peace education.[16] Nevertheless, in 1994 the ministry issued a new history curriculum that for the first time characterized Japan's role in World War II as one of aggression. That same year the Japanese supreme court ruled that government attempts to censor history textbooks were illegal. The war on the ground ended more than fifty years ago. The war waged in the Japanese national imagination—and the German one—may well go on indefinitely.

Progressive History and Dead Englishmen

The changing shape of national memory became a contentious issue in Great Britain in 1988 when Parliament instituted a new National Curriculum as part of a sweeping education reform measure. More than any other country, Britain parallels the United States in the circumstances under which school history aroused controversy in the 1980s and early 1990s. Both countries have traditionally had decentralized school systems, the national government leaving education policy mostly to regional or local authorities. Both countries worried that their competitive edge as industrialized democracies was slipping relative to countries such as Japan and South Korea, where the central government had more control over what children should know and be able to do. Both countries witnessed a resurgence of political conservatism that raised questions about the purposes of history and civic education. And both countries found appalling evidence that children were losing touch with the past, oblivious, for example, to the identity of Franklin Roosevelt or Winston Churchill. Britain, however, went about reforming history education in a way that most Americans would question. Indeed, the British case is a cautionary tale of how democracies ought not to make decisions about common cores of learning.

Until 1988 England's education structure was more decentralized than any system on the European continent. The Department of Education and Science (DES), headed by a government Cabinet minister, had general responsibility for education policy. The department did not, however, prescribe curriculum, not even the basic subjects that had to be taught. Under British law the only compulsory course was religious education. The key institution for schooling has been the Local Education Authority, which is similar to the school district in the United States. Funded by a combination of government grants and local property taxes, these agencies build state-maintained schools, manage them, and hire and pay teachers.

Before 1988, the staffs of individual schools had much leeway to determine subject matter. This freedom, however, was a matter of tradition not law. By the 1970s, the practice was coming into question amid much public grumbling about British education in general. Business and industrial leaders complained that the schools were failing to turn out young adults with the technological and management skills on which the country's competitiveness in world markets depended. In 1982, only about 29 percent of sixteen-year-olds were in school, and only 17 percent of seventeen-year-olds—far lower percentages than in the United States. Only about 1 percent of eligible students actually went on to higher education.[17] Critics identified all sorts of problems plaguing the system. One was the country's apparent curricular confusion: no universal standards of competence, no national system of assessment, no compulsory education in math, science, English, history, or foreign languages. Britain's curriculum, the *Economist* charged, was "diffuse and sometimes uncoordinated to the point of chaos."

Beginning in 1979 Prime Minister Margaret Thatcher launched the Conservative Party's dual mission to transform the British economy and to curtail state interference in the free operation of the market. Like some conservative commentators in the United States, critics within Britain's New Right movement called for a strong central command system for schools that would promote traditional values, social discipline, and effective channeling of students into appropriate economic and social niches. They also demanded a return to the strict teaching style of earlier times and denounced practitioners of progressive "child-centered" methods, which encouraged students to think critically about national policies and traditions.

Meanwhile, teachers responded warily to talk of a national curriculum. Few opposed the idea of a loose framework of principles and basic subjects comparable to the educational "constitutions" of some countries on the European continent, so long as the teaching community got to take part in writing it. On the other hand, educators were well aware of the neoconservative urge to refashion the nation's cultural destiny. The same Thatcher government that prized individualism, personal responsibility, and economic freedom also funneled new decision-making powers into its central ministries, including the DES. It also repeatedly cut back national budgets for education, allowed teachers' salaries to erode, and tried to marginalize the National Union of Teachers. Educators had good reason to wonder how a centrally imposed curriculum might affect their professional freedom and creative initiative.

After nearly eight years of debate within Thatcher's Cabinet, the Tory-dominated Parliament passed an omnibus Education Reform Act in the summer of 1988. The statute profoundly altered not only curriculum but also school and university finance, parental choice, religious education, and the prerogatives and responsibilities of the Local Education Authorities. The section of the law instituting the National Curriculum specified precisely ten subjects, including history, that were to be taught in all state-maintained schools in England and, with certain special provisions, in Wales. (Scotland had its own education authority and curriculum.)

Parliament's reform transformed England overnight from a country with a haphazard curriculum to one with standards of learning more tightly prescribed than those of many countries of Europe. One British educator went so far as to suggest that the plan "was remarkably similar to Joseph Stalin's curriculum for Soviet schools."[19] His point here was not that conservative ministers were Stalinists but that a government-mandated syllabus might seem more compatible with the interests of an authoritarian government than a liberal democratic one. The writer went on to observe that while a post-perestroika teachers' congress in Moscow was calling for a new educational system prizing "liberation, openness, respect for the dignity of the human being," the English National Curriculum was instituting "restrictiveness, the proliferation of bureaucracy, and the subordination of individual well-being to economic demands."[20] The good news for history educators was that their subject was now for the first time made compulsory at every grade level for children in England and Wales between ages five and sixteen. This plan represented a far greater commitment to the subject than was found in most of the United States. But whose history should be taught? And to what national purpose?

The debate over school history had in fact been going on for two decades. One educator recalls that when he studied the subject,

> the content was largely British, or rather Southern English; Celts looked in to starve, emigrate or rebel; the North to invent looms or work in mills; abroad was of interest once it was part of the Empire; foreigners were either, sensibly, allies, or rightly, defeated. Skills—did we even use the word?—were mainly those of recalling accepted facts about famous dead Englishmen.[21]

Recognizing that young Britons so loathed this approach to learning that they were escaping history classrooms at the earliest possible age, usually fourteen, reform-minded educators launched an ambitious project in the early 1970s to put some life into history education. The project advocated a "new history," arguing that the "dead Englishmen" approach bored students silly because teachers asked them to sit still and absorb information but seldom *do* anything challenging or stimulating. The new progressive methodology claimed that children, even in the primary grades, should be encouraged to develop critical thinking skills and habits of mind in relation to the discipline of history itself. They should grapple with such concepts as causation, learn how to interpret documents, do historical detective work, and sharpen their historical imaginations. Equipped with these mental tools, they might find their history studies engaging and would be much better prepared for lifelong learning about the past.

The new history methods, which on the whole promoted a balance between memory work and analytical reasoning, attracted little public controversy in England for almost a decade and a half. By the mid-1980s, however, neoconservatives were challenging the entire approach, charging that history education was not only in a mess, a point on which most citizens concurred, but that progressivist methods made the problem worse: Teachers were abandoning the schools' main mission to transmit to children the country's proud heritage and to reaffirm those collective memories that would make young people loyally and confidently *British*.

The most vocal critics declared that thinking skills were not particularly necessary or appropriate for acquiring the sort of knowledge they had in mind. The past, they argued, should be taught "for its own sake," meaning essentially that every sixteen-year-old awarded a diploma should possess a mental treasury of teacher-delivered and universally shared facts, mostly about the history of Britain and its place in the world. Knowledge and appreciation of the national heritage required not skills of research and interpretation, but qualities of industry, discipline, obedience, and civic pride. Children do not need to know how to evaluate historical information in order to memorize the "facts" of the Model Parliament, the Spanish Armada, the Fashoda Affair, or Dunkirk. They do not need interpretive skills to recount the major deeds and reigning dates of the various King Henrys.

Traditionalists also rejected the teaching practice known as "empathy." Encouraging children to identify in some sense with groups or individuals who lived in the past was a widely used and entirely conventional classroom strategy in the United States as well as Britain. It encouraged students to understand why human beings acted as they did by taking into account the context in which events occurred—the values, options, contingencies, and limitations of a past time and place. Most educators believed that children who cultivated such a sensibility would be more humanely educated. Empathizing with peoples of the past, one British educator wrote, "might, just sometimes, help us choke back mockery, give condemnation second thoughts, halt prejudice in its tracks, put a brake on violence, and if not in others, at least in ourselves."[22] Traditionalists, however, regarded the empathy technique as so much touchy-feely progressivist nonsense because it invited students to express what they thought about past events rather than having them commit to memory the "factual" version of the British national story. Not interested in understanding what the empathy skill was really about, they lampooned it out of all recognition: "Imagine you are Mary, Queen of Scots, after the discovery of the Throckmorton Plot. How do you feel?"[23]

Traditionalist reaction to the emphasis on historical thinking reflected larger social anxieties. In the United States, disputes over history were invariably linked to public perceptions that society was moving too fast and in the wrong direction. Likewise in Britain, the New Right controlled the government, but it did not drive the speeding train of economic and cultural change. In the mid-1980s, the economy was in recession, technology was lagging, immigrants were pouring in from many lands, and the country's marriage to the European Economic Community was deeply troubled. Like the United States, Britain faced painful questions about its social and cultural identity. But much more than the United States, Britain suffered the anguish of diminished esteem among the rich and powerful nations of the world. A smashing victory over Argentina in the 1982 Falkland Islands war gave nationalists a surge of adrenaline but in the end only drove home the more obvious fact that the glory days of the British Empire were gone.

Traditionalists shared with many other neoconservatives a sense of "moral panic," an abiding worry that Britain's greatness had been eclipsed.[24] If the country were not to go to the dogs, they argued, then the ancestral values and memories that constituted an acceptable definition of Britishness had to be aggressively affirmed. Progressive history, they complained, taught children to question national orthodoxies, value contrasting perspectives, and analyze social and cultural differences. In an unpredictable and dangerous world, this was the last thing children should be instructed to do. Schools, rather, ought to administer strong doses of *amor patriae* and fortify pupils with an impermeable, well-anchored, positive history that would motivate them, whatever their color or ethnic origin, to obey the law, honor the queen, and lead productive lives. "If we taught our children history with a little more honest and unaffected pride in our national achievement," one critic wrote, "we should not need episodes like the Falklands War to lift national morale and make us believe in England again."[25]

Thus, when Parliament instituted the National Curriculum in 1988, the first skirmishes in the history curriculum war were already being fought. Like all the mandated-subject projects, the one for history was organized from the top down. The history task force called together to draft the new curriculum reported directly to the secretary of state for education and had just ten members, all government appointees. Only two members were teachers, thus limiting the influence of the one professional group that presumably knew most about classroom history. Moreover, leading national professional groups such as the Historical Association had no formal representation. Kenneth Baker, Thatcher's education secretary, made statements supporting the traditionalist approach even before the committee got down to work. "The programs of study," he urged, "should have at the core the history of Britain, the record of its past and, in particular, its political, constitutional and cultural heritage."[26]

However, when the task force published its draft Interim Report in the summer of 1989, it revealed that it had a mind of its own.[27] The committee's recommendations by no means mirrored the traditionalist agenda. In the outlines of specific study topics about 40 percent of the material was British history; the other 60 percent was European and world history (including the United States) and a range of subject options. The committee also recommended five "attainment targets" designating particular historical thinking skills that students should master. The group made a brief stab at compiling discrete lists of facts for all children to learn at particular age levels. This exercise ended in futility. The committee concluded that children's progress in history should be measured in terms of their growing intellectual skill and understanding, not in the number of prescribed information bits they store in their brain from one year to the next. Indeed, an inventory of facts stipulated by the DES would amount in effect to official, canned-in-London history. Duncan Graham, chairman of the government's new National Curriculum Council, pointed up the absurdity of the issue when he reported that his staff found comic relief in trying to guess how Margaret Thatcher's list of acceptable historical facts might compare with that of Neil Kinnock, the leader of the opposition Labour Party."[28]

The task force, then, resisted factoid history and insisted on the inseparability of knowledge and critical skill. But because its mission was to produce course outlines, not just general or voluntary guidelines, it made numerous subject-matter choices. Many conventional topics were included, such as Victorian Britain and the American Revolution. But others—the Protestant Reformation, World War I, the Holocaust, and the history of Ireland—did not get in. Social history, including the experience of Britain's growing racial and ethnic minorities, was virtually absent.

In the ensuing months, public response to the Interim Report was lively. Members of Parliament convened special meetings, history teachers held regional conferences, and traditionalists and progressive educators fired salvos at each other in the popular press. On the whole, school leaders thought the document offered a sensible platform for professional discussion. Even so, nearly everyone had a bone to pick: The report was a ragbag of subjects, it left out the English Reformation, it tiptoed around World War II, it ignored the rise of fascism, it mythologized Winston Churchill, it was too dull. Welsh, Scots, and Northern Irish complained that the curriculum was much too English.

The Thatcher government also had an opinion. John MacGregor, the new education secretary, insisted that secondary schooltime devoted to British history be increased from 40 to at least 50 percent and that "essential historical knowledge," that is, hierarchically arranged compilations of specific facts, be incorporated into the program, not only to oblige children to master prescribed knowledge but also to create a fixed body of information on which they could be tested.[29] Response to MacGregor's criticisms were predictably impassioned. "So, we history teachers will soon be legally bound to teach particular named bits of history. Will we and many other history teachers either have to break the law or leave teaching?"[30] The *Times* of London observed that governments come and go and that the historical imaginings of one are likely to be very different from those of its successor: "There is something which is both ludicrous and sinister in the idea of the genial ... Mr. John MacGregor, with ambitious civil servants at his elbow, deciding what periods of history children in English schools should be obliged to study.... The idea that British history belongs to the government of the day—to the Secretary of State for the time being—is, and ought to be, deeply repugnant."[31]

In this clamorous atmosphere, the history task force went back to work to complete its Final Report. Meanwhile, the traditionalist forces mobilized. Early in 1990, a small group of university professors, teachers, Peers of the Realm, and New Right personalities formed the History Curriculum Association, a society dedicated to making "the need to learn facts a central part of teaching [history] and [to challenge] a trend in schools to emphasize the skills of collecting and evaluating evidence."[32] Or, in the words of one organizer, the association aimed to defend the "national memory, what makes Britain British" against the stratagems of skills-oriented "educationists."[33]

In staking out its position, this group had a powerful ally in London, the prime minister herself. "Instead of teaching only what are called themes," a Conservative member of Parliament asked in the Commons, "why cannot we go back to the good old days when we learnt by heart the names of the kings and queens of England, the feats of our warriors and our battles and the glorious deeds of our past?" Agreeing emphatically with the questioner, Thatcher declared, "Most of us are expected to learn from experience of history and we cannot do that unless we know it. Children should know the great landmarks of British history and they should be taught them at school."[34] As brief as Thatcher's remark was, the traditionalists responded with delight, the popular press proclaiming that she had put herself emphatically on the side of "facts" in the curriculum debate. The *Times*, on the other hand, remarked that the possibility of the government interfering in the development of the history syllabus "is enough to make one shudder. This was always the potential downside of the idea of a national curriculum."[35]

Thatcher spoke in the Commons about a week before the task force's Final Report was published. This document was a more nuanced and comprehensive product than its predecessor and incorporated many changes. British history was increased to 50 percent, though sections on other parts of the world were also filled out. Social, cultural, and economic history made something of a comeback, but not much. The report trimmed down the critical skills recommendations. It also reiterated the view, however, that learning to think historically assumes students must work with solid historical knowledge but also that "without understanding, history is reduced to parrot learning and assessment to a parlor memory game."[36]

Because of Thatcher's intervention, the Final Report was certain to make good copy. Naturally, it got teachers talking. On the one hand, most supported the curriculum's mandate of history for all children ages five to sixteen. On the other hand, many teachers wanted less designated content and more latitude for exercising their own professional judgment. Some teachers sighed in relief that their favorite lessons—the Reformation, World War II, the Holocaust—were now "in." Others smarted that their choice topics were still "out." Some American history was included, but as one educator observed, "In studies of the United States virtually nothing of interest seems to have happened west of the Mississippi, and not much west of the Appalachians."[37] The Historical Association endorsed the report partly out of fear that if the history community rejected it, the Right might succeed in demanding something far worse.[38]

Whatever intelligent discussion teachers were having, the popular media lost no time firing up the controversy, drastically oversimplifying the issue as a political confrontation between hostile forces. On one side was the New Right, which, according to the tabloid press, wanted British history glorified and piles of facts dumped on children's heads like multicolored confetti. On the other side were the progressive "educationists," who were alleged to believe that children should receive passing grades for expressing "hurt feelings." Operatives from rival political groups fed the dailies with provocative sound bites. A spokesman for the Labour Party charged Thatcher with subversion of the National Curriculum "to make it more a vehicle for indoctrination than for education."[39] On the traditionalist side, the History Curriculum Association and several New Right leaders issued a stream of criticism, insisting that children learn inspiring facts about Alfred the Great, Elizabeth I, and the Battle of Bosworth Field, not the gloomy record of social conflict, struggle, and change.[40]

At one point in April, Thatcher hinted obliquely that perhaps the history report should be junked and the work begun again.[41] Did she mean that history might better be eliminated altogether from the list of required subjects? Up to this point university historians had paid little attention to the history battle and were generally unaware of the school curriculum in history.[42] By comparison with the long walk that historians in America had taken from social studies education, British scholars appeared to have moved to a separate planet. Now, however, the academic community roused itself, fearful that young Britons might enter university knowing no history at all. One hundred and fifteen Cambridge University history dons wrote to the education secretary urging him to accept the framework of the Final Report.[43] Academics of Right and Left joined forces to plead for the sanctity of history as a basic subject.[44]

MacGregor's immediate task was to prepare proposals to lay before Parliament. With the task force out of the picture, he and his civil servants devised a compromise plan that significantly tilted the Final Report to the traditionalist side. Thatcherite intellectuals and politicians would presumably find his changes acceptable. MacGregor's revised "Proposals for History for Ages 5–16," which appeared in the summer of 1990, held British history to 50 percent of the total curriculum. Teachers were instructed in general terms to introduce gender issues and differing social and cultural perspectives, though little content was specified. For the Right the big issue remained the critical thinking recommendations. Here, the proposals stipulated that historical "knowledge" be made a category of learning and assessment distinct from "understanding."

The various compromises that the minister, the DES, and the history task force hammered out over a tumultuous eighteen months saved history as a basic subject and put the curriculum on track for implementation. The traditionalists were not completely happy but believed that their ideological message—"facts" over skills, and British history over the rest of the world's—would now be delivered to the schools. Most history teachers, convinced that the skills-knowledge dichotomy was bogus, resigned themselves to push ahead, less disturbed about the new curriculum's design than about the government's refusal to give them much role in creating it. Parliament approved the National Curriculum for history in March 1991, and it came into force for children ages five to fourteen the following September. Public controversy died down and stayed quiet for about a year and a half.

For teachers the new syllabus was not all bad news because history now had a firm place in state-maintained schools. Even so, anxieties ran high. Government funding was inadequate to realize the curriculum's goal, primary teachers felt meagerly trained in history, and fears loomed that national assessments would eventually drive teachers to "teach to the test." Educators also complained that the curriculum prohibited them from covering subjects they considered important. Despite the country's rapidly changing demographic profile, for example, the new program nearly excluded study of ethnic and religious minority communities and their historical experience. Teachers in Leicester, Bradford, and other English cities who presided over classrooms filled with the children of Muslim, Hindu, and Sikh families might have wondered if the curriculum was missing something vital.

A shadow of public doubt also spread over the National Curriculum in general. Schools reported that the academic day was too short to accommodate all the content the curriculum demanded. Teachers protested that the programs in almost all subjects were overstuffed and excessively complex. English opinion, the government was forced to recognize, tended to sympathize with educators who believed the curriculum had been developed in too much of a hurry. The decisive episode was the government's first attempt to carry out national assessments. In 1993, the National Union of Teachers in both England and Wales launched a successful boycott of the tests on the grounds that supervising and marking them made impossible demands on teachers' time. As a Carnegie Foundation report observed, "The boycott of the tests was effectively a boycott of the curriculum itself, and the action amounted to civil disobedience on a national scale. The government was powerless to stop it."[45] The National Curriculum seemed to be disintegrating even as it was being introduced.

The Conservative Cabinet had little choice but to call for a thorough review of the entire structure. The government appointed a new national commission, which, after eight months of consultations, polls, and reviews presented recommendations to slim the curriculum down and simplify assessments. History was designated for heavy trimming and erased altogether as a required subject for fourteen- to sixteen-year-old students. The Tory leadership, having no desire to see the national curriculum wrecked for good, quickly accepted the proposals, and new task forces were appointed to hammer out the details.

In contrast to the history committee appointed in 1988, the new one included eight classroom teachers among its fifteen members. This group completed its work in less than two months, and in May 1994 the secretary of state for education accepted its recommendations without contention. The new document cut many topics and much verbiage from the old version. British history held about 50 percent of the total, though the range of topics on other parts of the world shrank. The report instructed teachers to impart "*detailed* factual knowledge and understanding," but it made no concession to the traditionalist demand for lists of mandated information.[46]

Most teachers and much of the public thought that the revised curriculum was a big improvement. In the meantime, however, another media war quickly broke out. Throughout the spring of 1994, the popular press published story after story rehashing the same issues: facts versus skills, British history versus non-British history, political history versus social history. Traditionalists gave interviews protesting once again the absence of lists of required names and events for students to memorize. Great facts of British history were now "out," the conservative *Sunday Telegraph* proclaimed, and study of exotic foreign societies was "in."[47]

A traditionalist teacher who served on the task force complained that no one listened to his ideas and that the new plan included far too much "sociological baggage," which in his view included social, technological, religious, and virtually any kind of history other than political. If only the central political narrative could be held steady, he and other New Right intellectuals argued, then England might march unwaveringly into the future, irrespective of the rampant, chaotic changes that were afflicting both the United Kingdom and the world. Schools, the traditionalists argued, should help children focus their gaze on immutable images, symbols, and historical certainties that would ratify the traditional "we-ness" of the British people, untainted by class conflict, cultural dissonance, or moral relativism. As one commentator describes this creed: "Britain is unique and it should be considered an honor and a privilege to be born a Briton or, even better, an Englishman. The image is of an independent island race cut off from mainland Europe, proud and fierce, critical of 'foreigners' and their habits."[48] Students, then, should spend less time situating Britain's past within the broad landscape of European and world history and more effort digging deep into the island's political and cultural soil, thereby discovering how distinctive and exceptional their nation is.

Meanwhile, some history professionals complained that amid all the controversy over student knowledge of Guy Fawkes, Titus Oates, and the Wars of the Roses no one seemed to notice the serious impoverishment of world history in the revised program. Despite the flood of recent immigration and the myriad ways that Britain's past intersected with global developments, children were going to spend little time studying the world beyond the English Channel. "There is no way," one school headmaster protested, "that it is in the interests of British school children in the 1990s not to do a significant amount of European and world history."[49] Or as the head of an immigrant organization remarked, "If there is a problem in the schools, it is the lack of teaching about cultures like Islam and Hinduism— or their presentation in a stereotyped way."[50] Some teachers professed that they would have to add their own material to the curriculum to do justice to the country's cultural diversity.[51]

Despite such protests, multiculturalism by no means dominated the media debate—in marked contrast to the scene in the United States. English traditionalists represented the nation's history as if it were purely Anglo-Saxon and centered on the southeastern portion of the island. They tended to dismiss not only West Indian, South Asian, and other relatively new communities but even the historical contributions of Scots, Welsh, and Irish. This unicultural vision of the past did not, however, stir up much public passion, and the idea of creating a national curriculum that genuinely integrated ethnic or intercultural history into the larger story appears not to have taken up much time in the meetings of either of the two task forces. In short, multiculturalism as an educational issue had not as of 1995 implanted itself on the British consciousness nearly as powerfully as it had on that of America.

Public disagreement over non-British history in the curriculum focused mainly on subject-matter percentage counts rather than on the nature of the world history to be taught. As we saw in earlier chapters, educators in the United States began in the 1960s and 1970s to wrestle with the problem of conceptualizing and teaching world history as something other than either a grab bag of "global cultures" or "Western Civ" disguised as world history. In England, by contrast, even the most articulate advocates of non-British history appear to have demanded little more than study units on a variety of civilizations and cultures chosen from a master list, itself limited and arbitrary.

On the other hand, the American controversy over the importance of teaching the Western tradition had no parallel in the British debate. As we have seen, the very concept of Western civilization as a school subject was invented in the United States in the early twentieth century and served to link the experience of a large but still young nation to the much weightier civilization of Europe, especially of England. Ironically, this concept is alien to British history education, and phrases that have pervaded culture-war discourse in the United States—"Western tradition," "Western heritage," or simply the "West"—are virtually absent from both the National Curriculum and the debate over it. British traditionalists, who might have been expected to reciprocate their American counterparts by demanding the history of the West over that of Africa or Asia, argued in fact for no such thing. Rather they wished to accentuate the historical and cultural *differences* between the citizens of Britannia and everyone else in the world, not only Sri Lankans and Senegalese but French, Italians, Americans, and even Irish.

In the media uproar of 1994, the John Major government kept largely silent. After all, the Conservative Party had every reason to get the new guidelines for all the required subjects out to the schools, thereby putting an end to the agony of the previous six years. In January 1995, the department of education published the revised curriculum in a single volume of 222 pages. The government also announced emphatically that none of the programs should be revisited any time before the end of the millennium. The new course outlines began going into effect in the fall of 1996.

The British history war thus finally petered out at the very moment when controversy was heating up in the United States over the National History Standards. Looking back on the battle, British history teachers could at least feel pride that their subject had a secure place in all public schools, an achievement the United States has so far been unable to match. However, the new program, despite repeated draftings and redraftings, was still arbitrary and somewhat disjointed, the result of compromise among parties with decidedly different visions of the aims of history education. The curriculum also represented, whatever negotiations took place, a project of the central government and its Conservative leadership, not an achievement of the historical and social studies professions of England and Wales. With the exception of a few appointees to the task force, the history-teaching community and its professional organizations had no systematic role in the development process other than a reactive one. Rather, the most conspicuous actors were the prime minister, the secretary of state for education, and an array of civil servants and political appointees, as well as various professional educators who had degrees in subjects other than history.

What would the British curriculum have looked like if at the outset the government had put the project in the hands of a wide spectrum of organizations representing teachers, scholars, parents, and other interested citizens—which, as we will see, was the model adopted for developing national history standards in the United States? The task might have taken longer to accomplish but the guidelines might have incorporated more richly than they did the fruits of national and international scholarship of the previous several decades. The curriculum might also have more effectively reflected Britain's changing demographic, cultural, and social complexion, rather than marginalizing the country's remarkable social history and the historical roles of citizens of South Asian, West Indian, Middle Eastern, and other foreign descent. Furthermore the curriculum writers might have framed the British past within the wider contexts of European, Atlantic, and world history rather than perpetuating the anachronistic "little England" notion that the island's modern development had little to do with global events.

Public contests over history in the schools are characteristic not of totalitarian regimes but of countries where democracy is either blooming or persevering. Even so, the central government has been a major player in most countries where history wars have occurred. The United States, by contrast, established long ago the political tradition that education policymaking should mainly be the business of states and localities, not a ministry of education on the banks of the Potomac. Thus in 1989, when President George Bush and the nation's governors announced a major initiative to develop national education standards, they understood that although government might give material support to subject-based projects, the endeavor should not be under the supervision of the White House, the Department of Education, the Congress, or any other federal agency. In contrast to England's curriculum strategy, the American project involved Washington bureaucrats hardly at all and organizations of teachers, academics, and public interest groups by the dozens.

CHAPTER 7

Setting National History Standards

If the [history] standards were hijacked at all, they were hijacked by
America, through an admirable process of open debate that could proba-
bly only happen in the United States.

—Carol Gluck, Columbia University,
New York Times, November 19, 1994

"The time has come," declared President George Bush and the nation's governors in September 1989, "to establish clear national performance goals, goals that will make us internationally competitive [and] second to none in the twenty-first century."[1] In a country where state and local school control was as venerable as the town meeting, this manifesto was a historic first. Governors were already initiating state-wide education reform programs and candidate Bush had told voters he was eager to be the "education president." However, the sight of the nation's chief executive and the National Governors' Association (NGA) assembling to proclaim an ambitious *national* effort on behalf of excellence in education for all children was indeed big news.

Americans greeted this agenda with guarded anticipation. Nobody wanted high government officials to lay down rules about what and how to study history, science, civics, or anything else. Nobody thought that the nation's best teachers and scholars should be mere observers in the fight against educational mediocrity. Americans traditionally approached education reform differently from the citizens of other nations and they intended to do so again.

Genesis of the National Education Standards

In his 1990 State of the Union Address, President Bush announced six National Education Goals, jointly developed with the nation's governors.[2] Hammered out in long working sessions in which Bill Clinton, then governor of Arkansas and cochairman of the NGA, actively participated, the goals were intended neither to mandate a national curriculum nor to force specific reforms on states and local districts. Their purpose, rather, was to inspire new ideas in education at the federal, state, and local levels lest the United States lose its global economic leadership. "Today," the secretary of education announced, "a new standard for an educated citizenry is required, one suitable for the next century. Our people must be as knowledgeable, as well trained, as competent, and as inventive as those in any other nation. . . . America can meet this challenge if our society is dedicated to a renaissance in education."[3]

Goal 3 was pivotal to this aim. It proposed that by the year 2000, "American students will leave grades four, eight, and twelve having demonstrated competency in challenging subject matter including English, mathematics, science, history, and geography; and every school in America will ensure that all students learn to use their minds well, so they may be prepared for responsible citizenship, further learning, and productive employment in our modern economy."[4]

Five objectives elaborated upon that goal. One stated that "the percentage of students who demonstrate the ability to reason, solve problems, apply knowledge, and write and communicate effectively will increase substantially." Another affirmed that "all students will be knowledgeable about the diverse cultural heritage of this nation and about the world community." These two objectives alone marked the American project off from Britain's Education Reform Act of 1988, which said nothing about cultural diversity or global understanding.

For the next two years, the Bush administration, notably Secretary of Education Lamar Alexander, Deputy Secretary of Education David Kearns, Assistant Secretary of Education Diane Ravitch, and National Endowment for the Humanities (NEH) Chairman Lynne Cheney moved the National Goals program forward with bipartisan support. At the state level, strong leadership came from both Republican and Democratic governors, including Roy Romer of Colorado, Bill Clinton of Arkansas, John Ashcroft of Missouri, Evan Bayh of Indiana, and Carroll Campbell of South Carolina. All of them had tackled problems in education and understood the roadblocks to change and the clarity of purpose required to achieve results.

Romer, a Democrat and committed advocate of voluntary national standards and assessments, was the first elected chairman of the National Education Goals Panel (NEGP). This body, a group of governors and Bush officials, was given responsibility for overseeing and reporting annually on progress toward the National Education Goals.

The nation's bipartisan leaders enjoyed broad public support for their joint undertaking. A Gallup Poll in 1989 had asked whether the public wanted its schools to conform to national achievement standards, to adopt a standardized national curriculum, and to develop national testing programs to measure academic achievement. Respondents expressed surprisingly strong support for these measures, despite the hallowed traditions of local control of education.[5] Two years later, another Gallup Poll revealed that support was growing. Of those interviewed, 81 percent now backed national achievement standards and goals, 68 percent favored a national curriculum, and 77 percent wanted national testing. When asked if they approved testing programs in the subjects specifically identified in the National Education Goals (English, mathematics, science, history, and geography), the number in favor rose to 88 percent.[6]

Moreover, this support represented the entire spectrum of the American population: all major ethnoracial groups; all age groups; Republicans, Democrats, and independents; all occupational groups and income levels; and adults with or without children. Public opinion was moving swiftly in a direction that would have been unthinkable a decade earlier. As Ernest Boyer, head of the Carnegie Foundation for the Advancement of Teaching, observed: "Today Hondas and Toyotas and Japanese VCRs have us really worried about the national competitiveness, and that's more important than whether we have local governance. . . . All of this suggests there has been a sea change in the way Americans think about education."[7]

In 1991, confident of broad public backing for his agenda, President Bush launched America 2000, a comprehensive, long-range plan "to move every community in America toward the National Education Goals."[8] At its core, the plan recommended the development of "world class" standards in English, mathematics, science, history, and geography and of voluntary achievement tests to assess progress toward these goals.[9] Under Secretary Alexander's leadership, America 2000 was expected to achieve significant improvement in the nation's schools by the end of the millennium. Individual initiative and local control were expected to play essential roles in reaching these goals.

The federal role, while limited, was to be proactive. Washington, Alexander said, "can help by setting standards, highlighting examples, contributing some funds, and pushing and prodding—then pushing and prodding

some more."[10] The federal government would act as the "catalyst for change
... by working closely with governors and educators to define new world-
class standards." The government would also "develop voluntary—and the
president stresses that word—national tests for fourth, eighth, and twelfth
graders in those core subjects. . . . We have," concluded Alexander, "embarked on a new voyage in the American experience."[11]

Support for federal leadership in this "new voyage" came from many directions. The National Alliance of Business endorsed a high-stakes national
assessment system funded by federal money and given national priority by
both Congress and the Bush administration.[12] The term "high stakes" stood
for use of student performance results as one criterion for college admission and employment. The alliance cautioned, however, that the assessment
system should be used to lift *all* students to a high level of achievement with
respect to the national standards, that care be taken to ensure that the tests
do not discriminate on the basis of race or ethnicity, and that more resources be devoted to those students who have difficulty mastering the subject matter. Improving the school curriculum and teaching so that all
students might have the opportunity to meet challenging standards would
not come without costs.

NEH Chairman Lynne Cheney also endorsed internationally competitive "high-stakes" examinations. Noting the standards of achievement to
which students in Britain, Japan, and continental Europe were held, she
asked, "Do we expect our students to know American history as well as
other countries expect their students to know it? Do we expect our students
to know the history of other nations in anything approaching the detail
with which they are expected to know ours?"[13] Examinations in European
countries, Cheney further noted, asked students to explain complex historical issues in essays designed to "demonstrate whether they can organize
their thoughts, make analyses, and mount arguments."[14] Achievement on
high-stakes tests in this country, Cheney argued, would serve as a valuable
credential for students wanting to enter the workplace or college. Such
gatekeeper exams would give schools the incentives they now lacked. They
would also ensure equity because high expectations and incentives would
no longer be reserved largely for honor students or the college-bound. Unlike the National Alliance of Business, however, Cheney saw no special
need to ensure equity of opportunity for all students to achieve the high
standards that national tests would demand.

Chester Finn, former assistant secretary of education in the Reagan administration and codirector of the Educational Excellence Network, produced a more comprehensive and provocative argument for high-stakes
assessment and student accountability.[15] "Nationwide tests for all young

Americans, at whatever ages or grade levels, would be a truly epochal change in the nature and functioning of our education system," he wrote. The burden of such a policy change "must be borne by the executive branch, which is, after all, collaborating with the governors in this massive goal-setting project."[16] To connect tangible rewards to students who did well and real costs to those who failed, Finn recommended going beyond jobs and college admissions. Public agencies, for example, might grant or withhold work permits and driver's licenses according to students' scores. Like Cheney, Finn wanted all students held to the same high standards. He recognized, however, that students differed in ability, aspirations, and commitment, and might require different paths to reach the same goals. Schools must, he advised, offer enough different teaching methods and resources to bring all students to the same high standards. But he counseled no delay in national testing until those resources and strategies were in place and equally available to all students.

The governors also advised action.[17] No national agenda for school reform, however, could proceed without congressional financial support. Thus far Congress had not been invited to participate in the deliberations. Members of Congress had already heard warnings and protests, however, from education, civil rights, and advocacy organizations about the validity, equity, and fairness of high-stakes testing tied to standards.[18] Many in Congress feared that without adequate funding to ensure equal opportunity for all students to acquire the appropriate knowledge and skills, these tests would only worsen the life chances of economically disadvantaged youth. Other members, including Representative Bill Goodling of Pennsylvania, the ranking Republican on the House Education and Labor Committee, questioned the uses to which test results would be put. "As a former teacher, I've always preached that the purpose of assessment should be to see where you failed to get a point across to the student so you can go back and fix it," he explained. "I am concerned about whether [tests] will be used for learning purposes or scorekeeping purposes. That's why I urged ... move slowly."[19]

Congress, seeking to slow the rush to national testing until it had examined the full range of issues, formed the National Council on Education Standards and Testing (NCEST) with the support of the Bush administration and the governors. In June 1991, Congress charged the council to advise on the desirability of national standards and tests and to recommend long-term policies for such an agenda.

Composed of thirty-two members appointed by the secretary of education and the majority and minority leaders of the House and Senate, the council scrambled to meet its six-month deadline to submit a report.

Governors Romer, current chairman of the NEGP, and Campbell, who would succeed him in that position, cochaired the council. Members included an imposing array of federal and state legislators, Bush officials, business leaders, teachers' union officials, school administrators, classroom teachers, and testing and education policy experts. Meeting eight times in public sessions carried live on C-SPAN, the council heard the testimony of a stream of experts and special task forces. Sessions were at times stormy. The contentiousness of the agenda, the openness of the deliberations, and the wide range of viewpoints expressed ensured that controversies would be bluntly aired and consensus hard won.

The council's report, released on January 24, 1992, endorsed national education standards, a national system of assessments but not a single national test, and "school delivery standards"—a highly contentious recommendation whose purpose was to "attest to the provision of opportunities to learn and of appropriate instructional conditions to enable all children to reach high standards."[20] The report also recommended the formation of a National Education Standards and Assessment Council to coordinate the development of the new standards and tests and, in cooperation with the NEGP, to judge them for certification as "world class."

The report tried to lay to rest worry over federal control of the reform agenda by stipulating that the standards written for the five core subjects be national, not federal, and voluntary, not mandated by Washington. Though the Gallup Poll found in 1989 and 1991 that a large majority of the public wanted children all across America to study the same things in school, the council deferred to the long tradition of state and local control over curriculum. It declared that standards should provide focus and direction but not constitute a national curriculum. Finally, such standards must be dynamic, with provisions for their continuing development and revision in the years ahead. To demonstrate the feasibility of these recommendations, the council cited the work of the National Council of Teachers of Mathematics in producing challenging national math standards, and noted that various states and local districts were slowly but surely taking voluntary steps to modify their math curricula to conform more closely to these standards.

The council's report also strove to find an acceptable compromise on the thorny issues that national testing raised. To measure the progress of individual students, schools, districts, and states, the council recommended a system of multiple assessments that would be developed by states, commercial publishers, and others; be voluntary and not federally mandated; and, eventually, be considered for use for such high-stakes purposes as high school graduation, certification for employment, continuing education, and college admission.

Even these attempts to offset concerns, however, fell under the shadow of the larger social questions. Would all children be assured equal opportunity to master challenging subject matter? Would all schools be held equally accountable for "delivering" high standards to young learners? As the council neared completion of its work, two of its members—Marshall Smith, dean of Stanford's School of Education, and Keith Geiger, president of the National Education Association—joined other prominent educators in submitting to Congress and the American public a statement that argued strongly for "1) preserving local involvement in standards-setting and assessment, 2) ensuring that tests are not used to administer high-stakes consequences to students and schools, and 3) calling attention to equity concerns in the availability of educational resources."[21] Released on the same day the council's report was made public, this statement was something of a bombshell. Deciding that these assessment issues had not been satisfactorily resolved, the House of Representatives deferred approval of the council's recommendations and instituted its own hearings to investigate the issue further.

Democrats in the Senate were already drafting education legislation that supported several of the NCEST recommendations, including the National Education Standards and Assessment Council and school delivery standards to ensure all students equal opportunity to learn. In their wing of the Capitol, House Democrats, offended by the prospect that national tests might damage rather than elevate the life prospects of children from low-income school districts, instituted legislation that would have limited any implementation of national assessments to the research-and-development phase. The compromise bill, however, never reached the president's desk. It was killed by Senate Republicans to avoid an election-year presidential veto of an education measure the Bush administration did not like.[22]

For the time being, high-stakes national assessment was dead. The *Wall Street Journal* carried Chester Finn's outrage: "Three promising education reform ideas are under siege in Washington: national school standards, exams keyed to those standards, and the use of exam results for such purposes as college admission and employee selection. Surrounding these proposals and trying to cut their supply lines are an army of education establishmentarians, academics and congressmen." Instead of decisive movement forward, Finn continued, "the commission's recommendations are being pilloried by agents of the status quo. If they have their way, particularly with a Congress that has long been skittish about testing and the 'outcomes' orientation that these convey, an important opportunity will be lost."[23]

Toward National Standards in History

Although the national assessment agenda of America 2000 had been way-laid, the national standards movement forged ahead. By spring of 1992, both Congress and NCEST had joined the NGA and the Bush administration in supporting national standards for the five core disciplines. Indeed, con-stituencies of these curriculum fields were already seizing the initiative, even before the council brought in its report. Inspired by the success of the National Council of Teachers of Mathematics in developing national stan-dards, organizations in science and science education formed a coalition to develop guidelines. The Department of Education (ED) funded this enter-prise in September 1991, even as NCEST was getting under way. To some observers it appeared that the horses were already out of the barn and gal-loping up the trail, while the wranglers hired to organize the drive had yet to saddle up.

National Standards for History were soon off and running as well. The council had appointed as one of its working groups a History Task Force, chaired by member Lynne Cheney. The task force's members in-cluded Charlotte Crabtree, then director of the National Center for His-tory in the Schools (NCHS), a Cooperative Research Program of UCLA and the NEH. The task force meeting, held in October 1991, was charged with excitement, for assembled that day in the Hyatt Regency Hotel on Capitol Hill were some of the nation's strongest supporters of history in the schools. During several hours of lively interchange, the task force affirmed its support for the development of national history standards.[24] It recom-mended that these standards address world as well as U.S. history, that they include interpretation and analysis, not just basic facts, and that they incor-porate civic education, economic history, art history, literature, and geogra-phy. The task force also affirmed that the writing of the standards should be a consensual process, open and public, and should include teachers, profes-sional associations, groups with relevant expertise, and the public. It further recommended that the standards be developed in several stages so that they could be revised and refined. Last, it suggested that *Lessons from History*, a curricular guideline that the NCHS had just completed, be used as one of several major resources in standards development.[25]

At noon in the hotel's dining room, bustling with congressional aides, lobbyists, and other Beltway power-lunchers, Crabtree joined Cheney and several of her NEH officers. "Would the NEH be interested," Crabtree asked, "in reviewing an application from the center for funding to adminis-ter a national consensus-building project to develop national history standards consistent with the recommendations of the task force?" Just a month earlier, Lamar Alexander had agreed to fund the organizations collaborating to develop National Science Standards. Diane Ravitch, deeply committed to the idea of history standards, had encouraged Crabtree to submit a similar proposal to the Education Department in behalf of history. Given the relationship between the NEH and the NCHS, however, Crabtree approached Cheney instead. The response was warm and encouraging. Yes, indeed, Cheney agreed, draw up a proposal, but do it quickly. The NEH Advisory Council would meet in January, and at least a month was needed to conduct an external review of the application before the council considered the matter.

Thus encouraged, Crabtree, along with Gary B. Nash, who was then associate director of the center, proceeded to test the waters. It was by no means certain that the many scholarly, professional, and public interest organizations with a stake in history education would be interested in collaborating with the NCHS. Without such a broad-based effort, however, the project would go nowhere. History was too contentious a field for any single agency to construct standards for the entire country.

The history center faced a number of uncertainties. Members of the National Council for the Social Studies (NCSS), for example, were actively lobbying Congress and NCEST to add social studies to the five disciplines identified in America 2000. As we saw earlier, many social studies professionals had greeted the history reform campaigns of the 1980s with great skepticism and sometimes hostility. Some social studies advocates were even seeking to remove history and geography from America 2000 and replace these disciplines with social studies. This, they argued, would ensure the integrated, contemporary, problems-oriented approach that they favored. Because of these ideological tensions, whose origins harked back to the 1920s, Crabtree and Nash were by no means certain that the twenty-six-thousand-member NCSS would participate in the project.

Nor were academic historians unanimously convinced that they should join this enterprise. A number of highly politicized controversies—over, for example, the commemoration of the Columbian Quincentennial, the revision of the New York state curriculum, California's 1990 state adoption of new history-centered textbooks, and Afrocentrism in the schools—had exposed the difficulties of reaching consensus on such questions as "Whose history shall be taught?" "How can Western Civ and world history be reconciled?" "How can the booming field of women's history be fully incorporated into the curriculum?" Historians were not reluctant to address these questions. But seeing that national political leaders had initiated the standards movement and that government agencies were funding the projects, many scholars feared the imposition of tradition-bound interpretations of history that would marginalize the rich scholarship of the postwar era.

For historians, the prospect of national history standards represented both an opportunity to bring recent scholarship into the schools and a danger that this scholarship would be rejected by standards writers hostile to it. Among historians, debates over new scholarship are a normal part of academic discourse. Thrust into the public arena, however, such debates had a history of becoming politically divisive, particularly when critics hurled invectives of "political correctness" at defenders of a more inclusive reading of the nation's past. Had historians been working with the schools all along, this new research might have filtered down to school texts and classroom teaching much earlier. Historians, however, were only now returning from the "long walk" they had taken away from the schools. If at this juncture they refused to participate in writing the standards, they risked cutting themselves off from the schools once again and surrendering their influence on the project.

Perhaps the strongest argument bringing all these players together was the simple fact that the train was leaving the station. History standards were clearly on the country's agenda and strongly supported by the public, the governors, Congress, and the Bush administration. The matter boiled down to who would write them. Those who were at first reluctant about the wisdom of this enterprise soon decided that they might compromise their own best interests if they failed to join in. If the cards were being dealt, why would historians or social studies educators not want seats around the big table?

Within a week the NCHS had received favorable replies from several key organizations: the Council of Chief State School Officers (CCSSO), an alliance of the state superintendents of all fifty states; the Association for Supervision and Curriculum Development (ASCD), a 155,000-member association of school leaders; the Organization of History Teachers (OHT) and the National Council for History Education, a membership organization of scholars and teachers of history. The NCSS and the Council of State Social Studies Specialists (CS4) soon agreed to take part.

With this early backing assured, the history center drew up its application and submitted it to the NEH. The proposal followed the recommendations of NCEST's History Task Force.[26] The NEH Advisory Council favorably reviewed the application in January, and Cheney approved it. Meantime, ED officials approached her with the request to cosponsor and cofund the project. An agreement was quickly struck. On December 16, 199. Secretary of Education Alexander and Chairman Cheney announced the award. The National History Standards Project had been launched.

The Building Blocks of Consensus

The first task of the standards project was to form a National Council to set policy, serve as a sounding board for criticisms and critiques, and decide when the standards were ready for publication. The composition of the council was crucial. Nash and Crabtree, project codirectors, thought the group should include academic historians as well as teachers, women as well as men, and people of differing views on the history wars under way since the 1980s. They also agreed that the council should represent a wide range of interests and perspectives among scholars, teachers, and advocates of history education, but not a microcosm of American cultural politics from the far Right to the extreme Left. Nash and Crabtree wanted to seek consensus, not referee boxing matches or mop up blood. It was inadvisable, they agreed, to bring to the table the most fervent ideologues at either end of the political spectrum. That decision was one the funders, after some persuasion, accepted.

Following days of negotiating, Lynne Cheney, Diane Ravitch, and the project's two codirectors settled upon the names of twenty-eight individuals, many of them nominated by Cheney's officers. All twenty-eight accepted appointment.[27] They included the elected presidents of the eight large-membership organizations most directly involved in the teaching of history, officers of the Social Studies Development Center at Indiana University, supervisory staff of county and city school districts, veteran K–12 classroom teachers, and distinguished scholars in the history of the United States and other world areas. Two members of NCEST and several participants in the work already under way for the 1994 National Assessment of Educational Progress in U.S. history were also included. To avoid the appearance that the federal government was creating the standards, the council included no members of Congress or other government entities. Project officers appointed by the two funding agencies would attend all meetings as observers, but not participate actively in the deliberations. Crabtree and Nash, responsible for administering the project, served as the council's cochairs.

To reach out to an even broader range of organizations, the NCHS organized a National Forum, with representatives from twenty-four major education, parent-teacher, and public interest associations having a stake in history in the schools.[28] Advisory in its function, this body provided important counsel for the project and access to the larger public. A look around the table at the first meeting of the forum revealed a microcosm of America itself. There were Sister Catherine McNamee, president of the

National Catholic Educational Association; Clifford Trafzer of the Native American Heritage Commission; George Nielsen representing the Lutheran Schools, Lutheran Church–Missouri Synod; Ngueyn Minh Chau of the National Association for Asian and Pacific American Education; Mabel Lake Murray of the National Alliance of Black School Educators; Sara Shoob of the National Association of Elementary School Principals; Chester Finn of the Educational Excellence Network; and so on around the huge table.

In addition to the council and the forum, nine focus groups, chosen by the leaders of the major educational organizations, were recruited to provide important advisory, review, and consulting services.[29] The "Big Nine," as the codirectors called them, would undertake reviews of one draft after another of the standards. Finally, the NCHS formed three curriculum task forces, totaling more than fifty members, to draft the standards for grades K–4 and for grades 5–12 in U.S. and world history. Composed of both veteran teachers from Alaska to Florida and recognized scholars with deep commitments to history education in schools, these groups would work for more than two years to devise the standards and create teaching examples to illustrate how teachers might put the guidelines into practice.

Debating Multiculturalism

During the thirty-two months of deliberation, members of these groups differed sharply and passionately on some of the fundamental questions that the council and forum had to confront. One of the most divisive was multiculturalism: the question of how and to what extent the standards should include the historical experiences of racial, ethnic, and religious minorities, as well as women and the working classes. As we have seen, multiculturalism in the curriculum became a hot issue in the early 1980s as the harvest of new research in social and cultural history became more widely known and as the country's demographics rapidly changed.

When the council and forum met jointly for two days in April 1992, the multiculturalism question came up in one presentation after another.[30] Several speakers argued that the new standards should be required to do a much better job than curricula or textbooks had so far done at including the experiences of African Americans. Adelaide Sanford, a member of the New York Board of Regents and representative of the National Association of State Boards of Education, argued that the history written for the school directly contributed to the oppression of citizens whose experiences had been marginalized, distorted, trivialized, and ignored. "When expressed through the lens of those who have not distinguished themselves from the oppressing class," she remarked, "even the patches and bits of the history of people of African ancestry that are inserted into the pages of recorded history" are unsatisfactory.[31] Inclusivity is important, Sanford stressed, but the quality of the history that is included—its truthfulness and its reflection of the new historical scholarship—must count most in national standards setting.

Mabel Lake Murray concurred, urging the council to develop standards infused with the historical record of African American struggles, accomplishments, and civic contributions. "The promise of the 1960s was eliminated by the backlash of the 1970s, the elections of the 1980s and the Supreme Court of the 1990s," she said. "We are in deep trouble. It may have to do with the fact that there's an exclusionary education in our schools, one which excludes [the experiences of] black people from the very beginning, from kindergarten through the grades."[32]

Cynthia Neverdon-Morton, of the Association for the Study of Afro-American Life and History, quoted W.E.B. Du Bois: "Would America have been America without her Negro people?"

> For us this statement poses our first concern with standards, and that is that the centrality of the Afro-American experience must be carefully considered. . . . We must also, we believe, include in standards not only African American history, the life and culture and story of her people, but we also must promote greater inclusion of the histories of others, including those who were here before Columbus, the drama of immigration that continues to unfold, and the issues and complexities of cultural diversity.

From quite a different ideological direction came the statements of participants who deeply feared that multiculturalism in history education might cause a disintegration of national unity. Mark Curtis, representing the Atlantic Council of the United States, warned: "The so-called multicultural agendas in history threaten to balkanize American society. They will serve to drive people apart and will diminish the critical importance of teaching about our common American heritage."

Sam Banks, a council member and Baltimore schools administrator, replied: "To argue that multicultural education will bring about balkanization just cannot be sustained. The concepts of 'liberty and justice for all' should mean *all*. But reality has not squared with that promise. To argue now that including the history of all will somehow disrupt the body politic is . . . balderdash."

Chester Finn submitted a written statement that echoed Curtis's warning against multicultural excess:

We must teach about diversity, to be sure, but must never lose sight of what binds us together as a nation ... the great unifying Western ideas of individual freedom, political democracy, and human rights. . . . We agree wholeheartedly that in the past schools did not present history in a very balanced way. . . . But the solution to this problem is not ... to turn things around 180 degrees and blame, or even worse, ignore Western tradition.[33]

Taking the floor, Finn pushed the point further:

I want to emphasize that because these standards are going to be voluntary and not compulsory, their impact is going to depend on their acceptance by the general public—by grocers and legislators and bus drivers and ordinary folk who are going to have to find them compatible with their view of what is important in history, or these standards might as well not be developed because they will have passing little impact on the country. Mollifying factions who come to the table at education meetings isn't the same as developing standards for history that will have an impact upon how it is learned around this country.[34]

Banks, incensed by what he saw as Finn's effort to exclude large sectors of the American people from "the general public," charged:

Your point carries the considerable risk of what de Tocqueville called the "tyranny of the majority." If it were left to the "American public"—i.e., the larger white society—to decide, the view of many would be that all is well, there are no problems, the history I learned in school is good enough for me, and we don't need to talk about Native Americans, or black Americans, or Asian Americans, or women, for when you do, you disrupt the social order and balkanize American society.[35]

Some observed that the nation has never been unified as long as many Americans suffered discrimination and exclusion in violation of the nation's ideals. The specter of balkanization, they argued, was only a political ploy of those who resisted an inclusive curriculum.

Ruth Wattenberg, of the American Federation of Teachers (AFT), offered some recent data relevant to the dispute. AFT's New York affiliate had just completed a statewide survey that demonstrated public support for inclusiveness in the curriculum.[36] When asked, "Do you think it very important, somewhat important, or not important at all that public schools teach the common values and heritage that we share as Americans?" a majority of respondents said it was very important.[37] When asked, "Do you think it very important, somewhat important, or not important at all that public schools teach the separate histories and differences of America's ethnic and racial groups?" large majorities also judged this content to be important.[38] Asked whether students should be taught "*both* the traditional events of American history *and* the contributions and experiences of America's ethnic and racial populations," respondents overwhelmingly said yes. To the degree that these findings reflected national opinion, Finn's portrayal of the public as resistant to socially inclusive standards appeared to be inaccurate.

Mary Futrell, a forum participant representing the Quality Education for Minorities Network, spoke for the broad view of the nation's self-image:

> America is changing, and it's changing very dramatically. We must stop accepting this red herring that multiculturalism will destroy America. No, it will not. Those of us who support inclusivity also believe strongly in the principles and values that have traditionally defined America. We also talk about *unum*, about America being one. But how do we define "one"? Does it include me, a black, southern, Baptist woman? Does it include my ancestors? Does it include the Indian, the Hispanic, and white Americans? If we want people to support the values that we cherish, then we cannot exclude them. We must include them.[39]

James Gardner, deputy executive director of the American Historical Association (AHA), was equally forceful. "We would not be part of any standards project that does not address the multicultural aspects of our history," he said, "We don't see this as an option or an alternative but the reality of our past."[40]

As far as the council was concerned, the preponderance of opinion was clear. At a meeting on May 1, 1992, it drafted fifteen criteria to guide the development of the standards. Criterion 7 stated: "The history of any society can only be understood by studying all its constituent parts. As a nation—polity and society—the United States has always been both one and many. Therefore Standards for United States history should reflect the nation's diversity, exemplified by race, ethnicity, social status, gender, and religious affiliation. The contributions and struggles for social justice and equality by specific groups and individuals should be included."

Criterion 8, on the other hand, emphasized the commonalities in American society: "Standards in United States history should contribute to citizenship education through developing understanding of our common civic identity and shared civic values within the polity, through analyzing major policy issues in the nation's history, and through developing mutual respect among its many peoples." Submitted to national reviews throughout the next two years, these two criteria continued, with minor changes, to command wide support.

The council certainly took an accurate measure of professional opinion and public sentiment on the question of inclusive history. And though debate was contentious, it never degenerated into rancorous disputes over how much of the curriculum should be awarded to one ethnic group or another. Consensus on these issues had been reached. The charge made two years later that the standards' inclusionary thrust was the result of Bill Clinton's election in 1992 and subsequent capitulation to the excessive demands of various ethnic factions was simply untrue.

Western Civ or World History? A Battle Joined

Though the council and forum reached agreement on the balance between *unum* and *pluribus* in the U.S. History Standards, the search for consensus on world history was long and tortured. When the project began, neither Crabtree nor Nash saw much hint of the trouble ahead. The idea that young Americans should learn history on a world scale, rather than exclusively the U.S. or European past, was by the late 1980s commonplace in education. In 1987, the National Governors' Conference warned that the fifty states have never "been so exposed to the competitive forces of international commerce" and urged all states to "maintain an international perspective in all decisions, ranging from how we market our goods to how we educate our children."[41] The following year brought the recommendation from the Bradley Commission that schools teach the global past, arguing that "world history is inadequate when it consists only of European history plus imperialism, just as it is inadequate when it slights European history itself."[42]

By this time, virtually all textbooks for the high school world history course boasted "global coverage" in some measure. Except in Advanced Placement European history courses and some independent schools, the Western Civ textbook was a curricular relic. To be sure, a great distance had yet to be covered between education manifestos on the importance of international education and the realities of collegiate and in-service training which failed to give teachers sufficient help in moving beyond the old Western-Civ-as-world-history paradigm. However, this was precisely the sort of problem the national history standards project had been organized to address. The National Education Goals had been clear on this matter, emphasizing that by the year 2000, "all students will be knowledgeable about the diverse cultural heritage of this nation and about the world community."[43] NCEST's History Task Force, which Lynne Cheney chaired, had been even clearer, recommending that "the standards should have a global dimension, and include world as well as United States history."[44] The national council understood from the beginning that its mission was to write standards in both U.S. and world history. The problem arose in disagreements over how world history was to be defined and how much of it students should learn.

One ideological viewpoint was associated with a group of education critics that might be labeled the "humanist Right." William Bennett, Allan Bloom, Lynne Cheney, and Gertrude Himmelfarb were among its most prominent voices. As we saw in Chapter 5, this group argued that education in the humanities should be mostly concerned with imparting ideals and knowledge rooted in Western civilization. Our European political, philosophical, literary, and aesthetic heritage was, Bennett wrote, "the glue that binds together our pluralistic nation."[45] These critics warned, however, that America's cultural unity was threatened by young scholars of Marxist, feminist, and ultraliberal persuasions who since the 1960s had been taking over the universities and replacing study of the West with the divisive curriculum of race, class, and gender.[46] The humanist Right's agenda was to shore up Western studies in the nation's colleges and universities and stop the assaults they claimed were being made to "drop the West." However, not all of them, certainly not Cheney, favored a curriculum exclusively Western in orientation.

A minority of the leading critics in this camp had been educated as historians. (Bennett's degree was in philosophy; Cheney's in English literature.) As a group they mostly talked about Western values and traditions and had little to say about history as most historians viewed it: that is, as the study of change in human society and how developments in the various spheres of human experience—not only political and intellectual, but also social, economic, scientific, environmental, and so on—combined to make the world what it is today.[47]

John Patrick Diggins, for example, has argued that history is not so much the study of change as it is the examination of essential attributes that civilizations do or do not possess. In a recent article reflecting a particularly anachronistic form of cultural essentialism, he lists the fundamental characteristics of West and "non-West." The West, he declares, represents

"liberty and democracy," "science and technology," and "work and produc-
tivity." The non-West (the great majority of the world's population) represents "patriarchy and hierarchy," "sorcery and totems," and "hunting and
gathering."[48]

A second group actively working for the primacy of Western studies in
the schools was centered at the national headquarters of the AFT under the
leadership of Albert Shanker. An influential union organizer since the 1960s,
staunch anticommunist, and strong presence in the Democratic Party,
Shanker had used his AFT presidency to move his own program for education reform. It was an agenda often at odds with the rank-and-file membership. "The gap between what Al believes and the way his union acts,"
Chester Finn has commented, "is a big and important problem. It's why I
find it far easier to agree with Al than to admire . . . his organization."[49]

Shanker employed Paul Gagnon, a historian at the University of Massachusetts, Boston, and principal investigator for the Bradley Commission, as
consultant to his Education for Democracy Project, which was undertaken
in the mid-1980s—before the Cold War ended. The project published a series of booklets, two of them authored by Gagnon, which defined the West
not so much in terms of the humanistic tradition (than as) the alliance of
democracies that had defended, and was still defending, humankind against
fascist and communist totalitarianism. *Education for Democracy*, a statement of
principles published in 1987 by the AFT in association with the Educational
Excellence Network and Freedom House, argued that democracy's survival
cannot be taken for granted and that its endurance depends on "transmitting to each new generation the political vision of liberty and equality that
unites us as Americans."[50] For this purpose, history—more specifically, the
history of Western democracy—should be at the core of the curriculum.
This statement did not ignore study of the non-West, but it viewed the
world in Cold War terms: a tripartite universe made up of the Western
democracies, the communist bloc, and the Third World, the last categorized
indiscriminantly as the part of the world "where so many live amid poverty
and violence, with little freedom and little hope." It also argued that students could learn all they needed to know about other cultures by studying
"at least one non-Western society in depth."

This viewpoint, like that of the humanist Right, accepted the notion that
the history of Europe and North America together had an enclosed, linear
character, as if the Western experience from ancient Athens to the present
could be understood without much reference to the rest of the world. Indeed, Gagnon made the decidedly ahistorical argument that "the purpose
of world history is precisely to capture the essence of each major world
civilization."[51] He wrote to Crabtree in 1991,

I still don't believe in the integrated approach [to world history] throughout a text or a course because integration destroys the integrity of each
civilization's own story. Yes, I know the loudest talk is about intercultural
influences, and [William] McNeill thinks only of that. But I believe that
the most important thing about any given civilization is what it does to
itself.[52]

Gagnon's position contradicted the fundamental assumption of the contemporary historical discipline that civilizations do not possess "essences"
or fixed and unitary "stories" but rather that the histories of civilizations are
played out in social contexts larger than themselves, that all elements of
culture change over time, and that no civilization possesses preprogrammed
or culturally "genetic" traits such as love of freedom or a propensity for
authoritarian rule. Gagnon's premise, however, allowed him to argue that
democracy was uniquely part of the "essence" of the West and, for that reason, "it simply makes no sense for our schools to start anywhere but with the
Western experience."[53] Both the AFT and the humanist Right believed that
students should concentrate their studies upon the political, philosophical,
and aesthetic truths expounded in the classic texts that issued from ancient
Athens, Renaissance Italy, seventeenth-century England, and other carefully selected locales, most of them in Europe. The sweeping events and
transformations occurring in the world at large were to them of far less
importance.

Contrasting assumptions guided those advocating the "new world history." These were educators who had been teaching the subject in high
schools and colleges since the 1980s or earlier and could see no turning back
to the days of Western Civ. Most of them shared the views of Cheney,
Gagnon, and Ravitch that schools must provide more and better history. Almost none of them were apostles of "extreme relativism" or multicultural
victimology. They were not interested in bashing Western civilization as
evil and oppressive nor ranking civilizations according to which had
achieved the greatest glories or committed the worst crimes. And they actively supported teaching classic Western philosophy, literature, and art,
though not necessarily only in the context of the world history course.

On the other hand, they also questioned the notion, as Peter Stearns put
it, that "God decreed two different histories, one ours and one theirs."[54]
They proposed that young Americans are likely to understand the power
and appeal of modern democracy more clearly if they study it not simply
as an internal attribute of Western civilization, but as a set of ideas and
practices that went out from Europe to the world in the seventeenth and

eighteenth centuries and that peoples on all continents came to grips with throughout the nineteenth and twentieth.

These teachers contended furthermore that a world history program that failed to situate the study of any civilization—Western or non-Western—in the larger context of global or interregional change was deficient preparation for living and working in today's global economy. Social studies education, they argued, must stress not only European ideas and political institutions but also the big changes—demographic, social, economic, technological, and so on—that have shaped and been shaped by human endeavor. For example, historians have understood for some time that China nearly brought off something akin to an industrial revolution between the tenth and twelfth centuries and that that empire remained an economic powerhouse among the states of Eurasia and Africa for hundreds of years more. China's economic and military subordination to Western nations in the nineteenth and early twentieth centuries was a relatively brief episode in its long history. China, the argument runs, is now becoming an economic giant once again. American students need to know about China's long-term history of technological innovations, international trade, and economic growth, not in order to grasp the "essence" of Chinese culture but to understand events that significantly affected the direction the human venture was taking.

When he was president of the Social Science Research Council in the late 1980s, Frederic Wakeman warned that we must "remember that 'culture' is itself no longer the sort of thing anthropologists once took it to be: homogeneous, local, well-bounded, and in clear one-on-one correspondence with distinct social units." The world rather has become "deterritorialized," a concept that applies not only to "transnational corporations and money markets, but also to ethnic groups, sectarian allegiances, and political movements, which increasingly operate in ways that transcend specific territorial boundaries and identities."[55] If world history were confined largely to the political master narrative of Europe, how could young Americans possibly understand the developments, ancient and modern, that brought the world to such a condition?

When the council and forum met early in April 1992, discord over the meaning of world history quickly surfaced. Ruth Wattenberg argued that the World History Standards should have an exclusive, overarching theme—the history of democracy. "To grasp these complicated matters," she said, "students need to know and understand a great deal about democracy's roots in Egypt, Greece, and Rome, about its evolution in England and Europe, and about how it has unfolded here.... They need to understand the ideologies, institutions and practices that drive and sustain dictatorships of left and right."[56]

Finn vigorously supported this AFT position. At the same time he attacked cultural relativism, apparently believing that many history teachers and some council members championed the extremes of such an ideology:

> The full story of democracy, neither disguising nor apologizing for its innate superiority to other forms of government, should be the centerpiece of our teaching of history.... There exists today a very dangerous form of pedagogy: one that treats all assertions, however absurd, as equally valid; all information, however spurious, as equally trustworthy; all doctrines, however illogical, as equally worthy of attention; all systems of government, however they have fared historically, as equally valid and praiseworthy. This relativism denies students the moral and intellectual basis on which to evaluate ideas and threatens to erode support for our democratic system of government.... An honest, open, sensible focus on democracy would restore to the study of history the very foundation and direction that this fashionable relativism threatens to destroy.[57]

Other forum members agreed that the story of democracy was indeed important, but too small a vessel to convey all that students need to know about the human past. They held varied views, however, on what the vessel's contents should be. Bill Honig, California's superintendent of public instruction, argued that the history of democracy should be one of several themes in world history. Sara Shoob of the National Association of Elementary School Principals, was even more direct. "While we *must* teach the history and values of Western civilization, we must also teach children about the history and cultures of other nations and about the contributions that a wide variety of people have made to our culture."[58]

Some speakers took a resolutely global view, arguing that the AFT's restrictive world history approach was akin to demanding that math instruction be limited to algebra or science education to the study of chemistry alone. Nguyen Minh Chau of the National Association for Asian and Pacific American Education insisted that "the world history curriculum must be comprehensive and inclusive."[59] Mark Curtis, of the Atlantic Council, warned of the growing impact of international events on Americans' lives. "As a consequence," he said, "knowledge and understanding of history, and the history of international affairs in particular, is essential in preparing competent citizens and leaders for the future."

Marilyn Jo Hitchens of the World History Association contended that the curriculum should be neither a roundup of the histories of various nations nor a global issues course. Rather, "the story of world history is that of human change brought about by man's ongoing fashioning of his environment, and the political, economic, and social systems devised to accomplish that." Howard Spodek, a member of the AHA's focus group on standards, questioned whether "government, and in particular the establishment of democracy" should be the organizing theme.[60] History, he advised, is "more fruitfully [understood] in terms of the *many motivating forces* in human life and the ways in which individuals and groups have sought to attain them."

Clearly forum members were all over the map on the question of what "world history" means. Seeking to find some commonalities among these diverse views, the council, at its May 1992 meeting, wrote a first draft of criteria for world history standards. Criterion 9 stated in part: "Standards in world history should include the history of other democratic systems (e.g., European); the ideologies, institutions and practices that inform democratic and authoritarian forms of government; and the political aspirations of peoples in the nonwestern world." Criterion 13 read, "Standards in world history should include both the history and values of western civilization and the history and cultures of other societies, with the greater emphasis on western civilization, and on the interrelationships between western and nonwestern societies."

Both criteria set off a firestorm. James Gardner of the AHA staff wrote to the council that he found neither one acceptable. The expression "nonwestern" in Criterion 9 should be replaced with "Africa, Asia, and Latin America." Criterion 13 was "entirely problematic." He further warned that the AHA "was not likely to be part of standards with the sort of bias proposed here."[61] The AHA focus group concurred. "World history must be conceived as a truly global history, not as the history of Western civilization with occasional side glances at other cultures 'affected' by the West."[62]

The ASCD focus group agreed. "Adopting Criterion 13 as it is now stated," their report said,

> will open up a "multicultural minefield." The current emphasis among history and social studies teachers is to move away from an ethnocentric approach to history.... It is important that students display equal understanding of their own Western values and culture as well as those of non-Western societies.[63]

By June 1992, a large number of reviewers had weighed in on these and other issues, submitting more than five hundred pages of analysis and recommendations. The council was under great pressure to reach consensus on the standards criteria because the three task forces of teachers were about to converge on UCLA to begin the work of drafting the standards. William McNeill, widely regarded as the founder of the world history movement, counseled strongly against giving Western civilization greater emphasis than others, "at least for the period before A.D. 1500." The West, he pointed out,

> is not privileged. Indeed, we are a minority in the world and ought to know it. For the past five centuries there is reason of course to make European expansion central to the study of World History—because it was. Before that time, however, other civilizations enjoyed primacy and Europeans were comparatively backward—and acknowledged it by borrowing what they could from afar. This sort of interchange among peoples is, in my view, the main thread of World History and ought to be followed as such.[64]

McNeill's views carried much weight. Consequently, Criterion 13 was changed to delete the reference to "greater emphasis on western civilization." The criterion now read: "Standards in world history should include both the history and values of western civilization and the history and cultures of other societies, and the relations among them." The teacher task forces were left to work out the problem of how much attention to give to the various civilizations. Because no voices rose in opposition to this line of action, the council so agreed.

Though Wattenberg's and Finn's proposal to organize world history around the study of Western democracy did not prevail, Criterion 9 was revised to encourage the study of political history in world as well as in U.S. history. "Standards in world history," it now stated, "should include different patterns of political institutions (including varieties of democracy and authoritarianism) and ideas and aspirations developed by civilizations in all parts of the world. Standards in United States history should address the history of the nation's democratic system, its historical origins and intellectual roots, and the continuing development of its ideals, institutions, controversies and practices."

Back to Summer School

Assuming—erroneously, as it later turned out—that problems with the criteria were now solved, the council authorized the curriculum task forces to assemble at UCLA in July 1992 to begin writing standards. Drawn from schools throughout the nation, the forty teachers formed working teams. UCLA made available to them library collections and a bank of computers. Professors of history from various universities mingled with teacher groups, guiding them through the scholarship of recent decades and suggesting approaches to complex historical problems. In lively give-and-take sessions, teachers and professors of history worked each day to determine what young Americans should know about world and U.S. history. The insights of the veteran classroom teachers were critical to the project's success.

That summer the U.S. group, chaired by Nash, completed first drafts of standards and illustrative teaching activities for two eras of U.S. history. Progress on world history proved more difficult. The problem lay not so much with the task force as with the council's failure to develop more than general criteria to guide the summer's work.

The previous spring, the council had asked members of all the participating organizations to review *Lessons from History*, one of the volumes recommended by the NCEST History Task Force as a starting point for the standards. Reviews ranged from enthusiastic endorsement to outright rejection of *Lessons'* approach to world history. Fearing future problems in gaining consensus, the council decided to begin afresh. It developed criteria to advise the task force but had insufficient time to work out detailed guidelines. The teachers labored that summer to agree on a world history framework, but they also ran out of time.

In September, the council gave general approval to the draft standards in U.S. history and recommended disseminating that material for national review while proceeding with development of the remaining eras. World history was still the great puzzle. Recognizing the problems the task force had encountered, the council decided to establish an ad hoc world history committee to hammer out a framework with Michael Winston, vice president emeritus of Howard University, as chair. Members included three elementary and high school teachers from the task force, six historians from the council, and three more with working connections to such groups as the College Board's Pace Setter Project in World History. Four other respected world historians consulted with the committee and reviewed its work.[65]

Meeting three times in as many months, the Winston committee composed a document that the council enthusiastically endorsed in January 1993. Dividing the long sweep of human history into several major eras, the report provided lists of important questions to guide the task force in writing standards. While giving significant consideration to the West, the report included all other major civilizations and the interactions among them. It did not, however, project "identity politics" onto the world stage, assigning so much space to Civilization A and so much to Culture B. Proceeding era by era rather than culture by culture, it made the crucial points that societies have always developed within cultural, economic, and political contexts larger than themselves and that understanding large-scale changes and turning points (such as the worldwide spread of technological innovations or democratic ideas) requires a wider screen than any single civilization.

A Battle Rejoined

The Winston report could not have come at a more timely moment. Even while the committee was writing it, the old war over the place of Western civilization in the World History Standards had reemerged, but this time with the potential to shatter the coalition of groups working on the project. At its September 1992 meeting, the council had taken up a memo from the AHA's James Gardner requesting further revision of Criterion 13 so that the statement would endorse the study of values not only in Western civilization but in other societies as well.[66] The council made the change with two dissenting votes.

Six weeks later, Robert Blackey, vice president of the AHA's Teaching Division, informed Crabtree and Nash that the division was "adamantly opposed" to the Eurocentrism contained in Criterion 13, even as amended in September, and that the AHA was likely to oppose any document that contained such language.[67] Unless this problem was resolved, Blackey warned, his division would convey its concerns to the funders of the history standards project and make AHA's opposition public. In the meantime, he would present to the AHA Council a recommendation for withdrawal from the project altogether.

The council was caught between the AHA leaders' intransigence and strong opposition from certain council members to any further compromise. Nash, attempting to fashion a way out of the impasse, acknowledged that the views of the nation's oldest and largest historical association could not be lightly regarded. He reminded the council of Lincoln's reputed remark when, at the start of the Civil War, reporters asked the president if God was on the side of the Union. Lincoln quipped that he hoped so but that he *must* have Kentucky. Pondering this bit of wisdom, the council agreed to invite the AHA officers to its February 1993 meeting to try to resolve the issue.

The association accepted the offer, though in the meantime three of its elected officials wrote to the council to reiterate their concern over Criterion 13.[68] Its juxtaposing of "Western civilization" and "other civilizations," they wrote, established a two-tiered conceptualization that conveyed an "unintended and inappropriate signal of 'Eurocentric bias' at odds with the concept of cultural interdependence and the global approach advocated by specialists in the field." To resolve the dispute, they proposed compromise language that council member Carol Gluck had advanced at an earlier meeting. She suggested shifting the wording from "Standards in world history should include both the history and values of western civilization and of other societies, and the relations among them" to "Standards in world history should treat the history and values of diverse civilizations, including those of the West, and should especially address the interactions among them."

At its February meeting, the council reached no consensus on Criterion 13. Rather, it agreed to revisit this issue following a national review of the criteria and standards completed so far. The heat of this conflict over the words, syntax, and commas of a three-line statement clearly demonstrated to all present how deep were the associations in this country between our national identity and the Western tradition.

Although the AHA leaders left the February session disappointed, the chances of finding a satisfactory resolution were advanced when the council adopted the Winston report at the same meeting. The council was in effect casting the die for an inclusive, global approach to the world history standards. In the ensuing months, the NCSS and the Organization of American Historians (OAH) joined the AHA and the ASCD in calling for revision of Criterion 13.[69] When the council met again in June 1993, it adopted the wording that Gluck had recommended.

After months of stormy confrontations, the "grand alliance" remained firm and the project moved forward. Reflecting later on these events, council member Fred Risinger observed that

> the issues embedded in this criterion threatened to destroy the coalition of organizations so carefully put together by the project co-directors....
> There were several times when I (along with other Council members) were ready to tell the AHA representatives that their concerns had been heard and that they were welcome to stay or leave, but that the Council's work was moving forward. Fortunately, [others] were more patient than I. As I reread [the criterion] today, it sounds so non-controversial.[70]

Perhaps the larger point was that agreement on this issue, though protracted and messy, was a characteristically American exercise in civil discourse. It was a *public* debate among educator-citizens, not a closed-door wrangle settled by high officials of state.

Historical Facts or Historical Thinking:
Dispelling a False Dichotomy

Besides confronting issues of multiculturalism and global history, the council was also obliged to scrutinize fundamental assumptions about the relationship in history education between content mastery and critical thinking. Back in the nineteenth century, historians had founded their profession on the idea that history was an "argument with the past," a process of reconstructing, analyzing, interpreting, and contesting events that could never be wholly known or understood, simply because they could not be brought back intact into the living present. To be convincing, knowledge of the past had to be based on evidence, but facts were useful only insofar as they helped explain something that people cared about. For a hundred years or more, history educators have been finding their subject worth teaching precisely because it required of their students reflective thought and lively dispute.

Even so, American culture has also exhibited a contrasting tradition, the idea that history, especially the history of the nation, consists of "the truth," a body of fixed information, objectively known, and that the job of educators is simply to train children's memories in the facts they need to be loyal and industrious citizens. We have seen in earlier chapters how this line of thinking usually carried with it the naive notion that previous generations of Americans were all in agreement on the national narrative; that only the present community of intellectuals encourages students to question hallowed traditions and "plain truths." A certain amount of analytical thinking might be allowed, traditionalists reasoned, but students must absorb a rich fund of "basic facts" before starting to think about them. Pour in the facts and, when the brain is brimming over, students might then use their heads to consider what the facts signify.

For experienced social studies teachers the importance of facts—that is, historical evidence, authentic information, and specific names, times, and places—was never in question. Teachers also knew, however, that passive learning and excessive attention to fragmented factoids simply turn students off. "Drill the facts" history flew in the face of a half century of research into how learning occurs and how information and ideas are remembered.

The council had no trouble agreeing in general on what history teachers should strive to achieve. Good teaching, it asserted, should give students opportunities to examine the historical record for themselves, raise questions about it, and marshal evidence in support of their answers. Students should consult journals, diaries, government documents, artifacts, historic sites, and elderly citizens, approaching these sources imaginatively and comparing different points of view. Good teaching, moreover, should encourage pupils to reflect on the interpretative nature of history, analyze and compare historians' competing views, and thereby hone skills of critical judgment. Good teaching should equip students with a solid knowledge base of information, but also demonstrate that facts are only the raw material of historical understanding.

The agreement of the council and the forum on this broader definition of historical literacy put them squarely behind every commission that had addressed pedagogical reform in recent decades. The National Education Goals had called upon the schools to ensure that all students learn to use their minds well—to reason, solve problems, apply knowledge, and write and communicate effectively.[71] Similarly, the NCEST History Task Force that Lynne Cheney chaired called for standards that "encourage interpretation and analysis as part of the study of history, and not just the learning of basic facts."[72]

Though broad agreement existed among the project's participating groups on the need for investigative, analytical history education, a good deal of collegial nudging and elbowing still occurred over the proper relationship of thinking skills to content. At its June 1993 meeting, the council considered more than five hundred pages of recommendations received from the April–May 1993 national review of the 327-page draft document. Unlike earlier drafts, this one included three standards in historical thinking: *conducting historical inquiries and research, engaging in causal reasoning*, and, *engaging in sound historical interpretation*. With few exceptions, reviewers judged these standards to be inadequately developed. They recommended greater specificity as well as clarification of how these skills would be related to the content of U.S. and world history.

School supervisors and curriculum specialists urged the council to develop stand-alone thinking standards that would elaborate on the meaning of these skills. They were convinced that many teachers had no clear understanding of what historical thinking involved or of how students might demonstrate it. Other participants, however, feared separating subject matter from analytical skills. The CCSSO recommended merging content and skills in the standards to "avoid creating a false dichotomy between the two." Thinking skills, the CCSSO argued, are the *tools* students use to bring meaning to inert facts. But students must have something to think about, and "the key to engaging in critical thinking is depth of content."[73] The NCSS also insisted on the marriage of content and thinking skills, arguing that "content without process too easily becomes meaningless."[74]

Recognizing that emphasis on these skills would require a new approach to history teaching, both groups urged the development of examples that would show teachers how to unify analytical and content standards in their lessons. The National Math Standards included lengthy "vignettes" to illustrate implementation. As teachers reviewed the new drafts of the history standards, they found teaching examples such an invaluable part of the book that they demanded even more. The council decided to oblige. If teachers found the activities a boon, they would use the standards, and not shove them in their bottom desk drawers—the fate, too often, of curriculum guidelines emanating from district and state offices.

Over the next eight months, Crabtree and Nash worked with the assistance of council members to draft five standards in historical thinking:

1. Chronological thinking—understanding the temporal order in which events unfolded and knowing how to measure and calculate calendar time;
2. Historical comprehension—understanding the "who, what, when, where, and why" of historical trends and events, and learning how to draw on literature, music, art, maps, primary documents, and mathematical data in the study of history;
3. Historical analysis and interpretation—differentiating between historical facts and interpretations, considering multiple perspectives, evaluating debates among historians, assessing the credibility of historical accounts, and respecting the provisional nature of historical interpretations;
4. Historical research capabilities—developing the skills to gather, organize, analyze, and interpret historical data;
5. Historical issues analysis and decision making—identifying issues that people have confronted in the past and present, bringing historical perspectives to bear on these issues, considering alternative actions people might have taken, and assessing the consequences of decisions made.

Teachers in the task forces created teaching examples for each of these standards and linked them to the content guidelines for U.S. and world history. A national review of the five standards in April 1994 indicated that a consensus was emerging. The OHT judged that the "revised History Thinking Standards have transformed what was one of the weakest sections of the previous report to a new area of strength. We are pleased to endorse this section of the report without any suggestions for revision."[75] The OAH found the standards "clear, accessible, and substantive. Expectations were set very high, but this was admirable. Students should be challenged, and the Standards do just that."[76]

The CS4 reported unanimous support for the skills standards from across the nation.[77] "Historical thinking is wonderful in the document," was the report from Colorado.[78] "The thinking standards are the most important part of the entire document" was the assessment from Maryland.[79] "My overall reaction to this section is YES!" said the report from Maine.[80] Hawaii, California, Missouri, Michigan, Wyoming, and others concurred. The support of these leaders was particularly gratifying because they were the social studies line officers who would later have much to say about the use of the guidelines in their own states.

History for Young Children

A critical decision confronting the project was how to design history standards for children in kindergarten through fourth grade. No one on the council questioned the importance of history for children. That battle had been won in the curriculum guidelines adopted shortly before by such bellwether states as Florida and California. The long drought of history education for the youngest children was coming to an end. Only one question remained: how best to formulate standards that would help children take their first steps into the American and global past.

Accordingly, the NCHS and the council formed a K–4 task force of teachers with special expertise in working with primary pupils. Sara Shoob, an elementary school vice principal from Virginia, chaired the group with the assistance of Crabtree and Linda Symcox, assistant director of the NCHS. Understanding the importance of a unified curriculum for young children, the task force held meetings with project leaders developing national standards in geography and civics to foster links among the three disciplines. Agreements reached over the next two years produced a document that was spared virtually all the rancor later visited upon the U.S. and World history standards for grades 5–12. Displeasing almost nobody, the K–4 guidelines attracted no attention from the media.

The media should have taken notice. Basic principles guiding the development of the K–4 standards went beyond the traditional "expanding environment" pedagogy, which from the 1930s had prescribed that youngsters study their family in first grade, their neighborhood in second, their community in third, and their state in fourth. The premises of this curriculum were fast collapsing as American classrooms filled with children newly arrived from virtually every part of the world, and as movies and TV regularly introduced youngsters to distant times and places. Collapsing too were the hoary assumptions that historical perspectives were beyond children's ken. New understandings of children's capabilities were fast expanding the reach of the K–4 curriculum beyond the "here and now" to the distant and the long ago.

For these reasons, the K–4 task force affirmed the ability of young children to differentiate time present, time past, and time long, long ago—the earliest stages of chronological thinking. It stressed the importance of centering young children's studies on people—the history of families and individuals, ordinary and extraordinary, who once lived in children's own community, nation, and world. It endorsed the power of stories, myths, legends, and biographies to capture children's imagination and immerse them in the recent and long-ago past. It emphasized the importance of introducing historical artifacts, illustrations, written records, and historical sites to give children access to the lives of people in the past. And it affirmed youngsters' ability to formulate questions for study, marshal information, compare and contrast past and present, explain historical causes and consequences, and create historical narratives of their own.

The Council Confronts D-Day

In May 1994, the council assembled for its thirteenth and final meeting. National reviews of the latest drafts of the U.S. and K–4 standards had been completed just one month before. The time had come to decide upon publication. Present on this important occasion were members of the forum, the chairs of the nine focus groups, and a number of teachers and historians from the three task forces. Representatives of the two funding agencies were there as usual, as were the executive directors of the organizations participating in the project. Following their normal procedures, the cochairs opened the meetings to the press, the public, and any interested groups. Ross Dunn was attending his first and only council meeting. He had worked with two standards drafting groups the previous summer and fall, and the codirectors had invited him to serve as a coordinating editor to lead small groups in refining the world history document.

Support for publication of the U.S. standards—the fifth draft, reflecting two years of revisions made in response to public reviews—was broad-based and enthusiastic. Joyce McCray, executive director of the Council for American Private Education, summed up her organization's endorsement in a single word: "Bravo!"[81] The private schools, she said, judged these standards to be for *all* the nation's children, inclusive of our "great democratic values," yet they were flexible enough to permit private schools to develop their own religious values as they saw fit. The private schools, she assured the council, "support the process and are going to support the product as well."[82]

Sister Catharine McNamee, president of the National Catholic Educational Association, reported its assessment of the standards as a very positive contribution, challenging yet attainable, and a valuable resource for teachers.[83] Ruth Kurth of the Lutheran Education Association reported that teachers found the standards to be an excellent resource, usable and easily understood.[84] Administrators judged them to be comprehensive and well-written. The Lutheran University Professors Division appraised the standards to be "of great academic value for religious schools" and said that although they gave less attention than the group would have liked to the importance of religion in U.S. history, they offered "enough flexibility to enable [the schools] to demonstrate the enormous influence religion has had on the personal lives of Americans and on the nation."

Ruth Wattenberg echoed McCray's assessment in her opening remarks: "Bravo! I really think you have done a tremendous job in pulling together an extremely admirable document and we are very, very excited about it."[85] Judging the standards to be "a terrific resource for teachers," her report on behalf of the AFT concluded, "For the most part, these standards simply represent what a good history education should contain; there are not many standards that critics could point to and say they are not essential to a good history education."[86]

The CS4 reported "unanimous support for the U.S. history standards," and concluded that the document "breathes with a love of history and a sense of [its] importance as a field for life-long learning."[87] The AHA applauded improvements in the fifth draft and urged timely publication. Both the K–4 and the U.S. standards, the OAH reported, "met with general approval."[88] The OHT gave its unanimous endorsement.[89]

Various critical suggestions came forth to trim, expand, or modify particular historical content in the U.S. document. Nash assured the group that such recommendations would be addressed in subsequent weeks. Chester Finn, however, had more sweeping objections.[90] "What I believe can only be fairly termed political correctness and relativism rears its head in too many places," he said. "We've got the usual manifestations of excessive attention to fashionable groups and obscure individuals who need to be there for proportional purposes." He urged the council to consider how these standards would "go down with the Chamber of Commerce? With the American Legion? By callers to the Rush Limbaugh show? By people running for office against the governors, legislators and school board members on whose watch these standards are incorporated into the schools of, say, Tennessee?" Finn recommended considering how the Wichita Rotary Club or the "worst critic among Rush Limbaugh's audience" was likely to react and tailor the standards accordingly.

No one rose to second Finn's views, but a number made rejoinders. Sam Banks pointed out that "these standards have never been directed to proportionality but to *inclusiveness*, to a factual rendering of our history."[91] McNamee urged that there "not be any reduction in the emphasis . . . on cultural diversity, or on the contributions of various ethnic and racial groups that make up our American society. I would not like to see any of that changed or reduced."[92] Janet Crouse reported that the "National PTA appreciates the focus on diverse racial and ethnic cultures." Respecting and valuing cultural differences, the association advised, "requires confronting events in our own history not worth celebrating. Ultimately it requires learning that diversity does not divide us in a democracy but strengthens us."[93] The Lutheran Education Association representative cautioned against "dumbing down" the national standards in the mistaken belief that they would then be more acceptable to the citizen Chester Finn characterized as "Joe Six-Pack." "I think these standards will stand on their own," Kurth said. "Maybe it's time . . . that we remember the general public is intelligent and will react sensibly to good curriculum materials."[94]

Later events suggest that some council members were more sympathetic to Finn's opinions than they indicated during the meeting. His blunt words were indeed a portent of the political melee shortly to come. At the moment, however, the U.S. and K–4 standards were clearly sailing through this review. Sherrin Marshall, the project officer for the ED, concluded the day's session on a high note:

> I wanted to say what enormously high regard I have for this Project. Being very familiar with the other standards projects, I have had a chance to compare how this one has worked and I think that much of the contentiousness, as your [codirectors] today referred to it, has come from the fact that this Project has been extremely open about involving many groups, many individuals, many points of view. It's important for us all to remember as this Project comes to a close that consensus means that we don't always all get our way and get it to work out exactly the way each of us would individually like. This whole process of "give and take" is, I think, going to have a lot to do with the ultimate success of these standards.[95]

If "give and take" was required for success, the World History Standards had seen plenty of it already. Following approval of the Winston committee's helpful guidelines in February 1993, the world history task force had worked hard to make up for lost time. Although a year behind the U.S. group, it had by the May meeting completed standards and teaching examples for all but the twentieth-century era. The draft had benefited from multiple council reviews and reactions at a number of professional conferences. But it was far too long and still needed work, and the task force knew it. Now, as the council turned to that document, nerves noticeably tightened.

Throughout part of the second and all of the third day, members of the council, forum, and task force engaged one another in friendly but intense debate on the conception and form of the world history draft. Theodore Rabb, a council member and professor of European history at Princeton, urged a sharp tightening of the entire document by developing the "connective tissues" that would support a coherent world history course. He also found weakness in the document's "diminishment of Western history" in the later eras, and urged greater attention to that tradition. John Patrick, director of the Social Studies Development Center at Indiana University, agreed, arguing, "If we would foster a global-centric view of history, we necessarily must show the profound impact of Europe and things European on the shape of today's world." Several historians called for improvements in the non-Western content as well. For example, Carol Gluck urged significant changes in what she saw as serious problems in the treatment of nineteenth-century Japanese history.

One member wondered whether the task force ought to rethink the document from the ground up. Sensing an opportunity to roll back decisions the council had reached a year earlier, advocates of a return to the Western-Civ-as-world-history model enthusiastically supported this idea. As he had a year earlier, Bill Honig argued in favor of a thematic approach to world history focused on the development of democracy and modernization as a way to unify the document and increase its emphasis on Western achievements. This turn in the discussion sent protests ricocheting around the room. Representatives of the NCSS, the CCSSO, and the AHA all rose to oppose any retreat from the global approach agreed upon two years earlier and reaffirmed by the council in 1993. Don Woodruff, Jean Johnson, and Gloria Sesso—teachers who had helped develop the standards and had witnessed the strong support the drafts received at teachers' conferences—spoke heatedly in their defense.

At this tense moment, Rabb assured the council, "We are in very fundamental agreement around this table. No one that I heard has argued for a return to the 'rise of the West' narrative." Rabb's statement served to turn the discussion to serious consideration of how specific eras in the current draft should be improved. Jeff Thomas, the project officer for NEH, urged the council to proceed with publication of the guidelines. "In many respects," he said,

I consider this, from a layman's point of view, a remarkable document. It is remarkable in its ambition, in its clarity, in the degree to which you have been able to obtain the consensus, the enthusiasm of teachers and, to perhaps a lesser extent, of scholars around a good deal of this material. I would simply echo what Ted [Rabb] has said and what Carol [Gluck] and others have said. It is incumbent upon you to get the history right. But once you do that, I would go out on the streets with this document and say, 'This is our first shot.' Even when it goes out on the street it will still be a first draft. And then a couple of years later there will be a second draft. This is not the last word on this. Other projects have gone through this same process with this same kind of internal discomfort with one aspect or another of the project, and yet they moved forward. So I would urge you to move forward.

John Patrick spoke up again, and his remarks served to end debate on the matter.

There is no doubt that this is not yet a perfect document. But there is also no doubt in my mind that it may be the least imperfect document that we can achieve at this time and within the time limits under which we work. We have four months to fix this document before we present it to the public for what I think is going to be one of the most exciting debates on history in the schools that we've ever had in this country. This is not a one-shot project. It is the beginning of a continuous discussion about priorities and strategies in the teaching of history in the schools.... So my conclusion is, let's go forward and fuel the debate we ought to have.

Patrick could not have been more prophetic.

One other decision the council made turned out to be fateful. Participating groups differed on the handling of the examples illustrating how teachers might use the standards. The AFT representative urged that in order to slim down the U.S. and world history guidelines the examples be published either at the end of the books or in a separate volume. Reactions were mixed, some supporting the recommendation, others arguing that it was important to keep the examples where they were for reasons earlier agreed to, namely "to help educators and citizens understand that the content standards were calling for a fundamentally different type of instruction [than was common in the schools] and to show that content knowledge was not being sacrificed" by the emphasis on historical thinking.[96]

The council's way out of this conflict was to recommend publication of three versions of the standards—a short "executive summary"; a "basic edition" of the standards for school boards, administrators, legislators, parents, and other interested citizens; and an "expanded edition" that would include the activities for teachers and curriculum developers. In other words, three audiences, three editions. The council also agreed that the project directors should publish the expanded edition first.

Summer's Windup

The summer of 1994 involved a whirlwind of revisions, reviews, and more revisions. Nash, who became director of the NCHS on Crabtree's retirement in June, arranged for editorial teams from each of the three task forces to come to UCLA to make final changes and ready the standards for publication in the early fall. The K–4 team, under the leadership of Sara Shoob, worked to accommodate suggestions for additional historical literature and for deeper scientific content (adding, for example, such twentieth-century achievements as those of Jonas Salk, Thomas Edison, the American space ventures, and the walk on the moon). The reviews of this document had already been highly favorable, and the team rapidly completed the work.

The U.S. task force spent much time on strengthening the standards' treatment of the American West and religion's role in American history. The teaching examples for the late twentieth century were far from complete, and this job was undertaken at breakneck speed. The team was guided not only by the recommendations received during the May council meetings but also by a number of letters received in the early summer. Diane Ravitch, for example, had written to advise changes in a small number of illustrative teaching activities where she found a partisan tone.[97] The editorial team worked to accommodate these concerns.

The most intensive task of the summer, however, was directed toward the World History Standards. To complete guidelines for the twentieth-century era, a team of about fifteen educators gathered at the NCHS offices for a week of intensive work with Dunn, Nash, and Symcox, assistant director of the center. To achieve the greater coherence Rabb had recommended, Dunn drafted a series of short statements to introduce each historical era and demonstrate how it addressed broad patterns of change in human society over the ages. By late June, a new draft was ready and mailed to all members of the council, the forum, the focus groups, and the officers of the organizations cooperating in this project.

By mid-July reports began arriving at the NCHS offices. Most were highly supportive but also constructively critical and insightful. The National Council for History Education reported, for example, that the "overwhelming opinion" of their focus group was that "the draft statement is an important and original achievement giving serious new direction to history education. Individual reports make suggestions that the drafters should consider, but the main lines of opinion are [that it is] a remarkable piece of work for which the authors deserve the profound gratitude of all of us who work as teachers in the field of world history—from Grade Five through graduate school."[98] The OHT wrote that it "applauds the innovative work on standards for teaching world history. We strongly endorse this articulation of the standards."[99] The CCSSO found the new draft to be "greatly improved over the last draft and far superior in design and direction, a true world history," with "religions treated very well, and good attention paid to civilizations and their interactions over time."[100]

Two council members who had found serious flaws in the May draft expressed support. Theodore Rabb called in to say, "I think we are really close to what I think will be the final version of the standards." He raised three minor points that were readily remedied.[101] Carol Gluck wrote that the revised standards "look 'worlds' better than the last set, and the introductions to each era are terrific."[102] Michael Winston was equally supportive, commenting that this latest version was "a significant improvement over its predecessors" and praising the introductions to each era. They "give focus to the standards and help readers to grasp a sense of how they work together as a coherent approach to a very untidy set of subjects, since world history is far from being a single subject."[103]

By contrast, Paul Gagnon, the AFT's close adviser, wrote a withering and uncompromising critique of the document, pronouncing it "deeply flawed" and deficient on recent history, European history, political history, and intellectual history. In his rejection of virtually every aspect of the consensus achieved, he argued that the standards diminished the ideas, institutions, and achievement of Western civilization by giving too much attention to Asia, Africa, and the Americas and to interactions among peoples. He judged the whole enterprise to be "a great chance lost."[104]

Gagnon's assessment was so contrary to fundamental decisions the council had made over two and a half years that to satisfy him would have required sacrificing the hard-won support of the vast majority of organizations, teachers, and scholars involved in constructing the standards. His critique was significant, however, because officers of the AFT and the Educational Excellence Network adopted it as their own. Albert Shanker wrote from AFT headquarters in August, "We associate ourselves completely with the comments of Paul Gagnon."[105] Chester Finn wrote that he was "largely critical" of the standards in world history and found himself "in complete agreement with [Gagnon's] every point."[106] Thus, the project

headed into its final phase with these three educators profoundly dissatis-
fied with the product.

Dunn, Nash, and Symcox spent much of August completing world
history revisions, continuing consultations by fax, phone, and E-mail, and
holding office meetings with task force members and academic advisers.
They strengthened guidelines for the study of Western democratic institutions, enhanced twentieth-century political history, and made numerous
small changes to ensure accuracy and clarity.

Favorable reviews of these revisions convinced the project directors
that the time had come to go to press. David Baumbach, an experienced
teacher and council member, read the changes and reported, "Overall, I
think the latest draft is superb."[107] Ramsey Selden, speaking for the CCSSO
announced, "This document will, as it should, set the standard for a true
world history."[108] Jerry Bentley, a Renaissance historian and editor of the
Journal of World History, wrote, "I enthusiastically endorse the draft standards, which I believe represent precisely the approach that American
schools should take to history instruction in the late twentieth century and
beyond."[109]

Comments from William McNeill, dean of the world history movement
since the 1960s, were truly poignant:

> The overall sense of a REAL world history is with me, overwhelmingly
> so. This is what my professional life was mainly directed towards and be-
> hold, you have now put it before the schools of this country as a standard
> to be striven after. What a heady prospect! If teaching actually follows this
> direction, then one of the things I felt we most needed will in fact be on
> its way to accomplishment. So I am indeed pleased and proud of this
> work. It represents an enormous advance on older visions of the human
> past.[110]

Looking back on the process by which the standards were developed
council member Mary Bicouvaris characterized it as a "near textbook version of conflict management."[111] The 1989 National Teacher of the Year and
a strong advocate of Western civilization curriculum, she had viewed the
entire project from within and indeed wrote her doctoral dissertation on it.
She observed:

> Listening to the testimonies of the representatives of the National Forum
> caused a swelling of emotions regarding the beliefs, hopes, and aspira-
> tions of the groups that make America. Only a steel heart and a closed
> mind would have been untouched by both those who articulated the idea

of *E Pluribus Unum*, and those who simply asked, "Let my people, too, into America's story."

Allowing full expression of many points of view, the project had, she concluded,

> fulfilled its mission of reaching broad consensus on the contentious issues of content vs. process, the place of western civilization in the teaching of world history, and the inclusion of minority contributions in the teaching of U.S. history. The army of participants in the process represented as broad a spectrum as one could expect to find in a project with limited time and resources, and the resulting national history standards are truly the product of their consensus.[112]

CHAPTER 8

The Right-Wing Assault

Now what I want is facts. Teach these boys and girls nothing but the
facts. Facts alone are wanted in life. Plant nothing else and root out
everything else. . . . This is the principle on which I bring up my own
children. . . . Stick to the facts, sir.

—Mr. Gradgrind's address at the opening of his school,
Charles Dickens, *Hard Times* (1854)

To judge by Lynne Cheney's *Wall Street Journal* article and Rush Limbaugh's subsequent radio and TV attacks in late October 1994, the about-to-be-published National History Standards were the product of a misguided effort or a widespread conspiracy. Either the nation's most honored teachers, scholars, and professional leaders had taken leave of their senses or Cheney and Limbaugh had something more than the historical education of American kids on their agenda.

History Standards Besieged

To those who had no copy of the standards, the choice was either to accept at face value Cheney's and Limbaugh's allegations or to await publication and judge for themselves. A few citizens, though they could not yet have seen the documents, jumped to conclusions even grimmer than Cheney or Limbaugh had made.

On November 8, the *Wall Street Journal* carried four letters to the editor under the provocative headline, "The History Thieves."[1] The first, by Balint Vazsonyi, senior fellow at the Potomac Foundation, likened the standards to "an amnesia-inducing drug, to be administered on a national scale without hypodermic needles." The standards writers, wrote Vazsonyi, had taken a page out of the book "developed in the councils of the Bolshevik and Nazi parties and successfully deployed on the youth of the Third Reich and the Soviet Empire. The recipe called for schools that dispense not knowledge but a compendium of selected events, personalities and interpretations. More important, knowledge was eliminated of such events and personalities as were deemed to have no usefulness by the ideologues of the Nazi or Bolshevik party (which also gave us the concept of political correctness). . . . Because it has worked every time, it is this same recipe [that the] 'National Standards' seeks to dispense to America."

Vazsonyi offered no specific examples from the standards of mind poisoning. Likewise, Kim Weissman and J. D. Dampman's letters gave no evidence to support their charges. "Now, thanks to Mrs. Cheney's revelations," wrote Weissman,

> we see the full scope of their subterfuge and their warped vision of America. We learn that their 'standards' are nothing more than a cynical ploy to indoctrinate children with their own hatred of America; to steal the American birthright from the children of our country; to teach our children to feel guilt over their own heritage. Now the special interest pressure groups seek, through Goals 2000, to complete the balkanization of America. The rising ethnic tensions and violence in America today are a direct result of the successes that the multiculturalists have already enjoyed. Are we prepared to allow the haters of America to dictate how American history will be taught to our children?

"Kudos to the clever crafters of the National Standards for United States History," wrote Dampman. "From the tone of Mrs. Cheney's editorial, I assume that these guardians of political correctness made little or no mention of the Declaration of Independence. . . . I am alarmed by a vision of a land filled with the Sierra Club's equivalent of the 'Hitler Youth.'" The history standards, it seemed, were fast becoming something of a national Rohrhach test, where critics freely projected their own deepest fears and discontents.

Attacks on the standards quickly became a media war, as conservative syndicated columnists immediately waded in. John Leo, Charles Krauthammer, and John Fonte all hit the op-ed pages in the first two weeks of November 1994. Krauthammer, under the eye-catching title, "History Hijacked," recalled the leaders in the Bush administration who had pushed for national standards to restore excellence in America's schools. "Beware what you wish for," Krauthammer wryly observed.[2] The National History Standards, he said, had been hijacked by the educational establishment and turned into a classic of political correctness. "The whole document strains to promote the achievements and highlight the victimization of the country's preferred minorities, while straining equally to degrade the achievements and highlight the flaws of the white males who ran the country for its first two centuries."

History standards and national politics
The Christian Science Monitor, September 21, 1995

"But even more corrosive than the ethnic cheerleading and the denigration of American achievements," Krauthammer continued, "is the [standards'] denigration of learning itself." He based this statement on a comment that Gary B. Nash, codirector of the standards project, made during a televised debate with Lynne Cheney. In arguing against the "traditional emphasis on dates, facts, places, and events," Nash had proposed

"[L]et's have them discuss really important, momentous turning points in American history." In place of the old "passive" history of events and facts, Krauthammer said, "Nash wants to have mock trials, to stage debates, to get kids 'even writing history themselves.' . . . but how can they discuss anything without first having mastered dates, facts, places, and events?"

Had Krauthammer consulted the documents themselves, he would have found that a major standard in historical thinking specifically called for students to "identify who was involved, what happened, where it happened, what events led to these developments, and what consequences or outcomes followed," in short, to base historical study firmly on rules of evidence. The standards, furthermore, encouraged students not only to identify the who, what, where, and when of the past but also to shape such raw evidence into patterns of meaning and thereby make sense of history. In effect, the guidelines warned that the easiest way to turn young people off to history is to set them to work merely memorizing information and loading it into workbooks. Krauthammer apparently did not believe that actively engaging students in the stuff of history—researching historical records and documents for themselves, re-creating significant historical events, and analyzing the past in essays of their own—would further the goal of historical literacy. His article drew outraged responses from historians and educators who wrote that he himself needed an education in what "historical thinking" was about.[3]

John Fonte, an education consultant who received a Ph.D. in history in the 1970s but had almost no publications in the discipline, reportedly identified himself in a meeting of the conservative National Association of Scholars as "the person who did the analysis of the standards for Cheney." She soon appointed him executive director of a committee she was forming to assess all national standards. Fonte's indictment, carried by a number of newspapers in early November, sounded much like Cheney's article. Though acknowledging the importance of including "previously neglected groups and individuals," and stating that we "should examine our country's tragedies as well as its triumphs," he condemned just such inclusions in the standards as proof these documents were "steeped in political correctness."[4] For the standards to mention Harriet Tubman or stress the importance of the Seneca Falls women's suffrage convention of 1848 was in Fonte's view "politically correct" rather than recognition of a memorable figure and a momentous political convention in American history.

John Leo joined the fray in a *U.S. News & World Report* article titled "The Hijacking of American History."[5] Though Leo discussed some of the historical content of the standards, like Cheney he drew on the teaching examples for evidence as if they were the standards. He found it offensive, for example, that one teaching activity for grades 7–8 included among the heroic figures of the American Revolution a poor shoemaker (Ebenezer McIntosh) and a woman (Mercy Otis Warren). For Leo, the standards' writers found room for McIntosh (who led the Stamp Act Riots in Boston that launched the revolutionary movement) because he "fits right in as a sort of early Abbie Hoffman and Jerry Rubin."

"No uprising or rebellion seems to go unmentioned in these history standards," Leo continued, "from the important ones (Shays', Nat Turner's) to Leisler's and the Paxton Boys' (don't ask). And it certainly makes sense. If you view America as inherently oppressive, then the only possible national story line is the gradual rise of more and more rebellions against the selfish and hypocritical ruling white elites." What Leo did not note was that the Leisler and Paxton rebellions (included in the teaching examples only, but also in most high school American history texts) were to be "assessed by students for what they revealed of tensions in the English colonies." Leo also failed to mention that Nat Turner's historic slave uprising of 1831 was a rebellion against the landed slaveholders of Virginia.

Leo, like other critics on the Right, grimaced at the mention of Native Americans. "By the allocation of the text, America today seems to be about 65 percent Indian," Leo informed his readers, "with most of the rest of us black, female or oppressive." Fonte cited the mention of Speckled Snake in a teaching example on Cherokee resistance to forced removal during Andrew Jackson's presidency. In fact, Americans of the 1830s knew the name well enough since Speckled Snake was a powerful leader of one of the nation's most populous Indian nations. Concluding his assessment, Leo rendered his verdict: "This won't do. The whole idea was to set unbiased national standards that all Americans could get behind. Along the way, the project was hijacked by the politically correct. It's riddled with propaganda and the American people would be foolish to let it anywhere near their schools."

One critic found the standards "often inspired." But he also judged them to be "loaded with revisionism," including, for example, "no end of stuff about the mistreatment of Japanese Americans" during World War II.[6] In fact, one of the most massive violations of civil rights in American history was presented in one nine-word component of a standard, plus suggested classroom activities that encouraged students to ponder the fragility of civil liberties during wartime.

As the first wave of criticisms blanketed the nation's newspapers and magazines, most Americans keeping up with current events might easily have concluded that what critics dubbed "UCLA's History Standards" were equivalent to the treason texts of the 1920s and 1930s. For citizens who might have missed the press barrage, *Reader's Digest* reprinted Lynne Cheney's article in the January 1995 issue, which arrived in millions of American homes before Christmas 1994.

Through November and December the airwaves covered the controversy, broadcasting both crossfire-style debates and talk shows in which hosts such as Rush Limbaugh railed against the standards and invited call-in commentary. Oliver North and G. Gordon Liddy lambasted the "standards from hell" on their radio shows and sympathized with indignant listeners, most of whom had not seen the books. The Department of Education (ED) in Washington informed Nash that its switchboards were flooded with calls from people angrily asking, "Why are the Feds telling our schools that our kids can't learn about George Washington anymore?"[7]

Adversarial debates at least gave each side a chance to present its views. For weeks, Nash and Cheney duked it out on TV and radio. In one twenty-four hour period beginning on October 26, they went at each other on PBS's *McNeill-Lehrer Report*, ABC's Peter Jennings' *World News Tonight*, the Pat Buchanan radio show, and Bryant Gumbel's *Today* show. Over the next few weeks, Cheney debated other historians such as Joyce Appleby, 1997 president of the American Historical Association (AHA), Alan Brinkley, an American historian at Columbia, and Eric Foner, who had just finished a term as president of the Organization of American Historians.

Answering the Critics

The fury and the speed with which conservatives rallied to Cheney's cause momentarily stunned those involved in the standards project. Nash remembers having lunch with Sheldon Hackney, Lynne Cheney's successor as chairman of the National Endowment for the Humanities (NEH), two months before the standards came off the press. Hackney asked whether any controversy might be expected. Trained to look backward, Nash proved a poor crystal-ball gazer. The U.S. standards, he said, were unlikely to be controversial, given the praise for them in public hearings and reviews over the preceding year, the sense of goodwill and accomplishment within the National Council for History Standards, the affirmations of support from almost all of the organizations participating in the work, and the strong praise voiced by the project officers from the two funding agencies—the NEH and the ED. Moreover, the ED had informed Nash of its intent to place the standards on the Internet for ready access by schools and school boards throughout the nation.

When media attention stoked the controversy, the project leaders were

compelled to respond. Serious misrepresentation of what the standards actually said could not go unanswered. At the same time, however, neither the
project directors nor the participating organizations claimed that these
books were faultless or likely to satisfy everyone. As Carol Gluck, a member of the council, noted, "Consensus does not mean unanimity. The new
history standards were wrestled into their present shape through a lengthy
national dialogue. It is inconceivable that everyone involved would agree
with the final product, which in a decentralized system is not final anyway."[8]
Indeed, the preface to each volume specifically stated:

> In undertaking this process, it was widely agreed that the History Stan-
> dards, as finally drafted, would in fact mark a critical milestone but not
> the final destination in what must be an ongoing, dynamic process of im-
> provement and revision over the years to come. History is an extraordi-
> narily dynamic field today, and standards drafted for the schools must be
> open to continuing development to keep pace with new refinements and
> revisions in the field.[9]

One beneficial side effect of media attention to the critics on the Right
was that responsible journalists, educators, and other citizens were encouraged to scrutinize the books for themselves. These careful probes resulted
not only in recognition of the strengths of the guidelines but also in sound
critical commentary identifying some of the problems in the texts that indeed needed to be addressed.

In the early weeks of the controversy many op-ed writers and talk-show
hosts threw grenades at the standards without reading them, but metropolitan editorial boards and journalists did their homework. These editorials and news reports highlighted misrepresentations of the guidelines and
acknowledged the merits that reviewers found in the books. Though some
journalists perceived some bias or excessive coverage in the teaching examples, they also pointed out that the standards were voluntary and not mandated for the schools, leaving to teachers the choice of what to accept or to
reject.

"We are happy to report that this new inclusiveness [of long-neglected
groups]," said an editorial in the Los Angeles Times, "entails no new, politically correct exclusions."

> When the guidelines suggest that a fifth-grader, to demonstrate knowl-
> edge of the Constitution, be ordered to "draw upon a variety of historical
> sources such as paintings, biographies of major delegates, and narratives
> of the Constitutional Convention to construct a description of who

the delegates were and why they were assembled in Philadelphia," nobody is airbrushed out of the famous paintings. The framers are all still there. . . . As for the Constitution, would that college graduates could all meet the standards for knowledge of the Constitution that are set here![10]

"Cheney, Rush Limbaugh and other detractors of the new standards should be embarrassed," was the editorial opinion of the *Minneapolis Star Tribune*:

With a nit-picking focus on whiffs of political correctness, critics like Cheney have missed the new standards' huge contribution—a whole new pedagogy, far more rigorous, challenging and involving than the dates and names approach of past classroom practice. . . . The scope of world history is much broadened, so that students will no longer be strangers to America's neighbors and world trading partners. . . . That is manifestly the right choice at this point in the American journey. . . . [S]chool districts that choose to adopt these voluntary standards will discover lively history classrooms full of intense debates far more enlightened than the ones already taking place on talk radio.[11]

A *Seattle Post-Intelligencer* editorial focused on the World History Standards and their critics.

The new voluntary standards for teaching world history . . . make significant recommendations that should help broaden Americans' understanding of the world they live in. Such broadening is an act of self-interest, given this nation's need to compete in ever-more interdependent world markets. Yet some narrow-minded critics seem to assume that adding to the study of history the values of other important but neglected cultures somehow diminishes our own Western civilization. . . . This is xenophobic trash. . . . One critic, Gilbert Sewall, . . . complained that some of the guidelines present American and European history "in a fairly unflattering light." History teachers are not press agents. Their business is not flattery; it's to present information.[12]

The *Lincoln Star* of Nebraska agreed. "The standards are intellectually demanding. . . . They do expect senior high students to begin exploring the shades of truth, to look at how the values of a bygone era affect behavior of that time, to learn the difference between facts and interpretations of those facts." The *Star* commended the guidelines for promoting "a broader, more thoughtful look at America's past. The Civil War becomes the story of

black Americans, of white Americans, of Southerners and Union supporters, of foot soldiers and officers, of women on the home front and the battle front. The materials offered in the guidelines better reflects the variety
and complexity that is America than does much of today's public school
curriculum."[13]

An editorial in the *New York Times* emphasized the teaching approach
contained in the standards.

> Reading the standards and support materials is exhilarating. Students will
> rejoice in learning from them, teachers will cherish using them. . . . The
> treasures . . . are found among the 2,600 sample assignments that accom-
> pany the standards. . . . Ms. Cheney skips over these jewels. She also
> ridicules through misrepresentation. . . . Most of what annoys conserva-
> tives can be remediated. For every mock trial of John D. Rockefeller on
> charges of amoral business practices can be added another exercise that
> celebrates the growth of individual freedom and wealth.

The *Times* thought that the standards demanded more than most students could accomplish. "Yet," it concluded, "if this government-sponsored
project errs by demanding too much, that in itself might herald a welcome
change for America's primary and secondary schools."[14]

The *Chicago Tribune* carried a strong endorsement of the standards in an
op-ed page article by Douglas Greenberg, director of the Chicago Historical Society. The guidelines, he wrote, present

> a breathtaking narrative of the American past that reflects the best recent
> scholarly work, as well as more traditional approaches. Far from a simple-
> minded attempt to debunk American history, the document sets loftier
> goals that involve teaching young people to think effectively about his-
> tory. It addresses candidly, and unashamedly, those aspects of our past of
> which we cannot be proud. Slavery and the vicious racism that accompa-
> nied it receive full treatment here, but so does the Constitution and the
> Bill of Rights.

Greenberg noted that the standards drew attention to the role of ordinary people in American history, but argued that

> it does not do so at the expense of the Washingtons, Lincolns and Roo-
> sevelts, who were so influential in shaping our national experience.
> In short, the new U.S. standards offer a balanced view of our national
> history that neither reflexively dismisses nor uncritically praises our ac-

complishments as a people. This bracing approach to America's past promises to excite the imagination and to stimulate the intelligence of school children. [Cheney] is using the standards as an excuse to initiate a discussion that has nothing to do with education and everything to do with politics.[15]

Like the history war in Britain, the standards controversy was not mainly an argument among educators but a popular media event. To succeed as national news for an extended period, the elements of the controversy had to be stripped down, polarized, and translated into provocative sound bites and snappy visual images. In media confrontations the critics had the easier part. They were on the offensive and loaded their indictments with culture-war fighting phrases ("multiculturalists," "revisionists," "politically correct liberals," "educational establishment").

The educators called upon to defend the guidelines in the public arena had a harder job. They were on the defensive, usually called upon to respond to charges. Extreme or misleading accusations had to be answered with reasoned explanation, especially since few citizens had actually *read* the standards in the early months of the controversy. The popular media, however, had little patience for extended academic discourse on the difference between "standards" and "teaching examples" or the importance of teaching about the Ottoman Empire as well as the Italian Renaissance.

In the early days of the controversy Cheney got off a number of well-crafted zingers that could not easily be challenged without explanation. For example, she protested that the U.S. guidelines never identify George Washington as our first president. The charge seemed formulated to suggest that the authors of the standards were either incompetent or wished to conceal facts about Washington from American children. In the narrowest sense Cheney was not wrong; no standard specifically stated that Washington was our first president. But students were asked to examine major issues confronting the young country during his presidency, and much material on him as "father of our country" was to be found in the separate book of K–4 standards. The two books taken together encouraged students to study his life, military leadership, and presidency through stories, biographies, documents, national symbols, and library research. But it was difficult to explain all this in a few seconds of broadcast time.

During the last weeks of 1994, associates of the National Center for History in the Schools (NCHS), as well as teachers and academic historians, began writing op-ed articles. They also started submitting pieces to professional journals and humanities-oriented discussion groups on the Internet in order to engage teachers and scholars in a more dispassionate debate

than was occurring on network radio and TV. There emerged from these efforts a fuller and more systematic rebuttal of the unfounded charges the
critics had made.

In attacking the standards, commentators on the Right linked them to
radical trends in postmodernism, feminism, and multicultural approaches
to education. They characterized the standards as the work of a small band
of radical 1960s-generation professors, centered at UCLA and deeply dedicated to intellectual deconstructionism. In one of his attacks, John Leo
advised readers that "U.S. history is now being written from the counter-
cultural perspective by oppression-minded people who trashed the dean's
office in the 1960s (or wish they had)." In another piece, he declared that the
standards got "to be so bad" because "most of the power and control of the
drafting process stayed in the hands of academics with a heavy ideological
agenda" to "take the West down a peg" and "romanticize the Other."[16]

In demonizing the guidelines, critics found it useful to claim that the
standards were written not just by a rogue group of historians but by a
UCLA cabal in particular, or even by one or two people. John Fonte
repeatedly referred to the guidelines as the "UCLA Standards" and, like
Cheney, assiduously avoided any mention of the central role that schoolteachers played in the project. Nash became "the chief architect" and "main
author" of the standards, thereby shrouding the roles of teachers, administrators, and curriculum experts.

Carol Gluck spoke from firsthand knowledge. "I watched the debate
unfold. Over more than two years, nearly six thousand teachers, administrators, scholars, parents and business leaders had their say in the drafting."
If the standards were hijacked at all, she concluded, "they were hijacked by
America, through an admirable process of open debate that could probably
only happen in the United States."[17] The "actual writing of these standards,"
Gluck pointed out, was the work of "battalions of classroom teachers from
all over the country." But who were these teachers? What were their pre-
dispositions, political and otherwise? Were they alienated, disillusioned
Americans? Kirk Ankeney, a vice principal in the San Diego City schools
recalls the team of teachers he worked with to draft standards for American
history: "Off the top of my head I'm remembering teachers such as David
here in California, Mark up in Washington, Earl in Chicago, Helen there in
Michigan, Gloria on Long Island, John in New Jersey, Melvin in Philadelphia, Bill over in Maryland, Dan down in Florida, Angeline in Colorado
and John in New Mexico."[18] The K–12 teachers who worked on the project
were there because of their reputations as creative and committed professionals. As Ankeney points out, "there was no philosophical or political litmus test or paper screening applied to the educators who came to work on
the standards. . . . The topic of one's political beliefs never came up.[19]

Even so, did the task forces have a particular political or philosophical slant? It seems likely that a large majority of the teachers and scholars who joined the committees were of moderate to liberal political persuasion if their commitment to ethnically inclusive American history, international education, and teaching based on thoughtful inquiry was any indication of their politics. Altogether the participants probably spanned the central part of the political spectrum; ideologues of either right or left were not to be found. It is clear that most K–12 teachers had little investment in post-modernist, deconstructionist, Afrocentric, New Leftist, or radical feminist theory. On the other hand, virtually all of them were dedicated, up-to-date practitioners of the discipline of history. Insofar as they understood and drew upon the important contributions that writings in the fields of sociology, anthropology, economics, literature, and women's studies have made to the understanding of the past, they strengthened rather than weakened the standards. Not even the right-wing critics argued that schools should renounce all multicultural, international, or gender-oriented education.

The teachers who worked on the project were indeed puzzled by the critics' characterization of the guidelines' authorship. As task force members John Pyne, from West Milford, New Jersey, and Gloria Sesso, from Dix Hills, New York, wrote,

All of the classroom teachers who wrote the standards and developed the activities are mainstream educators with long experience in the classroom and are highly regarded by their colleagues, by students, and by parents. To be labeled as some sort of left-wing radicals by critics such as Mrs. Cheney is an injustice to classroom teachers everywhere.[20]

Sesso and David Vigilante, high school history teachers who worked on the classroom activities on McCarthyism (about a page worth of material that the Right fiercely maligned as evidence of America bashing), were well known for leading teams of students to honors in national competitions in Washington on knowledge of the Constitution and Bill of Rights. A member of the world history task force, an active Republican, vented his frustration with ideologues who attacked the project he and other teachers had labored with for three years:

I would suggest that Fonte et al. had best get out of the way because they will become mere bumps in the road paved by teachers who want to teach and who need the guidance and wisdom that the standards present. . . . Jefferson [would] be proud because we will be helping to prepare better citizens, citizens who are mature enough to look beyond "myths" and can admit to our failures as a nation, . . . citizens who will help to make the history of our nation richer through the truth, learning, and understanding [of] "real" history.²¹

Substance and Mirage

The Right's accusation that the standards were the work of "multicultural" radicals at UCLA was nearly synonymous with their charge that the guidelines were, in Cheney's words, "politically correct to a fare-thee-well." We have described how the words "politically correct" began to be used in the late 1980s as a slogan of derision, referring to "a kind of regimented sympathy shown to the nation's minorities and women."²² Public fights over political correctness in the schools, universities, government, and press have invariably been wars of exaggeration. "If the key to the art of demagogy is oversimplification," Todd Gitlin writes, "the crusade against PC was a master exhibit. It suited ideologues of the Right to brandish the term relentlessly, collapsing affirmative action, curriculum revision, and speech regulation codes into a uniform enemy, lumping together nonsensical 'Afrocentrism' with serious scholarship, and referring darkly to a 'new McCarthyism.' "²³

As the critics denounced the standards as a left-wing plot to "degrade the achievements and highlight the flaws of the white males who ran the country for its first two centuries,"²⁴ teachers and other citizens who ordered and read the books began contacting the NCHS to ask what all the fuss was about. They had discovered that the U.S. guidelines included pages upon pages of teaching topics and examples that most Americans would regard as conventional—the early European explorations, the American Revolution, the creating of the Constitution, the settling of the West, the impact of the New Deal, the world wars, the role of religion in American life, and so on. One of the standards on the Civil War, for example, featured fourteen teaching examples that encouraged students to use biographies, historic documents, narratives, novels, maps, photographs, and memorabilia to examine the Emancipation Proclamation, Lincoln's leadership, the Gettysburg Address, war technology, military commandership, and combat conditions.

Cheney had charged that the U.S. standards failed so much as to mention the Constitution. This was pure sophistry—and deliberate misrepresentation. The only truth to the charge was that the *word* Constitution did not appear in any of the thirty-one main standards headings. In fact, a major standard (see pp. 202–3) called for students to develop understandings of the Continental Congress, the Constitution, the debates leading to ratification, the Bill of Rights, and the founding of the Supreme Court. These understandings were all explicitly identified under the major standard that read: "Students should understand the institutions and practices of government created during the revolution and how they were revised between 1787 and 1815 to create the foundation of the American political system."

Equally misleading was Cheney's charge that the "foundings of the Sierra Club and the National Organization for Women are considered noteworthy events, but the first gathering of the U.S. Congress is not." True, the guidelines recognized the National Organization for Women in one sentence of a standard dealing with the emergence of the modern women's movement, and mentioned the Sierra Club in one teaching example for grades 5–6 only. But they devoted five pages to the accomplishments of the first Congress, including its approval of the Bill of Rights, adoption of Hamilton's economic program, and development of the Supreme Court.

The guidelines were far more inclusive of the experiences of American men and women of all classes and origins than they would have been had they been written, say, thirty years before. The teachers who did the drafting took very seriously the instructions of the National Council to develop standards that reflected the nation's diversity as well as its commonalities, the struggles of specific groups for freedom and equality as well as the development of our common civic identity, the lives of ordinary men and women as well as the careers of political and economic decision makers. These basic criteria were adopted when Cheney was still leading the NEH. That the standards should range across America's social, cultural, ethnic, religious, and economic landscape was also recognition of the new realms of research that had opened up since World War II and that represented the singular achievement of the historical profession during the past half century.

Such inclusiveness in the standards, however, became a major target of the critics' attention. In making their charges of excessive attention to minorities and women, they did not target the standards themselves, that is, the statements describing the historical understandings and thinking skills that students should acquire. Rather, they concentrated their fire on the "examples of student achievement," which were included in the books at the behest of K–12 professional organizations to give teachers practical ideas for implementing the standards. The critics' strategy was to find sentences and phrases that might be interpreted as biased or excessively multicultural, count up the number of times mainstream heroes were mentioned compared with lesser-known, minority-group, or sinister figures, then put all these pieces together to create a caricature of the standards specifically crafted to raise public ire.

202 HISTORY ON TRIAL

STANDARD 3

Students Should Understand: *The institutions and practices of government created during the revolution and how they were revised between 1787 and 1815 to create the foundation of the American political system.*

Students Should Be Able to:

3A Demonstrate understanding of government-making, at both national and state levels by:

[5-12] Analyzing the arguments over the Articles of Confederation. [Examine the influence of ideas]

[9-12] Comparing at least two state constitutions and explaining why they differed. [Analyze multiple causation]

[7-12] Assessing the accomplishments and failures of the Continental Congress. [Evaluate major debates among historians]

[7-12] Assessing the importance of the Northwest Ordinance. [Interrogate historical data]

3B Demonstrate understanding of the issues involved in the creation and ratification of the United States Constitution and the new government it established by:

[5-12] Analyzing the factors involved in calling the Constitutional Convention, including Shays's Rebellion. [Analyze multiple causation]

[7-12] Analyzing the alternative plans considered by the delegates and the major compromises agreed upon to secure the approval of the Constitution. [Examine the influence of ideas]

[9-12] Analyzing the fundamental ideas behind the distribution of powers and the system of checks and balances established by the Constitution. [Examine the influence of ideas]

[9-12] Comparing the arguments of Federalists and Anti-Federalists during the ratification debates and assess their relevance in late 20th-century politics. [Hypothesize the influence of the past]

3C Demonstrate understanding of the guarantees of the Bill of Rights and its continuing significance by:

[5-12] Analyzing the significance of the Bill of Rights and its specific guarantees. [Examine the influence of ideas]

[9-12] Analyzing whether the Alien and Sedition Acts (1798) threatened those rights and the issues they posed in the absence of judicial review of acts of Congress. [Evaluate the implementation of a decision]

[9-12] Analyzing issues addressed in recent court cases involving the Bill of Rights to assess their continuing significance today. [Identify relevant historical antecedents]

▸tudents Should Be Able to:

3E Demonstrate understanding of the development of the Supreme Court's powers and significance from 1789 to 1820 by:

`7-12` Appraising the significance of John Marshall's precedent-setting decisions in establishing the Supreme Court as an independent and equal branch of the U.S. government. [**Assess the importance of the individual**]

`9-12` Tracing the evolution of the Supreme Court's powers during the 1790s and early 19th century and analyzing its influence today. [**Explain historical continuity and change**]

3D Demonstrate understanding of the development of the first American party system by:

`9-12` Explaining the development of the two-party system, although political factions were widely deplored. [**Analyze multiple causation**]

`5-12` Comparing the leaders and the social and economic composition of each party. [**Compare and contrast differing personalities, behaviors, and institutions**]

`7-12` Comparing the different views of the two parties on the central economic and foreign policy issues of the 1790s. [**Compare and contrast differing sets of ideas**]

The Constitution and Bill of Rights in the National History Standards

Cheney and her researchers came up with the names of some historical ʒiants—Robert E. Lee and the Wright brothers, for example—about whom ₁o teaching examples were written, and then publicized those omissions as f the writers had deliberately expunged white male achievers from the hisory that schools would henceforth teach. In fact, the examples were writen to illustrate how the standards might be used and were never intended ₁o mirror all their content. The critics, however, suggested that any great American leader left out of the examples was destined to be ignored enirely in American schools and textbooks, as if teachers would not dare inroduce their students to personages not mentioned in the examples.

Any citizen who read the documents would have found that white males, he category of the great majority of public personalities in American hisory, comprised also the great majority of all persons mentioned in the exmples—Columbus, Washington, Franklin, Jefferson, Hamilton, Madison, ℩om Paine, Patrick Henry, Lincoln, Woodrow Wilson, Teddy Roosevelt, ⸱DR, Kennedy, Nixon, Reagan, and so on. Indeed more than seven hundred white men, living and dead, were identified, many times the grand total of all women, African-Americans, Latinos, and Indians individually named. Few names appeared in the actual standards statements, but those that did were *all* white males.

If the critics ignored these facts, they also ignored the evidence that the standards themselves clearly called for understanding important leaders in the nation's history. One of the Civil War standards, for example, asked students to evaluate "how political, military, and diplomatic leadership affected the outcome of the war." The first teaching example suggested that teachers have their students "explain how the military leaders and resources of the Union and the Confederacy affected the course and outcome of the Civil War. Compare population, armies, and leaders of the Confederacy with those of the Union at the beginning of the war." Robert E. Lee was not mentioned by name, but neither was Ulysses S. Grant. History teachers understood that the military leadership of the Union and Confederacy certainly included their highest ranking generals. Outrage over General Lee's omission was a political ploy, not an exposé of a real problem.

The critics also censured the standards for including in the classroom examples so many people whom, in their view, no one had ever heard of. The implication here was that the authors were packing the standards with the names of obscure blacks, women, Indians, and social reformers in order to satisfy the demands of politically correct interest groups. Leo, for example, made great fun of the inclusion of Ebenezer McIntosh, dismissing him as "a brawling street lout of the 1760s who whipped up anti-British mobs and sacked the homes of various colonial officials," an "anti-elitist, anti-oppression and pro-uprising gang member."[25] McIntosh was indeed all of those things, an urban hell-raiser and revolutionary. Until the well-to-do colonial politicos whisked him off the public stage, McIntosh led the popular protests against Britain's burdensome Stamp Act and helped politicize Boston working folk in the decade leading to the Revolution. For teachers, the story of McIntosh made terrific classroom copy. For Leo, perhaps the Revolution might better have been fought without Revolutionaries.

In the media war over who was "in" and who was "out"—or, as one popular magazine put it, who was "hot" and who was "not"—Cheney's most widely publicized allegation (a charge still being repeated in the press in 1996) was that Joseph McCarthy was mentioned nineteen times and the Ku Klux Klan seventeen times. How could children be taught to love their country if such unpleasantness was brought to their attention? In fact, the U.S. guidelines contained no extended narrative discussion of either McCarthy or the Klan. All references to the senator from Wisconsin were concentrated on two pages of the standards, mostly in the teaching examples. The Klan was similarly presented. (See pp. 208–9 for the single mention of the KKK in the standards and note the last teaching activity that alone accounts for eight of the seventeen references to the Klan totted up by Cheney.)

The Right's indictment of the standards as grim and gloomy raised once again the issue that had been at the heart of most controversies over history teaching since the nineteenth century. Should classrooms emphasize the continuing story of America's struggle to form "a more perfect union," a narrative that involved a good deal of jostling, elbowing, and bargaining among contending groups? A story that included political tumult, labor strife, racial conflict, and civil war? Or should the curriculum focus on successes, achievements, and ideals, on stories designed to infuse young Americans with patriotism and sentiments of loyalty toward prevailing institutions, traditions, and values?

Though not made explicit in the introduction, the standards did indeed embody a point of view on these questions. It was not that children should be discouraged from loving their country or taking pride in its accomplishments. Quite the contrary. The idea suffusing the standards from beginning to end was that the continuing struggle to put constitutional, democratic, and Judeo-Christian ideals into practice was itself the story worth telling, the story most likely to inspire in young Americans the will to nurture, protect, and make more perfect the national union. What the critics refused to recognize or failed to understand was that the greatest theme in American history is not a steady cavalcade of purposeful progress but creative reform and ingenious reinvention.

Al Shanker recognized the importance of this message when he wrote that the history of our nation

> is the story of democracy's transformation from a great idea into . . . the most successful multiethnic and multiracial society of our time. . . . But this continuing transformation did not take place without a long, painful and sometimes ugly struggle . . . by many people who tried to turn the promises of democracy into realities. . . . The struggle to define our democracy still continues and it will as long as our country does. It has helped turn abstract principles like equity, justice, individual rights and equality of opportunity into political movements, laws, programs and institutions—concrete things. And if our children walk away from an American history course without understanding this, the history they have studied is a travesty.[26]

Treatment of the KKK and McCarthyism are cases in point. The rise of the Klan during Reconstruction was a grim story indeed, and the story gets grimmer when the KKK became a national movement in the 1920s, recruiting more members in Indiana than in Mississippi. McCarthyism involved corrosive innuendoes that ruined the reputation of many loyal Americans. These *were* somber episodes in American history. But the teachers who wrote the standards assumed that students might be taught valuable lessons, indeed feel national pride, when they discovered how Americans recognized injustice when they saw it and acted overwhelmingly, in time, to oppose both McCarthyism and the ideology of the Klan.

The guidelines aimed to help students understand the principles that the Founding Fathers set forth to organize national life. Was it dismal and dreary to say that the struggle to attain these ideals has been painful, sometimes bloody? Was it inadmissible to suggest that the agenda set two centuries ago has not been fully accomplished? Should high school literature classes banish *Huckleberry Finn, The Grapes of Wrath, Native Son,* or *To Kill a Mockingbird* from classrooms because they present a less than cheery view of American life and therefore might sap children's patriotism? Literature is about triumph and tragedy, cowardice and heroism, achievement and failure, the light and the dark. So is history. This was one of the standards' key messages.

Historian David Kennedy found in this message not only a "faithful reflection of recent trends in historical scholarship" but also "an unmistakable reflection of the historical moment in which we are fated to live."[27] The document, he affirmed, "does have a tone, and a decidedly modern one. To call that tone 'politically correct,' whether in its strident or deferential variations, is a cheap shot, incomplete and misleading."

Kennedy recognized the importance the standards placed upon historical study in shaping "political intelligence" and pointed out the criterion that called upon schools to "address the struggle to narrow the gap between [the nation's] ideals and practices." Yet the document, he observed, "pays considerably more attention to analyzing the messy practice of democracy than to explicating those ideals" that were given "exceedingly short shrift." This approach, he said, leaves "the reader ... with a far more vivid sense of the conflicts that have riven American society than of the common values and shared ideas that have traditionally been thought to have united it." He concluded that the standards were true to their time, reflective of the "seismic upheavals in American society" of the past forty years rather than the "serene and soothing certitudes" represented in traditionalist histories of the 1950s.[28]

Critics on the Right saw these matters differently. To them, revisionist history was simply an assault on objective truth, and therefore a weapon to be used in the war against the standards. In the 1980s and 1990s, the culture wars subjected this phrase to an odd transmutation. To scholars and educators, revisionist history was work that challenged older interpretations of past events and proposed fresh ones, just as research in chemistry and physics challenges older formulas and suggests new ones. Historians might cling to established explanations of the way things happened, but none, at least not in the twentieth century, regarded the idea of reinterpreting the past as subversive.

No one involved in writing the standards regarded the recommendation that students "hold interpretations of history as tentative, subject to changes as new information is uncovered, new voices heard, and new interpretations broached" as anything other than a vital and valuable skill students should acquire. Is all history "socially constructed"? Yes, in the sense that once the present disappears into the past, it can never be fully recovered. It is historians' mission to reconstruct the past as best they can using the research tools and sources of information available. In the culture wars, however, conservative fears of postmodernism and its supposed denial of verifiable truth and objective reality brought revisionism *per se* under attack. Revisionism became a pejorative word, and revisionists were denigrated as people who went about manipulating the "facts" and demolishing the known past.

The National Standards for World History sustained a lighter barrage of attacks in the media than did the U.S. guidelines. In history wars of the past, the teaching of world history or Western civilization had not often aroused public controversy, though the disputes over Afrocentrism and the Columbian quincentennial are exceptions. Textbooks and curriculums on world history, geography, or culture rarely touch the raw nerves of national identity and patriotic feeling the way American history does. Slavery, labor reform, religious conflict, the Civil War, the dropping of the atomic bomb are all issues that readily set Americans to arguing with one another over our usable past. The Sung empire, the Italian Renaissance, or the Algerian Revolution are rather less likely to be objects of history war—at least in the United States.

Even so, the World History Standards did take political hits. As Chapter 7 has shown, the controversy began in meetings of the National Council, where those standards excited more controversy at that stage of development than did the U.S. guidelines. The world history volume appeared several weeks later than the U.S. book, and when it did, the residue of discord from the council meetings spilled quickly into the open. Among the most vocal critics of the new handbook were Gilbert Sewall and Elizabeth Fox-Genovese, both council members, who made press statements highly critical of the standards. David Battini, a council member and a teacher from upstate New York, also complained that the standards had not turned out

Students Should Understand: *How the United States changed from the end of World War I to the eve of the Great Depression.*

Students Should Be Able to:

3A Demonstrate understanding of the cultural clashes and their consequences in the postwar era by:

7-12 Examining the "red scare" and Palmer raids as a reaction to Bolshevism. [**Marshal evidence of antecedent circumstances**]

5-12 Analyzing the factors that lead to immigration restriction and the closing of the "Golden Door." [**Interrogate historical data**]

7-12 Examining race relations, including increased racial conflict, the resurgence of the Ku Klux Klan, and the emergence of Garveyism. [**Analyze cause-and-effect relationships**]

7-12 Examining the clash between traditional moral values and changing ideas as exemplified in the Scopes Trial and Prohibition. [**Examine the influence of ideas**]

9-12 Analyzing the emergence of the "New Woman" and challenges to Victorian values. [**Examine the influence of ideas**]

| Grades 5-6 | **Examples of student achievement of Standard 3A include:** |

♦ Examine the effects of "nativism" and anti-immigrant attitudes. Looking at census charts, compare rates of immigration before and after the passage of restrictive laws in 1921 and 1924. *Why did nativists feel that immigration was harmful and had to be restricted in the early 1920s? Who did they think should live in this country? Why did Congress pass laws to sharply limit immigration from southern and eastern Europe? Did these laws further restrict the immigration of Asian peoples?*

♦ Assess the spread of the Ku Klux Klan's influence in different sections of the country in the 1920s. Analyze photographs showing cross burning, the march in Washington, D.C., and violence against African Americans and immigrants. *How did the Ku Klux Klan regard African Americans, Asians, southern and eastern European immigrants, and Jewish and Catholic Americans?*

♦ Draw historical evidence from narratives, stories, diaries, and photographs to describe how women's lives changed after World War I. *How did women contribute to improvement in schools, hospitals, settlement houses, and social agencies? How did the spread of electrification and growing use of household appliances like the refrigerator, washing machine; and vacuum cleaner improve the life of homemakers?*

♦ Use historical fiction such as *Shadrach's Crossing* by Avi to examine smuggling during Prohibition.

The Ku Klux Klan in the National History Standards

Examples of student achievement of Standard 3A include:

♦ Debate the proposition: In order to defend American society from the threat of communists it may become necessary to restrict civil liberties.

♦ Construct a sound historical argument, or conduct a Socratic seminar on the topic: "Immigration restrictions of the 1920s rendered the Statue of Liberty obsolete." *Did the quota system discriminate against particular groups of immigrants? How did the restriction of European immigration affect Mexican American immigration?*

♦ Assess the degree to which the rebirth of the Ku Klux Klan exemplified hostility toward people of color, religious minorities, and immigrants in many parts of American society. *What accounts for the development of large Klan organizations in northern states?*

♦ Construct a historical narrative comparing attitudes toward women with changing values and new ideas regarding such things as employment opportunities, appearance standards, leisure activities, and political participation.

Examples of student achievement of Standard 3A include:

♦ Analyze the major causes of the Red Scare and explain the role of J. Edgar Hoover and Attorney General A. Mitchell Palmer in contributing to the hysteria. Draw historical evidence from speeches, political cartoons, news reports, editorials, and journal articles to analyze how words and images were used to stir fears of Bolshevism and foreigners. *To what extent was Bolshevism a real or imagined threat to the United States? How effective was propaganda in winning public support for the Palmer raids?*

♦ Draw evidence from the Sacco and Vanzetti trial proceedings and commentary by journalists to analyze the issues raised by the celebrated case. *How did the Sacco and Vanzetti case relate to the Palmer raids? Did Sacco and Vanzetti get a fair trial?*

♦ Use statistical charts and the immigration laws of 1917, 1921, and 1924 to explain the changes in the ethnic composition of immigrants and the fears it represented. *What factors contributed to the passage of restrictive immigration laws in the twenties? How was "American" being defined?*

♦ Draw historical evidence from biographies, newspapers, and works of authors reflecting different attitudes on race, such as Madison Grant, Thomas Dixon, James Weldon Johnson, W. E. B. Du Bois, and Claude McKay, to construct a historical narrative assessing the impact and consequences of racism in the postwar era. *What were the underlying causes of the northern race riots of the postwar era? What were the origins and goals of the Garvey movement? How successful was Marcus Garvey?*

♦ Gather evidence from a variety of sources including the Ku Klux Klan's book of rules (The Khloran) and descriptions of Klan ceremonies to examine the purposes and goals of the "New Klan." *To what extent did the "New Klan" differ from the earlier Klan? How did the ritual and ceremonies of the Klan appeal to a need for community? To what extent were the immigration laws related to the revival of the Klan? What was the role of women in the "New Klan"?*

to his liking. According to Lynne Cheney, one of the council members told her that those who advocated adequate attention to Western civilization had been "iced-out" of the discussions by militant multiculturalists linked to the AHA.[29]

The Right's accusation that AHA radicals "hijacked" the writing of the standards was fanciful. Most of the teachers who did the drafting were not even members of that organization, and anyone who glanced at the list of established scholars and teachers who made up most of the council would find such an assertion baffling. In fact, most of the non-American historians on the council were nominated by Cheney herself.

In the best culture wars tradition, however, conservative commentators, following Cheney, picked up the early complaints about the World History Standards and ran with them. The critics asserted that the guidelines had two major deficiencies: one, they minimized and denigrated the role of Western civilization in world history, and two, they included way too much "arcana" about other parts of the world that American children need not know about. "This global historical revisionism is totally unbalanced," Sewall declared to a conservative London newspaper. "It compresses Western achievement in a poor and unflattering light that makes all the former colonial powers come off very badly, in particular Britain."[30] John Leo characterized the world history book as "a great heap of data. . . . Somewhere buried deep within the pile is Western civilization, which seems to be on a par with the Kush and the Carthaginians. In the multicultural view, all cultures are equal."[31] Cheney told *USA Today* that in the standards "everything is the same as everything else—gender relations under India's Gupta Empire, political and cultural achievements under Shah Abbas in Persia, and oh yes, the Magna Carta."[32]

However citizens might disagree over the relative weight the standards gave to various regions and peoples, the charge that the guidelines marginalized Western civilization seriously misrepresented them. Across the eight eras of world history, about 40 percent of the material was concerned with Western civilization as conventionally defined; that is, ancient Greece and Rome, as well as medieval and modern Europe. In Era 7, which covered the period from 1750 to 1914, when Western power and influence in the world were at their height, material on Europe and European involvement abroad constituted more than 60 percent of the content. In the era from 1000 to 1500 C.E., European history was given relatively less weight because at that time the continent's impact on world events relative to other civilizations and regions was smaller. In other words, the standards aimed to highlight those topics of greatest import to humankind during the era in question, not just the themes of the distant European past that loom especially large in the

Western imagination. In response to a *Wall Street Journal* editorial that branded the standards "a jungle of runaway inclusiveness," William Mc-Neill wrote:

> Had you looked through the volume you ridicule, you would find that classical Greece and Rome, the rise of Christianity and the European Middle Ages are carefully presented and situated in the context of Eurasian and world history. . . . There is no anti-Western bias here; and the roots of our own political institutions in the classical and Christian past are faithfully set forth. We are the heirs of that Western past, and of all the rest of the world as well. For that reason the study of history in our schools cannot overlook the achievements of Asians, Africans and Amerindians—as once was done—and remain true to the facts, or help to guide our nation's present and future encounters with other peoples.[33]

Other critical assertions were equally unsustainable if set against the evidence in the book itself. Sewall's charge that "the Industrial Revolution . . . is given short shrift" is a case in point.[34] The standards identified industrialization as one of the two great revolutions of the 1750–1914 period and devoted a major standard to it. Unsupportable too was Albert Shanker's characterization of the World History Standards: "Everything that is European or American, or that has to do with white people is evil and oppressive, while Genghis Khan is a nice sweet guy just bringing his culture to other places."[35] Such an indictment contradicted the evidence. In the section on the Mongols, for example, the standards and examples referred to their conquests, destruction, and terror and invited students to analyze Genghis Khan's famous remark that "man's highest joy is in victory: to conquer one's enemies, to pursue them, to deprive them of their possessions, to make their beloved weep."

Attempting to expose "politically correct" content, the critics often picked out a detail, then hammered it to the media over and over again. For example, Era 7 of the book had a standard asking students to "demonstrate understanding of the causes and consequences of European settler colonization in the 19th century."[36] This standard drew attention to a major movement in world history, the migrations of peoples of European origin to other temperate regions of the northern and southern hemispheres. The topic aimed in part to help students better understand America's westward movement by recommending comparative study of similar treks across Argentina, Siberia, South Africa, Australia, and other places.

One of the standard's subheadings called on students to compare "the consequences of encounters between intrusive European migrants and

indigenous peoples" in a number of different regions. In working with draft
material from teachers, Ross Dunn recalls editing the sentence in question
and using the word "intrusive." At the time he had in mind such events as
the French invasion of Algeria, the Dutch takeover of the Cape of Good
Hope, and the early encounters between British newcomers and aborigines
in Australia. It was clearly a bad decision, however, because the statement
appeared to describe every European immigrant who came through Ellis
Island as an "intruder" on American soil. Recognizing a hot button issue
when they saw one, critics pronounced this sentence symptomatic of the
standards' anti-Western revisionist tone. On the floor of the U.S. Senate and
many times in the press well into 1996, the "intrusive Europeans" phrase was
offered as a single example of the unsoundness of the entire book. (When
the NCHS revised the standards, "intrusive" was removed.)

Criticisms in the media must be situated within the larger context of the
long-running debate over the place of the Western cultural heritage in
schools and universities. As reported in Chapter 7, Bennett, Cheney, and
other humanists of the Right thought that a curriculum centered on the
West strengthened the vital chain connecting American institutions and
values to a much wider civilized tradition that cherished natural law, rational science, freedom, individualism, and democracy. The American Federation of Teachers' leaders and their consultant Paul Gagnon believed
that to educate young citizens, the curriculum must emphasize the history
of Western democracy, though time should be given to studying at least one
non-Western society in depth. The harshest critics of the World History
Standards, however, seemed to want not only a Western-centered curriculum but a triumphalist version of it. Fox-Genovese, for example, lamented
that

> nowhere in those standards ... will you find any mention of the fact that
> it was the Western tradition that first produced the idea of individual
> freedom. Nowhere will you find that it was in Christianity that the con-
> cept of individual freedom originated. That slavery is evil is a Western
> idea. Because the bias of the standards is so weighted against the United
> States and the West, you will find no acknowledgment of the fact that we
> have produced what no other country and tradition has.[37]

Whatever historians might find problematic about this argument, it
clearly projected "identity politics" onto the globe. Here was the notion that
national history standards should take on the task of ranking peoples and
civilizations according to who came up with which idea first and who did
not, an enterprise designed not to teach children the meaning of freedom,

lavery, or Christianity in world history but to rhapsodize over Western
noral successes.

The standards included an array of topics dealing with democracy, freedom, liberalism, and other political issues that figured large in the Western
experience. But as one teacher observed, "Won't students cultivate a deeper
appreciation of the power of the democratic and liberal ideas that arose in
Europe in the 17th and 18th centuries if they investigate the ways in which
peoples of Latin America, Asia, and Africa grappled with those ideas in the
9th and 20th centuries?"[38] Or as historian Hanna Holborn Gray of the University of Chicago wrote,

> The "national standards" for world history have been rather curiously
> criticized for departing from Western civilization. This is odd, since
> world history presumably must contain more than that of the West and
> since the West has indisputably been located in and deeply shaped by a
> larger global history. Its development is incomprehensible outside that
> context. . . . By comparative inquiry we seek to understand ourselves as
> well as others.[39]

The hostile op-ed essays that came out in the late months of 1994 made
one other accusation that confused many Americans. Warning that the
standards were destined to be certified under the Goals 2000 legislation,
critics protested that the document would thereafter become the nation's
"official knowledge," dictating textbooks and teachers' lesson plans. In fact,
the thinking skills section of the standards cautioned students against
acceptance of any form of official history. Moreover, these charges ignored
the fact that the standards were entirely voluntary and that at no time were
states or local school districts under any federal mandate to implement
them.

The Story Behind the Story

If suspicion was building that Cheney's real goal in her crusade against the
history standards was political, her tactics in late 1994 strengthened such
speculation. She followed almost to the letter the *modus operandi* Speaker of
the House Newt Gingrich urged Republicans to pursue in challenging their
opponents: a strategy set out in the training manual of GOPAC, the political action committee Gingrich had formed, in which candidates were advised "to 'go negative' early," to "never back off," and to "use minor details
to demonize the opposition."[40]

Statements attributed to John Fonte reinforced the suspicion that Cheney's agenda was political. An observer at the convention of the National Association of Scholars, meeting in Boston shortly after the November 1994 election, informed Nash of a session led by Fonte in which he regaled his audience with the story that just after the national election Cheney was with Newt Gingrich in his limo listening to Rush Limbaugh and called him on the car phone to help him heap abuse on the standards.[41] Fonte reportedly explained that Cheney was organizing an effort to get Congress to disavow the standards and was starting that very week to visit as many members of the House and Senate as she could. Members of the association were asked to contribute to this lobbying effort and, further, to get to school officials through their local chapters. Fonte reportedly also sought their assistance in a strategy to reach textbook publishers, particularly in Texas and California, in order to make the National History Standards so controversial that no publisher would touch them.

Shortly after this meeting, *Education Week* published an announcement of a panel that Cheney was creating to critique all the national education standards.[42] The Committee to Review National Standards would be based at the American Enterprise Institute, where Cheney coordinated her campaign. The announcement reminded readers that she had been highly critical of the history standards and was concerned that the National Education Standards and Improvement Council (NESIC) created by Goals 2000, the Educate America Act signed into law by President Clinton in March 1994, would "routinely certify standards that are not up to par." Cheney was forming her committee, the announcement said, "to analyze the standards and the Goals 2000 legislation; to build alliances with groups interested in the standards issue; to work with members of Congress as they consider the standards; and to provide educators, parents, and policymakers in the states with information about the standards." Funding from The Reader's Digest Association had been arranged. Nearly three years later, as this book went to press, however, the committee had made no report.

By the end of 1994, the scope and intensity of the crusade against the history standards led many to ask how to account for the determination of Cheney and her supporters on the cultural Right. These standards, after all, were well under development before she left office as chairman of the NEH. Moreover, at the time of her retirement she was on record praising both the standards and the NCHS.

In October 1992, for example, on the release of the first draft of the U.S. History Standards, Cheney wrote Crabtree a two-line memo: "What nice work you do! I've been saying lately that the best grant I've ever given is to your standards-setting project."[43] This particular draft of the standards included the same two eras of U.S. history—Era 3 (the American Revolution and New Nation) and Era 4 (National Expansion and Reform, 1801–61)— and the same standards and teaching examples for these eras that would be the focus of Cheney's attacks two years later. In December 1992, in her public announcement of her pending resignation as NEH chairman, she singled out two grants among the hundreds she had signed as evidence of her achievements: one to fund Ken Burns's Civil War documentary series and the other to found the National Center for History in the Schools at UCLA.[44] By this time, the standards for Era 5 (the Civil War and Reconstruction) and Era 6 (Development of Industrial United States) had also been drafted.

By January 1995 it was clear that Cheney's campaign involved far more than her attack on the history standards. In company with such leading conservatives as Newt Gingrich and Lamar Alexander, she had moved to the forefront of the Republican drive to dismantle the NEH, the National Endowment for the Arts (NEA) and the ED as well as to return all education matters—standards included—to the states.[45] In short, she joined the assault on the national education reform agenda launched in 1989 by President Bush and the National Governors' Association (NGA). Why did this movement, undertaken with broad bipartisan support and endorsed by two successive presidential administrations and the general public, come under such fierce conservative attack in 1994? What accounted for this turnaround by Republicans who had been at the helm of national education reform from 1989 to 1993?

The answer lies in part in the difficulties of translating that agenda into law. Though the education legislation initiated by Democrats in 1992 died in the Senate for lack of Republican support, hopes were high that the Goals 2000 education bill would fare better with a Democrat in the White House. First presented on Capitol Hill in April 1993, that bill did not, however, win passage until a year later and then only after months of bruising political controversy. The issues over which these legislative battles raged and the terms on which they were finally resolved were one factor contributing to conservative demands in 1994 that the federal government vacate the field and return education matters to the states.

The fiercest battle raged over national testing. Many educators, civil rights activists, and their supporters in the Democratic Party called attention to the handicap that high-stakes testing would place upon students enrolled in poorer schools with their outdated textbooks, dearth of library and technological resources, inadequate in-service training for teachers, and limited curriculum. If students were to be held accountable for achieving high standards, then the states had to give students an education that accorded all of them equal opportunity to reach those standards. The argument was strongly supported by House Democrats, who in early 1993 sent the initial bill back to the White House with the demand that provisions ensuring equity for all students in the conditions of schooling—the so-called "Opportunity to Learn (OTL) Standards"—be strengthened. "We do not want to go to national testing until we are sure children have an opportunity to learn the material," said Jack Jennings, general counsel to the House Education and Labor Committee.[46]

Opponents saw these matters differently. Advocates of national testing felt the OTL Standards were a ploy to derail such tests until equity had been achieved in all schools in any given state—a utopian vision that essentially would derail testing indefinitely.[47] Others feared that the OTL Standards, though termed "voluntary" in the bill, would be made mandatory and imposed upon states through federal legislation later drafted to deny education funding to any state that failed to apply those standards to all schools.[48] But most indicative of the fault lines developing over Goals 2000 were the mounting concerns of the nation's governors, who worried that the OTL standards could be used to dictate the resources to be provided by state and local government to every school in the country and would almost certainly lead to a wave of finance-equity lawsuits.[49] Evidence of these dangers, they said, was already appearing in House amendments to the bill that would give the proposed NESIC authority to certify state as well as national OTL guidelines.

On May 5, 1993, two governors who had been in the forefront of the national standards movement—Roy Romer, the chairman of the NGA, and Carroll A. Campbell, vice chairman—released a letter they had written to Secretary of Education Richard Riley, expressing the concerns of some governors that giving certification authority to NESIC would constitute federal intrusion into an area that had historically been a responsibility of the states.[50] Though supporting much that was in Goals 2000, they expressed their belief in the "need to preserve the opportunity for diversity" in state approaches to meeting the National Education Goals and to ensuring "that every student is given the opportunity to meet the high standards proposed by this legislation."[51] In a separate letter to Riley, Campbell argued further that the revised bill "comes dangerously close to derailing our hard-won emphasis on student achievement . . . and threatens to turn the clock back on four years' worth of bipartisan teamwork."[52]

The House Education and Labor Committee proposed another amendment to the president's bill that would limit federal education funding to those states that met nationally approved OTL standards. Clinton, sensitive to the governors' concerns, intervened. On June 3, 1993, he urged House

Democrats to halt their efforts to revise his bill and to return to the version he had submitted to them. "Amendments which require states, as a condition of federal support, to commit to specific corrective actions for schools that fail to meet these standards go too far. The requirements will impede states' efforts to focus accountability on results" and would be "a disincentive for states to participate in reform efforts. I urge you not to support amendments that expand the definition or role of opportunity-to-learn standards."[53]

The legislative year ended with no agreement on Goals 2000, but with the promise of Senator Edward Kennedy, chairman of the Senate Labor and Human Resources Committee, that he would introduce in January 1994 a revision—a bill that would be more acceptable to the governors and Senate Republicans.[54] Renewed efforts culminated in March in a House-Senate Conference agreement on a compromise version of the bill.

As finally passed and signed into law later that month, the Goals 2000 Educate America Act formally authorized the National Education Goals Panel and wrote into law eight subjects in which students were to demonstrate competency over challenging subject matter: the original five subjects of mathematics, science, history, geography, and English, and now economics, civics, and foreign languages. The act created NESIC, with authority for certifying voluntary national content and performance standards in the academic subjects; voluntary state standards and assessments "comparable to [the national standards] or higher in rigor and quality"; and voluntary national OTL standards. Significant federal funds were to be made available to states whose education reform plans were approved by NESIC or the ED. Finally, the legislation authorized grants for the development of OTL guidelines.

Educators across the nation celebrated passage of Goals 2000. Typical of their responses was that of Pascal D. Forgione Jr., the superintendent of public instruction for Delaware. "We now have a compact and partnership that will begin to allow us to work collaboratively together," he said. "It's a wonderful affirmation that we're heading in the right direction."[55] Thomas C. Boysen, commissioner of education for the state of Kentucky, judged Goals 2000 to be "as important as anything that's happened [in federal education legislation] in the last 30 years."[56]

But critics on the conservative Right were marshaling their forces to dismantle not only this act, but also the ED, which would administer it. Their opportunity lay, as they saw it, in the coming November elections and the installation of Republican majorities in Congress strong enough to reverse education policies enacted by Democratic majorities during the previous thirty years.

No organization would be more important in this effort than the Christian Coalition, which was mobilized as a formidable voting force by televangelist Pat Robertson and his executive director, Ralph Reed. As a condition of their support for Republican candidates and voter drives, the coalition made clear its expectation of reciprocal backing for its education agenda: abolishing the ED, transferring its funding to families and local school boards, repealing Goals 2000, and enacting school-choice legislation through a tax-supported voucher plan extending parental choice equally to public, private, and religious schools. In addition, the coalition called for abolishing the NEH and the NEA, and for converting these agencies into "voluntary organizations, funded through private contributions."[57]

At the core of this agenda was the belief that the public schools were operating under the control of a distant education establishment that was at best out of touch with the traditional values of American families and at worst at war with them. A key element in the agenda to "strengthen families and restore common sense values" was wresting control of schools from the "education bureaucrats," "experts," and the National Education Association—the nation's largest teachers union—which, they charged, had usurped power over the school curriculum and the values it transmitted. The coalition contended that the ED's most recent attempts to grasp power "came in 1993 and 1994 with the passage of the 'Goals 2000' program," an "extraordinary usurpation of the American tradition of local control of education."

Speaking directly to the congressional leadership, Ralph Reed stated, "There is no deadline or specified time period during which these items are to be enacted. But Congress would be well advised to act with all due and deliberate speed."[58] The Republican leadership heard and heeded the message. In their Contract with America, House Republicans pledged to bring to a vote within the first hundred days of the 104th Congress a Family Reinforcement Act that would, among other things, "strengthen the rights of parents in their children's education," including their rights "to protect their children against education programs that undermine the values taught in the home."[59] The specific goals of zeroing out the ED and the national endowments would become part of the larger Republican agenda to slash the federal deficit and to "return government to the people" by privatizing federal agencies deemed unnecessary and shipping other federal programs along with their funding back to the states.

In making its case for getting Washington entirely out of education, the coalition declared, "There is perhaps no better proof of the danger of federal involvement in education than the recently released model national history standards." On this point, the coalition was not alone. Phyllis Schlafly, in her nationally syndicated radio broadcasts and in *The Phyllis Schlafly Report*, a monthly newsletter published by the Eagle Trust Fund, reported that "The whole idea of the Federal Government writing or financing public school curricula is an elitist, totalitarian notion that should be unacceptable in America."[60] Her strongest attack was directed against the "leftwing, revisionist" National History Standards, which, she claimed, were permeated with "hostility to Western/Christian civilization," "multicultural items that have had little or no importance in American History," and a "radical feminist ideology based on victimology." "It is," she said, "a grievous disservice to American schoolchildren, as well as historically false, to view the entire panorama of American history as one long conflict about race and gender, in which all ethnic groups except white males are portrayed as victims."

Like Cheney, Schlafly supported her charges with isolated teaching examples pulled out of context or misinterpreted. "Completely ignoring the historical fact of the dominance of the Christian religion in America and its moral values and traditions," she charged, "the student is taught an anonymous quotation from an 18th century New Yorker asserting that 'the only principle of life propagated among the young people is to get money.' "[61] In fact, that one quotation (a contemporary criticism of secularism) lay among many pages of standards encouraging students to analyze thoughtfully the religious heritage and ideals of Puritan New England and their lasting impact on the nation; such Protestant tenets as the covenant of grace and the doctrine of sanctification; such readings as John Winthrop's "A Model of Christian Charity," John Milton's *Paradise Lost*, and Jonathan Edwards's sermon "Sinners in the Hands of an Angry God"; and such evangelical movements as the First and Second Great Awakenings in eighteenth- and nineteenth-century America.[62] The quotation Schlafly found offensive had been included both to engage students in analyzing changing values in eighteenth-century urban America as the burgeoning economy brought riches to the new entrepreneurial class and to illustrate why religious leaders, in the vanguard of the First Great Awakening, thundered against the sins of a people falling away from God in their pursuit of wealth.

Leaders of the Christian Right did not inform their flocks that the standards included, for public school instruction, sacred texts, beliefs, and teachings of the great religions of the world. Amid all the harsh criticism—from Dobson's Focus on the Family, from Gary Bauer's Family Research Council, and from the Christian Coalition—was no acknowledgment that the guidelines included such biblical readings from the Hebrew Bible (the Old Testament in the Christian Bible) as the Creation accounts in Genesis, the Ten Commandments, the Psalms, and the books of the Torah,

Ezra, and Nehemiah.[63] Nor did these critics mention the Christian texts presented in the standards—both the teachings of Jesus of Nazareth as recorded in the gospels of the New Testament and the letters of Paul the Apostle, such as Colossians 3:12–17, Galatians 5:13–14, and 1 Corinthians 13:1–13, concerning the moral Christian life.[64]

Like the Christian Coalition, Focus on the Family also used the standards as a handy rallying cry in mobilizing its membership to work for repeal of Goals 2000. "One of the most frightening examples of the potential [of Goals 2000] for damage," it warned, "became clear with the release of the proposed history standards."[65] Bauer and the Family Research Council produced their own alternative to the National History Standards under the title, *Let Freedom Ring! A Basic Outline of American History.*[66] This pamphlet was, in fact, akin to a table of contents that one might have found in a textbook written decades ago. The advertisement for *Let Freedom Ring!* in the *Washington Times* on February 21, 1995, included a photo of the U.S. moon landing and a caption declaring, "They promised us the Moon, But they Missed!" The text below charged that

> Bill Clinton and his Department of Education promised us national education standards so our kids could compete in a world economy. But the biased national history standards they actually funded completely omit any references to the U.S. Apollo program that landed Americans on the moon! They include "Soviet gains" in space while highlighting America's Challenger disaster. They emphasize U.S. failures and injustices but leave out many important achievements.[67]

In fact, the history standards did include the impact of late-twentieth-century space exploration, biotechnology, and the new physics, and they specifically referenced the moon landing and the achievements of John Glenn and Sally Ride.[68] Nowhere in any of the three volumes was reference made to the Challenger disaster or to Soviet gains in space. But in an interview carried in the same issue of the *Washington Times*, Gary Bauer, who had been White House domestic policy adviser in the Reagan administration, repeated the charges, adding: "It is just another example of how bizarre the history is that the other group has formulated. Their outline is consistent with what I found at the Department of Education in the '80s—that American textbooks already were tending to magnify America's flaws and belittle her achievements."[69]

Linking the standards to the Family Research Council's larger political agenda, the *Washington Times* ad concluded with the warning, "This is the inevitable result of Big Government trying to man our local schools from Washington D.C. . . . That's why Family Research Council is fighting right now to return the critical decisions in education to parents and locally elected school boards. Help us shut down the U.S. Education Department with its bloated $30 billion budget."

Abandoning Old Allegiances, Accommodating New Politics

The condemnation by conservatives of federal agencies and programs in education, the arts, and the humanities placed both Lynne Cheney and Lamar Alexander in a politically vulnerable position. After all, Alexander had been at the helm of the ED and Cheney at the NEH during the years when their agencies generously funded the very federal programs now under attack. Commentators would soon link Alexander's change of position to his presidential aspirations for 1996.[70] How much of Cheney's attacks, critics asked, could be traced to her need in this new political climate to disassociate herself sharply from a program she herself had launched? Some observers wondered if her position on the history standards was not connected to the "political plans of her husband, Bush administration Defense Secretary Dick Cheney, who frequently [was being] mentioned as a possible Republican presidential candidate in 1996."[71]

Whatever her motivations, Cheney now claimed that the NCHS had failed to produce the kind of document they had promised her and that "only a distant relationship" existed between the standards and the center's earlier volume, *Lessons from History*.[72] "The people at UCLA did not deal honestly with me," she wrote in a letter to the *Seattle Times*.[73] She had, she said, been "promised X and given Y." Or, as she asserted many times on talk shows and in the press, "I was flimflammed."[74]

In fact, these charges distorted what the codirectors of the project had agreed to in their application for the grant and had negotiated in their follow-up conferences with Cheney's NEH staff. As Nash and Crabtree later reminded critics, Cheney had agreed to fund a national consensus-building *process*, not a particular product.[75] "A process as broadly participatory and genuinely responsive to reviewers as this one [had been] could not guarantee in advance a particular product," the codirectors explained. "It would have been improper, in the first place, for a federal official to have made any such demands of the distinguished historians, veteran teachers, and hundreds of supervisors, administrators, parents, librarians, economists, and other concerned citizens who actively participated in this process." Cheney may have changed her mind concerning the merits of

what this process produced and may even have deeply regretted ever having gotten involved, now that the election of 1994 had changed the political
landscape. But her role as chairman of the NEH had never endowed her, in
columnist Meg Greenfield's phrase, with the powers of the nation's cultural
commissar.[76]

CHAPTER 9

Inside the Beltway

The dogmas of the quiet past, are inadequate to the stormy present. . . .
We must disenthrall ourselves, and then we shall save our country.

—Abraham Lincoln,
Annual Message to Congress, December 1, 1862

O ne of the main complaints of the culture warriors on the Right is that "tenured radicals" who are said to control the nation's campuses have politicized literature, history, anthropology, women's studies, and even science. These warriors, whose own work is highly polemical, call for neutral, objective academic studies. They ignore the fact that around the world and across the disciplines teachers and scholars have conceded "the impossibility of any research being neutral" and have accepted the pivotal notion "that knowledge-seeking involves a lively, contentious struggle among diverse groups of truth-seekers."[1] Furthermore, in the history wars, it would be hard to imagine a more thoroughly politicized strategy than the fierce attacks on the National History Standards.

In this chapter, we go inside the beltway that circles the nation's capital to document the efforts to defuse the controversy over the standards, the U.S. Senate's extraordinary intervention in the controversy, the teaching profession's response, and the efforts of those who created the guidelines to further the consensus-building process for improving history education in America's schools.

Washington Pow-Wows

About a week after Cheney's op-ed piece appeared in the *Wall Street Journal,* Nash spent two days in Sacramento working with Charles Quigley, head of the project to develop National Civics Standards and director of the Center for Civic Education in Calabasas, California. Quigley's organization would present the civics standards to the secretary of education on November 15, and the press would laud them. But now Nash and Quigley found themselves laying plans to reach the nation's elected representatives to tell them how Cheney's distortion of the history guidelines was misleading the public and undermining the momentum that had been gathering for higher standards in all disciplines.

If anyone knew how to get people inside the Washington beltway to take a look at the Right's campaign of disinformation, it was Quigley. For years, he had made it his business to cultivate staffers on Capitol Hill who dealt with educational policy. He had built a highly successful program for teaching constitutional and civic issues in the schools and had secured annual appropriations from Congress to support his center. With a background in philosophy and education, he had left teaching some twenty-five years earlier to give his full time to the cause of civic literacy.

Quigley promised to get to work on "the problem." He had read the history standards with general satisfaction and understood that the civics guidelines, along with those for geography, science, and the arts, might go down the drain if the ultraconservative attack on history soured the entire educational climate. The need now was to avert more media attention. Nash had already debated Cheney on a half-dozen television newscasts and radio talk shows. In this drive-by debate, sound bites ruled. Quigley understood that this was hardly the way to get the public to think about what it means to study history and to recognize that three decades of scholarship had brought to light many forgotten Americans whose memories had been so poorly served in earlier textbooks.

Quigley and Nash met with three public relations specialists from the Department of Education (ED) on November 16, little more than a week after the election of 1994, when the Republicans took control of the Senate and captured the House for the first time in forty years. Newt Gingrich was going to be Speaker of the House, and Republicans would enjoy a majority on all House committees. What was not clear was the degree to which the conservatives' agenda to halt the national standards movement and repeal Goals 2000 would move forward.

The history flare-up was not making the officials at the ED feel any better. "We're getting pummeled," one officer reported. "Phone calls are pouring in from people enraged because beltway bureaucrats are telling us that George Washington can't be taught in the schools anymore." These officers believed the smear campaign was outrageous, but they argued that the best tactic was to demonstrate how Cheney and her friends were deceiving the public. It was good folk wisdom that the American people, basically fair-minded, did not like to be deluded. Now show them. But try to lower the temperature a few degrees. One ED officer reminded Nash that in a tough debate with Cheney reasonableness and equanimity were the best course. Invoking an old Sam Rayburn quip, he advised: "Never get into a pissing match with a skunk."

Quigley and Nash then parleyed at the National Trust for Historic Preservation with the directors of the other standards projects. Also present were Republican and Democratic staffers working with the House Education and Labor Committee, representatives from the National Endowment for the Humanities (NEH), and Jennifer Davis, special assistant to Secretary of Education Richard Riley. Quigley set the tone for the meeting by stating what was on everyone's mind: The savaging of the history standards might wash away the work of thousands of educators over three years to lift performance in the nation's classrooms. We were all in the same boat, he observed, and if one goes down, all go down. Jack Jennings, the longtime Democratic staffer on education issues, warned that the Republican revolution might bring heavy attacks on the Goals 2000 programs and that the history standards promised to be a handy bloody flag for right-wing freshman representatives to wave in the air.

The group urged Nash, who was fast becoming the polecat of the standards movement, to write fact sheets refuting the most flagrant charges against the history guidelines. These broadsides, a call for truth in advertising, could be used to expose Cheney's misrepresentations. Nobody in the room, including key Republican staffers, thought the problem was "standards from hell" but rather media manipulation born of questionable motives and little regard for the challenges that teachers face every day of the week.

Two days later Nash and Quigley met with Victor Klatt, John Barth, and Lynn Selmser, Republican staffers for the House Education and Labor Committee, now rechristened by Gingrich the Economic and Educational Opportunities Committee. These were the key figures who would advise the incoming Republican committee chair. Experienced in education issues, they had looked carefully at the history standards. Barth, who had directed the Valley Forge Historical Center, regarded himself as something of an expert on Early American history. He was prepared to put Nash's feet to the fire by throwing every charge that had been made against the standards in op-ed and talk-show "exposés." The spirited discussion went back again and again to *Exploring the American Experience*, the U.S. history guidelines, in order to see what the printed pages actually said as opposed to what the critics alleged. At the end of the meeting, Barth and Klatt promised to think carefully about the position the Republican majority ought to take. But they were guarded about promising anything—candidly reminding Nash and Quigley that the Republicans' day in the sun had arrived, that far-Right party members were riding the crest of the Gingrich wave, and that the history standards were turning out to be appealing fodder.

In the meantime, orders for the standards were pouring into the National Center for History in the Schools (NCHS). Angry letters were also arriving from people who had obviously never read the books but nevertheless accepted the fulminations of Cheney, Rush Limbaugh, Oliver North, and G. Gordon Liddy. One scatological letter bearing the seal "Arbeit Macht Frei" (the slogan of the Nazi death camps) poured out a jumble of barely literate hate phrases against women, Jews, and blacks. Dunn received a message suggesting that General Washington's troops at Valley Forge should have had the history standards to keep their campfires going. Other letters expressed shock that historians—or simply Nash since he had been fingered as the main author of the books—could visit such a plague on the nation's children. NCHS replies proposing that angry or dismayed correspondents actually read the standards (and get a refund if they found the books contaminated) went unanswered. On the other hand, as weeks passed and thousands of books went out from the center, not one purchaser asked for money back.

It was also clear that the overwhelming majority of educators, especially those who had read the books, were not buying the Cheney line. In the previous six weeks, Nash had on five occasions shown the standards to teachers and historians at meetings: the Boston University Annual Humanities lecture, the American Association of Higher Education in Washington, the National Council for the Social Studies in Phoenix, a New Jersey social studies teachers conference in Princeton, and the Council of State Social Studies Specialists in Dallas. Among all kinds of educators ranging from curricular reform specialists to classroom teachers, the response was the same: the Cheney-led blitzkrieg might be winning the media war but was losing badly with teachers. They had the wisdom and independence of mind to use new curricular materials selectively and reject whatever they thought was poorly constructed, distorted, or false.

Nash and Quigley went to Washington again in mid-December for another round of talks. By this time, the political pundits had appreciated how profoundly the November 1994 elections were affecting Congress. Some seventy new Republican members had declared all-out war on social welfare capitalism and many programs that had enjoyed bipartisan support. Further complicating matters was the vow of the Gingrich battalion to eliminate not only the NEH and the National Endowment for the Art (NEA), but also public radio and television, and the Goals 2000 programs

The history standards were clearly being singled out and hung albatross-like on the NEH and the ED.

When Nash, Quigley, and the other directors of standards projects met again at the National Trust for Historic Preservation on December 14, the main topic was how to repulse the opponents with a combination of rebuttals and more effective public relations strategies to reach mass audiences. Quigley had decided to check his own reading of the history standards by asking two political scientist friends—one conservative, one liberal—to appraise them. Both gave enthusiastic support. The more conservative evaluator, former dean of the faculty at Johns Hopkins University, opened his critique with these words: "One walks away from this publication [the U.S. standards] in awe of the team and principal authors who brought it together. It inspires admiration for the breadth of the coverage and its intellectual depth and sophistication." This reviewer had criticisms and suggestions but ended by observing that the book was "of very high intellectual caliber and all who participated deserve credit for contributing to a major step in precollegiate education in United States history."[2]

The next morning Quigley and Nash met with Representative William Goodling, a seven-term Republican from central Pennsylvania who had once been a high school history teacher. Also present in Goodling's office were Representative Dale Kildee, the Democrat from Detroit who was outgoing chair of the Education and Labor Subcommittee, and Representative Randy "Duke" Cunningham, a Republican from California, who growled, "Left, left, left—these damned history standards," as he entered the room. Plopping down at a battered piano, Goodling belted out an old hymn and pronounced the meeting convened.

Quigley pointed out that the standards themselves had never been attacked but that a few dozen of the teaching examples were said to be biased. When Cunningham declared that the standards should just get the facts straight and recommend which facts were most important to learn, Kildee asked if he had compared accounts of yesterday's congressional proceedings in the *Washington Post* and *Washington Times*. "History isn't like math where two plus two equals four," Kildee wryly suggested. "It's a lot more than facts, and they don't always add up to the same sum."

The group agreed that Nash should send a stripped-down version of the standards, without the teaching examples, to every member of Congress. With it would go a letter stating that the NCHS would convene a meeting in Washington in early January and invite some of its most visible critics to engage in a discussion with representatives of the project. Goodling agreed to send a "Dear Colleague" letter to every member of the House outlining this procedure and suggesting a cooling-off period.

Later, Quigley and Nash met with staffer John Barth in the Rayburn

cafeteria in a further attempt to get history back on track. Barth, who played
the leading role in advising Goodling in the following months, openly
scorned Cheney, whose attacks, he thought, were disingenuous and politically motivated. The next morning they met with staffers of Democratic
Senators Claiborne Pell of Rhode Island and Edward Kennedy of Massachusetts, and Republican Senators Nancy Kassebaum of Kansas and James
Jeffords of Vermont, members of the Senate's Education, Arts, and Humanities Subcommittee. Gathering in the office of David Evans, a Pell adviser on education issues who enjoyed bipartisan admiration for his
professionalism, Nash and Quigley learned that the problem for Senate
staffers, like other civil servants, was not the history standards but rather the
political attacks on them. Indeed, one officer reported, Kassebaum had
taken the books home to read and found them rigorous, enlightening, and
praiseworthy. Cheney was not held in much repute. It took only half an
hour to agree that the Goodling gambit was workable, that a letter should
go out from the four senators calling for close attention to the history standards themselves rather than the sound bites, and that a January meeting
should bring the standards coordinators together with some of the critics.

In Los Angeles, Nash wrote the agreed-upon letter to members of Congress. It was to be released just before Christmas with attached "Dear Colleague" memos from Goodling, Pell, Kennedy, Jeffords, and Kassebaum.
The letter promised that a "basic edition" of the National History Standards, not to include the hundreds of "examples of student achievement,"
would be published within a few months and would incorporate modifications, rephrasings, and fine-tuning suggested by organizations and task
forces that had participated in the original consensus-building process. "We
are confident," Nash wrote, "that our ongoing efforts to develop broad-
based consensus in the area of history will result in a book that will be a
great resource for teachers, curriculum specialists, and parents." The letter
concluded with word that Nash was organizing a meeting where "a small
group of historians and teachers who collaboratively drafted these books"
would confer with some of the "principal critics." Unfortunately, this letter,
though hand delivered to the key House and Senate staffers, never reached
members of Congress. This may have been because Goodling and the Senate advisers decided to wait until after the Christmas intersession. But other
forces were at work.

The Brookings Showdown

A new and revealing chapter in the history war opened on January 12, 1995,
when representatives of the history standards project met with a group of

critics at the Brookings Institution in Washington. Around the table sat four individuals who had played key roles in developing the standards: Nash, Dunn, Joyce Appleby, and Donald Woodruff. The invited critics included Albert Shanker, president of the American Federation of Teachers (AFT); Shanker's lieutenant, Ruth Wattenberg; Diane Ravitch, who had reviewed an early draft of the U.S. standards and made criticisms that she felt had been only partially addressed in the final edition; Elizabeth Fox-Genovese and Gilbert Sewell, two members of the National Council for History Standards who had become public critics after publication; and Joy Hakim, a former journalist who had written a series of books for children with inspiring stories on American history.

In a second ring of chairs around the table sat observers from the ED, the NEH, and Democratic and Republican staffers from the House and Senate. Also on hand were Christopher Cross, president of the Council for Basic Education (CBE), a reporter from *Education Week* who had followed the history standards story for three years, and other interested parties, including the education director at Pew Charitable Trusts. One final participant was John Fonte. Lynne Cheney had been invited by phone to attend but instead sent Fonte, who arrived unannounced.

Though convinced that the history guidelines were basically sound, Quigley was most interested in reaching terms of compromise that would prevent media fulminations from lethally wounding the entire standards movement. The discussions were vigorous, candid, tense, and for the most part polite. Some of the critics came to do serious business. Others saw the meeting as a chance to heighten the controversy and to contest basic decisions about the organization and approach of the standards that the National Council, with the endorsement of the project's participating organizations, had made months or even years earlier. For example, the fifteen criteria that the council had adopted to guide the development of the U.S. and World history standards were not anticipated to be "on the table" at this meeting. Even so, some of the critics obliged the group to listen to their objections to Criterion 1, which reads: "Standards should be intellectually demanding, reflect the best historical scholarship, and promote active questioning and learning rather than passive absorption of facts, dates, and names."

This criterion had never been controversial at the council meetings. Shanker, however, protested the statement, insisting that it devalued the importance of children knowing facts. He cited the standards on World War I in the world history guidelines, arguing that nowhere were teachers instructed to teach the main "facts" of the war. Nash replied that the key phrase in the criterion was "passive absorption of facts" and wondered if Shanker was indeed advocating the stultifying classroom methods of old.

Dunn remarked that the history standards were in fact rich in subject matter but that facts must be set in contexts of historical narratives and patterns of cause and effect to have any meaning for children. Nevertheless, Fox-Genovese supported Shanker with the comment that children should learn facts first and analyze and interpret their meaning later. Even Quigley suggested that Criterion 1 was indeed a "red flag" in the controversy, though the statement had never been a subject of contention in any public forum. Nash reiterated that the NCHS was not prepared to put the basic criteria up for auction, and finally the group turned to other matters.

Wattenberg expressed again her consistent view that the world history guidelines should focus mostly on the history of Europe, bringing into question the project's understanding that the World History Standards would be global in scope. Sewell, who had become one of the most quotable critics in the weeks following Cheney's article, reiterated his views that the World History Standards were full of non-Western "esoterica" and (privately to Dunn) that such subjects as the Bantu migrations (the four-millennia movement that culturally and economically transformed the southern half of the African continent) had no business being part of K–12 history education. He also charged that the World History Standards took a "world cultures approach" when in fact in their conceptualization and organization they flatly contradicted the bland and ahistorical "world cultures" courses that had for so long dominated junior high and middle schools. Hakim complained that the history standards, which for the most part took the form of listings of topical guidelines, were "boring," as if they should somehow be unfavorably compared with her sprightly and lavishly illustrated textbooks. Ravitch made constructive suggestions and worked to move the process ahead.

John Fonte, who announced himself as "representing Mrs. Cheney," did not speak at length but repeated his press comment that the standards were "flawed from beginning to end." He zeroed in on a piece of phrasing that referred to the nation's "many peoples" as evidence that the standards writers wished to divide the country into warring ethnic and racial groups. (Fonte would publish an article on this issue the next year in *National Review*, by which time the NCHS had already removed the offending "s" from "people" in the criterion.) He also highlighted another phrase to expose the "political correctness" of the standards, a reference to "white Americans, motivated by land hunger and the ideology of 'Manifest Destiny,'" expanding westward in the nineteenth century. This statement appeared in the introduction to one of the eras of U.S. history, not in a standard. Even so, on this point the book was indeed vulnerable. One member of the NCHS team replied that such blanket or stereotypical references to racial groups should certainly be deleted from a revised edition. It was subsequently done.

Nash summarized the criticisms and indicated how the project coordinators intended to proceed. He stressed that the meeting had been convened because those who developed the standards regarded the endeavor as a continuing process and that it was important to be as responsive to criticism of the published standards as the project had been to reviews of the five drafts that had been widely circulated and critiqued before publication. He also reaffirmed the NCHS's intention to publish as soon as possible a "basic edition" that excluded the examples of student achievement. He confirmed the plan "to have established a broad-based panel of noted scholars and teachers to make recommendations regarding changes in the light of the criticisms and to seek foundation support for this effort." Finally, he reminded the critics that revisions would certainly be made on the basis of responsible criticism, but that they would have to be consonant with the general structure and governing criteria of the original standards and must not compromise the creative consensus that underlay the books.

At a press conference immediately following this meeting, Fonte handed reporters a statement, printed on the letterhead of Lynne Cheney's Committee to Review the Standards, asserting that the history guidelines were fatally flawed and that no progress had been made at the Brookings Institution meeting. An NEH press officer pressed Fonte to acknowledge whether his statement had been prepared before the meeting actually took place. To the amazement of those present, Fonte admitted that he had written it "that morning." Within a few days it would become apparent why he did not hesitate to mock further consensus building. He was helping to prepare a speech for Republican Senator Slade Gorton of Washington to be made on the floor of the Senate.

The 99-1 Senate Vote: A Lesson in Procedural Politics

Joyce Appleby was upbeat about the Brookings meeting, believing that the NCHS had demonstrated to the assembled education officials and congressional staffers its openness to criticism and revision. Dunn and Nash were somewhat discouraged, citing the time wasted on challenges to the criteria and finding Shanker, Wattenberg, Fox-Genovese, Sewell, and Fonte to be more interested in sabotaging the project than in developing a thoughtful revision. Nevertheless, the NCHS was ready to move quickly ahead until, six days later, the roof nearly fell in.

Fonte reportedly had been a speech writer for Senator Gorton at one time. Now, as he publicly stated, he provided most of the material and large chunks of a speech Gorton would present to the Senate on January 18.[3] Judging from information provided Nash, Fonte may have done more. How

U.S. senators' speeches are written is not always easy to know. It is, however, questionable whether Gorton wrote his. The telephone log at the NCHS indicates that Gorton's staff asked for a copy of the history standards the day before the speech, suggesting that no one in the office had yet read them. Moreover, the leading Democratic Senate staffer on education issues told Nash that Cheney and Fonte had put Gorton up to the performance.[4]

The Senate at this time was bogged down in a three-day debate over the Unfunded Mandates Bill (S.1), part of the Republicans' Contract with America. Gorton rose to request the reading of an amendment he had drafted titled "National History Standards." It would, if adopted, have prohibited both the National Education Goals Panel (NEGP) and the National Education Standards and Improvement Council (NESIC) from certifying the National History Standards; denied the award of any federal money to the NCHS; stipulated that any national standards in history established under Goals 2000 not be based on standards developed by NCHS; and specified that the recipient of any federal money for the development of standards should "have a decent respect for United States history's roots in western civilization."[5]

By proposing this secondary amendment to the Unfunded Mandates Bill, Gorton was using a tactic that had a long history in American congressional politics: The legislator attaches a rider to a major bill with the aim of pushing through, usually in the later stages of debate, a pet project extraneous to the issue at hand or, as in this case, language targeted to discredit a foe, imagined or real.

Gorton's speech delivered on behalf of his amendment bore all the trademarks of Fonte's attacks against the standards. What, Gorton asked,

> is a more important part of our Nation's history for our children to study—George Washington or Bart Simpson? Is it more important that they learn about Roseanne Arnold or how America defeated communism as the leader of the free world? . . . According to this document . . . the answers are not what Americans would expect. With this set of standards, our students will not be expected to know George Washington from the man in the Moon. According to this set of standards, American democracy rests on the same moral footing as the Soviet Union's totalitarian dictatorship.[6]

In Orwellian twists of language (see p. 233 for how Gorton distorted references to *The Simpsons* and *Roseanne*), Gorton ticked off the identical charges that Cheney had made in the *Wall Street Journal*, contending in his speech that "the Constitution is not mentioned in the 31 core standards."

Students Should Be Able to:

3A Demonstrate understanding of the international background of World War II by:

[7-12] Analyzing the factors contributing to the rise of Fascism, National Socialism, and Communism in the in the war period. **[Analyze multiple causation]**

[7-12] Explaining the breakdown of the Versailles settlement and League of Nations in the 1930s. **[Challenge the arguments of historical inevitability]**

[9-12] Explaining President Roosevelt's emphasis on hemispheric solidarity as exemplified in the Good Neighbor Policy. **[Draw upon data in historical maps]**

[7-12] Analyzing the reasons for American isolationist sentiment in the interwar period and its effects on international relations and diplomacy. **[Analyze cause-and-effect relationships]**

[5-12] Evaluating the Roosevelt administration's response to aggression in Europe, Africa, and Asia from 1935 to 1941. **[Formulate a position or course of action on an issue]**

[7-12] Analyzing the growing tensions with Japan in East Asia. **[Marshal evidence of antecedent circumstances]**

♦ Organize a cultural jamboree in which the food, music, and art of various ethnic groups are demonstrated.

♦ Create a list of sports and entertainment figures used to advertise specific products. *Do you think this is a good use of sports and entertainment figures? Why or why not?*

Grades 7-8 — Examples of student achievement of Standard 2E include:

♦ Examine the influence of MTV (Music Television) on popular culture. *What is the role of image in the success of popular music figures? How does Madonna symbolize the popular culture created by MTV?*

♦ Using examples from the local community, examine how ethnic art, music, food, and clothing have been incorporated into the mainstream culture and society.

Grades 9-12 — Examples of student achievement of Standard 2E include:

♦ Drawing on the works of artists such as Willem DeKooning, explain how abstract expressionism is an art form illustrating changing societal concerns.

♦ Analyze the reflection of values in such popular TV shows as *Murphy Brown, Roseanne, Married With Children,* and *The Simpsons.* Compare the depiction of values to those expressed in shows like *Ozzie and Harriet, The Honeymooners, Father Knows Best, My Three Sons, All in the Family,* and *The Bill Cosby Show.*

♦ Evaluate the effect of women's participation in sports on gender roles and career choices. *How are images of women changing because of their involvement in sports?*

Roseanne and *The Simpsons* in the National History Standards

Further, he claimed, "Paul Revere and his midnight ride will never capture the imagination of our children," and "Ben Franklin's discovery of electricity will not encourage young scientists to seek out their own discoveries that can change the world." Gorton declared that the World History Standards "whitewash the less attractive historical backgrounds of many non-Western civilizations" and consign Western civilization to burial "as a relatively minor element of the world we live in today." The senator demanded that this "ideologically driven, anti-Western monument to politically correct caricature" designed to "destroy our Nation's mystic chords of memory" be regarded as "a horrendous threat to the vitality and accuracy of American history education." The standards, "beyond any hope of salvaging," should be terminated, "junked in total," and "recalled like a shipload of badly contaminated food."[7]

Some senators rose in support of the amendment, but others opposed it. Senator Pell said, "This amendment is an unwarranted governmental intrusion into what is basically a private effort. It also constitutes micromanagement to a degree that is neither wise nor necessary." Pell reminded his colleagues that the NCHS leadership had met with critics shortly before and had agreed to consider revisions. "Their commitment," Pell went on, "is to remove historical bias and to build a broad base of consensus in support of the proposed standards." Democratic Senator Jeff Bingaman of New Mexico echoed Pell in declaring that Congress had no business "directing the National Education Goals Panel, made up primarily of Governors in this country, directing them as to what action to take or not to take on specific standards."[8]

Senator Jeffords opposed the amendment, observing that criticism of the standards had been "focused not on the standards themselves but upon the examples of activities for students in each grade level. Of the thousands of examples not more than 25 were considered controversial. . . . The Center for History in the Schools is reviewing and altering its work. This, in fact is and should be, the appropriate process and primary purpose of public commentary." Jeffords went on to criticize Gorton's attempt "to step in and derail" the movement for higher school standards. Senator Kassebaum stated that she would support the amendment, not because she favored "prohibiting a federally authorized council from certifying a particular set of voluntary standards" but because she intended to introduce legislation to abolish NESIC, the proposed body that would have had authority to "certify" standards.[9]

It was Bingaman who stepped forward with a temporizing measure. Mindful that the Republican majority had the votes to pass the amendment, even if every Democrat voted against it, he offered an alternative—a kind of Hobson's choice. If Gorton scaled back his rider to a sense-of-the-Senate resolution, which would not have binding legal force, then Democrats would vote for it, however offensive it might be to them. The legislators could then get back to the business at hand, which was unfunded mandate reform. Gorton agreed, and thus the Senate passed by a vote of 99–1 a resolution stating that NEGP and NESIC should not approve or certify the standards developed by the NCHS, that future national guidelines for history should "not be based on standards developed primarily by the NCHS prior to February 1, 1995," and that any new project supported by federal funds should show "a decent respect for the contributions of Western civilization." (Senator Bennett Johnston of Louisiana cast the only dissenting vote, though not because he supported the standards.) As amended, the resolution omitted Gorton's original stipulation barring federal funds to the NCHS.

To well-informed observers in the Senate gallery, it was obvious the action had been hasty and purely procedural. The Senate had held no hearings on the history standards; the Subcommittee on Education, Arts, and Humanities had taken no action; and not one of the teachers and scholars who had produced the guidelines had been consulted. It was also apparent that most of the senators voted on the resolution without having opened a copy of the documents at issue. Patty Murray, Gorton's Senate colleague from Washington, admitted that she voted for the resolution without ever having seen the standards "in order to move the debate back to the unfunded mandates bill that was on the floor at the time."[10] Senator Paul Sarbanes of Maryland wrote to a constituent:

> While I, and a number of my colleagues, opposed the Gorton amendment as introduced, it was likely that the amendment would have been adopted if put to a vote. Consequently, I supported efforts to change the amendment to a non-binding "sense of the Senate" resolution.... Further efforts to jeopardize the National History Standards may be mounted and, in this regard, it is most helpful to have the benefit of your thoughtful comments.[11]

Less than two weeks after the Senate passed the resolution, it voted to strip its Unfunded Mandates Bill of all extraneous provisions, including the resolution disapproving the history standards. Later, the House took up the bill but never introduced the history standards issue at all. Nevertheless, a chill wind blew through the NCHS office in Los Angeles. The world's most powerful deliberative body had intervened in support of the most fervent critics of the standards to tell the nation's teachers and academic historians that its guidelines for schools had been written irresponsibly and malevolently.

The Senate vote by no means convinced all Americans that the standards were "fundamentally flawed," as Fonte described them. NEH Chairman Sheldon Hackney stated in a press release: "In the case of the history standards, the way some people have politicized the discussion is a real disservice to the nation; the discussion has become more of a 'drive by debate' than a thoughtful consideration. School reform is much too important to be made a hostage in the culture wars."[12] In the ensuing days press support of the guidelines probably exceeded the attacks. An op-ed piece by Helen Wheatley, a historian at Seattle University, was published in a large newspaper in Senator Gorton's state, exposing point by point how his speech distorted both the content and meaning of the standards. "By voting to reject the standards," Wheatley noted, "the Senators also rejected the work of the National Education Association, the National Association of Elementary School Principals, the American Association of School Librarians, the American Association for State and Local History, and numerous other organizations."[13] Historian Eric Foner wrote to the *New York Times* that behind the congressional action lay

> an ominous precedent—the Senate manipulating Federal funds to promote an official interpretation of American history. This kind of thing used to happen regularly in other countries, but until recently was held to be inappropriate for a society that values freedom of thought. . . . I find it hard to understand why conservatives like Ms. Cheney, who favor a radical reduction in the Federal Government's powers, are not disturbed by this governmental attempt to dictate how scholars and teachers ought to interpret the nation's past.[14]

Harold Hyman, president of the American Society for Legal History and a professor of constitutional history at Rice University, wrote Texas Senators Phil Gramm and Kay Bailey Hutchison:

> The contributors of the National History Standards have dealt remarkably even-handedly with the many controversial matters that these areas of academic inquiry and analysis necessarily embrace. In my judgment a heavy burden of proof rests, therefore, upon those who suggest that the existing version of the National History Standards is ideologically flawed. Conversely, a weighty duty exists on such persons to produce superior alternative analyses that are verifiable from evidence, not from present-minded goals or footnoted sentimentalisms.[15]

One educator who had taught history for twenty years at Friends Seminary in New York City and contributed to development of the World History Standards wrote Gorton:

> On what evidence did you base your [speech]? Did you or any of your staff actually read the proposed standards? ... The teachers who participated in the democratic process that resulted in scholarly accurate and pedagogically innovative content standards in history were proud to offer our time and experience as part of a process that certainly "manifested a decent respect for the democratic process."[16]

Gorton's action represented an effort by a federal legislator to propose that Congress determine whether particular subject matter should be taught in American public schools. In effect, his amendment would have put Congress in the position of judging whether history standards developed by any state or local jurisdiction—the city of Seattle, for example—using federal funds they had received under Goals 2000 were properly respectful of U.S. history, ideas, and institutions "to the increase of freedom and prosperity around the world." Presumably, the Seattle schools might come under congressional censure or perhaps court action if its standards taught students that U.S. occupation of Cuba, the Philippines, or other lands at the end of the nineteenth century involved imperial motives. Clearly, if part of the Republican agenda in the 104th Congress was to get the federal government off the backs of state and local school authorities, Gorton was not advancing it.

The Senator's amendment also indicted the historical scholarship on which the standards were based, an action akin to condemning science standards in modern physics or chemistry because they were based on such "revisionism" as Einstein's theory of relativity. The senator demanded that the history standards be "stopped, abolished, repudiated, repealed." But who would do the repudiating and repealing in the absence of a federal agency with the centralized power to dictate curriculum? And if some government agency could be invested with the authority to remove thousands of copies of the history standards from libraries, schools, curriculum specialists' offices, or teachers' homes, what penalty would be imposed on those who found the books useful and refused to surrender them?

Bashing the history standards was certainly not the whole objective of Gorton's initiative. The larger strategy seems to have been to fight the culture wars, specifically to strike a blow against any federal education or cultural agency that might be linked to the guidelines, and to undermine any effort to set national standards, over which ideologues of the Right felt they had no control.

Historians and Teachers Rally

When the history standards war broke out, the history profession largely re-acted to the right-wing media blitz with puzzled silence. Most regarded the controversy as unfair and unwelcome, but in the first month or two they stood on the sidelines. History teachers and scholars were busy with their classes and research. The majority of scholars were not involved with his-tory education in the schools, and few were accustomed to being in the pub-lic eye. Most had suffered nothing more unpleasant in their professional roles than an adverse review of their latest book, and even hostile review-ers of their work were unlikely ever to have charged them with "kidnapping history" or being "history thieves."

As recounted in Chapter 8, a handful of historians, mostly those involved in developing the standards, came forward quickly with op-ed essays, let-ters, and media appearances. Theodore Rabb mused, "Something strange is going on when a normally invisible historian of Early Modern Europe sud-denly has a constantly ringing telephone.... The callers' interest, of course, is not history but the politics of history."[17]

The steady drumbeat of criticism convinced the history profession that its work over recent decades was under indictment. Consequently, his-torians and teachers took up their pens to produce short, thoughtful essays on the guidelines and how they might affect classroom practices.[18] At the University of California, Davis, Ruth Rosen surveyed the scene created by the media war and wrote, "What the right really hates about this new his-tory is that it has been written by some of the same people who fought against segregation and gender discrimination, who protested the Vietnam War, and gave birth to the environmental and gay-rights movements.... It is a generation that believes the democratic promise of America, magnifi-cent as it is, is still unfolding and has yet to be realized by everyone."[19] Brian Copenhaver, a historian of European philosophy in the sixteenth and sev-enteenth centuries and provost of UCLA's College of Letters and Science, put it:

> I write and teach about Renaissance history. I've also read the new na-tional history standards, so wildly misread by John Fonte, by Lynne Cheney, and by a few others whose distortions twist these important vol-umes beyond recognition. As a student of the Renaissance, I study a small group of people, ... [whose] genius ... was to speak persuasively to the present and the future through the past. Our memory of Erasmus, More, Machiavelli, Milton and others educated by them shows how their Re-

naissance has endured. One of the basics in their educational program, however narrowly conceived, was to tell the truth about history—a lesson that Ms. Cheney and Mr. Fonte apparently skipped. The humanists created a strong intellectual solvent in their historicized curriculum. History, told truly and fully, always cuts through the muck eventually.[20]

Thirteen recent presidents of the American Historical Association and the Organization of American Historians (OAH) weighed in with their collective judgment that "the claim that the standards represent a p.c.-inspired effort to distort the histories of the United States and Western Civilization cannot be sustained by a careful examination of them." The history standards, they wrote, "beyond their comprehensiveness, . . . also include wonderful ideas for introducing literature, biography, and art into history instruction as well as concrete proposals for getting students to appreciate that historical understanding involves both knowing and thinking."[21] Arnita Jones, executive director of the OAH, lamented the way conservative critics were creating "a serious misunderstanding, if not demonization, of several decades of scholarship in American history."[22]

After the Senate resolution in January 1995, entire history departments began writing their senators to express their shock at Congress's irresponsible action. Stanford's history department unanimously signed a letter that the history standards "are a serious and responsible attempt to present issues and problems which historians now address. . . . This was an intensely American process in which many voices were heard on matters of great importance."[23] Oberlin's historians "deplored the politically motivated attacks" on "well-balanced guidelines. . . . We would be delighted to find our Oberlin classrooms full of students whose historical knowledge had been shaped at the K–12 level by these Standards."[24]

Entire faculties at some universities criticized the Senate intrusions. The faculty senate of the State University of New York, representing twenty-four thousand faculty and professional staff, chided the Senate for "unwarranted and potentially harmful political and legislative interference in the academic freedom and responsibility of scholars and teachers in the field of history . . . to seek truth, engage freely in the interchange and dissemination of ideas, and pass on their findings to others."[25] A month later, the faculty senate of the City University of New York transmitted a resolution to New York's two senators, expressing its belief that the vote "represents an unwarranted and potentially harmful legislative interference in the academic freedom and responsibility of scholars and teachers."[26] These two faculty groups represented not only humanists and social scientists but also schools of education, law, medicine, business, dentistry, engineering, and the arts.

They embodied intellectual and political viewpoints running from one end of the spectrum to the other.

The NEH under Fire

In their attempt to bury the National History Standards, the culture warriors were after much bigger prey: the NEH, the NEA, the ED, and the Corporation for Public Broadcasting. Less than a week following the Senate action on the history standards, Lynne Cheney spoke out again in the *Wall Street Journal.* In a punchy op-ed piece titled, "Kill My Old Agency, Please," she cited the history standards and other NEH-funded projects she didn't like as evidence that "a prolonged period of postmodernism," which teaches that "objectivity is an illusion," had poisoned both the NEH and the NEA. Therefore these organizations should be abolished. Projects, she declared, that serve "our national heritage and the heritage of Western civilization" such as preservation of the papers of Benjamin Franklin should be turned over to private enterprise.[27]

On January 24, Cheney appeared as a witness, along with William Bennett, Charlton Heston, and others, before the House Subcommittee on Interior Appropriations to discuss future funding of the two endowments. She made her usual charges against the history standards, citing the way they turned out as good reason for abolishing the NEH. Most of the Republican-led committee was ready to say "Amen" to her invective, but David Skaggs, Democrat of Colorado, challenged Cheney's statement that if fifth- and sixth-grade classrooms base their study of World War II on the National History Standards, children will learn nothing about Japanese atrocities, only about the tragedy of a Japanese girl who died painfully of leukemia in the aftermath of the atomic bomb attack on Hiroshima. Skaggs pointed out that this little girl's story was not a standard at all but rather a book cited in one of the teaching activities. The relevant standards (see pp. 242–43) called for, among other things, student understanding of "the international background of World War II" and "the global scope and human costs of the war." Based on his own review of the guidelines, Skaggs observed that the standards "suggest a much broader breadth of understanding of the war and the end of the war" than Cheney alleged. Her reply to that, a reply preceded by three months of continuous public commentary on the standards, was, "Maybe I read them too quickly."[28]

Three days later, Frank Rich, a columnist for the *New York Times*, reported on the Cheney-Skaggs exchange, wondering whether her opposition to the U.S. History Standards, whose development she had earlier praised, lid not result from the project going bad but because "she will stop at nothing to be a major player in the Gingrich order? The evidence suggests that she deliberately caricatured her own former pet project as politically correct so it might be wielded as a Mapplethorpe-like symbol to destroy the agency she so recently championed."[29]

Refereeing the Controversy

Though historians stepped forward after Gorton's hostile initiative, nobody had illusions that single voices or even large organizations could match the media reach of Rush Limbaugh on radio and TV or Lynne Cheney and John Leo in *Reader's Digest* and *U.S. News & World Report.* To counter the tactics of the right-wing strategists something more would be required. The most promising plan was to invoke a time-honored American tradition: a blue-ribbon commission composed of nonpartisan, visible, and respected figures who could independently assay the problem, consider all the facets of the controversy, and make recommendations in the service of better history education.

The NCHS had agreed in principle to such a plan at the Brookings meeting. One or two of the critics present had suggested that the review panel be composed of traditionalist or conservative scholars on the premise that the original volumes were the work of "UCLA ultra-liberals" and that standards revised by a committee of right-to-center representatives would find wide acceptance in the nation's schools. The idea went nowhere at Brookings, but the Senate action may have inspired some critics to think the standards might now be turned over to a group of "patriotic" writers. At one point, a staffer for Senator Gorton suggested that perhaps conservative foundations should be approached to conduct any proposed review and thus prevent the panel from being stacked with liberals.[30]

Indeed, one day after the Senate's censure, Ruth Wattenberg, the AFT official who accompanied Al Shanker to the Brookings meeting, wrote to an officer of a foundation that showed interest in an independent review and that would later help fund the CBE project. Arguing that "this existing document [the standards], with this immediate parentage, is DOA" and that questions should be raised as to "whether there's any use to a revision effort," Wattenberg urged the foundation to support the idea of asking "some outsiders to take the next crack at revision." These "outsiders" were to be "centrist and conservative historians" who don't share the "perspective" of Nash and others associated with the NCHS. This panel's revised version

STANDARD 3

Students Should Understand: *The origins and course of World War II, the character of the war at home and abroad, and its reshaping of the U.S. role in world affairs.*

Students Should Be Able to:

3A   Demonstrate understanding of the international background of World War II by:

[7-12]   Analyzing the factors contributing to the rise of Fascism, National Socialism, and Communism in the in the war period. [**Analyze multiple causation**]

[7-12]   Explaining the breakdown of the Versailles settlement and League of Nations in the 1930s. [**Challenge the arguments of historical inevitability**]

[9-12]   Explaining President Roosevelt's emphasis on hemispheric solidarity as exemplified in the Good Neighbor Policy. [**Draw upon data in historical maps**]

[7-12]   Analyzing the reasons for American isolationist sentiment in the interwar period and its effects on international relations and diplomacy. [**Analyze cause-and-effect relationships**]

[5-12]   Evaluating the Roosevelt administration's response to aggression in Europe, Africa, and Asia from 1935 to 1941. [**Formulate a position or course of action on an issue**]

[7-12]   Analyzing the growing tensions with Japan in East Asia. [**Marshal evidence of antecedent circumstances**]

Grades 5-6   **Examples of student achievement of Standard 3A include:**

▶ Use political and physical maps to examine the global involvement of nations and people before World War II. Identify the geographic features that affected the U.S. policy of isolationism before World War II. Locate countries in the Western Hemisphere affected by Roosevelt's Good Neighbor Policy. Locate countries that were affected by prewar events such as the Japanese invasion of Manchuria, Italian invasion of Ethiopia, foreign involvement in the Spanish Civil War, the Munich conference over Czechoslovakia, and German demands for the Polish Corridor. Locate countries that formed the Allied and Axis powers at the beginning of World War II.

▶ Locate Pearl Harbor and describe the events that brought the United States into World War II in 1941.

World War II in the National Standards for United States History

would then be published "with Gary's group getting due credit for their initial work."[31] Here Wattenberg revealed that AFT's central leadership wanted not only a massive rewriting of the World History Standards but also major changes in the U.S. guidelines, which she had previously praised.

This attempt to steer the standards in a radical new direction seemed disingenuous. The National Council had, over the course of thirty-two months, processed and profited from repeated national reviews, "centrist"

4B Demonstrate understanding of the global scope and human costs of the war by:

[5-12] Explaining the major turning points of the war, and describing the principal theaters of conflict in Western Europe, Eastern Europe, the Soviet Union, North Africa, Asia, and the Pacific. [Interrogate historical data]

[5-12] Analyzing how and why the Nazi regime perpetrated a "war against the Jews," and describing the devastation suffered by Jews and other groups in the Nazi Holocaust. [Analyze cause-and-effect relationships]

[7-12] Comparing World Wars I and II in terms of the impact of industrial production, national mobilization, technological innovations, and scientific research on strategies, tactics, and levels of destruction. [Marshal evidence of antecedent circumstances]

[7-12] Assessing the consequences of World War II as a total war. [Formulate historical questions]

Grades 5-6 | **Examples of student achievement of Standard 4B include:**

♦ On a world map locate the turning points for the United Nations forces during World War II. *How important were these battles in changing the course of the war?*

♦ Drawing on books such as *Hear O Israel* by Terry Walton Treaseder, *Don't Say A Word* by Barbara Gehrts, *Gideon* by Chester Aaron, *Twenty and Ten* by Claire Hachet Bishop, and *Number of Stars* by Lois Lowry, describe the experiences of Jews living under the Nazi regime and the Holocaust.

♦ Review the treatment of children during the Holocaust and share poems from the book *I Never Saw Another Butterfly.* Illustrate one of the poems.

♦ As part of a group draw up a Declaration of Human Rights for Children. Discuss: *Would it be possible for the world to honor such a document? Is there such a document in existence today? Who wrote it? Would there ever be situations when human rights should not be honored?*

♦ Use books such as Monika Kotowska's *The Bridge to the Other Side* to discuss the human costs of war and the resulting social problems.

♦ Draw on books such as Eleanor Coerr's *Sadako* to discuss the costs of dropping nuclear bombs on Japan. Read *Sadako and the Thousand Paper Cranes.* Make origami cranes and write on them a personal message for world peace. Display in the classroom.

historians and teachers had participated in the project in large numbers, and all the major professional organizations involved in their development, except the AFT, stood solidly behind what had been done. Moreover, advising that the "next crack" at the standards be awarded to a commission of conservative scholars ignored another fact: historians or teachers identified with the radical Left of the political spectrum had never been involved in the standards project. If conservatives should have the next crack, when should prominent Marxist, New Leftist, Afrocentrist, and radical feminist scholars get their turn?

The principal leader in putting an independent review plan into action was Robert Schwartz, director of educational programs at the Pew Charitable Trusts. For years, Schwartz had quietly been making grants to organizations and individuals whose proposals promised to strengthen American education, whether in schools, museums, or neighborhood sites. Through his efforts, the Ford Foundation, the John D. and Catherine T. MacArthur Foundation, and the Spencer Foundation agreed to be cofunders. All four organizations were convinced that torpedoing the standards was not in the nation's interest and certainly not in the interest of the campaign against historical illiteracy.

Schwartz obtained the agreement of the CBE in Washington to undertake the responsibility of forming the commission, providing staff, and publishing the final report. CBE was an apt choice, for it had been involved for four decades in efforts to improve precollegiate education, had a reputation in Washington as a highly professional organization with moderate Republican leadership, and had as its current president a man who had been the chief Republican House of Representatives staffer on education issues during the Nixon and Ford years. Christopher Cross, Schwartz thought, would have the confidence of even the Gingrichites.

Cross's task was to assemble two panels of unassailable, fair-minded, and knowledgeable persons. One would deal with the U.S. History Standards, the other with the World History Standards. To chair the world history panel, Cross secured the services of Stephen Muller, president emeritus of Johns Hopkins University, whose career had been spent as a political scientist of Latin America and a team builder and negotiator at Hopkins. To lead the U.S. history panel, Cross found Albert Quie, a Midwestern Lutheran minister who had served nine terms in the House of Representatives, followed by a term as Republican governor of Minnesota. Cognizant that the panels were certain to find themselves in the public gaze, Cross gathered together a range of accomplished people of varied intellectual and political sensibilities.[32]

Through the summer and early fall of 1995, the commission held three-day sessions in Philadelphia, Washington, and Williamsburg, Virginia. Participants say the sessions were vigorous, intellectually stimulating, and contentious, yet held together by a common understanding that the panelists' job was to offer constructive suggestions to defuse the controversy and get better history education back on track. Robert Bain, a teacher on the world history panel, reported that the meetings were not droning committee affairs but exhilarating, far-ranging seminars on global history and how to teach it.

Doling Out Scorn

While the commission was at work, the Senate Majority Leader spoke at the annual meeting of the American Legion in Indianapolis on Labor Day, 1995. Sounding much like a man who had read Cheney, Fonte, and Leo's criticisms but not the National History Standards themselves, Bob Dole found the guidelines not simply wrongheaded or unbalanced but downright treasonous. "Worse than external enemies," he said.

Dole was following the Nixon strategy of running for president: Zig sharply right to win nomination, then zag back to the center to win the election. The Right had played the game of bogus populism for some time, claiming that its authoritarian impulses were the people's democratic sensibilities while charging that liberals—who had historically stood for American labor, for the rights of women and minorities, and for equal opportunity—were actually elitists. "There is a shocking campaign afoot," Dole charged, "among educators at all levels—most evident in the national history standards . . . to disparage America and disown the ideas and traditions of the West." Moreover, "the purpose of the National History Standards seems not to teach our children certain essential facts about our history, but to denigrate America's story while sanitizing and glorifying other cultures."

That the Lutheran Education Association, the National Catholic Educational Association, the Native American Heritage Commission, and over two dozen other not-very-radical groups had supported these standards was probably unknown to the Legionnaires. But Dole, indulging in a ritualized recitation of charges suitable for preelection speeches to a sympathetic audience, did not tell them. Instead he claimed that the educators who perpetrated the history standards were the "intellectual elites who seem embarrassed by America."[33] The "embarrassed by America" crowd came, in fact, from nearly every state, from towns large and small, from places unlikely to harbor teachers bent on attacking American values and encouraging students "to disparage America and disown the ideas and traditions of the West."

Confusing the picture of who wrote the history standards, Dole vowed that "the federal government must end its war on traditional American values." Perhaps some in the audience knew that these guidelines, along with the other standards, were completely voluntary; were not endorsed by the NEH or the ED, and were never submitted for review to any government agency. But to Dole, it seemed essential that he not allow other Republican aspirants to get to his right. And one of them was getting there fast, including a position on the standards.

Pat Buchanan had made it clear, even before the guidelines appeared, that he had no interest in the inclusion of African Americans, women, and other forgotten groups in the history textbooks that children learn from. Early in the history standards war, he had served as cohost for a Washington radio program where Lynne Cheney and Gary B. Nash were the guest pugilists. Buchanan accused Nash of leading a bead-wearing sandaled crowd of leftover sixties radicals who had no faith in America and enjoyed teaching children to malign their country. "They're trying to poison the minds of American children against the history and heritage of this country," Buchanan told audiences in his stump speeches in the winter of 1995–96. "That's what these elitists are doing in these universities that do those kinds of textbooks and guidelines, and that's coming right out of the Department of Education."[34] On the campaign trail, he promised once elected president to abolish the NEH, NEA, and ED. As for the history standards, they should be recalled—a line that Cheney began using about the time it became clear that the standards were selling briskly, despite the media blitz.

The Clinton Administration Runs for Cover

When President Clinton and Secretary of Education Riley received an advance copy of Dole's Labor Day speech, they "panicked," as one of Clinton's supporters told Nash. Even before Dole addressed the Legion, Riley's public relations team had a press release ready. "The President and I do not think the history standards are the basis for a good curriculum in the schools," the secretary announced. A few days later, at the National Press Club, Riley emphasized that his department "had nothing to do with them" and allowed that "they portray American history in a bad light, and that is a mistake."[35]

Riley's comments represented a striking turnabout. A year earlier, shortly after the history standards were first attacked, his department released a statement declaring that the "proposed U.S. History Standards ... represent[s] the work of a wide cross-section of historians and teachers who have participated in this effort to encourage and advance the study of history in the American classroom." The release advised citizens to regard the books "as the starting point of a reasonable and disciplined dialogue among historians, teachers, and the American public to ensure a broad national consensus. The imperfections inherent in a document of this nature will be sorted out during this dialogue and the result should be a balanced view of American history that reflects our best traditions and values."[36] A few weeks later, when queried at a press conference about the standards, Riley called them "a very innovative approach" and added, "I see some real value in approaching history in an interesting way, but since I have not read the standards, it is impossible for me to make a personal observation on whether they're good, bad, or indifferent."[37]

Between November 1994 and January 1995, Riley's lieutenants met and talked with Nash many times without ever suggesting that their boss thought that standards from hell had been loosed on the American schools. At a meeting in March 1995 with Nash and Quigley, they expressed their support for the guidelines and their intention to find ways to combat Cheney and her allies. Assistant Secretary of Education Thomas Payzant uttered no condemnation of the standards when late that month he addressed the annual meeting of the OAH on the subject of the controversy.

Six months later, when Nash phoned both Jennifer Davis, Riley's special assistant, and Kevin Sullivan, public relations officer, to express his dismay at Riley's denunciation of the standards, the ED position had clearly changed. "We're blocking for the president," Sullivan explained. "You know there's an election coming up." Nash pointed out that blocking below the knees costs fifteen yards for unsportsmanlike conduct and suggested that a statesmanlike posture, in the face of Dole's attacks, might be to explain to the American people that a blue-ribbon commission was examining the standards and the controversy and was about to release its findings to the public. Sullivan and Davis protested that they had to do what they had to do, that Clinton could not afford to have this issue held against him while under attack on other fronts. Nash wondered aloud if Riley's primary responsibility wasn't the education of American children rather than the reelection of Bill Clinton.

Teachers who served on the task forces that created the standards wrote angrily to Riley, tasking him for his turnabout. Sue Rosenthal, a 20-year veteran in the Philadelphia schools, spoke her mind:

> I am writing to protest in the strongest terms the words you have spoken in your biased attack on the National U.S. and World history standards. . . . I have never been more honored to be a part of any group [the world history task force]. What an extraordinarily qualified and dedicated assemblage of teachers! . . . The intellectual honesty of the U.S. Secretary of Education should overcome the temptation to seek political favor or pander to special interests."[38]

David Vigilante, a nationally decorated "teacher of the year," expressed to Riley his "astonishment and regret that you have succumbed to political

HISTORY ON TRIAL

pressure," pointing out that "blanket condemnation of the History Standards plays into the hands of those who advocate a 'smiling face' history
purged of all but sidebars and occasional pictures which recognize the diversity of this nation."[39]

Shortly after, the *Congressional Quarterly Researcher*, which publishes
in-depth reports on pertinent issues in play in Washington, devoted
twenty-two pages to the subject. The report reminded readers that U.S. history "has sparked controversies for almost as long as history has been taught
in schools." It reviewed the new scholarship about women, African Americans, and others left out of older textbooks and described the "search for
consensus."[40]

Six weeks later, *Education Week* published an analysis of the controversy
with the title "Playing Games With History." Readers were reminded that
in October 1994, Cheney trashed the U.S. History Standards in the *Wall
Street Journal* and blamed Clinton officials. A telling insert called "Myths
and Realities" (see p. 250) lined up Cheney-initiated charges with what the
researchers actually found in the history standards. "Many of the rebukes,"
they wrote, "which have attained near-mythical status" echoed examples
given in Cheney's (*Wall Street Journal*) piece, and resurfaced in Senator Gorton's speech where he tried "to persuade the U.S. Senate to censure the
standards."[41] Like the *Congressional Quarterly Researcher*, the report detailed
the involvement of thirty national educational organizations and quoted
Cheney's comment in August 1992 that "it may be the single most important
legacy that those of us who have been working on education reform since
1983 leave—the idea and the fact of externally set standards."[42]

The History Standards Revised

At the same time that Senator Dole was likening the history standards
to an alien invasion and Secretary Riley was on the verge of reporting them
to the national Center for Disease Control, Nash and the staff at UCLA
were awaiting word from the CBE panels on their preliminary recommendations. On October 11, following their third session, the panels gave a
preview of their report-in-progress at a press conference at Colonial
Williamsburg. Sketching their major findings and criticisms, the panelists
recommended that the standards be revised—not radically overhauled or
returned to the drawing board—and declared that a new edition "would
make appropriately high academic demands on American students and
contribute in important ways to developing a responsible and productive
citizenry."[43]

Noting that "the overwhelming majority" of negative remarks about the guidelines had been directed not against the actual standards but against the teaching examples, the panelists also recommended that all the activities be deleted from the revised edition. This should be done, they counseled, because the examples were being misperceived as a "national curriculum," were the subject of numerous contentions over "bean counting" of historical names, and included flawed language of one sort or another. The commissioners affirmed that the standards, detached from the activities, "provide a reasonable set of expectations for learning and a solid basis for strengthening history teaching."

The commission also called for a number of improvements: expanded treatment of certain subjects, clarification of certain concepts, elimination of biased language, and more effective connection of ethnic and gender issues to their wider historical contexts. Though the news release cited the "intrusive European migrants" phrase in the world history guidelines as evidence of loaded language, the panels strongly endorsed the standards' approach to world history and observed that the balance in treatment of the West and other parts of the world was about right. What the commissioners did not say was also of great importance. They did not criticize the first edition for being too inclusive of women and minorities, for stressing social history too much, for expunging white males, for deprecating Western civilization, or for neglecting George Washington and the Constitution. In no sense did they legitimize Lynne Cheney's view that the standards were "politically correct to a fare-thee-well" or John Fonte's statement that they were "seriously flawed . . . from start to finish."[44]

The news release suggested that the project would be vindicated in the main. The educators who had collaborated in writing the original guidelines would not find their work rejected, and indeed should be congratulated for building a framework for student achievement on a half century of historical scholarship and pedagogical practice. In subsequent days, the announcement received wide though not sustained national coverage. The particular take on the report depended on the newspaper. The Associated Press put a negative spin on it, listing the criticisms, largely ignoring the supportive recommendations, and implying spuriously that the original guidelines had neglected the "Founding Fathers" and "documents like the Declaration of Independence."[45] Lynne Cheney faulted the CBE panels' finding that "the proposed standards provide a solid basis for strengthening history teaching," and said, "There are a multitude of other alterations that the CBE should insist upon."[46] Most papers accurately reported the panels' report. The *Los Angeles Times* ran an editorial concluding that the "review panels have largely validated the views of those who endorse these

Myths *and* Realities

After Lynne V. Cheney wrote a blistering op-ed piece for The Wall Street Journal *in October 1994, other editorials and columns began appearing nationwide that were also highly critical of the U.S. history standards.*

Many of the rebukes, which have attained near-mythical status, echoed examples given in Cheney's piece. In his speech to persuade the U.S. Senate to censure the standards, Sen. Slade Gorton, R-Wash., also sounded similar chords.

While many of the criticisms are technically correct, they mischaracterize the scope, content, and tenor of the document. Here are a few examples.

MYTH:

○ The U.S. Constitution merits no mention in the 31 standards, although it does appear in the supporting materials.

REALITY:

○ This is one of the few times when Cheney distinguishes between the standards and the teaching examples. The word "Constitution" does not appear in the 31 sentences that constitute the first part of each standard. One of the 31 sentences, however, alludes directly to the document: Students should understand "the institutions and practices of government created during the revolution and how they were revised between 1787 and 1815 to create the foundation of the American political system." Under each of the 31 sentences are subsections that specifically address the Constitution and the Bill of Rights. All told, the Constitution is mentioned 177 times throughout the document.

○ Sen. Joseph McCarthy, the Cold Warrior whose ruthless pursuit of real and imagined Communist agents and sympathizers in the 1950s has been largely repudiated, and McCarthyism are mentioned 19 times—a telling example of how the standards set a negative tone about the United States.

○ McCarthy and McCarthyism are indeed mentioned 19 times—all in a two-page section on the Cold War. Seventeen of the citations are in teaching examples, which are divided into different activities for grades 5-6, 7-8, and 9-12. The writers do not use pronouns for the senator or the campaign that bears his name. Consequently, in one teaching example alone, McCarthy's name or its derivative comes up five times, and, in another, the words appear four times. Moreover, the emphasis is not so much on McCarthyism as it is on students' ability to understand the climate that allowed it to develop and thrive and the reasons for its repudiation.

○ George Washington makes only a fleeting appearance and is never described as the first president of the United States.

○ Washington's name appears only a few times in the teaching examples in the era covering the American Revolution and the forging of a new nation. One example asks students about the major issues confronting the "Washington administration," and an engraving of Washington's inauguration is included. But teachers would have a hard time addressing some of the standards themselves unless they talked about the first president. For example, one standard says that students should be able to analyze "the character and roles of the military, political, and diplomatic leaders who helped forge the American victory." Meanwhile, Thomas Jefferson, arguably the most important Founding Father, is cited time and again. Besides, Washington is a staple of the K-4 volume that students are expected to have completed before they reach the U.S. document for 5th to 12th graders.

○ Albert Einstein makes no appearance at all.

○ While Einstein, a native of Germany, is not in the U.S. standards, he appears in the world-history volume in the standard on changes in science and the arts in the first half of the 20th century and in the accompanying teaching examples.

Myths and realities in the National History Standards
Education Week, November 15, 1995

standards" and that the CBE's effort ought to "push these worthy—and ambitious—standards toward widespread adoption."[47]

For his part, Riley issued a wary statement reaffirming his support for academic standards in general and commending CBE's work as "an important step forward in the resolution of the controversy." His statement went on, however, to proclaim that children "must have a full understanding and appreciation of the Constitution and the Bill of Rights," even though the original history standards urged precisely that.[48]

Although CBE did not publish its special report on the standards until January 1996, it provided the NCHS with advance versions, as well as comments by individual panelists, in order to help get the revision process under way. When the standards-writing project started in 1992, participating groups had understood that owing to the continuing stream of new scholarship, national history guidelines would have to be "an ongoing, dynamic process of improvement and revision over the years to come."[49] The project's original blueprint, however, did not provide for either organizational machinery or public funding for changes or updates. The original ED and NEH grants for the project had been used up months before. In the fall of 1995, neither agency was about to touch the history standards, even though Clinton and Riley no doubt hoped that CBE's intervention and a subsequent revision would get the conservative culture warriors off the administration's back.

By this time the NCHS staff was serving teachers in a variety of ways around the country, and filling the continuous flow of orders for the standards and the center's other educational materials. The Rockefeller and Spencer foundations provided money to revise and print the new edition. These grants were modest compared to the original federal money for the project, but the funders understood that the CBE's work would be pointless in the absence of sufficient money to carry through on the recommendations.

Following the press conference, Nash consulted widely to determine the timeliest and most collegial way to get the new edition out. Neither money nor time was available to reconvene the original National Council, large teacher task forces, or focus groups representing the major professional organizations. In any case, nearly all of the associations that had participated in writing and reviewing the first edition had expressed their approval of it.

Between November and the end of February 1996, the NCHS carried out most of the CBE panels' recommendations for changes in the U.S. and World history standards. Throughout the previous year it had kept a careful record of critical reviews of the standards in the popular and professional press, as well as useful comments received from teachers, historians, and other citizens. Nash, Dunn, and Linda Symcox, working with small task forces of secondary and collegiate educators, now supervised the process of sifting through, discussing, and reformulating numerous recommendations. Comments on the CBE report were solicited from the members of the original National Council and the heads of the participating groups. Nash and Dunn also consulted a number of teachers and experts around the country for advice.

Late in December, the NCHS formed a new advisory board (half of whose members were K–12 teachers), and the following month convened this group in Los Angeles to review a draft of the new edition. The CBE's *History in the Making: An Independent Review of the Voluntary National History Standards* was published at the end of January, but because the organization had cooperated closely with the NCHS in providing advance drafts and individual panelists' critiques, the revision was by this time nearing completion. The document went to press in March and was published on April 3, 1996.

The new Basic Edition of the National Standards for History combined the standards for K–4, U.S., and world history in a single volume. The teaching activities, which accounted for about half the text in the three original volumes, were deleted. The standards for K–4 remained unchanged from the first edition because they had not been controversial (even Lynne Cheney praised them), and the CBE panels had no charge to review them. The standards on "historical thinking" underwent only minor revisions to sharpen language or add a few skills that students should cultivate. No modification was made to the "criteria for the development of standards," except that in Criterion 9 a reference to America's "many peoples" was changed to "many people."

The revised U.S. History Standards for grades 5–12 incorporated a variety of changes. Among the major modifications were new elements encouraging study of the impact of science and technology; addition of several statements on immigration and its relationship to the forging of national identity; amplification of the themes of economic opportunity and democratic evolution; greater attention to the European background of North American settlement and economic history; and more nuanced treatment of Soviet-American conflict after World War II. In all ten eras of history a number of statements were reformulated to ensure that references to women and to ethnic and racial minorities were contextualized in relation to particular historical developments or social environments, thus avoiding the faulty notion that women, African Americans, Latinos, or other categories constituted homogeneous groups that thought or behaved deterministically or possessed self-contained histories separate from the broad streams of the American past.

At the end of the U.S. section of the book a new standard was added that bid students to explore issues in the national past that might include the history standards controversy itself: "Evaluate the continuing struggle for *e pluribus unum* amid debates over national vs. group identity, group rights vs. individual rights, multiculturalism, and bilingual education." Perhaps better than any other, this statement captured the spirit of the entire project because it implied that students should not regard a publicly controversial document like the standards as a historical scripture to be memorized and recited but, on the contrary, as an interesting artifact of the recent American past to be scrutinized and debated.

In revising the World History Standards, NCHS followed most of the CBE report's suggestions. The panel supported the validity of genuinely globe-encircling history, as this teaching field had evolved in the 1980s and early 1990s, and it found little evidence that Western civilization had been marginalized or bashed in the first edition. Its recommendations, therefore, aimed not to take the standards back to 1950s Western-Civ-as-world-history but to make them even more effectively globe-encompassing and useful for young Americans poised on the doorstep of the twenty-first century.

The revised World History Standards in the Basic Edition thus included several new features as well as an assortment of minor revisions and corrections. Twentieth-century world history, which had been treated as a single era in the first edition, was divided into two sections with the break at 1945. In each of these eras, material was expanded on a variety of subjects to provide more comprehensive guidelines for study of the past one hundred years. New standards were added to several of the eras to encourage study of "global trends" in addition to developments within civilizations or nations. Guidelines were bolstered for Russian, Southeast Asian, Sub-Saharan African, and Pacific Oceanic history, as well as for the Scientific Revolution, the Enlightenment, and the role of science, technology, and medicine in the modern world. Statements were added at several points in the document to underline study of institutional and intellectual continuities within the Western tradition as well as modern experiments with democracy in all parts of the world. Finally, two new features were added: a short section that demonstrated the applicability of the standards to four different curricular approaches to world history and a new standard titled "World History Across the Eras" that aimed to stimulate exploration of long-term changes and recurring patterns in the human record.[50]

As soon as the new Basic Edition appeared, the NCHS started filling orders from all parts of the country. With foundation support, the center worked with the American Association of School Administrators to send free copies of the book to each of the nation's sixteen thousand school districts. In a cover letter, Paul Houston, executive director of the association, and Christopher Cross informed the nation's school administrators that the revised standards were "the result of excellent scholarship, sensitivity to many points of view, and our growing knowledge of teaching practice. In this concise volume," they continued,

> the new history standards provide a rich resource for teachers, administrators, and state and local education agencies. School systems across our nation will likely consider this work in designing history courses and in developing curriculum guidelines or state and local standards.[51]

The NCHS assured the CBE commission that it would not reprint the first edition because the new book superseded it. But Nash and his associates rejected the "defective Corvair" theory that the first editions of U.S. and World history standards should be "recalled" or withheld from teachers, libraries, or any citizens who wanted them. If anything, these books had become an important artifact of American history and a collector's item. When the new edition was imminent, the NCHS found that orders for the first edition surged, notably from teachers who wanted to get their hands on the practical teaching activities before they disappeared from the market.

In contrast to the events of 1994, no media explosion followed publication of the new Basic Edition. Most major newspapers reported the event and printed a sample of major changes in the new version.[52] Many of the articles quoted two Republicans who had scrutinized the revisions. "This version of the history standards," commented Albert Quie, "represents a tremendous improvement over the way history is taught in America's schools. Teachers, parents, and students will all benefit tremendously if schools choose to use these voluntary teaching standards." Christopher Cross called the revised standards "excellent" and judged that they "will serve schools well as a guide to improving the teaching of U.S. and world history."

James McPherson, Civil War historian at Princeton University, praised the standards as "intelligently conceived, lucid, fair-minded, and balanced ... [and] the best hope for the achievement of [historical] literacy in our schools." Linda Kerber, president-elect of the OAH, called the guidelines "conservative in the best sense of the word, encouraging in the next generation precise and complex knowledge of the past."[53]

The general drift of editorial opinion was that the NCHS had responded in good faith to the review, that the guidelines were improved, and that even though a strong federal role in education standards setting might be absent for the time being, states and schools would be well advised to draw on the new volume as an important source of ideas for teaching and curriculum development. For example, the *Washington Post* declared that if the fight the standards occasioned was inevitable, a symptom of divided times, fair-minded people should consider the exercise useful and be willing to count the document as its fruit. Whatever people's feelings about the wisdom of mandating such outlines nationally, the document can be useful to teachers. It should be made widely available.[54]

Marshall Smith, an undersecretary of education, issued a brief statement declaring that the revised U.S. standards "represent a solid and more balanced approach to what constitutes American history." Stressing once again that neither history standards nor any other academic guidelines were mandated or required by the federal government, Smith affirmed that "the worth of these standards will be decided in the free market place of ideas as teachers, parents and principals at the state and local level begin the process of writing new state standards."

The press comment that more than any other helped to preempt another round of history war was an op-ed piece by Diane Ravitch and Arthur Schlesinger Jr. that appeared in the *Wall Street Journal*, Lynne Cheney's usual platform, on the same day the Basic Edition came out. The authors affirmed that they had been critics of the standards, believing that the earlier volumes had failed "to balance *pluribus* and *unum* and to place the nation's democratic ideals at the center of its history." Indeed, during the months of controversy Ravitch had criticized the U.S. standards repeatedly, both in print and before a committee of Congress. Though at one point she appeared to be running with Cheney when she cited the Senate vote as if it constituted an informed judgment of the guidelines, she also made clear, in opposition to Cheney, that the nation needed national educational standards and that the history project should be thoughtfully revised, not scrapped. Schlesinger had communicated his reservations about the first editions of the standards to the NCHS mostly in private, and he wrote in May 1996 that the initial media attack had been a "vociferous overreaction" and the Senate's censure vote "absurd."[55] Now both he and Ravitch, who was a member of the CBE panel that reviewed the U.S. history document, concluded that the revised standards "are rigorous, honest, and as nearly accurate as any group of historians could make them. They do not take sides, and they pose the most fundamental questions about our nation's history. In our judgment, they will make a solid contribution to the improvement of history education in American schools."[56]

Even two of the more conservative commentators said in so many words, "enough already." John Leo seemed to have forgotten his acid remarks about the first edition in his *U.S. News & World Report* columns. He declared the new standards "much better" and let it go at that.[57] George Will devoted a column to the issue, first reviewing Cheney's major charges against the first edition, but then announcing that the revised standards "probably merit a passing grade" and that they provide some evidence "that the historians' profession is not incorrigible or impervious to arguments congenial to conservatives." He concluded with an expression of hope that national standards in any subject would "annoy multiculturalists."[58] Rush Limbaugh apparently made no comment at all about the new edition.

At the AFT, Shanker and Wattenberg declared that the U.S. History Standards "had improved substantially." They also said that in the World History Standards "the PC problem is essentially remedied." Wattenberg complained that the World History Standards still had a "big problem" because "there is no focus," a comment she did not clarify.[59] Of the many academic historians and teachers who had written in support of the first edition, few went into print following publication of the revision. After the first few days and the weighing in of Ravitch, Schlesinger, Will, Leo, and a few others, the popular media quickly lost interest.

That left Cheney and her allies. The former NEH chair declared that although the revised standards "made some improvements," they were "still highly unsatisfactory."[60] In early May she published another op-ed piece in the *Wall Street Journal*, criticizing the new edition and professing again her latter-day conversion to the view that national standards in any form were a terrible idea.[61] She took great exception to an introductory statement in the World History Standards that "at the beginning of the 20th century, Western nations enjoyed a dominance in world affairs that they no longer possess." The statement clearly referred to the fact that in 1900, Europeans and North Americans together dominated most of the world—either politically or economically—and called upon students to investigate how this hegemony arose and why it did not endure. Jacob Weisberg remarked in *New York* magazine that this proposition was "so obviously true as to be hardly worth discussing."[62] Cheney also charged that the new edition ranked the 1930s Depression, an unpleasant episode, as important as the American Revolution, a glorious one. The statement in the revised standards actually reads: "In its effects on the lives of Americans, the Great Depression was one of the great shaping experiences of American history, ranking with the American Revolution, the Civil War, and the second industrial revolution." Weisberg asked, "Anybody got a problem with that?" Arthur Schlesinger found Cheney's whole set of objections to the new edition "very feeble."[63]

A harsh attack by John Patrick Diggins on the revised standards appeared in the *New York Times*. His op-ed piece thoroughly confused the first edition of the standards with the second and endorsed a Latin American writer's questioning of whether pre-Columbian Mexico "could even be regarded as historical."[64] In two college graduation speeches Senator Kay

Bailey Hutchison lambasted the new guidelines as "slightly less awful" than the old ones. She declared that "when we revise our history, we devalue our culture" and that "laid bare, the past really *is* one thing after another—in a specific order."[65] The chairman of the University of Texas at El Paso history department subsequently wrote Hutchison, wanting to know why she would "suggest that students should not engage in serious historical analysis nor examine complexities in the historical record."[66] In the ultra-Right *Washington Times*, Robert Holland attempted to discredit the entire project to revise the standards on the grounds that the CBE had been "swallowed by The Blob" of "education-establishment orthodoxy" and that the organizations funding the effort—Ford, MacArthur, Spencer, and Pew—were merely "a gaggle of left-wing foundations."[67]

Within a month or so of the Basic Edition's publication, the year-and-a-half media debate about the standards petered out, and the guns of this history war nearly fell silent. In a wider context, the first half of 1996 was also a period when American public opinion made one of its typical swings back toward the center: the Republican revolution in Congress was grinding to a halt, and President Clinton's popularity ratings were rising even as Newt Gingrich's plummeted. Cheney's new book *Telling the Truth*, which included a recital of her charges against the standards, was, according to one publishing company official, a "non-starter."[68] In the presidential primary campaigns Pat Buchanan and Lamar Alexander took a few swipes at the standards in their stump speeches, but the issue no longer gave much value for money. In the Republican and Democratic party conventions in July and August, history standards never came up.

In September, however, House Republicans ventured forth one more time in an effort to derail the guidelines. Nine months earlier, some 112 members of that body had signed a resolution by Lamar Smith of Texas expressing the House's "disapproval" of the National History Standards because they presented "an inaccurate, misleading, and distorted characterization of United States history and world history." The chairman of the House Committee on Economic and Educational Opportunity never brought it to the floor for a vote. The influence of Christopher Cross and Albert Quie helped forestall this resolution.

Now Smith resumed his attack. Above the signatures of fifty-one House members, Smith urged Nash to notify everyone who had received copies of "these discredited guidelines" that "they are not official" and that the revised standards, which "remain controversial," should "be distributed with a caveat" that "they are not official or improved national standards."[69] Nash's response reminded Smith that consensus had been achieved in creating the standards; that the new edition included substantial changes, thus widening the consensus through the support of former critics; and that hardly anyone needed to be reminded that the standards were not "official."[70] In distributing complimentary copies of the Basic Edition to the nation's sixteen thousand school districts, the American Association of School Administrators had already made that point in its cover letter, cosigned by its executive director and the president of the CBE.

The real purpose of Smith's attack, it appears, was to warn off states from consulting the history standards. Smith wrote the governors and the fifty state superintendents of instruction about the guidelines and included a copy of his letter to Nash. In the interest of "our nation's proud history," he explained, he wanted "to make sure that you are aware of their potentially detrimental impact on the children of your state." Charging that the standards had been sent to their schools "under the pretext that they were official, government approved standards," Smith labeled the new edition "no more than a facade."[71]

Few state officials were fooled. Typical of their responses was a letter from Wisconsin's state superintendent, John T. Benson, who wrote Smith, "I must make it clear that we also never assumed that [the National History Standards] were official" and added his concern "about the many ways in which educational issues are becoming politicized."[72] The history war was not yet ended, but the controversy was dying down.

CHAPTER 10

Lessons from the History War

The rages of the ages will inform.

—Thomas Hardy

One of the signs of emerging democracy in countries that until re-cently have been ruled by authoritarian governments is that citizens start arguing publicly about history. In authoritarian regimes, those in power routinely represent the national past in any way they like, and the public is instructed to swallow the story. The government's legitimation of its powers and the versions of the past taught in schools go hand in glove. In a genuine democracy, no such imposition of "official history," of whatever stripe, is possible. Citizens value independence of thought, and scholars de-mand the freedom to follow where the data and their own insights lead them. This is the way of a democracy.

The culture wars in recent years have tested American democracy. We have come alarmingly close to muzzling museums that dare to broach sen-sitive historical topics. Most taxpayers do not object to government finan-cial support for museum exhibitions, editions of the papers of important historical figures, and symposia or performances on a variety of topics in communities large and small. But we have reached a perilous state when exhibits treating the historical experiences of little-noticed Americans are dismissed as politically correct and held hostage to partisan skirmishing. In the wake of the controversies over the *Enola Gay* exhibition and the "Amer-ica as West" show, many curators are self-censoring for fear of bringing trouble to their doors or losing financial support. Curators around the country ask themselves: Is a historical exhibit not presentable unless it passes a congressional litmus test? This is dangerous and self-defeating. Neil Harris, a cultural historian at the University of Chicago, asks: "Is it possible for museums deliberately to avoid all controversy in their choice of exhibitions" unless they settle for presenting "a set of sacred objects and sealed-off interpretations?"[1] This is not the way of a democracy.

The Costs of Politicizing Education

As we have seen, authoritarian states don't have history wars, but democracies frequently do. Controversies over what the schools teach, however, have followed a different course in the United States from those in democracies with a strong central ministry of education. In Britain, the government directed the rewriting of the history curriculum and pronounced that all state-supported schools would be obliged to teach it. The ensuing controversy pitted a Conservative Party government, which held particular ideas about versions of the past to be taught, against citizens who saw things otherwise.

In the United States, the country was largely united in supporting education reform from 1989, when President Bush and the governors launched their program, until 1995, when the Republican Party's leadership backed away from this ambitious agenda. As Chapter 7 has demonstrated, both the governors and the public at large coalesced behind the idea of instituting "world class" standards. Such breadth of consensus for *national* standards in math, science, English, history, and geography was unprecedented. Local control and decision making on curriculum matters had been the U.S. pattern since public schools were first established, and on this policy conservatives, moderates, and liberals had long agreed.

By the close of the 1980s, however, Americans had come to share the belief that their schools were in deep trouble, that national achievement levels had fallen alarmingly below those of other industrialized nations, and that this country's global economic leadership was seriously at risk. For the first time, Americans accepted the idea that the initiative to address these problems must begin at the national level, with the states, localities, and federal government joining in a grand collaboration to set the schools on the road to excellence. In contrast to Britain, this effort was undertaken in a spirit of genuine bipartisanship, with Republicans and Democrats working in harmony to achieve goals widely shared across the political spectrum.

By 1995, however, that consensus had collapsed, a victim of the Republican right wing's success in winning control of its party and the Congress. As the GOP lurched to the right, moderates were either swept along or out, and the bipartisan education campaign that had started only five years earlier ground to a halt. Perhaps nothing more dramatically demonstrated this turn of events than Lynne Cheney and Lamar Alexander's sudden reversal of position. By 1995, they were not only disavowing initiatives they had once championed but were leading the charge to dismantle the agencies they had earlier directed.

Education reform became thoroughly politicized. The two major parties now clashed over the Republican Right's plans to close the Department of Education (ED) and repeal the Goals 2000 Educate America Act that Congress had passed in March 1994. The following year, the act became the special target of conservatives determined to return all education matters to the states. Their position was strongly influenced by the religious Right, which played no small role in demonizing Goals 2000 as a violation of parental rights and denouncing the history standards as evidence that the statute was a "corrupting influence" on children.

The federal government had taken no part in developing the history standards, except for funding. Even potential "national certification" of the standards was to be conducted by an independent, nongovernmental agency in cooperation with the National Education Goals Panel, a nonfederal body largely composed of members of the National Governors' Association (NGA). Furthermore, Goals 2000 made clear that use of the standards by local schools was purely voluntary. No move was ever taken to create a national history curriculum or impose one on the country.

None of these facts slowed the Right's onslaught, much of it conducted in what historian Richard Hofstadter termed the "paranoid style in American politics." The Clinton administration, finding Goals 2000 under siege and having no particular commitment to the history standards, abruptly abandoned them for the greater gain it saw in trying to insulate its education program—and itself—from attack. Consequently, the government made weak noises in support of the heavyweights on the Right, who seemed to be holding much better political cards than the professional academic associations or the National Center for History in the Schools (NCHS).

One of the paradoxes of the history standards controversy was the critics' charge that the guidelines would impose an "official history" on the schools. In fact, the professional and public interest organizations that developed them would never have agreed to any narrowly defined or nationally prescribed curriculum. Moreover, the standards on historical thinking contradicted the whole notion of government-approved history. Those standards stressed the responsibility of a democratic society to rethink the meaning of the past over and over again and to examine both the conflicting arguments historians make and the multiple perspectives of historical actors themselves.

A second paradox of the controversy was that, however much conservative critics might demand the return of education to local communities, it was they, like the conservative Right in England, who longed for "official history"—but with the subject matter prescribed by *them*. Conservative critics had long argued that the history project had not "gotten it right" and that if they could establish a committee of like-minded traditionalists, this group would produce standards acceptable to the nation. They soon had opportunities to try.

In Virginia, Republican Governor George Allen pulled back the work of the professional educators commissioned to produce state standards and in January 1995 released what came to be known as the "Allen plan"—a "back-to-basics" approach crafted by a small group representing the state's conservative and Christian activists and advocates of home schooling.[2] The resulting firestorm could be heard nationwide. The Virginia Association of School Superintendents, teachers organizations, PTA groups, and leading Republican moderates in the state legislature united in opposition to standards they condemned as "bankrupt," "abysmally bad," and a retreat from "modern academic principles."[3] Critics, outnumbering supporters of the Allen plan by 2 to 1 margins in public hearings, asserted that the 179-page document's emphasis on rote memorization of facts, its failure to develop higher-level thinking, and its "outdated view of the world" would return Virginia's schools to the 1920s. Lynne Cheney, by contrast, announced her support of the Allen plan and charged, "When members of the education establishment encounter a curriculum that actually expects students to know a few names and dates..., they slam the concept of 'critical thinking' down on the table like a trump card.... The hope is that the good citizens of Virginia will neither be intimidated by the vituperation being slung about nor hornswoggled by talk about how damaging it is actually to expect students to command facts and master skills."[4]

Moderate Republicans in the Virginia legislature, strongly opposed to the Allen plan, called upon the state board of education to establish a new task force to rewrite the standards.[5] In what was widely held to be a setback for conservatives, the Virginia Department of Education responded by withdrawing the contested social studies standards, and the board's president announced that a new task force would start over.[6] The compromise standards, worked out over the next two months and adopted by the board in June 1995, gave something to everyone.[7] "It'll be the best we can get," allowed Michelle Easton, an Allen appointee on the board. "It's much improved," was the judgment of the president of the Virginia Education Association. "We can live with it."[8] School people were pleased that the emphasis on memorizing facts was gone, that historical content had been deepened, and that the historical thinking skills of the National History Standards were now reflected in the revised document.[9] However, they swallowed hard over the virtual invisibility of the nation's minorities in the state's U.S. History Standards and looked to the counties and local schools to rectify that problem. Allen aides also accepted the pact. "While it's not 100 percent of what Governor Allen asked for," his press secretary said, "it certainly is consistent with the governor's philosophy and goals of achieving high education standards."[10]

Even as Virginia was working out a compromise acceptable to its warring parties, Massachusetts was plunged into a history war of its own. Initially, a statewide committee, working under the leadership of the state superintendent of instruction and with plenty of teacher, scholar, and citizen input, drafted new state standards. However, John R. Silber, the governor-appointed chairman of the state Board of Education, peremptorily dismissed the draft and, acting like an education czar, appointed a small committee of stalwart conservatives to redesign the state history standards.

The resulting framework, like that commissioned by Virginia Governor Allen, produced a fracas of its own. Reflecting one side of the argument, Diane Ravitch wrote to the Massachusetts board that the new guidelines "would ensure that Massachusetts will be one of the very few states in the nation to adopt a first-rate curriculum framework in [this] field of study."[11] Opposing the new version were hundreds of teachers, school administrators, district superintendents, scholars, and citizens who publicly protested the draft document as traditional, fact-driven history "heavily focused on European events and doctrines" and developed without benefit of public participation. Harvard professors Henry Louis Gates Jr. and K. Anthony Appiah agreed, declaring that "since these documents essentially detail what Massachusetts students must know, it is vital that the frameworks propose a content that is global and reflects the rich diversity of our American heritage."[12]

More than two hundred educators and parents who shared this view submitted statements to the board. Dan French, director of instruction and curriculum in the Massachusetts Department of Education, summed up professionals' reactions. "This is a dumbing down of the discipline. It reduces history to a set of unrelated facts, memorization, and it's not very interesting. The current draft pushes us back to a 1950s approach to history and the social sciences." Silber's actions in overturning "the work of previous committees and the input of thousands of educators and residents" so frustrated and angered French that he resigned his post. Reviewing this turn of events, a writer for *Education Week* observed, "While states throughout the nation have been able to forge at least a grudging consensus on what students should know in the various disciplines, when it comes to history there has been one public squabble after another."[13]

Four new drafts and half a year later, the state was still in an uproar. By spring of 1997, the state legislature's Education Committee had weighed in, demanding a reconstituted committee and yet another draft, the eighth in this interminable wrangle. At the April 1997 board meeting, Silber obligingly discharged the committee of three and announced the formation of yet another small task force, assigned to bring in a new version by June. The project was now three years behind schedule and threatening to derail the state's $2 billion dollar Education Reform Act.[14] Critics of the National History Standards were learning that consensus is not easily won, certainly not by imposing the will of a small, nonrepresentative committee on an entire state.

Chester Finn offers a different approach to standards writing than that tried by any state. He rejects the idea that officials, experts, or teachers, whatever their political orientation, should have the responsibility. Rather, he takes a position that Louis Menand describes as "fake populism": Let committees of "bus drivers, policemen, shopkeepers, engineers, preachers, and orthodontists" or perhaps "the first hundred people in the Boston phone book" do the job.[15] In developing the history standards it might have been a good idea to have an electrician or two sit on the National Council to minimize professional jargon and provide occasional reality checks. We doubt, however, whether Finn's board of bus drivers and dentists would have been much interested in writing guidelines for school history. Nor would it be easy to find a committee of history teachers eager to write vocational standards for engineers. In any case, if a group that largely excluded history educators wrote standards, to what extent would teachers give them credence? Nor would the public stand for any single group's version of standards being pressed on all the nation's school districts.

One of the avowed purposes of those who attacked the standards was to make them so controversial that no textbook publisher or local school board would touch them. They did score successes here and there. In some communities where Cheney's criticisms resonated, jittery school boards and administrators ignored the standards or attempted to limit their use.

On the other hand, if the market provides a measure of consumer interest and confidence in a product, the standards were making an impact where it most counted—among the nation's teachers and school leaders. By late 1996, more than forty thousand copies of the first edition of the standards had been ordered, many in bulk quantities by state and local departments of education for use by teachers drafting new curriculum guidelines for their districts. Furthermore, despite the war launched against the standards, not one teacher, school district, or other purchaser returned a single copy or requested a refund. Orders came in steadily for the revised

Basic Edition as well. By spring 1997, more than seventy thousand copies of the original and revised editions of the history standards were in circulation, either through distribution to the nation's sixteen thousand school districts by the American Association of School Administrators or by direct purchase.

Putting their weight behind the history standards, the National Council for the Social Studies (NCSS) began marketing the revised edition as part of its publications series, along with the History Center's two related volumes, *Bring History Alive! A Sourcebook for Teaching United States History* and *Bring History Alive! A Sourcebook for Teaching World History*—two books that presented hundreds of teaching examples illustrating how the standards might be used in the nation's classrooms. At the same time, the 155,000-member Association for Supervision and Curriculum Development began selling *Content Knowledge: A Compendium of Standards and Benchmarks for K–12 Education.*[16] This volume, developed with funding from the ED, devoted nearly one-third of its 605 pages to a presentation of the original National History Standards, modified to "benchmark" the standards to specific grades. Critics on the Right were still hoping the history standards would soon disappear. These actions of two of the nation's leading professional organizations, however, demonstrated that the guidelines were in fact a growing influence in history and social studies education.

The View from the States

The fear of many educators that the history controversy might undo the entire movement to improve academic standards also proved false. In spring 1996, the NGA and major corporate leaders joined in an Education Summit to proclaim their shared commitment to developing state education standards and assessment programs, along with needed technological resources, to bring their states up to "world class" achievement levels. In many of these states, work in drafting new state standards and curriculum frameworks was already under way, inspired by national Goals 2000 legislation and by the national standards now available for most of the core subjects of the curriculum. But Goals 2000 and national education standards had become victims of a bruising war fought over a false issue, "Who controls the schools, the states or the feds?" Rather than allow national education reform to founder in this highly politicized war, the nation's governors returned to the agenda they had helped President Bush launch seven years earlier.

In recommitting themselves to the development of "world-class" education standards, the governors had much to build upon. Six months earlier, for example, Frank Klajda, state specialist in social studies education for Arizona, had released the results of a national survey he conducted of the Council of State Social Studies Specialists, the curriculum leaders for social studies in the fifty states.[17] Thirty states reported that their departments of education were developing new curriculum frameworks and standards in social studies education and three more reported that they expected to start soon. Of the thirty states already at work, twenty-eight were using the National History Standards, among them California, Colorado, Delaware, Michigan, Minnesota, Wisconsin, Utah, New Jersey, and New York.

School leaders, in short, were proceeding in exactly the manner that experienced educators, knowing how change in schools actually occurs, always expected they would—selectively and incrementally, consulting the National History Standards as advisory documents and taking from them what they found appropriate to their own projects and circumstances. The process of curriculum change is neither wholly "top-down" nor wholly "bottom-up," but a combination of both: "top-down" in the sense that new ideas often come from higher levels in the system or from outside the system altogether; "bottom-up" in the sense that no lasting change occurs unless local schools and school districts buy into those ideas, modify them to their own specifications, and make them their own.

National standards offered the schools the academic and professional expertise in history that few local districts or even states could hope to assemble for themselves. But national standards, as well as state standards, can never take into account the specific circumstances, needs, and preferences of every locality and must, for that reason, be open to modification as needed. California has long recognized this fact and offered its state curriculum frameworks as advisory documents that local districts might modify. Similarly, in the wake of Virginia's 1995 compromise on the Allen plan, bellwether districts like Fairfax County were already planning some modifications of the Virginia state plan in developing their own standards. The road to effective curriculum change, in other words, is a two-way street, with national and state standards offering "top-down" resources for desired change, and local districts actively partnering in this endeavor through "bottom-up" initiatives specifically responsive to their own needs and perspectives. Critics who protested that national standards would lead to federal control over schools not only misjudged how schools make decisions in this nation. Had they succeeded in burying the standards, they would also have destroyed a set of valuable academic resources for the improvement of education.

With the renewed commitment of the NGA to high academic standards, 1996 turned out to be a busy year for standards writing in both states and localities. The Council of the Great City Schools reported that 77 percent of the nation's largest districts were working on new content standards. Moreover, 69 percent of those districts reported that they were basing their guidelines on both national and state standards, while an additional 9 percent had based their work solely on national standards.[18] The American Federation of Teachers (AFT) conducted its own survey of the trend and reported that forty-eight states plus the District of Columbia were developing standards.[19] *Education Week,* in collaboration with the Pew Charitable Trusts, released a report early in 1997 indicating that most states were developing standards for the core subjects of the curriculum, and gave them an overall grade of B for the effort they were making.[20]

Questions remained, however, about the rigor of these standards and about the commitment of states to prepare teachers to implement them and to hold schools and students accountable for meeting them. One widely held fear was that the protracted media crisis over the National History Standards would persuade state education agencies or other standards project leaders to create documents so general as to be of little practical use to teachers and parents. Now, as states undertook the development of standards, AFT's Educational Issues Department reported that many of the state standards being written in 1996 were so "nebulous and lacking in specific criteria" that teachers would simply put them on the classroom shelf.[21]

The AFT based its judgment on whether these standards were "written in clear, explicit language, firmly rooted in the content of the subject area, and detailed enough to provide sufficient guidance to teachers, curriculum and assessment developers, parents, students, and others."[22] Though only twenty states were found to have developed social studies standards that could be rated "satisfactory" on these criteria, even fewer were judged "exemplary"—Virginia and California in the case of states that provided "grade-by-grade" standards, and Florida and the District of Columbia in the case of those that had developed standards organized into "grade clusters" (e.g., grades 9–12).

At a national press conference in March 1997, Wisconsin Governor Tommy G. Thompson and IBM Chairman and CEO Louis V. Gerstner Jr. announced that the governors expected their states to complete work in setting high academic standards within two years. "Achieve," the nonprofit, nongovernmental entity the governors had established to monitor progress and share information among the states was now up and running. Thompson predicted a lively competition among the states, not unlike that played out on their athletic fields. No way, he jested, was Wisconsin going to be found wanting when compared with Iowa. Governor Terry Branstad, he ventured, undoubtedly felt the same way. It was an upbeat news conference, but it left one important question unanswered: How could the unsatisfactory condition of so many of the state standards be turned around?

Meantime, Behind the Classroom Door . . .

As the clamor of the history war rose and then subsided and states busied themselves drafting new guidelines, teachers continued to face their classes each day. In fact, the controversy itself revealed just how much good teaching was going on. For years education critics had filled the media with claims that public school teachers were mediocre if not incompetent. Yet in covering the standards war, the press found abundant evidence that history teachers in any number of schools were creating exciting learning environments for their students and, despite enormous odds, instilling in many of them a lifelong love of the subject.

Many teachers interviewed in the media were already using the National History Standards to validate their classroom practices and to harvest new ideas for bringing history alive. In the *New York Times*, Jo Thomas reported examples of exhilarating teaching and learning. "Far from the glare of the political debate," she wrote, "visits to six high schools in the New York metropolitan area found that history teachers in the classroom are already embracing the spirit of the standards."[23] At Stuyvesant High School in Manhattan, Thomas found two classes of students crowded into one room to debate whether Alexander Hamilton's vision during the founding years of the new American republic was the right one for its time.

"Hamilton was a stand-up politician," argued Eugene. "His views, which may have been monarchist and pro-British, alienated his comrades at the Constitutional Convention, but this did not stop him."

He went on to praise Hamilton's support for Federalism and his insistence that the central government assume the debts of the states.

"States like Virginia, which had paid their debts, now had to pay for others," Elaine retorted. "His economic policies benefited merchants at the expense of farmers."
"Hamilton protected an infant democracy," Christina argued.
"He protected the rich," Elaine shot back.

Ultimately, judged on evidence, reason, delivery, pertinence, and quality of rebuttal, the moderator decided that the anti-Hamilton arguments had won by a narrow margin.[24]

In Warren Donin's class, students debated whether the word "holocaust" appropriately described the experiences that Africans suffered in the Atlantic slave trade, or whether using such a term trivialized the horrors of Nazi exterminations. The students did not conclude the debate within the class hour but carried it out to the hallway. A *Times* photo captured the students arguing passionately in the corridor, a scene that strikingly illustrates the power of history to capture students' attention and engage their minds.

When Thomas visited Gloria Sesso's class at Half Hollow Hills East High School in Dix Hills, Long Island, students were examining the aftermath of the French and Indian War and the rising tensions between the English Parliament and the American colonies. Sesso posed a question: "England has a program. They propose a Stamp Tax to help pay for the war. The colonists think the Stamp Tax is tyranny. Who do you think has the stronger argument? Who's right? Who's being tyrannical?"

To provide her students with facts to support their analysis, Sesso handed out photocopies of arguments for and against the Stamp Act that were written at the time. Hands waved in the air.

"The British case is destroyed by the colonists' case," said Duane Koh. "Everyone in England could have a say in Parliament, but a colonial person had no representative in Parliament. The colonists were right."

"The colonists were English," said Matthew Wurse, disagreeing.

"They were English, but now they're Americans," David Scheine said. "They have a different society."

Sesso would not allow the students to avoid grappling with the central issue.

"Is it tyranny? Patrick Henry gets up and says we should tax ourselves. All of a sudden George Grenville is being hung in effigy. . . . In Massachusetts, they go to Governor Hutchinson's house screaming, 'Liberty! No stamps!' and they burn it down because he's in cahoots with the Stamp Tax. . . . Who's exercising tyranny here? England or the mob burning down the house?"

Sesso drew in almost every pupil. One student later told Thomas, "In most other classes, teachers tell you something, and you daze out." In history class, she said, "You're up. People want your opinion. It makes you want to understand it."

Thomas did not find all the classrooms to be this successful. In one room the teacher plunged too quickly into a lesson requiring students to take the roles of laborers and managers, then negotiate a dispute set in the late nineteenth century. Their teacher had not prepared them to understand factory conditions or the processes of labor negotiations of that time. In another classroom, the teacher divided students into groups to analyze the New Deal but failed to provide them with needed resources on the complicated policies enacted by the Roosevelt administration. In both situations the problem was that the teacher had inadequate knowledge of how to approach lessons like these and how to give students adequate resources to make the lessons work.

As everyone who worked on the standards project understood, the publication of the new guidelines would not by itself lead to better history instruction. Teachers must know their subject thoroughly. And they must have opportunities to develop effective teaching skills. Students must have adequate time and resources for serious learning. School reform is a many-faceted undertaking. Standards are essential, establishing classroom goals for teachers and achievement targets for students. Excellence in history education, however, will not come on the cheap. The full story of this nation's commitment to educational excellence has yet to be written. Only the first episode—stormy to be sure—is now over.

Beyond History War

Throughout most of the twentieth century, an era when public school and university education in the United States expanded at a rate unmatched anywhere in the world, academic historians and social studies professionals looked at one another across a wide gorge of mistrust, misunderstanding, and indifference over the teaching of the past to young Americans. We have shown how the promising alliance between the scholars and the schools went off track shortly after World War I and why the estrangement, despite individual efforts here and there to span the gulf, lasted so long.

Only in the 1980s, in the midst of revelations of an appalling disconnect between Americans and their own history, did K–12 and university professionals begin to collaborate again. The nation's collective memory appeared to be at risk, and the keepers of the past—scholars, teachers, public historians, and museum heads—began to recognize that they must work together more closely if young people were going to graduate from high school knowing anything more than gross superficialities about the past.

The project to write national history standards strengthened the cooperative trend among educators because it brought together a large team of historians, teachers, curators, and other interested citizens, along with their professional organizations. The ensuing attack on the standards, which aimed to obliterate them, in fact reinforced the new alliances. The hostile critics, in challenging the importance of a history education that is at once inclusive and global, reflective and analytical, helped significantly to repair the long-troubled relations between historians and social studies educators.

In other words, the history standards tempest, whatever damage it did, had a silver lining. At all levels, history educators have recognized more clearly their common goals and how much they need one another to protect the gains, however insufficient, that the field had made since World War II. In constructing the standards, historians came to appreciate the deep commitment of social studies professionals to giving young Americans the skills of critical investigation, analysis, and judgment. And the social studies community came to understand better than before that historians are not "fact chasers" and that for a long time they have drawn liberally on all the social sciences to shape and reshape their own discipline. Global educators in the social studies know better today that historians are not on the whole rigidly Eurocentric and that few of them any longer define world history as merely the parade of Western progress. Historians dedicated to advancing the teaching of non-American, comparative, and global subjects are realizing the benefits of working with internationally minded organizations such as the NCSS and the Council of Chief State School Officers.

Today, more K–12 teachers and university scholars are joining one another's professional organizations. More teachers and scholars are talking history with one another via E-mail. More history specialists are making themselves directly available to schoolchildren in classrooms or through electronic hookups. More school groups are crowding into historical sites and museums. More university and college instructors are meeting with middle and high school teachers, not to give "sage on the stage" lectures but to collaborate as professional partners in designing new courses and programs.

Acrimonious as it was, the media debate over the standards has strengthened all of these tendencies. To cite one example, in 1995 the Rockefeller Foundation, directly in response to the standards controversy, funded the Organization of American Historians to offer grants of $500 to college and university history departments to assemble local teachers to discuss both the history standards and better ways to teach American and world history to children and college students. Meetings were subsequently held on campuses across the country, bringing together K–12, community college, and university educators who in many cases had never met each other before. They strengthened scholar-teacher networks and stimulated new plans for long-term partnerships to improve history education. In coming years this kind of collaboration can do much to rejuvenate America's historical memory, and it should have more lasting significance than the testy exchanges that took place on talk shows and the floor of the U.S. Senate in 1994 and 1995.

Finally, the controversy aroused greater public awareness of the breadth, depth, and singular achievement of historical research and writing during the past forty years. Similarly, it put a spotlight not only on the critics of the standards but also on dedicated history teachers who argued publicly that students will learn more history and understand it better when they are permitted to think, investigate, and interpret, rather than merely memorize and recite.

Lively debate over the meaning of the past and its relation to today's affairs does not signal national disunity and deterioration; rather it is a sign of a vibrant democracy. On the other hand, when these debates become rancorous and politicized, they threaten to impede the national mission to cure ourselves of historical amnesia. Teachers and scholars, liberals and conservatives, must work together to meet the challenge that President Bush and the nation's governors made in 1989 to educate children both *to know* and *to be able to do:* to know the grand sweep of our nation's and our world's history—its pivotal events, long-term transformations, great landmarks, achievements, catastrophes, heroes, and villains; and to be able to think reflectively on all these things—to develop the skills to find and use historical information, follow a historical argument, expose bias and bogus logic, grapple with the "whys" of the past, and relate the lessons of history to contemporary events and trends.

To accomplish these ends, and to diminish harsh rivalries over the purposes and methods of history education, certain tendencies already in play need to be encouraged.

First, as a nation we should commit ourselves enthusiastically and unreservedly to a history education that is fit for a democratic society. This means abandoning the notion that teachers or education authorities should designate certain historical facts, events, deeds, ideas, or interpretations as off limits to analysis or reassessment. By the same token, no historical representations or explanations—even those dearest to the hearts of liberals, conservatives, Afrocentrists, Eurocentrists, or postmodernists—should be held publicly sacrosanct and indisputable. We should give up all projects to write the final and definitive version of our nation's or our world's history or to identify and settle on the five hundred, one thousand, or ten thousand historical "facts" that every American should know. Leave such stipulation to authoritarian states, which have always imposed that kind of curriculum. Our collective memory is bound to change as the issues that matter to us a a nation change. Historical research will continue to yield new information and interpretations. In a democracy where five major newspapers often offer five conflicting slants on a single event (and the government a sixth one!), Americans will keep rewriting history. To invoke historical revisionism as a form of foul play serves democracy poorly.

Second, we should end the futile struggle among educators and policy makers over whether we should teach more historical "content" and less "historical thinking" or vice versa. This is a false dichotomy, as good teachers have always known. Facts, to be useful, must be embedded in some context or pattern of meaning. In turn, students shape meaning by applying reason, analysis, and judgment. Some education critics have repeatedly protested curriculum frameworks and guidelines that emphasize "learning processes" and "historical thinking" without giving equal emphasis to the content to be learned. They have argued that teaching children to think is pointless unless we give them something (historical content, subject matter) to think about. The criticism is valid, and states and school districts should bear in mind that content-impoverished history standards have little pedagogical value for either teachers or students. However, a distinction must be made between standards that prescribe lists of facts to be memorized or conclusions to be accepted and frameworks that identify specific topics, themes, peoples, and periods worthy of inclusion in a curriculum.

Equally important is recognizing that teaching children historical subject matter has no point if we do not ask them to reflect on it. Research has shown clearly that students remember history better when they are given the opportunity to weigh, analyze, and interpret it. Likewise, they master skills of inquiry more effectively if they bring those skills to bear on historical subject matter that is concretely located in time and space, that has narrative power, and that can be meaningfully related in one way or another to children's daily experience and the world in which they live. No history curriculum reform that builds a wall between knowledge and skills can have lasting success.

Third, we must nurture the flourishing new alliances between schools and universities. As more and more young Americans go on to higher education, we must continue to found programs and institutions that will link teachers, history departments, schools of education, libraries, historical societies, historical sites, museums, and computer resources. Postsecondary institutions, especially public ones, should periodically ask themselves how well their curriculum serves the needs of future teachers who will have to teach the historical subjects that states or school districts require. If a new middle or high school instructor, just beginning to teach, is asked to take on a broad course in world history, for example, then that teacher should come away from college carrying not only notebooks full of classroom techniques and knowledge about one part of the world or another but also intellectual strategies for conceptualizing, organizing, and selecting content for that course: that is, ideas for making world history intelligible and engaging.

For their part, legislatures and school boards should insist that new history teachers be well trained in the discipline. An old joke among educators is that half the history teachers in the United States have the same first name—"Coach." Whether or not history teachers make good coaches, they must be more than minimally qualified in their field if American children are to become intellectually mature and historically literate. New teachers should have a solid base of historical knowledge but also an understanding of how to expand that base from year to year and how to translate knowledge into good classroom practice. Although 40 percent of the nation's history teachers have a bachelor's degree in the subject, just as many have had no formal study in history at all.[25] In Denmark, by contrast, a minimum qualification for high school history teachers is a master's degree in that subject.

Fourth, the last few decades have witnessed a remarkable effort to broaden the scope of history education to ensure that the experiences of all classes, regions, and ethnoracial groups, as well as both genders, are included in it. This represents a commitment to multiculturalism as originally defined and least open to dispute. Indeed, it expresses an allegiance to the democratic notion that our history should reflect the experiences, contributions, aspirations, and travails of all the nation's people. A glance at current textbooks, syllabi, and teacher-training programs shows that we continue to make progress in realizing this imperative goal, though the subject matter of many books still in use in the schools is too restricted.

Some Americans have argued that particular ethnoracial groups and non-American cultural traditions deserve "histories of their own" in the K–12 curriculum. Though most schools lack the time and resources to make much room for Asian, African American, women's, or other special history courses, the study of particular countries, cultural groups, and world regions is perfectly valid. Danger arises when we presume that students can gain adequate understanding of specific groups apart from larger contexts of social reality; that, for example, women's history can be understood exclusive of men, labor history exclusive of corporate capitalism, or Latino history exclusive of the wider American population. Historians and social scientists have long recognized that human institutions, ideas, social arrangements, and economies change over time and that the historical experiences of aggregates such as nation-states or ethnoracial groups intersect and run together in all sorts of untidy and complicated ways.

A primary goal of history education, therefore, should be to help young

Americans understand that we do indeed live in a world that has always been complicated, but that those complexities can in some measure be analyzed, explained, and understood. We confuse and delude young Americans if we teach them that any group in this country, whether colonial landowners, middle-class women, sharecroppers, or Plains Indians, possesses a past of its own distanced from the pasts of other groups, or that particular civilizations have self-contained linear histories that can be understood in terms of purely internal mechanisms and in isolation from the human community at large. Such an approach is simply not consonant with the way events, processes, and trends play themselves out from one historical period to the next.

We must aim, rather, for a history curriculum that embraces yet goes beyond the admirable goal of representing a diverse variety of groups and cultures. Such a curriculum would aim not merely to determine which groups or civilizations to include and how much time in the school year to award to each. Rather, it would identify the most important developments, processes, and transformations that we would like students to understand, formulate the historical questions we most want them to address, work out the humanistic and social scientific vocabulary we want them to be able to use, and create stimulating lessons that lead them to explore the broader landscapes in which groups, societies, and peoples interact. If pursued honestly, such an approach would produce unequivocally inclusive history. This is so because the questions we most need to pose in our history and social studies classrooms, whether in the political, social, economic, ecological, or any other sphere, require a broader stage of inquiry than the experience of any single ethnoracial or national community.

The presentation of American history in our schools has already made considerable progress along these lines. World history courses, however, continue to rely too heavily on "civilization of the month" approaches that fail to give proper attention to comparative study, patterns of change that link to our own time, or interregional and transnational developments that have shaped the contemporary world. The last few years have seen a significant increase in the number of books, articles, panels, institutes, and programs bringing K–12 and postsecondary educators together to formulate a world history that goes beyond both the traditional Western Civ and the more recent "diverse cultures" models. The efforts of these historians are directed toward building a curriculum that is genuinely global but nonetheless coherent, rigorous, and engaging. To accept the notion that humankind's past as such is unintelligible, or that genuine global history is too far-reaching or complicated to bother with, would do a grave injustice to the children who will live and work in the twenty-first century.

Fifth, progress toward more unified, integrated histories of the United

States and the world should help to reconcile the differing views of committed multiculturalists and those Americans who believe classrooms should emphasize the study of democracy's evolution and the Western heritage. Multiculturalists should recognize the counterproductivity of placing excessive emphasis in the curriculum on differences, distinctions, and separate experiences among social groups or cultural traditions, or on searching for the essential traits and unique achievements of this civilization or that. This approach may sometimes actually alienate children from interest in such groups and traditions because the presentation is so relentlessly focused on the Other, who is to be appreciated and tolerated but understood nevertheless as fundamentally different from themselves. Rigidly dividing the world into self-contained cultures may also seriously obstruct students' understanding of the large-scale, transnational, and culturally interconnected processes that help explain the history of our nation and world.

Those who advocate putting the Western heritage at the center of the curriculum should consider two things. First, though studies of European history—its events, turning points, ideas, philosophies, religions, literature, and art—are certainly worthwhile and important, we mislead students if we fail to make clear that European history is not synonymous with the history of humankind. Moreover, European history alone will not give children the expansive knowledge base and conceptual architecture they need to understand the increasingly global issues of their day. It is not that children must study "other cultures" besides the West, but that they should be able to situate the study of any historical problem in its proper context, a setting that for many of the most important questions is the world as a whole. Second, the study of democracy and its attendant ideas—popular sovereignty, individual rights, constitutionalism, electoral politics, and civic participation—is vital indeed. The locus of a major part of that study will necessarily be Europe and North America. But students should also learn that although the specific institutions and ideas that we conventionally associate with democracy are largely of Western origin, democracy as a way of organizing government and society went out to the world in the eighteenth and nineteenth centuries. Peoples of Latin America, China, the Middle East, Russia, Sub-Saharan Africa, and other places began experimenting with it and adapting it, whether successfully or not, to their own cultural and social circumstances. Democracy, in other words, belongs to the world, and it is within the framework of world history that schoolchildren should investigate it. If we teach about democracy to show how political and social progress is an exclusively European or American story, then we will never give students an understanding of the extraordinary appeal that democratic ideas and institutions have had on every continent in the past two hundred or three hundred years.

Publicly engaged citizens of the coming century who recognize that both the United States and the West are situated and always have been situated in the world will be better prepared for the challenges ahead. Citizens possessing such sensibilities, we believe, will be more likely to come effectively to grips with the great problems of surging nationalism, international migration, multipolar diplomacy, economic uncertainties, environmental transformation, and global culture. To prepare students for those challenges requires that schools offer young Americans an extensive, rigorous history education and one built on the premise of humankind's underlying unity.

"Can the scholar's history be the public's history?" asks historian Kenneth Moynihan.[26] This book endorses his view that professional historians and responsible teachers cannot "devote themselves to writing a catechism for someone's version of the civic religion" and term the result history. Yet for all the sound and fury of recent history wars, professional scholars and the public may be on converging paths. By the hundreds of thousands, the public is drinking in museum exhibits, historical movies, television documentaries, history enactments, and popular trade books based on new historical interpretations. Valuing both critique and commemoration, Americans are liberating themselves from the notion that history is an agreed-upon set of facts and a forever fixed story. Rather, they are coming to understand that history is "an ongoing conversation that yields not final truths but an endless succession of discoveries that change our understanding not only of the past but of ourselves and of the times in which we live."[27] One of the jewels in democracy's crown is an educated citizenry that welcomes new harvests of information, unsettling questions, and fresh visions that illuminate our past as well as our present condition.

Notes

PREFACE

1. Lawrence W. Levine, *The Opening of the American Mind: Canons, Culture, and History* (Beacon Press, 1996), xiv.

CHAPTER I

1. Lynne V. Cheney, "The End of History," *Wall Street Journal*, 20 Oct. 1994, A 26(W), A 22(E).
2. Rush Limbaugh, *See, I Told You So* (Pocket Books, 1993), 66; see also Mike Wallace, "Culture War, History Front," in Edward T. Linenthal and Tom Engelhardt, eds., *History Wars: The Enola Gay and Other Battles for the American Past* (Henry Holt, 1996), 171–98.
3. Transcript of Rush Limbaugh radio program, 24 Oct. 1994. Subsequent quotations on this and following page are from his television program, 28 Oct. 1994.
4. James A. Morone, "The Corrosive Politics of Virtue," *The American Prospect*, 26 (May–June 1996): 32–33.
5. Quoted in Todd Gitlin, *The Twilight of Common Dreams: Why America Is Wracked by Culture Wars* (Henry Holt, 1995), 81.
6. Ibid.
7. Edward Hallett Carr, *What Is History?* (Vintage Books, 1961), 16.
8. H. Stuart Hughes, *History as Art and as Science* (Harper & Row, 1964), 4–5.
9. Joyce Appleby, Lynn Hunt, and Margaret Jacobs, *Telling the Truth about History* (Norton, 1994), 255.
10. Carr, *What Is History?*, 10.
11. Turner, "Social Forces in American History," *American Historical Review* 16 (1911): 226.
12. Becker, "Everyman His Own Historian," *American Historical Review* 37 (1932): 231.
13. Christopher Hill, *The World Turned Upside Down: Radical Ideas during the English Revolution* (Temple Smith, 1972), 13–14.
14. Becker, "Everyman His Own Historian," 235.
15. Lawrence W. Levine, "The Unpredictable Past: Reflections on Recent American Historiography," *American Historical Review* 94 (1989): 671.
16. Joan Wallach Scott, "History in Crisis? The Others' Side of the Story," *American Historical Review* 94 (1989): 690.

17. Appleby, Hunt, and Jacobs, *Telling the Truth*, 252.

18. Roberto Peccei and Fred Eiserling, "Literacy for the 21st Century," *Los Angeles Times*, 26 Feb. 1996, B5.

19. William H. McNeill, *Mythistory and Other Essays* (University of Chicago Press, 1986), 5–6.

20. Peccei and Eiserling, "Literacy for the 21st Century," *Los Angeles Times*, 26 Feb. 1996, B5.

21. Quoted in Robert Fullinwider, "Patriotic History," in Fullinwider, ed., *Public Education in a Multicultural Society: Policy, Theory, Critique* (Cambridge University Press, 1996), 204.

22. Ernest Lavisse, quoted in Michael Kammen, *Mystic Chords of Memory: The Transformation of Tradition in American Culture* (Knopf, 1991), 289.

23. James Loewen, *Lies My Teachers Told Me: Everything Your American History Textbook Got Wrong* (New Press, 1995), shows the sanitizing of American history in school textbooks, but all but two of the twelve books he examines were published more than ten years ago.

24. Mark Twain, "To the Person Sitting in Darkness," 1901, quoted in Gary B. Nash, *American Odyssey: The United States in the Twentieth Century* (Glencoe/McGraw Hill, 1997), 300.

25. Quoted in Marcus Cunliffe, *George Washington: Man and Monument* (Collins, 1959), 21.

26. John Adams to Elbridge Gerry, 2 May 1785, Adams Papers, Reel 364.

27. Quoted in Cunliffe, *George Washington*, 159.

28. Adams to Benjamin Waterhouse, Oct. 29, 1805, in Worthington Chauncey Ford, ed., *Statesman and Friend: Correspondence of John Adams and Benjamin Waterhouse, 1784–1822* (Little, Brown, 1927), 31.

29. Jefferson to James Madison, 14 Feb. 1783, in Julian P. Boyd et al., eds., *The Papers of Thomas Jefferson*, 60 vols. (Princeton University Press, 1950), 6:241.

30. Nathanael Emmons, *A Discourse, Delivered on the Annual Fast in Massachusetts, April 9, 1801* (Nathaniel Heaton Jr., 1801), 22.

31. Bessie L. Pierce, *Attempts to Control the Teaching of History in the Schools* (n.p., 1925), 4–8.

32. Quoted in Stuart McConnell, *Glorious Contentment: The Grand Army of the Republic, 1865–1900* (University of North Carolina Press, 1992), 226.

33. Quoted in ibid., 224–25.

34. Mildred Lewis Rutherford, *A Measuring Rod to Test Text Books, and Reference Books in Schools, Colleges and Libraries* (n.p., 1919), 3, 5.

35. Bessie Louise Pierce, *Public Opinion and the Teaching of History in the United States* (Knopf, 1926), 146, 148–49.

36. Ruth Miller Elson, *Guardians of Tradition: American Schoolbooks of the Nineteenth Century* (University of Nebraska Press, 1964), 76.

37. Frederick Law Olmsted, *A Journey in the Seaboard Slave States with Remarks on Their Economy* (Dix & Edwards, 1856), 214–15.

38. Quoted in Kammen, *Mystic Chords of Memory*, 21.

39. Elson, *Guardians of Tradition*, 285.

40. Ibid., 337.

41. Lawrence A. Cremin, *American Education: The Metropolitan Experience, 1876–1980* (Harper & Row, 1988), 545.

42. Elson, *Guardians of Tradition,* 338–39.
43. Newt Gingrich, *To Renew America* (HarperCollins, 1995), excerpt reprinted in *Los Angeles Times,* 31 July, 1995, B5; Robert Dole speech in Indianapolis, Sept. 4, 1995, transcript from Federal Document Clearing House, p. 5.
44. Arthur M. Schlesinger Sr., *In Retrospect: The History of a Historian* (Harcourt, Brace & World, 1963), 71–72, 104–5.
45. Hill, *The World Turned Upside Down,* 13.
46. Levine, "The Unpredictable Past," 675.
47. Hill, *The World Turned Upside Down,* 14.
48. Levine, "The Unpredictable Past," 675.
49. Appleby, Hunt, and Jacob, *Telling the Truth,* 3.
50. Lawrence W. Levine's *The Opening of the American Mind: Canons, Culture, and History* (Beacon Press, 1996) is a rich new contribution to the arguments over historical scholarship in this century.

CHAPTER 2

1. For the state of history in the schools on the eve of the Civil War, see William F. Russell, "History in the Curriculum of the High School," *The History Teacher's Magazine* 5 (1914): 311–17.
2. Joyce Appleby, Lynn Hunt, and Margaret Jacobs, *Telling the Truth about History* (Norton, 1994), 105–6.
3. David Saville Muzzey, *An American History* (Ginn, 1911), 618.
4. Muzzey to Carl Becker, 16 Oct. 1920, quoted in Peter Novick, *That Noble Dream: The "Objectivity Question" and the American Historical Profession* (Cambridge University Press, 1988), 229.
5. Muzzey, *An American History,* 25.
6. Ibid., 486.
7. Ibid. Muzzey's account of Reconstruction followed closely the work of his colleague William Dunning, who commanded this area of American historiography.
8. Charles A. Beard, *An Economic Interpretation of the Constitution of the United States,* (Macmillan, 1913).
9. Quoted in Ellen Nore, *Charles A. Beard: An Intellectual Biography* (Southern Illinois University Press, 1983), 63.
10. Ibid.
11. The phrases from the attacks on Muzzey and fellow historians are examined in Harold Rugg, *That Men May Understand: An American in the Long Armistice* (Doubleday, Doran, 1941), 136.
12. Charles Grant Miller, *Treason to American Tradition: The Spirit of Benedict Arnold Reincarnated in United States History Revised in Textbooks* (Sons of the Revolution in the State of California, 1922), 4.
13. Charles Grant Miller, *The Poisoned Loving-Cup; United States School Histories Falsified through Pro-British Propaganda in the Sweet Name of Amity* (National Historical Society, 1928), v–viii.
14. Miller, *Treason to American Tradition,* 6.
15. Ibid., 182.
16. Miller, *Poisoned Loving-Cup,* 165.

17. Bessie Louise Pierce, *Public Opinion and the Teaching of History in the United States* (Knopf, 1926), 18.

18. Ibid., 19.

19. Quoted in Michael Kammen, *Mystic Chords of Memory: The Transformation of Tradition in American Culture* (Knopf, 1991), 301.

20. Rugg, *That Men May Understand*, 194–201.

21. Quoted in Kammen, *Mystic Chords of Memory*, 485.

22. The book commissioned by the American Legion, which seems to have made little headway in the schools, was Charles F. Horne, *The Story of Our American People*, 2 vols. (United States History Publishing, 1925).

23. Bessie L. Pierce, *Citizens' Organizations and the Civic Training of Youth* (Scribner's, 1933), 329–33.

24. Quoted in Kammen, *Mystic Chords of Memory*, 486.

25. Charles A. Beard, "History in the Public Schools," *New Republic*, 16 Nov. 1927, 348.

26. William E. Dodd to Charles Barker, 28 Oct., 1932, quoted in Novick, *That Noble Dream*, 199.

27. Lawrence Cremin, *American Education: The Metropolitan Experience, 1876–1980* (Harper & Row, 1988), 545.

28. National Education Association, Committee of Ten on Secondary School Studies, Report of the Committee on Secondary School Studies (U.S. Government Printing Office, 1893), 166–67.

29. Ibid., 170.

30. Charles W. Eliot, *Educational Reform: Essays and Addresses* (1898), quoted in Lawrence W. Levine, "Clio, Canons, and Culture," *Journal of American History* 80 (1993): 855.

31. American Historical Association, Committee of Seven, *The Study of History in Schools* (Macmillan, 1899), 117–18.

32. Charles A. McMurry, *Special Method in History: A Complete Outline of a Course Study in History for the Grades Below the High School* (Macmillan, 1903), 2.

33. Ibid., 7–8.

34. Ibid., 17.

35. Hazel Whitman Hertzberg, "Are Methods and Content Enemies?" in *History in the Schools: What Shall We Teach?*, ed. Bernard R. Gifford (Macmillan, 1988), 20.

36. Quoted in Mark H. Leff, "Revisioning U.S. Political History," *American Historical Review* 100 (1995): 831.

37. John Higham, *History: Professional Scholarship in America* (Johns Hopkins University Press, 1983), 8.

38. Quoted in Hazel W. Hertzberg, "History and Progressivism: A Century of Reform Proposals," in *Historical Literacy: the Case for History in American Education*, ed. Paul Gagnon (Macmillan, 1990), 84.

39. American Historical Association, Commission on the Social Studies, *Conclusions and Recommendations of the Commission* (Scribner's, 1934).

40. American Historical Association, *Conclusions and Recommendations of the Commission*, 8.

41. Carlton J. H. Hayes, quoted in Novick, *That Noble Dream*, 192.

42. Novick, *That Noble Dream*, 134.

43. Quoted in ibid., 140.

44. Rugg, *That Men May Understand*, 176–83.

45.   Ibid., 186–95; Peter F. Carbone Jr., *The Social and Educational Thought of Harold Rugg* (Duke University Press, 1977), 16–21.

46.   Rugg, *That Men May Understand*, 173.

47.   Carbone, *Thought of Harold Rugg*, 23.

48.   Muzzey's junior and senior high history textbooks survived the attacks in the 1920s to dominate history education through the 1930s, 1940s, and 1950s.

49.   George H. Sabine, Arthur N. Holcombe, Arthur W. Macmahon, Carl Wittke, and Robert S. Lynd, *The Textbooks of Harold Rugg* (American Committee for Democracy and Intellectual Freedom, 1942), 25, quoting Rugg's *Teacher's Guide and Key*.

50.   Harold Rugg, *Changing Civilizations in the Modern World* (Ginn, 1930).

51.   Nore, *Charles A. Beard*, 114.

52.   *Report of the Proceedings of the Convention of the American Federation of Labor at Cincinnati, June 1922* (Washington, D.C., 1923), 23, quoted in Pierce, *Public Opinion and the Teaching of History*, 197.

53.   Ibid., 42.

54.   Rugg, *A History of American Civilization: Economic and Social* (Ginn, 1930), 198; idem, *Teacher's Guide for a History of American Civilization* (Ginn, 1931), 80–83.

55.   Carbone, *Thought of Harold Rugg*, 11.

56.   Diane Ravitch, *The Troubled Crusade: American Education, 1945–1980* (Basic Books, 1983), 90.

57.   Dan W. Gilbert, "Sovietizing Our Children," *National Republic*, 24 Aug. 1936, 16–17, 32; Orvel Johnson, "Red Mist over Philadelphia," ibid., Oct. 1936, 1–2.

58.   Rugg, *That Men May Understand*, 26.

59.   O. A. Armstrong, "Treason in the Textbooks," *American Legion Magazine* 29 (Sept. 1940): 8–9, 51, 70–72.

60.   S. Alexander Rippa, *Education in a Free Society: An American History*, 5th ed., (Longman, 1984), 298.

61.   Charles A. Beard and William G. Carr, "The Schools Accept New Jobs," *Journal of the National Education Association* 24 (April 1935): 117.

62.   "Book Burnings," *Time*, 9 Sept. 1940, pp. 64–65; *New York Times*, 6 June 1940; 23, Aug. 1940; 11 Nov. 1941; Rippa, *Education in a Free Society*, 298–99.

63.   Rugg, *That Men May Understand*, 71–72.

64.   Ibid., 73.

65.   Ibid., 6, 92–93.

66.   "The Crusade Against Rugg," editorial, *New Republic*, 10 March 1941, 327–28.

67.   Rugg, *That Men May Understand*, 16, 91–92.

68.   Quoted in Carbone, *Thought of Harold Rugg*, 28.

69.   Charles A. Beard, "Freedom of Teaching," *Social Frontier* (March 1935): 18.

70.   *The Textbooks of Harold Rugg*, 4–5.

71.   William Swinton, *Outlines of the World's History* (Ivison, Blakeman, 1874), 2.

72.   Ibid., 3.

73.   Philip Van Ness Myers, *General History for Colleges and High Schools*, rev. ed. (Ginn, 1917), 67.

74.   Ibid., 10.

75.   Quoted in Gilbert Allardyce, "Toward World History: American Historians and the Coming of the World History Course," *Journal of World History* 1 (Spring 1990): 51.

76. Ibid.
77. Ibid., 52.
78. Hertzberg, *Social Studies Reform, 1880–1980*, 57.
79. Cremin, *American Education: The Metropolitan Experience*, 545.
80. Philip D. Curtin, *Precolonial African History* (American Historical Association, 1974), 3.
81. Marshall G. S. Hodgson, *Rethinking World History: Essays on Europe, Islam, and World History*, ed. with introduction and conclusion by Edmund Burke III (Cambridge University Press, 1993), 6–7.
82. Carl L. Becker, *Modern History* (Silver, Burdett, 1931), 2.
83. Carlton Hayes et al., *World History* (Macmillan, 1932), 748.
84. Ibid., 729.
85. Lawrence W. Levine, *The Opening of the American Mind: Canons, Culture, and History* (Beacon Press, 1995), 56–57.
86. Gilbert Allardyce, "The Rise and Fall of the Western Civilization Course," *American Historical Review* 87 (1982): 705–6.
87. Hazel Whitman Hertzberg, "Are Method and Content Enemies?" in *History in the Schools: What Shall We Teach?*, Bernard R. Gifford, ed. (Macmillan, 1986), 33.
88. Allardyce, "Rise and Fall," 715.
89. Eric R. Wolf, *Europe and the People without History* (University of California Press, 1982), 5.

CHAPTER 3

1. Carl Bridenbaugh, "The Great Mutation," *American Historical Review* 68 (1963): 322–23, 328.
2. "Report of the History Department for 1956–57," A. Whitney Griswold Presidential Papers, Yale University, quoted in Peter Novick, *That Noble Dream: The "Objectivity Question" and the American Historical Profession* (Cambridge University Press, 1988), 366.
3. Novick, *That Noble Dream*, 323.
4. Ellen W. Schrecker, *No Ivory Tower: McCarthyism and the Universities* (Oxford University Press, 1986).
5. Daniel Boorstin, *The Genius of American Politics* (University of Chicago Press, 1953), 162, 179.
6. Michael Wallace, "Visiting the Past: History Museums in the United States," in Wallace, *Mickey Mouse History and Other Essays on American Memory* (Temple University Press, 1996), 13–15.
7. Novick, *That Noble Dream*, 362.
8. Both quotes are from ibid., 379.
9. Ruth Miller Elson, *Guardians of Tradition, American Schoolbooks of the Nineteenth Century* (University of Nebraska Press, 1964), 88–92.
10. Ibid., 99.
11. Ibid., 97–98.
12. Quoted in James Ford Rhodes, *History of the United States from the Compromise of 1850 to the Final Restoration of Home Rule in the South in 1877*, 8 vols. (Macmillan, 1906–1919), 6: 37.

13. Frances FitzGerald, *America Revised: History Schoolbooks in the Twentieth Century* (Little, Brown, 1979), 83.

14. Charles F. Horne, *The Story of Our American People*, 2 vols. (United States History Publishing, 1925), 2: 212.

15. Ibid., 267.

16. Samuel Eliot Morison and Henry Steele Commager, *Growth of the American Republic* (Oxford University Press, 1930), 415, 418.

17. W.E.B. Du Bois, *Black Reconstruction: An Essay toward a History of the Part Which Black Folk Played in the Attempt to Reconstruct Democracy in America, 1860–1880* (Harcourt, Brace, 1935), 725, 727.

18. *My Country* (1948), quoted in *Social Studies Review*, 7 (Winter 1991): 10.

19. Frank L. Owsley, John Craig Stewart, and Gordon T. Chapell, *Know Alabama: An Elementary History* (Colonial Press, 1965), 176–78.

20. Leon Litwack, "Trouble in Mind: The Bicentennial and the Afro-American Experience," *Journal of American History* 74 (1987): 326.

21. Quoted in Novick, *That Noble Dream*, 352, from Kenneth Stampp, "The Historian and Southern Negro Slavery," *American Historical Review* 57 (1952): 619–20.

22. Novick, *That Noble Dream*, 350.

23. FitzGerald, *America Revised*, 108–9.

24. Ibid., 116–17.

25. Robert Sobel, Roger LaRaus, Linda Ann De Leon, and Harry P. Morris, *The Challenge of Freedom* (Glencoe, 1990), quoted in James Loewen, *Lies My Teacher Told Me: Everything Your American History Textbook Got Wrong* (New Press, 1995), 197.

26. FitzGerald, *America Revised*, 112–13.

27. Bruce Levine et al., *Who Built America: Working People and the Nation's Economy, Politics, Culture, and Society*, 2 vols. (Pantheon, 1989–92), 1: xii.

28. Allan Nevins, "American History for Americans," *New York Times Magazine*, 3 May 1942.

29. Hazel Whitman Hertzberg, *Social Studies Reform, 1880–1980* (Social Science Education Consortium, 1981), 67.

30. Ibid.

31. *New York Times*, 4 April 1943. Quoted in ibid.

32. Ibid.

33. Quoted in Novick, *That Noble Dream*, 369.

34. Quoted in ibid.

35. Quoted in ibid.

36. Edgar Wesley, *American History in the Schools and Colleges* (Macmillan, 1944), 4.

37. Chester M. Destler in American Historical Association, Annual Report, 1949 (American Historical Association, 1950).

38. Novick, *That Noble Dream*, 368.

39. Diane Ravitch, *The Troubled Crusade: American Education, 1945–1980* (Basic Books, 1983), 89.

40. Erling M. Hunt, ed., *Citizens for a New World*, 14th Yearbook of the National Council for the Social Studies (National Council for the Social Studies, 1944).

41. Hilda Taba and William Van Tils, eds., *Democratic Human Relations: Promising Practices in Intergroup and Intercultural Education in the Social Studies*, 16th Yearbook of the National Council for the Social Studies (National Council for the Social Studies, 1946), 352.

42. Stanley E. Diamond, *Schools and the Development of Good Citizens* (Wayne University Press, 1953); and Citizenship Education Project, *The Premises of American Liberty* (Teachers College, Columbia University, 1952).

43. Ray Allen Billington, *The Historian's Contribution to Anglo-American Misunderstanding,* Report of a Committee on National Bias in Anglo-American History Textbooks (Hobbs, Dorman, 1966), 2.

44. This account of the Meriden controversy is derived from Jack Nelson and Gene Roberts Jr., *The Censors and the Schools* (Little, Brown, 1963), ch. 1.

45. Ibid., 41–42; Lucille Cardin Crain, Magruder's attacker, is quoted on p. 41.

46. Ibid., 134; Dobie is quoted on p. 141.

47. Ibid., 132.

48. Ibid., 178.

49. *Goals for Americans: Programs for Action in the Sixties.* Report of the President's Commission on National Goals (Prentice Hall, 1960), xi.

50. Ibid., 3.

51. Ibid., 6–9.

52. Novick, *That Noble Dream,* 372.

53. *Goals for Americans,* 23.

54. Gilbert Allardyce, "Toward World History: American Historians and the Coming of the World History Course," *Journal of World History* 1 (Spring 1990): 45.

55. On Stavrianos's career as a world historian, see ibid, 40–62.

56. K. S. Latourette, "The Study of the Far East," *The Historical Outlook* 10 (March 1919): 131–32.

CHAPTER 4

1. Charles W. Colson, "When History Is Up for Grabs," *New York Times,* 28 Dec. 1995, A17.

2. For a scintillating discussion of this see David A. Hollinger, *Postethnic America* (Basic Books, 1995).

3. Lawrence W. Levine, "The Unpredictable Past: Reflections on Recent American Historiography," *American Historical Review* 94 (1989): 673.

4. Leo Tolstoy, *War and Peace,* trans. Constance Garnett (Heinemann, 1971), 889–90.

5. Joyce Appleby, Lynn Hunt, and Margaret Jacobs, *Telling the Truth about History* (Norton, 1994), 218.

6. Robert Darnton, *The Great Cat Massacre and Other Episodes in French Cultural History* (Basic Books, 1984).

7. Levine, "The Unpredictable Past," 673.

8. Thomas Paine, *Common Sense and Other Political Writings,* ed. Nelson F. Adkins (Bobbs-Merrill, 1953), 51.

9. Thomas Paine, "The Forester's Letters," #3, in *The Complete Writings of Thomas Paine,* ed. Philip S. Foner (Citadel Press, 1945), 2: 82.

10. Abigail Adams to John Adams, 31 March 1776, *Adams Family Correspondence,* ed. H. Butterfield Lyman (Belknap Press of Harvard University Press, 1963), 1: 370.

11. Hazel Whitman Hertzberg, *Social Studies Reform, 1880–1980,* (Social Science Education Consortium, 1981), 122.

12. James P. Shaver, "A Critical View of the Social Studies Profession," *Social Education* 41 (April 1977): 300–307.

13. Howard D. Mehlinger, "Social Studies: Some Gulfs and Priorities," in Howard D. Mehlinger and O. L. Davis Jr., eds., *The Social Studies,* Eightieth Yearbook of the National Society for the Study of Education, Part 2 (University of Chicago Press, 1981), 244.

14. Martin Mayer, *Where, When, and Why: Social Studies in American Schools* (Harper & Row, 1963), 6, 42.

15. Matthew T. Downey, ed., *History in the Schools* (National Council for the Social Studies, 1985), 6–7.

16. Quoted in Thomas C. Mendenhall, "The Introductory College Course in Civilization," *American Historical Review* 49 (Oct. 1943): 683.

17. Mayer, *Where, When, and Why,* 21.

18. Gilbert Allardyce, "Toward World History: American Historians and the Coming of the World History Course," *Journal of World History* 1 (Spring 1990): 55.

19. Leften Stavrianos, "Main Currents in World Thought," in *New Perspectives in World History, Thirty-Fourth Yearbook of the National Council for the Social Studies,* ed. Shirley H. Engle (National Council for the Social Studies, 1964), 11.

20. Mayer, *Where, When, and Why,* 30.

21. Alexander Clarence Flick, *Modern World History, 1776–1926* (F. S. Crofts, 1926), 485.

22. Hugh Trevor-Roper, *The Rise of Christian Europe* (Thames and Hudson, 1965), 9.

23. Philip D. Curtin, "African History," in Michael Kammen, ed., *The Past Before Us: Contemporary Historical Writing in the United States* (Cornell University Press, 1980), 114–15.

24. Gilbert Allardyce, "The Rise and Fall of the Western Civilization Course," *American Historical Review* 87 (1982): 716.

25. William H. McNeill, "Beyond Western Civilization: Rebuilding the Survey," *The History Teacher* 10 (1977): 510.

26. Ibid., 514.

27. Howard D. Mehlinger, et al., *Global Studies for American Schools* (National Education Association, 1972), 11–12.

28. Allardyce, "Toward World History," 58.

29. L. S. Stavrianos, "The Teaching of World History," *The History Teacher* 3 (Nov. 1969): 22, 24.

30. L. S. Stavrianos, *A Global History from Prehistory to the Present,* 4th ed. (Prentice Hall, 1988), xii.

31. Charles G. Sellers, "Is History on the Way Out of the Schools and Do Historians Care?" *Social Education* 33 (1969), 509–16; Peter Novick, *That Noble Dream: The "Objectivity Question" and the American Historical Profession* (Cambridge University Press, 1988), 372.

32. Richard S. Kirkendall, "The Status of History in the Schools," *Journal of American History* 62 (Sept. 1975): 557–70. All quotations that follow are from Kirkendall's report.

CHAPTER 5

1.   Henry Wallace, *The Century of the Common Man* (Reynal & Hitchcock, 1943), 5.

2.   Edward T. Linenthal and Tom Engelhardt, eds., *History Wars: The Enola Gay and Other Battles for the American Past* (Henry Holt, 1996), 7.

3.   Arthur Schlesinger Jr., "History as Therapy: A Dangerous Idea," *New York Times,* 3 May 1996, A11.

4.   Joyce Appleby, Lynn Hunt, and Margaret Jacobs, *Telling the Truth about History* (Norton, 1994), 289.

5.   Michael Zuckerman, "Myth and Method: The Current Crisis in American Historical Writing," *The History Teacher* 17 (1984): 221.

6.   Bernard Bailyn, "The Challenge of Modern Historiography," *American Historical Review* 87 (1982): 3.

7.   John Higham, "Beyond Pluralism: The Historian as American Prophet," unpublished paper delivered to the Organization of American Historians, April 1983.

8.   Mark H. Leff, "Revisioning United States Political History," *American Historical Review* 100 (1995): 833.

9.   Gertrude Himmelfarb, "Some Reflections on the New History," *American Historical Review* 94 (1989): 664.

10. Robert Fullinwider, "Patriotic History," in Fullinwider, ed., *Public Education in a Multicultural Society: Policy, Theory, Critique* (Cambridge University Press, 1995), 211.

11. Ibid.

12. Lawrence W. Levine, "The Unpredictable Past," *American Historical Review* 94 (1989): 673.

13. Appleby, Hunt, and Jacobs, *Telling the Truth,* 293.

14. Joan Wallach Scott, "History in Crisis? The Others' Side of the Story," *American Historical Review* 94 (1989): 682.

15. Stephen Burd, "Chairman of Humanities Fund Has Politicized Grants Process, Critics Charge," *Chronicle of Higher Education,* 22 April 1992, A32.

16. The two quotes are from Stanley Katz, president of the American Council of Learned Societies, and John Frohnmayer, Chairman of the National Endowment for the Arts, who was appointed by President Bush. Quoted in John K. Wilson, *The Myth of Political Correctness: The Conservative Attack on Higher Education* (Duke University Press, 1995), 62.

17. "Bennett Draws Fire in Stanford Talk Assailing Course Change," *Los Angeles Times,* 19 April 1988, I3.

18. Robert Marquand, "Stanford's CIV Course Sparks Controversy," *Christian Science Monitor,* 25 Jan. 1989, 13.

19. Quoted in Wilson, *The Myth of Political Correctness,* 78–79.

20. Todd Gitlin, *The Twilight of Common Dreams: Why America Is Wracked by Culture Wars* (Henry Holt, 1995), 168.

21. Quoted in William J. Bennett, *The De-Valuing of America: The Fight for Our Culture and Our Children* (Summit, 1992), 258.

22. Quoted in Wilson, *Myth of Political Correctness,* 78.

23. Wilson, *Myth of Political Correctness,* especially pp. 64–89; see also Dinesh D'Souza, *Illiberal Education: The Politics of Race and Sex on Campus* (Free Press, 1991), 59–93.

24. Wilson, *Myth of Political Correctness,* 84.

25. Ibid., 86.

26. National Commission on Excellence in Education, *A Nation at Risk: The Imperative for Educational Reform* (U.S. Government Printing Office, 1983), 5.

27. Gertrude Himmelfarb, *The New History and the Old: Critical Essays and Reappraisals* (Harvard University Press, 1987), 25.

28. E. D. Hirsch Jr., *Cultural Literacy: What Every American Needs to Know* (Houghton Mifflin, 1987), 1–2. Leading representatives for this camp came out of literature backgrounds more often than history.

29. Lynne V. Cheney, *American Memory: A Report on the Humanities in the Nation's Public Schools* (National Endowment for the Humanities, 1987), 6.

30. Lynne V. Cheney, *Telling the Truth, A Report on the State of the Humanities in Higher Education* (National Endowment for the Humanities, 1992), 7.

31. Ronald W. Evans, "Diane Ravitch and the Revival of History: A Critique," *Social Studies* 80 (May/June 1989): 85.

32. Ibid., 89.

33. Diane Ravitch, "The Revival of History: A Response," *Social Studies* 80 (May/June 1989): 90.

34. Diane Ravitch and Chester E. Finn Jr., *What Do Our 17-Year-Olds Know? A Report on the First National Assessment of History and Literature* (Harper & Row, 1987).

35. Ibid., 7.

36. Ibid., 17.

37. National Assessment of Educational Progress, *The U.S. History Report Card* (Office of Educational Research and Improvement, U.S. Department of Education, 1990).

38. Ravitch, "The Revival of History," 90.

39. Bradley Commission on History in Schools, *Building a History Curriculum: Guidelines for Teaching History in Schools* (Educational Excellence Network, 1988), 7–8.

40. Ibid., 6.

41. Ibid., 8.

42. National Commission on Social Studies in the Schools, report of the Curriculum Task Force, *Charting a Course: Social Studies for the 21st Century* (National Commission on Social Studies in the Schools, 1989).

43. Ibid., 14.

44. *History–Social Science Framework for California Public Schools: Kindergarten through Grade Twelve* (California State Department of Education, 1988).

45. Robert Reinhold, "Class Struggle," *New York Times Magazine,* 21 Sept. 1991, 28.

46. Diane Ravitch, "California Schools Gear Up to Fight Pervasive Public Ignorance of the Past," *Los Angeles Times,* 1 Jan. 1989, V3.

47. Evans, "Diane Ravitch," 88.

48. Lynne V. Cheney, "Memorandum to All NEH Staff," 1 Dec. 1992, released to press 2 Dec. 1992.

49. Frances FitzGerald, *America Revised: History Schoolbooks in the Twentieth Century* (Little, Brown, 1979), 83–105.

50. James W. Loewen, *Lies My Teacher Told Me: Everything Your American History Textbook Got Wrong* (New Press, 1995), 197.

51. Peter N. Stearns, *Meaning Over Memory: Recasting the Teaching of Culture and History* (University of North Carolina Press, 1993), 63–64.

52. Robert Roswell Palmer and Joel Colton, *A History of the Modern World,* 6th ed. (McGraw-Hill, 1984).

53. Reinhold, "Class Struggle," 26.

54. Gitlin, *Twilight of Common Dreams,* 13.

55. This argument was made, fervently but disingenuously, in Catherine Cornbleth and Dexter Waugh, *The Great Speckled Bird: Multicultural Politics and Education Policy-making* (St. Martin's Press, 1995).

56. Paul Boyer and Merle Curti, *The American Nation* (Holt, Rinehart, and Winston, 1994).

57. John Leo, "Affirmative Action History," *U.S. News & World Report,* 28 March 1994, 24.

58. Gilbert Sewall, "Triumph of Textbook Trendiness," *Wall Street Journal,* 1 March 1994, A18.

59. Paul Boyer, Letter to the Editor, *U.S. News & World Report,* 25 April 1994 and letter to Sewall from Little, Brown (provided by Paul Boyer to the authors).

60. Michel Marriott, "Afrocentrism: Balancing or Skewing History," *New York Times,* 11 Aug. 1991, 1; see also Molefi Kete Asante, *The Afrocentric Idea* (Temple University Press, 1987).

61. Asante, *The Afrocentric Idea,* 9.

62. Portland Public Schools Social Studies African American Baseline Essay, (1990).

63. Leonard Jeffries quoted in Jim Sleeper, "Blacks and Jews," *The Nation,* 9 Sept. 1991, 252. For two accounts of Jeffries, see Michael Eric Dyson, "Leonard Jeffries and the Struggle for the Black Mind" in *Reflecting Black: African-American Cultural Criticism,* ed., Michael Eric Dyson (University of Minnesota Press, 1993); and James Traub, "The Hearts and Minds of City College," *The New Yorker* 69, no. 16, 7 June 1993, 42–54.

64. Quoted in Andrew Sullivan, "Racism 101," *New Republic,* 26 Nov. 1990, 20.

65. Quoted in ibid.

66. Henry Louis Gates Jr., "Beware of the New Pharaohs," *Newsweek,* 23 Sept. 1991, 47; idem. "Pluralism and Its Discontents," *Contention* 4 (Fall 1992), 69–78.

67. Barbara Kantrowitz, "A is for Ashanti, B is for Black," *Newsweek,* 23 Sept. 1991, 45.

68. David L. Kirp, "The Battle of the Books," *San Francisco Chronicle,* 24 Feb. 1991, Image section.

69. Quoted in Roger Lane, *William Dorsey's Philadelphia and Ours: On the Past and Future of the Black City in America* (Oxford University Press, 1991), 278.

70. Carter G. Woodson, *The Miseducation of the Negro* (The Associated Publishers, 1933).

71. Martin Bernal, *Black Athena: The Afroasiatic Roots of Classical Civilization,* 2 vols. (Rutgers University Press, 1987, 1991).

72. Mary F. Lefkowitz, *Not Out of Africa: How Afrocentrism Became an Excuse to Teach Myth as History* (Basic Books, 1996).

73. David A. Hollinger, *Postethnic America: Beyond Multiculturalism* (Basic Books, 1995), 127–28.

74. Gitlin, *Twilight of Common Dreams,* 175.

75. Dinesh D'Souza, "Pride and Prejudice: The Errors of Afrocentrism," *American Enterprise* 6 (Sept./Oct. 1995): 54.

76. See Arthur M. Schlesinger Jr., *The Disuniting of America: Reflections on a Multicultural Society* (Norton, 1991) for an example of a work that exposes Afrocentric excesses but then lapses into Eurocentric triumphalism.

77. Kantrowitz, "A is for Ashanti, B is for Black," 48.

78. Quoted in *Time*, 26 Nov. 1990.
79. Carlos E. Cortes, "Backing into the Future: Columbus, Cleopatra, Custer, & the Diversity Revolution," *Humanities* 14 (1992): 1.
80. Thomas J. Schlereth, "Columbia, Columbus, and Columbianism," *Journal of American History* 79 (1992): 937.
81. Quoted in Eric Foner and Jon Wiener, "Fighting for the West," *The Nation*, 29 July 1991, 163.
82. William H. Truettner and Alexander Nemerov, "What You See Is Not Necessarily What You Get: New Meaning in Images of the Old West," *Montana: The Magazine of Western History* 42 (Summer 1992): 71, 77.
83. Andrew Gulliford, "Visitors Respond: Selections from 'The West as America' Comment Books," *Montana: The Magazine of Western History* 42 (Summer 1992): 78.
84. Edward T. Linenthal, "Can Museums Achieve a Balance Between Memory and History?" *The Chronicle of Higher Education*, 10 Feb. 1995, B1. The *Enola Gay* episode is exhaustively explored in Linenthal and Engelhardt, *History Wars*.
85. *New York Times*, 30 Jan. 1995, A14.
86. Paul Goldberger, "Historical Shows on Trial: Who Judges?" *New York Times*, 11 Feb. 1996, Sec. 2, 26.
87. Richard H. Kohn, "History and the Culture Wars: The Case of the Smithsonian Institution's *Enola Gay* Exhibition," *Journal of American History* 82 (1995): 1036.
88. Ellsworth Brown, president of AAM, quoted in Alfred F. Young, "S.O.S.: Storm Warning for American Museums," *OAH Newsletter* 22 (1994): 6.
89. Spencer Crew, "Who Owns History? History in the Museum," unpublished paper delivered at the American Historical Association annual meeting, Atlanta, Jan. 1996, 3.
90. Joan Wallach Scott, "The Campaign against Political Correctness: What's Really at Stake," *Radical History Review* 54 (Fall 1992): 66.

CHAPTER 6

1. "Students in a Moscow School Debate the Once-Undebatable," *New York Times*, 20 Oct. 1988, A1.
2. "Searching for Truth Amid Lies," *Los Angeles Times*, 19 Dec. 1991, A1.
3. "New Texts Reshape Past for Russians," *Los Angeles Times*, Part A, 25 Sept. 1994.
4. Ibid.; Janet G. Vaillant, "Reform in History and Social Studies Education in Russian Secondary Schools," in Anthony Jones, ed., *Education and Society in the New Russia* (M.E. Sharpe, 1994), 141–68.
5. "No More Lessons From the Revolution," *Los Angeles Times*, 21 Oct. 1996, A1.
6. See Jacqueline Dean and Roger Sieborger, "After Apartheid: The Outlook for History," *Teaching History* 79 (April 1995): 32–38.
7. "Reversing Apartheid's Lessons," *Los Angeles Times*, 11 Feb. 1997, A1.
8. "South Africa Tentatively Begins Struggle to Learn Its History," *International Herald Tribune*, 22 March 1995.
9. "Mexicans Look Askance at Textbooks' New Slant," *New York Times*, 21 Sept. 1992, A3; "Salinas Accused of Doctoring the Books on Mexico's History," *Los Angeles Times*, 22 Sept. 1992, H3.

10. Harvey J. Kaye, *The Powers of the Past: Reflections on the Crisis and the Promise of History* (University of Minnesota Press, 1991), 135–39.

11. Joyce Appleby, Lynn Hunt, and Margaret Jacobs, *Telling the Truth about History* (Norton, 1994), 291.

12. Gordon Craig, "The War of the German Historians," *New York Review of Books,* 15 Jan. 1987, 15–19.

13. See Robert G. Moeller, "War Stories: The Search for a Usable Past in the Federal Republic of Germany," *American Historical Review* 101 (Oct. 1996): 1008–48.

14. Quoted in Byron K. Marshall, *Learning to Be Modern: Japanese Political Discourse on Education* (Westview Press, 1994), 187.

15. "Right, Proper and Perplexed: Japan is Struggling to Reconcile Conflicting Views of Its History," *Financial Times,* 6 Aug. 1994, 9.

16. James L. Barth, "A Comparative Study of the Current Situation on Teaching about World War II in Japanese and American Classrooms," *International Journal of Social Education* 6 (Autumn 1991): 7–19.

17. George Thomas Kurian, ed., *World Education Encyclopedia* (Facts on File, 1988) 3: 1326–27.

18. "National Curriculum: Lots of Little Guinea Pigs," *The Economist,* 3 Dec. 1988, 66.

19. John White, "Educational Reform in Britain: Beyond the National Curriculum," *International Review of Education* 36, no. 2 (1990): 133.

20. Ibid., 142.

21. John Slater, *The Politics of History Teaching: A Humanity Dehumanized?* (Institute of Education, University of London, 1989), 1.

22. Slater, *Politics of History Teaching,* 8.

23. Andrew Roberts, "Take a Pride in History," *Sunday Telegraph,* 24 Nov. 1991, 27.

24. Keith Crawford, "History of the Right: The Battle for Control of National Curriculum History 1989–1994," *British Journal of Educational Studies* 43 (Dec. 1995): 434. Crawford borrows this idea from Stanley Cohen, *Folk Devils and Moral Panics: The Creation of the Mods and Rockers* (Martin Robertson, 1972). See also Denis Lawton, "Political Parties, Ideology and the National Curriculum," *Educational Review* 45, no. 2 (1993): 111–18.

25. A. N. Wilson quoted in Crawford, "History of the Right," 441.

26. Quoted in Duncan Graham, *A Lesson for Us All: The Making of the National Curriculum* (Routledge, 1993), 64.

27. Great Britain, Department of Education and Science, National Curriculum History Working Group, Interim Report, 1989.

28. Graham, *Lesson for Us All,* 65.

29. MacGregor to Saunders Watson, Interim Report.

30. Paul Grey and Rosemarie Little, letter, *Times Educational Supplement* (London), 25 Aug. 1989, 12.

31. "Too Many Eggs Spoil the Pudding," editorial, *Times Educational Supplement* (London), 18 Aug. 1989, 10.

32. "History Curriculum Should Emphasize Need to Learn Facts," *Independent,* 19 Mar. 1990, 3.

33. Ibid.

34. Quoted in D. McKiernan, "History in a National Curriculum: Imagining the Nation at the End of the 20th Century," *Journal of Curriculum Studies* 25, no. 1 (1993): 42.

35. "Tories Launch Their Biggest Takeover Bid—for History," *Times* (London), 1 April 1990.
36. Great Britain, Department of Education and Science, National Curriculum History Working Group, Final Report, April 1990, 7.
37. John Slater, "History in the National Curriculum: the Final Report of the History Working Group," in *History in the National Curriculum*, ed. Richard Aldrich (Kogan Page in association with the Institute of Education, University of London, 1991), 24–25.
38. Robert H. Phillips, " 'The Battle for the Big Prize.' The Shaping of Synthesis and the Role of a Curriculum Pressure Group: The Case of School History and the National Curriculum," *The Curriculum Journal* 3, no. 2 (1992): 245–61.
39. "History Inquiry Ignites Fierce Row in Britain," *Christian Science Monitor*, 24 April 1990, 4.
40. "Flexibility Urged over History Curriculum," *Daily Telegraph*, 4 May 1990, 4.
41. "What the Prime Minister Said," *Times Educational Supplement* (London), 20 April 1990, 3.
42. One ex-professor admitted that neither he nor his colleagues had "a clue what was being taught in schools." "Tories Launch Their Biggest Takeover Bid—for History."
43. "Flexibility Urged over History Curriculum," *Daily Telegraph*, 4 May 1990, 4.
44. "Historians Fear for Future of Their Subject in Schools," *Independent*, 20 June 1990, 6.
45. Kathryn Stearns, *School Reform: Lessons from England* (Carnegie Foundation for the Advancement of Teaching, 1996), 17.
46. Great Britain, Department of Education, "Revised National Curriculum for History," Jan. 1995.
47. "History Texts Drops 1666 and All That," *Sunday Telegraph*, 27 Feb. 1994, 7.
48. Crawford, "History of the Right," 447.
49. "Great Britons to Star in History Lessons," *Times* (London), 6 May 1994.
50. "Curriculum Man 'Stupid, Misguided,' " *Yorkshire Post*, 19 July 1995.
51. Josna Pankhania undertakes such a project in *Liberating the National Curriculum* (Falmer Press, 1994).

CHAPTER 7

1. U.S. Department of Education, *National Goals for Education* (U.S. Department of Education, 1990), 1.
2. Ibid.
3. Ibid.
4. Ibid., 5. Succeeding quotations from this document are from pages 5–6 of this document.
5. Stanley M. Elam and Alec M. Gallup, "The 21st Annual Gallup Poll of the Public's Attitudes Toward the Public Schools," *Phi Delta Kappan* 71, no. 1 (Sept. 1989): 41–56.
6. Stanley M. Elam, Lowell C. Rose, and Alec M. Gallup, "The 23rd Annual Gallup Poll of the Public's Attitudes Toward the Public Schools," *Phi Delta Kappa* 73, no. 1 (Sept. 1991): 41–57.

7. "Schools Face a Variety of Challenges," *Dallas Morning News,* 8 April 1990, J8.

8. Lamar Alexander, "A Message from the Secretary," Preface to *America 2000, An Education Strategy* (U.S. Department of Education, 1991).

9. *America 2000, An Education Strategy,* 11.

10. Ibid., 2.

11. Lamar Alexander, "A Commitment to Learn Will Make Us a Better Nation," *Daily News,* 18 Aug. 1991, 1, 4.

12. National Alliance of Business, "Policy Statement: A National Assessment System," unpublished paper of the NAB, n.d.

13. Lynne V. Cheney, *National Tests: What Other Countries Expect Their Students to Know* (National Endowment for the Humanities, 1991), 2.

14. Ibid., 4.

15. Chester E. Finn Jr., *We Must Take Charge: Our Schools and Our Future* (The Free Press, 1991).

16. Ibid., 177.

17. National Governors' Association Center for Policy Research and Analysis, *Time for Results: The Governors' 1991 Report on Education* (National Governors' Association, 1991), 2–7.

18. The National Center for Fair and Open Testing (FairTest), for example, organized a coalition of some thirty organizations to launch a Campaign for Genuine Accountability in Education to contest the idea that national tests would spur school reform, alert the Congress to issues of equity and fairness in testing, and issue criteria for the evaluation of testing programs. The organizations included the Children's Defense Fund, the NAACP, the Mexican American Legal Defense and Educational Fund, the Center for Women's Policy Studies, the National School Boards Association, the Council of Chief State School Officers, and the Association for Supervision and Curriculum Development.

19. "Legislation to Create National System of Standards, Assessments Under Fire," *Education Week,* 25 March 1992, 1, 31.

20. National Council on Education Standards and Testing, *Raising Standards for American Education,* A Report to Congress, the Secretary of Education, the National Education Goals Panel, and the American People. (U.S. Government Printing Office, 1992).

21. "Response to National Testing Proposals," a statement drafted by Theodore Sizer, Coalition of Essential Schools, and initially signed by 49 nationally prominent educators, scholars, and citizen activists, 24 Jan. 1992.

22. Robert Rothman, *Measuring Up: Standards, Assessment, and School Reform* (Jossey-Bass, 1995), 136. See also Chapter 5 of Diane Ravitch, *National Standards in American Education: A Citizen's Guide* (The Brookings Institution, 1995).

23. Chester E. Finn Jr., "Fear of Standards Threatens Education Reform," *Wall Street Journal,* 23 March 1992, A10.

24. History Task Force of the National Council for Education Standards and Testing, "Report of the History Task Force," in *Raising Standards for American Education,* K1–3.

25. National Center for History in the Schools, *Lessons from History: Essential Understandings and Historical Perspectives Students Should Acquire* (University of California, Los Angeles, 1992).

26. "Report of the History Task Force", K1–3.

27. Members of the National Council for History Standards were Charlotte Anderson, Joyce Appleby, Samuel Banks, David Battini, David Baumbach, Earl Bell, Mary Bicouvaris, Diane Brooks, Pedro Castillo, Ainslee Embree, Elizabeth Fox-Genovese, Carol Gluck, Darlene Clark Hine, Bill Honig, Akira Iriye, Barbara Talbert Jackson, Kenneth Jackson, Morton Keller, Bernard Lewis, William McNeill, Alan Morgan, John J. Patrick, Theodore K. Rabb, C. Frederick Risinger, Denny Schillings, Gilbert T. Sewall, Warren Solomon, and Michael R. Winston. Charlotte Crabtree and Gary B. Nash were cochairs of the council, assisted by Linda Symcox.

28. Represented in the forum were the American Association for State and Local History, the Association for the Study of Afro-American Life and History, the National Alliance of Black School Educators, the League of United Latin American Citizens, the National Association for Asian and Pacific American Education, the Native American Heritage Commission, the Quality Education for Minorities Network, the Council of the Great City Schools, the Council for American Private Education, the National Catholic Educational Association, the Lutheran Schools–Missouri Synod, the American Association of School Librarians, the National Education Association, the American Federation of Teachers, the National Association of State Boards of Education, the National Association of Elementary School Principals, the National Association of Secondary School Principals, the Center for Civic Education, the National Council for Geographic Education, the National Council for Economic Education, the Atlantic Council of the United States, the Council for Basic Education, the Educational Excellence Network, and the National Congress of Parents and Teachers.

29. These nine focus groups represented the membership of the Council of Chief State School Officers, the Association for Supervision and Curriculum Development, the American Historical Association, the Organization of American Historians, the World History Association, the National Council for History Education, the National Council for the Social Studies, the Council of State Social Studies Specialists, and the Organization of History Teachers.

30. Debra Viadero, "Issue of Multiculturalism Dominates Standards Debate," *Education Week*, 22 April 1992, 18.

31. Adelaide L. Sanford, "Recommendations to the National Council for History Standards," 24 April 1992.

32. Joint meeting of the National Council for History Standards and the National Forum for History Standards, audiocassette of meeting, 10 April 1992. This audiocassette is the source for the following quotations from participants at that meeting.

33. The Educational Excellence Network, "Recommendations to the National Council for History Standards," 24 April 1992.

34. Joint meeting of the National Council for History Standards and National Forum for History Standards, audiocassette of meeting, 10 April 1992.

35. Ibid.

36. New York State United Teachers, "Public Attitudes on the Debate over Multicultural Education in New York State." *1991 Education Opinion Survey. Final Report* (Fact Finders, 12 Nov. 1991), Section II.

37. Seventy percent of whites, 89 percent of blacks, and 87 percent of Hispanics agreed.

38. Eighty percent of whites, 93 percent of blacks, and 97 percent of Hispanics judged this content to be "very important" or "somewhat important."

39. Joint meeting of the National Council for History Standards and the National Forum for History Standards, audiocassette of meeting, 10 April 1992.

40. Ibid.

41. "Governors Assert Key to Prosperity Is a Global View," *New York Times,* 26 July 1987, 1.

42. Bradley Commission on History in Schools, *Building a History Curriculum: Guidelines for Teaching History in Schools* (Educational Excellence Network, 1988), 15.

43. U.S. Department of Education, *National Goals for Education,* 6.

44. National Council on Education Standards and Testing, *Raising Standards for American Education,* K–2.

45. William J. Bennett, *To Reclaim a Legacy* (National Endowment for the Humanities, Nov. 1988), 30.

46. See, for example, Roger Kimball, *Tenured Radicals: How Politics Has Corrupted Our Higher Education* (Harper & Row, 1990).

47. Harvey J. Kaye points out that William Bennett's NEH report, *To Reclaim a Legacy,* "is characterized by the virtual absence of any recognition that the constitution of the humanities includes social history." *The Powers of the Past* (University of Minnesota Press, 1991), 114.

48. John Patrick Diggins, "Can the Social Historians Get It Right?" *Society* 34 (Jan./Feb. 1997): 14.

49. Elaine Woo, "Al Shanker's Last Stand," *Los Angeles Times Magazine,* 1 Dec. 1996, 52.

50. American Federation of Teachers, Educational Excellence Network, and Freedom House, *Education for Democracy, A Statement of Principles* (American Federation of Teachers, 1987), 8.

51. Paul Gagnon, *Democracy's Untold Story, What World History Textbooks Neglect* (American Federation of Teachers, 1987), 40.

52. Paul Gagnon to Charlotte Crabtree, 31 Aug. 1991.

53. Gagnon, *Democracy's Untold Story,* 38.

54. Peter N. Stearns, "Teaching the United States in World History," *American Historical Association Perspectives,* April 1989, 12.

55. Frederic E. Wakeman Jr., "Transnational and Comparative Research," *Items* (Social Science Research Council) 42 (Dec. 1988): 87–88.

56. American Federation of Teachers, untitled paper presented to the National Council for History Standards, 10 April 1992.

57. The Educational Excellence Network, "Recommendations to the National Council," 24 April 1992.

58. Sara R. Shoob, "Setting Standards for History." Report of the National Association of Elementary School Principals, April 1992.

59. Joint meeting of the National Council for History Standards and the National Forum for History Standards, audiocassette of meeting, 10 April 1992. The following direct quotes are also drawn from this cassette.

60. Howard Spodek, "Reflections on and responses to *Lessons from History* from the National Center for History in the Schools, UCLA/NEH," 28 May 1992.

61. James B. Gardner to Charlotte Crabtree, 21 May 1992.

62. American Historical Association, "Report of the World History Focus Group of

the American Historical Association, National History Standards Project," 18 May 1992.

63. Association for Supervision and Curriculum Development Focus Group. "Review of the Criteria for Standards: Comments and Recommendations," 22 May 1992.

64. William H. McNeill, letter to the project codirectors, 8 May 1992, discussed in the council meeting 11–12 June 1992.

65. The World History Curriculum Committee consisted of Joan Arno, David Baumbach, Richard Bulliet, Ainslee T. Embree, Carol Gluck, Akira Iriye, Henry G. Kiernan, Colin Palmer, Theodore K. Rabb, Richard Saller, and Michael R. Winston, chair. Consultants were Philip Curtin, Ross Dunn, William McNeill, and Peter Stearns.

66. James B. Gardner to Charlotte Crabtree, 14 July 1992.

67. Robert Blackey to Charlotte Crabtree, 2 Nov. 1992.

68. Robert Blackey, Tom Holt, and Louise Tilly to Charlotte Crabtree and Gary B. Nash, 8 Feb. 1993.

69. National Council for the Social Studies Focus Group Report, May 1993; Organization of American Historians Focus Group Report, 19 May 1993.

70. C. Frederick Risinger, "The National History Standards: A View from the Inside," *History Teacher* 28, no. 3 (May 1995): 387–93.

71. U.S. Department of Education, *National Goals for Education,* 5.

72. "Report of the History Task Force," K3.

73. Council of Chief State School Officers Focus Group, "Report of the Meeting to Discuss March 1993 Progress Report and Sample Standards from the National History Standards Project," Washington, D.C., 15–16 April 1993.

74. National Council for the Social Studies, "Focus Group Report on the National History Standards Project," May 1993.

75. Organization of History Teachers, "Response to the Proposed United States History Standards from Reconstruction Through the Present," April 1994.

76. "Focus Group Report" of OAH's *OAH Magazine of History,* n.d.

77. Council of State Social Studies Specialists, "Focus Group Report, March 1994 Edition of the National History Standards," 13 May 1994.

78. Ibid.

79. Peggy Altoff, "Review of National History Standards," 27 June 1994.

80. Constance Miller Manter, "Responses to Review Categories for the National History Standards—U.S. History," 29 April 1994.

81. Joint meeting of the National Council for History Standards and National Forum for History Standards, audiocassette of meeting, 19 May 1994.

82. Ibid.

83. Ibid. Comments reported also in the written statement of the National Catholic Educational Association, "National History Standards," 19 May 1994.

84. Ruth J. Kurth, "Report on the National Standards Project for History from the Lutheran Education Association—LCMS," 31 May 1994.

85. Joint meeting of the National Council for History Standards and National Forum for History Standards, audiocassette of meeting, 19 May 1994.

86. Ruth Wattenberg, American Federation of Teachers, "Comments on the History Standards," 28 April 1994.

87. Council of State Social Studies Specialists, "Focus Group Report, March 1994 Edition of the National History Standards," 24 May 1994.

88. Eric Rothschild, OAH Committee on Teaching, "National History Standards Project," 30 April 1994.

89. Organization of History Teachers, "Response to the Proposed United States History Standards from Reconstruction through the Present," April 1994.

90. Chester E. Finn Jr., "Notes for National Forum/National Council History Standards Discussion," Washington, D.C., Education Policy Committee of the Educational Excellence Network, 19 May 1994.

91. Joint meeting of the National Council for History Standards and National Forum for History Standards, audiocassette of meeting, 19 May 1994.

92. Ibid.

93. Janet W. Crouse, chair, Education Commission, National PTA, "Report to National Council for History Standards," 19 May 1994.

94. Joint meeting of the National Council for History Standards and National Forum for History Standards, audiocassette of meeting, 19 May 1994.

95. National Council for History Standards, audiocassette of meeting, 20 May 1994. This audiocassette is also the source for the succeeding quotations from participants at this meeting.

96. "Summary of the CCSSO Focus Group Meeting for Standards in U.S. History," 26 May 1992.

97. Diane Ravitch to Charlotte Crabtree, 8 June 1994.

98. National Council for History Education, "Report of the Focus Group on World History," 11 July 1994.

99. Organization of History Teachers, "Response to the Proposed World History Standards, From Early Humans through the Present," 20 July 1994.

100. Ramsey Selden, CCSSO Focus Group, "World History Standards Critique: June 1994," 15 July 1994.

101. Regina Maguire, graduate research assistant to Professor Rabb, to Gary B. Nash, 15 July 1994.

102. Carol Gluck to Linda Symcox, 11 July 1994.

103. Michael R. Winston to Gary B. Nash, 25 July 1994.

104. Paul Gagnon, "Problems with World History Standards as prepared by the National Center for History in the Schools," 20 June 1994.

105. Albert Shanker, "Proposed World History Standards," memo to Charlotte Crabtree and Gary B. Nash, 9 Aug. 1994.

106. Chester E. Finn Jr., "Memorandum: Draft World History Standards," 7 July 1994.

107. David Baumbach, "Comments on Fifth Draft (August 1994) National Standards for World History, Exploring Paths to the Present," 11 Sept. 1994.

108. Ramsey Selden, "World History Standards Critique: Fourth [*sic*] Draft, August 1994," 29 Aug. 1994.

109. Jerry H. Bentley to John Mears, 12 July 1994.

110. William H. McNeill to Gary B. Nash and Charlotte Crabtree, 23 Aug. 1994.

111. Mary Vassilikou Bicouvaris, "Building a Consensus for the Development of National Standards in History" (Ph.D. dissertation, Old Dominion University, 1994), 125.

112. Ibid., 152–53.

CHAPTER 8

1. "The History Thieves," Letters to the Editor, *Wall Street Journal,* 8 Nov. 1994, A23.
2. Charles Krauthammer, "History Hijacked," *Washington Post,* 4 Nov. 1994, A 25.
3. See, for example, Joyce Appleby, "Lessons in History—Based on Facts," *Washington Post,* 19 Nov. 1994, A 15; and Warren Solomon, "If the Truth Were Told About U.S. History," *St. Louis Post-Dispatch,* 12 Nov. 1994, 15B.
4. John D. Fonte, "Rewriting History," *San Diego Union-Tribune,* 6 Nov. 1994, G 1.
5. John Leo, "The Hijacking of American History," *U.S. News & World Report,* 14 Nov. 1994, 36.
6. Peter Schrag, "What Should U.S. History Be?" *Sacramento Bee,* 2 Nov. 1994, B6.
7. Personal communication to Gary B. Nash from David Stevenson, Rita Lewis, and Kevin Sullivan, 16 Nov. 1994.
8. Carol Gluck, "History According to Whom? Let the Debate Continue," *New York Times,* 19 Nov. 1994, 15.
9. *National Standards for United States History: Exploring the American Experience,* Grades 5–12 Expanded Edition (National Center for History in the Schools, 1994), iii.
10. "Now a History for the Rest of Us," *Los Angeles Times,* 27 Oct. 1994, B6.
11. "Living History. New Standards Reflect Vital Reality," *Minneapolis Star Tribune,* 14 Nov. 1994, 8A.
12. "Broaden History," editorial, *Seattle Post-Intelligencer,* 12 Nov. 1994.
13. "History Guidelines Offer Good Ideas," *Lincoln Star,* 2 Feb. 1995, 14.
14. "Maligning the History Standards," *New York Times,* 13 Feb. 1995, A14.
15. Douglas Greenberg, "Face the Nation. Exposing the Chief Critic of the 'American Experience,'" *Chicago Tribune,* 9 Jan. 1995, 9.
16. John Leo, "History Standards Are Bunk," *U.S. News & World Report,* 6 Feb. 1995, 23.
17. Gluck, "History According to Whom?", 15.
18. Kirk Ankeney, "The Intersection of Pluralism and Democracy: United States History at the Crossroads," address at UCLA International Studies and Overseas Program Summer Institute, 22 July 1995.
19. Ibid.
20. John Pyne and Gloria Sesso, unpublished letter, 7 Feb. 1995.
21. Donald Woodruff to Charlotte Crabtree, Linda Symcox, Gary B. Nash, and Ross Dunn, 3 March 1995.
22. Joyce Appleby, Lynn Hunt, and Margaret Jacobs, *Telling the Truth about History* (Norton, 1994), 293.
23. Todd Gitlin, *The Twilight of Common Dreams: Why America Is Wracked by Culture Wars* (Metropolitan Books, 1995), 170.
24. Krauthammer, "History Hijacked," A25.
25. Leo, "Hijacking of American History," 36.
26. Albert Shanker, "America the Multicultural," *The New Republic* 204 (March 25, 1991): 47.
27. David M. Kennedy, "A Vexed and Troubled People," in *Exploring the National Standards for United States and World History, The History Teacher,* 28, no. 3 (May 1995): 417.
28. Ibid., 419–20.

29.   Lynne V. Cheney, "The End of History," *Wall Street Journal*, 20 Oct. 1994, A26.
30.   "British History Meets Its Waterloo," *Daily Telegraph*, 5 Nov. 1994, 1.
31.   Leo, "Hijacking of American History," 36.
32.   "Standards Push Wider View of World History," *USA Today*, 11 Nov. 1994, 1D.
33.   William H. McNeill, letter, *Wall Street Journal*, 11 Jan. 1995, 15.
34.   "It's a Small World, After All," *Newsweek*, 14 Nov. 1994, 59.
35.   "Historians Propose Curriculum Tilted Away from West," *New York Times*, 11 Nov. 1994, A6.
36.   *National Standards for World History: Exploring Paths to the Present*, Grades 5–12 Expanded Edition (National Center for History in the Schools, 1994), 234.
37.   "McCarthy, Seneca Falls and History," *Wall Street Journal*, 30 Dec. 1994, A8.
38.   Quoted in Gary B. Nash and Ross E. Dunn, "National History Standards: Controversy and Commentary," *Social Studies Review* 34 (Winter 1995): 11.
39.   Hanna Holborn Gray, "Why Any 'National Standards' at All?" *Washington Post*, 29 Jan. 1995, C7.
40.   Michael Kramer, "Newt's Believe It or Not," *Time*, 19 Dec. 1994, 44.
41.   Personal communication to Gary B. Nash from NEH staff member, 25 Jan. 1995.
42.   Lynn Olson, "Cheney to Start Review Panel," *Education Week*, 7 Dec. 1994, 9.
43.   Lynne V. Cheney to Charlotte Crabtree, 6 Oct. 1992.
44.   Lynne V. Cheney, "Memorandum to All NEH Staff," 1 Dec. 1992, released to press 2 Dec. 1992.
45.   See, for example, Lynne V. Cheney, "Kill My Old Agency, Please," *Wall Street Journal*, 24 Jan. 1995, A22 and Lamar Alexander, William J. Bennett, and Dan Coats, "Local Options: Congress Should Return Control of Education to States, School Boards—and Parents," *National Review*, 19 Dec. 1994, 42–44.
46.   "Clinton Package for Schools Has Chance to Pass," *Wall Street Journal*, 16 April, 1993, B1 (W), B1 (E).
47.   "Rolling Riley," *Wall Street Journal*, 19 April 1993, A14.
48.   *Department of Education Reports* 14, no. 17 (26 April 1993): 6.
49.   Julie A. Miller, "'Goals 2000' Gets Mixed Reaction from Lawmakers and Educators," *Education Week*, 12 May 1993, 18.
50.   *Department of Education Reports* 14, no. 20 (17 May 1993): 3–4.
51.   Ibid., 4.
52.   John Leo, "School Reform Remissions," *Washington Times*, 18 June 1993, F3.
53.   "President Clinton Urges Ford to Oppose House Activists," *Department of Education Reports* 14, no. 25 (21 June 1993): 2–3.
54.   "GOALS 2000 Fails to Pass This Year; Expected to Be Early Business in January 1994," *Department of Education Reports*, 29 Nov. 1993.
55.   Mark Pitsch, "With Students' Aid, Clinton Signs Goals 2000," *Education Week*, 6 April 1994, 1, 21.
56.   Ibid.
57.   *Contract With the American Family, A Bold Plan by Christian Coalition to Strengthen the Family and Restore Common-sense Values* (Moorings, 1995), chaps. 2 and 3. All succeeding references to the Christian Coalition's agenda are drawn from this same source.
58.   Ibid., xiii.
59.   *Contract With America, The Bold Plan by Rep. Newt Gingrich, Rep. Dick Armey, and the House Republicans to Change the Nation* (Times Books, 1994), 10, 79.

60. Phyllis Schlafly, "How the Liberals Are Rewriting History," *The Phyllis Schlafly Report* 28, no. 8 (March 1995).

61. Ibid., 2.

62. *National Standards for United States History,* 52–53, 58–61, 116–17.

63. *National Standards for World History,* 72–73.

64. Ibid., 88–89, 102–103.

65. Linda S. Page, *Making the Grade: What Goals 2000 Means to Our Schools* (Focus on the Family, 1995), 9. All succeeding references to the position of this organization are from this publication.

66. *Let Freedom Ring! A Basic Outline of American History* (Family Research Council, 1995).

67. *Washington Times,* 21 Feb. 1995, A3.

68. *National Standards for World History,* 282–83; *National Standards for History for Grades K–4: Expanding Children's World in Time and Space,* Expanded Edition (National Center for History in the Schools, 1994), 53, 67.

69. "Pro-family Group Proposes History Standards," *Washington Times,* 21 Feb. 1995, A4.

70. Mark Pitsch, "Alexander Has Change of Heart on Federal Role," *Education Week,* 6 March 1996, 1, 28–29.

71. "Battle over History May Itself Prove Historic," *Chicago Tribune,* 30 Oct. 1994, 1, 4.

72. Cheney, "The End of History," A26.

73. Lynne V. Cheney, "Wheatley Wrong to Indict Truthfulness of Others," Letter to the Editor, *Seattle Times,* 5 March 1995, 81.

74. "Up in Arms About the 'American Experience.' History Curriculum Guidelines Play Down Traditional Heroes and Focus on Negatives, Critics Say," *Washington Post,* 28 Oct. 1994, A3.

75. National History Standards Project, "Fact Sheet on National Standards for United States History," 16 Nov. 1994, 2.

76. Meg Greenfield, "The Cultural Commissars," *Newsweek,* 18 Dec. 1995, 76.

CHAPTER 9

1. Joyce Appleby, Lynn Hunt, and Margaret Jacobs, *Telling the truth about History* (Norton, 1994), 224.

2. Richard Longaker to Charles Quigley, "Observations Regarding National Standards for United States History," Dec. 1994.

3. Personal communication from Catherine Stimpson, former president of Modern Language Association, to Gary B. Nash; communication from Fonte to Nash at University of Southern California School of Education debate in July 1995.

4. Personal communication from David Evans to Gary B. Nash, 19 Jan. 1995.

5. U.S. Senate, Senator Slade Gorton of Washington speaking on National History Standards, *Congressional Record* (18 Jan. 1995), S1026.

6. Ibid., S1027–28.

7. Ibid., S1028–29.

8. Ibid., S1032–34.

9. Ibid., S. 1029–31.

10. "Don't Buy the Standard Line of Critics of History Project," *Seattle Times,* 1 Feb. 1995, B4; Also Helen Wheatley, "Teaching History: Critics of the New Standards

Distort the Facts," *Seattle Post-Intelligencer,* 19 Feb. 1995, D1; and Slade Gorton's reply, "History Standards Are Political Correctness Run Amok," 28 Feb. 1995, A7.

11.　Senator Paul S. Sarbanes to Jo Ann O. Robinson, Morgan State University, 16 March 1995.

12.　Press release, chairman of the National Endowment for the Humanities, 19 Jan. 1995.

13.　Helen Wheatley, "Teaching History," *Seattle Post-Intelligencer,* 19 Feb. 1995, D1.

14.　Eric Foner, "Historian, Show Decent Respect," *New York Times,* 31 Jan. 1995, A20.

15.　Harold Hyman to Senators Kay Bailey Hutchison and Philip Gramm, 22 Feb. 1995.

16.　Jean Johnson to Senator Slade Gorton, 25 Jan. 1995.

17.　Theodore Rabb, "Whose History? Where Critics of the New Standards Flunk Out," *Washington Post,* 11 Dec. 1994, C5.

18.　For example, see the essays in special issue of *The History Teacher* 28 (May 1995): 295–456.

19.　Ruth Rosen, "The War to Control the Past," *Los Angeles Times,* 24 Nov. 1994, B5.

20.　Brian Copenhaver to *New York Times,* 22 Feb. 1995, unpublished.

21.　AHA and OAH presidents to "Fellow Historians," 5 Jan. 1995. (Paper circulated at American Historical Association Convention and mailed to various people.)

22.　Arnita Jones, "Our Stake in the History Standards," *Chronicle of Higher Education,* 6 Jan. 1995, B1.

23.　Stanford Department of History Faculty to *New York Times,* 6 April 1995, unpublished.

24.　Oberlin Department of History Faculty to Senator John Glenn, 16 Feb. 1995.

25.　Resolution of the University Faculty Senate, State University of New York, 28 Jan. 1995.

26.　City University of New York Faculty Senate to Senators Daniel Patrick Moynihan and Alfonse M. D'Amato, 1 March 1995.

27.　Lynne V. Cheney, "Kill My Old Agency, Please," *Wall Street Journal,* 24 Jan. 1995, A22.

28.　House Subcommittee on Interior Appropriations, "Testimony of Members of Congress and Other Interested Individuals and Organizations: National Endowment for the Humanities, National Endowment for the Arts," 104th Cong., 24 Jan. 1995.

29.　Frank Rich, "Eating Her Offspring," *New York Times,* 26 Jan. 1995, A19.

30.　Kim Savage, UCLA Congressional Liaison Officer, to Gary B. Nash, personal communication, 31 Jan. 1995.

31.　Ruth Wattenberg to Robert Schwartz, 19 Jan. 1995.

32.　On the U.S. panel served Diane Ravitch; Cary Carson, vice president of Colonial Williamsburg; Harvard historian Stephan Thernstrom; Reed Ueda of Tufts University; Evelyn Brooks Higginbotham, historian of religion and African American history at Harvard; David Hollinger, University of California, Berkeley, intellectual historian; Jeannette LaFors, a teacher in the public schools in Palo Alto, California; and Rex Shepard, a social studies specialist in the Baltimore public schools. The World History panel was composed of noted historians in various areas and eras of history whose work transcended national boundaries: Allison Blakely, a professor of European and comparative history at Howard University; Philip D Curtin, a Johns Hopkins University historian of Africa and the Atlantic world and one of the pioneers of comparative and world history; Prasenjit Duara, a University of Chicago historian and authority on China; Michael F. Jimenez, an expert on the economic and social history of Latin America at the University of Pittsburgh; Ramsay MacMullen, professor emeritus in ancient Greek and Roman history at Yale; Joan Wallach Scott, an Institute for Advanced Study scholar known for her writings on French labor and women's history; and John Obert Voll, a leader in the world history teaching movement and a faculty member at Georgetown University and its Center for Muslim-Christian Understanding. The secondary school educators on the panel were Hilary Ainger, head of the Humanities Department at the United Nations International School; Robert Bain, a world history leader and teacher at John Carroll University and Beachwood High School in Ohio; and Marjorie Malley, a specialist in the history of science and an advocate of science and mathematics education. The twelfth member of the panel was A. Lee Blitch, an AT&T vice president and director of the company's telephone language interpretation services.

33. Transcript of Dole speech on Labor Day, 4 Sept. 1995, 5, 7; Gary B. Nash to Senator Dole, 30 Aug. 1995.
34. Buchanan stump speech, played on *News Hour with Jim Lehrer*, 31 Jan. 1996.
35. Department of Education press release, 4 Sept. 1995; and National Press Club comments on C-SPAN, 9 Sept. 1995.
36. Statement by Undersecretary of Education Marshall Smith, 26 Oct. 1994.
37. Quoted in Lyric Wallwork Winik, "We Are Responsible," *Newsday*, 19 March 1995, 6.
38. Sue Rosenthal to Richard Riley, 26 Sept. 1995.
39. David Vigilante to Richard Riley, 12 Sept. 1995.
40. *Congressional Quarterly Researcher*, 5 #36 (29 Sept. 1995): 850–71. The quotes are from p. 865.
41. Karen Diegmueller and Debra Viadero, "Playing Games with History," *Education Week*, 15 Nov. 1995, 29–34.
42. Ibid., 32.
43. "Review Panels Find History Standards Worth Revising," Council for Basic Education news release, 11 Oct. 1995.
44. Associated Press release, 12 Jan. 1995.
45. "History Standards Draw Barbs," Associated Press, 2 April 1996.
46. Lynne V. Cheney, "The National History (Sub)Standards," *Wall Street Journal*, 23 Oct. 1995, A16.
47. "Good Sense on Teaching History," *Los Angeles Times*, 13 Oct. 1995, B8.
48. U.S. Department of Education, "Statement by U.S. Secretary of Education Richard W. Riley Regarding Proposed Revisions of National History Standards," 11 Oct. 1995.
49. *National Standards for United States History: Exploring the American Experience* (National Center for History in the Schools, 1994), iii.
50. NCHS found several CBE recommendations ill-advised but these concerned deleting guidelines suggesting appropriate grade levels for study of specific historical topics and linking each topic to an apt historical thinking skill. The CBE panelists were satisfied with Nash's explanation that these pedagogical issues had been carefully discussed and resolved to the satisfaction of the major organizations responsible for curricular and pedagogical matters.

51.   Paul Houston and Christopher Cross, letter to the membership of the American Association of School Administrators, May 1996.

52.   For example, Jo Thomas, "Revised History Standards Disarm the Explosive Issues," *New York Times,* 3 April 1996, B10 (N), B8 (L); Rene Sanchez, "Revised Teaching Standards Shift Historical Emphasis," *Washington Post,* 3 April 1996; A3; "Revised History Standards Blunt 'Bias' Criticism," *USA Today,* 3 April 1996, 1D; Karen Diegmueller, "History Center Shares New Set of Standards," *Education Week,* 10 April 1996, 1, 14, 15; and "Rebirth of History Standards," *Los Angeles Times,* 14 April 1996, M4.

53.   All quotations are from UCLA press release, 3 April 1996.

54.   "History Standards, Take Two," *Washington Post,* 6 April 1996, A16.

55.   Arthur Schlesinger Jr., "History as Therapy: A Dangerous Idea," *New York Times,* 3 May 1996, A11.

56.   Diane Ravitch and Arthur Schlesinger Jr., "The New, Improved History Standards," *Wall Street Journal,* 3 April 1996, A22.

57.   John Leo, "Who's for a Little Tongue Violence," *U.S. News & World Report,* 15 April 1996, 23.

58.   George F. Will, "A Standard for History," *Washington Post,* 7 April 1996, C7.

59.   Diegmueller, "History Center Shares New Set of Standards," 1, 14, 15.

60.   Associated Press, "History Standards Draw Barbs," 2 April 1996.

61.   Lynne V. Cheney, "New History Standards Still Attack Our Heritage," *Wall Street Journal,* 2 May 1996, A14.

62.   Jacob Weisberg, "Old Ball and Cheney," *New York,* 27 May 1996, 20.

63.   Quoted in ibid., 27.

64.   John Patrick Diggins, "History Standards Get It Wrong Again," *New York Times,* 15 May 1996, A15.

65.   Kay Bailey Hutchison, commencement address, The University of Texas at El Paso, U.S. Senate press release, 18 May 1996.

66.   Kenton Clymer, Department of History, The University of Texas at El Paso, to Kay Bailey Hutchison, 14 June 1996.

67.   Robert Holland, "History Standards Stuck in PC Era," *Washington Times,* 28 May 1996, A13.

68.   Frank Rich, "The G.O.P.'s Bum Rush," *New York Times,* 7 Feb. 1996, A15.

69.   Lamar Smith to Gary Nash, 17 Oct. 1996.

70.   Nash to Smith, 8 Nov. 1996.

71.   Smith to superintendents of instruction, 24 Oct. 1996.

72.   John T. Benson to Lamar Smith, 15 Nov. 1996 (copy provided to Nash with letter from Benson to Nash, 6 Dec. 1996, where he expressed his opinion that "It is unfortunate that the politicization of the history standards is continuing").

CHAPTER 10

1.   Neil Harris, "Museums and Controversy: Some Introductory Reflections," *Journal of American History* 82 (Dec. 1995): 1102, 1109.

2.   "Battle over School Standards Resumes at Loudoun Hearing," *Washington Post,* 7 April 1995, B7.

3.   "Allen Plan Praised, Panned at Hearing," *Washington Post,* 30 March 1995, B6.

4. Lynne V. Cheney, "Gone Beserk over the Facts," *Washington Post*, 6 April 1995, A21.

5. "Allen's Education Plan Causes Division in GOP," *Washington Post*, 26 April 1995, B1.

6. "Revised Social Studies Standards for Va. Schools Dropped; Teacher Opposition Cited," *Washington Post*, 27 April 1995, A8.

7. *Standards of Learning for Virginia Public Schools* (Commonwealth of Virginia Board of Education, June 1995).

8. "Compromise Reached on Va. School Standards," *Washington Post*, 23 June 1995, C1, and Spencer S. Hsu, "Va. School Board Unanimously Approves 'Back to Basics' Standards," *Washington Post*, 30 June 1995, C3.

9. Personal communication from Noralee Frankel, parent in Fairfax County assisting in the development of the Fairfax County social studies standards and officer of the American Historical Association, 27 March 1997.

10. "Compromise Reached," C4.

11. Kathleen Kennedy Manzo, "In Massachusetts, Silber Goes to Battle over History Framework Draft," *Education Week*, 22 Jan. 1997, 19.

12. Ibid.

13. Ibid., 1.

14. Kate Zernike, "Showdown Looms over History Test Standards," *Boston Globe*, 14 April, 1997, A1.

15. Chester Finn, "On Governors and Ostriches," *Education Week*, 14 Feb. 1995, 44.

16. John S. Kendall and Robert J. Marzano, *Content Knowledge: A Compendium of Standards and Benchmarks for K–12 Education* (Mid-continent Regional Educational Laboratory, 1996).

17. Frank Klajda, "State Social Studies Development and National Standards," unpublished report, 25 Oct. 1995.

18. Council of the Great City Schools, *Becoming the Best: Standards and Assessment Development in the Great City Schools* (The Council, June 1996), iii, 9–12.

19. American Federation of Teachers, *Making Standards Matter, 1996.* An annual Fifty State Report on Effotts to Raise Academic Standards (American Federation of Teachers, 1996).

20. *Quality Counts: A Report Card on the Condition of Public Education in the 50 States.* A Supplement to *Education Week*, in collaboration with the Pew Charitable Trusts (*Education Week*, 22 Jan. 1997), 1, 32–35.

21. "Teachers Union Faults Efforts to Set Scholastic Standards," *San Diego Union-Tribune*, 5 Aug. 1995, A6.

22. AFT, *Making Standards Matter*, Part II.

23. Jo Thomas, "New Standards, New Looks: Despite Critics, Enlivening History," *New York Times*, 5 April 1995, A20. Copyright © 1995 by the New York Times Co. Reprinted by permission.

24. Ibid. The following quotations are also from this article.

25. David O'Shea, *Implementing the American History Curriculum in Public Senior High Schools* (National Center for History in the Schools, 1994), 110–11.

26. Kenneth J. Moynihan, "Can the Scholar's History Be the Public's History?" *Proceedings of the American Antiquarian Society*, 105, Pt. 2 (1995), 301–13.

27. Ibid., 311.

Index

Italicized page numbers refer to illustrations.

Index

Winston committee, 172–4, 181, 185
women('s): and American Revolution, 82,
  84, 85–6; historians, 55; history of, 23, 53,
  76–7, 92, 100–2, 157, 160, 162, 200–1, 204,
  209, 233, 246, 249, 252; movement, 65, 201;
  studies, 103, 107, 114, 199, 223; suffrage, 86,
  191; *see also* feminism
Women's Educational Equity Act, 88, 114
Woodruff, Donald, 182, 229

Woodson, Carter G., 120
Woodward, C. Vann, 62
world history, 46–52, 73, 89–95, 114–15;
  tenth grade, 49, 52, 67, 89, 90, 92, 94
World History Association, 111, 169
World War I, 51
World War II, 62, 65, 67, 124–5, 134–5, 242–3

Yale University, 55

A NOTE ABOUT THE AUTHORS

Since 1966 Gary B. Nash has taught American history at UCLA, where he has received a Distinguished Teaching Award and Faculty Research Lecturer Award. During 1994–95 he served as President of the Organization of American Historians. In 1997 he was elected to membership in the American Academy of Arts and Sciences, and is Director of the National Center for History in the Schools.

From 1962 to 1993 Charlotte Crabtree taught curriculum studies at UCLA, where she chaired the Division of Administrative, Curriculum, and Teaching Studies in the Graduate School of Education. She was founding Director of the National Center for History in the Schools and has served on the National Assessment Governing Board, the 1994 National Assessment of Educational Progress in U.S. History, and the California Curriculum Commission.

Ross E. Dunn is Professor of History at San Diego State University, where he teaches African, Islamic, and world history. He is also Director of World History Projects at the National Center for History in the Schools. In 1982 he was elected the first president of the World History Association.

A NOTE ON THE TYPE

This book was set in Janson, a typeface long thought to have been made by the Dutchman Anton Janson, who was a practicing typefounder in Leipzig during the years 1668–1687. However, it has been conclusively demonstrated that these types are actually the work of Nicholas Kis (1650–1702), a Hungarian, who most probably learned his trade from the master Dutch typefounder Dirk Voskens. The type is an excellent example of the influential and sturdy Dutch types that prevailed in England up to the time William Caslon (1692–1766) developed his own incomparable designs from them.

Composed by Creative Graphics, Inc., Allentown, Pennsylvania
Printed and bound by R. R. Donnelley & Sons, Harrisonburg, Virginia
Designed by Robert C. Olsson